This study analyzes the political and fiscal origins of the French Revolution by looking at the relationship between the royal government and privileged, corporate bodies at the local level. Utilizing a neo-Tocquevillian approach, it argues that the monarchy undermined its own attempts at reform by extending central authority, while at the same time it continued to rely upon corporate structures and monopolies to finance the state. The unresolvable, institutional conflicts had the effect of politicizing members of the privileged elite and eventually led many of them to embrace a rhetoric of citizenship, accountability, and civic equality that had far-reaching and unanticipated consequences. When Lille's bourgeoisie consolidated a municipal revolution in 1789, they followed a program that was politically liberal, but economically conservative.

Arranged as a series of case-studies, the book illuminates the structure of political power in the Flemish provincial estates, the growth of royal taxation, the problem of municipal credit, the role of venal officeholders, and the relationship of the revolutionary bourgeoisie to monopolies of the guilds.

The politics of privilege

The politics of privilege

Old regime and revolution in Lille

Gail Bossenga

University of Kansas

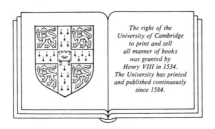

The right of the
University of Cambridge
to print and sell
all manner of books
was granted by
Henry VIII in 1534.
The University has printed
and published continuously
since 1584.

Cambridge University Press

Cambridge
New York   Port Chester
Melbourne   Sydney

Published by the Press Syndicate of the University of Cambridge
The Pitt Building, Trumpington Street, Cambridge CB2 1RP
40 West 20th Street, New York, NY 10011, USA
10 Stamford Road, Oakleigh, Melbourne 3166, Australia

First published 1991

Printed in Great Britain at the University Press, Cambridge

British Library cataloguing in publication data
Bossenga, Gail
 The politics of privilege: old regime and revolution in
 Lille
 1. France. Social conditions, 1715–1792
 I. Title
 944.034

Library of Congress cataloguing in publication data
Bossenga, Gail.
    The politics of privilege: old regime and revolution in Lille/
 Gail Bossenga.
        p.   cm.
    Includes bibliographical references and index.
    ISBN 0-521-39282-9
    1. Lille (France – Politics and government). 2. France–History–
 –Revolution, 1789–1799
 Causes. 3. Lille (France) – Economic
 conditions. 4. Economics–France–History – 18th century.
 I. Title
 DC195.L53B67 1991
 944'.28 – dc20   90-43043 CIP

ISBN 0 521 39282 9 hardback

UP

Contents

Figure

Tables

Preface

My interest in the relationship between the corporate bodies of the old regime and the origins of the French Revolution goes back to my days as a graduate student at the University of Michigan, specifically to a course with David Bien. The class was engrossed (or at least I was) with the problem of how notions of equality might have arisen in a society organized upon the antithetical principles of hierarchy and privilege. One solution, the most common proposed, was some variant of the "egalitarian outsider" theory of history. According to this historiographical scenario, unprivileged groups, chronically thwarted in their attempts at social mobility, rose up, armed themselves with the rhetoric of equality, and finally overthrew their privileged oppressors. As a specialist in ironical twists of history, however, Bien had an additional proposal: perhaps notions of equality were being formulated inside corporate bodies as well as in opposition to them. This I found to be such a preposterous idea that I immediately knew I had stumbled onto the subject of my doctoral research.

Since that time I have pursued various angles of the relationship of privileged corps to an egalitarian revolution, some more successfully than others. My approach has been that of the local study, and within that locality, of case studies of particular corporate institutions endowed with different ranks, powers, and rights. By restricting the study to specific corps, I found that I could investigate in a more detailed fashion the processes impinging upon these institutions, the rhetoric utilized to defend or attack their privileges, and the multiple allegiances generated through simultaneous membership in several of these bodies. My goal, ultimately, was to present a series of essays on the problem of privilege in the old regime from the perspective of local actors who witnessed the various stresses, strains, and uses to which corporate bodies were subjected. As such, the research was oriented heavily toward institutional factors, and, although I did not predict this when I began, the results led me to argue for the primacy of fiscal, political, and cultural reasons for the outbreak of revolution. Indeed, a central problem that I faced after completing my research was to interpret the connection, if any, between economic liberalism and the political origins of the Revolution, given that my evidence pointed so starkly away from a Marxist interpretation toward a Tocquevillian and Weberian one.

A number of individuals and institutions provided moral and material support without which this work would never have been completed. I would like to express my thanks to them all. David Bien, as noted already, provided the inspiration for this study, while Charles Tilly gave me invaluable advice on how to construct a viable agenda for my research. Both of these professors, as well as other members of my doctoral committee, Louise Tilly and Jacob Price, offered helpful comments for writing and revising the dissertation. My initial sojourn in Lille would have been less pleasant and productive without the warm hospitality of Pierre and Solange Deyon, and the friendship of Thorkil Jacobsen and Liana Vardi. I gained a number of insights from conversations with Wayne Te Brake and from discussions with Harry Liebersohn, with whom I had the pleasure of teaching a graduate course during my tenure as a Henry Luce postdoctoral fellow at the Claremont Graduate School. I received encouragement and suggestions from various members of a northern California reading group in French history, coordinated at the time by Lynn Hunt, and from my colleagues at the University of Kansas, Angel Kwolek-Folland, Ann Schofield, and, in particular, Beth Bailey. Jack Goldstone, Jim Riley, and Ran Halévi took the time to comment on portions of the manuscript. A number of reader's reports, all anonymous, recommended changes that helped me to produce a far more readable final text. The editorial support of William Davies has been appreciated.

At the doctoral level, my research was supported by grants from the Social Science Research Council, the French Fulbright, and the University of Michigan. I am also grateful for postdoctoral financial aid from the National Endowment for the Humanities, the American Council for Learned Societies, the Henry Luce Foundation, and a summer research grant from the University of Kansas. I owe a debt, for which this book will have to serve as repayment, to them all.

My family has weathered the process of completing this book with good humor and patience. As my daughter Laurna astutely observed, "children have more fun than adults, because when you are young you can play, but when you grow up, you have to write books." Our second, who has yet to make an appearance at the time of writing this preface, has reminded me again of the fundamental importance of the role of biology in history, at least in how quickly it gets written. Most important in this ongoing project has been the selfless help of my husband, Carl Strikwerda, who has alternately served as research assistant, proofreader, bibliographer, and sympathetic ear. One of the more remarkable achievements in this line of work proved to be his surprising ability to listen to the rise and fall of the ancien régime in Lille at least 256 times (after which we both lost count) and never once fall asleep. This book is dedicated to him.

Abbreviations

A.D.N.	= *Archives Départementales du Nord*
A.D.N., C.B.F.	= *Archives Départementales du Nord, série C, Archives du Bureau des Finances.*
A.M.L.	= *Archives Municipales de Lille*
A.M.L., A.G.	= *Archives Municipales de Lille, Affaires Générales*
A.N.	= *Archives Nationales*
B.M.L.	= *Bibliothèque Municipale de Lille*

1 Monarchy, privilege and revolution: the problem and setting

On 24 May 1667, Louis XIV's armies entered Walloon Flanders, and Lille's inhabitants, subjects of the Spanish Habsburgs, began to prepare for a siege.[1] The municipal magistrates hurried to secure provisions for the town, while the confraternity of St. Jacques met to say masses in honor of their namesake, the patron saint of Spain. As the conquerors approached, Lille filled with frightened peasants seeking refuge within the city's walls. On 10 August, the city was surrounded, and by the next day Lille's bourgeoisie was in arms. Five days later, as French soldiers tried to batter down the gate at Fives, the city's inhabitants held a solemn procession to celebrate the assumption of the Virgin and to implore the city's patron saint, Notre Dame de la Treille, for aid. Three thousand people with torches marched in front of priests carrying the Blessed Sacrament, while the governor, the magistrates of the town council, and the governor's court followed *en corps*. Wherever the procession passed, nothing could be heard but the sound of drums, the fanfare of trumpets, and the peal of carillons and bells. When the procession reached the marketplace, a company of armed bourgeois stood ready. As soon as the Blessed Sacrament passed by, they fired their muskets into the air, and at the same time "a huge standard or banner was put at the very top of the Tower of Saint Estienne, with the Cross of Burgundy in the middle to tell the enemies that we still had Spanish and Burgundian hearts and not French, and that the besieged were all ready to die for their king...rather than to become slaves under the laws of another."[2] After witnessing the French army on the field for a while, however, Lille's governor decided that discretion was the better part of valor. On 27 August 1667, he surrendered.

The next day twenty-four heralds with trumpets, flutes, and drums announced the entrance of Louis XIV into the city. A great number of nobles adorned with lace, gold and silver, accompanied the satisfied king who rode into the city on his horse "like a Caesar." At the gate, the municipal magistrates of Lille presented their new sovereign with the keys to the city, after which the royal entourage went to hear a mass at the Church of St. Pierre. Having rendered homage to God, the king retired to

1

the chapel of Notre Dame de la Treille, Lille's protectress, where, surrounded by images of divine authority, Louis received the oath of loyalty from the municipal officials and confirmed the city in all its traditional rights, usages, and privileges. Thus the victorious Sun-king continued a long-standing tradition whereby each of Lille's new sovereigns, personally or through a representative, solemnly swore to uphold the city's customary rights and prerogatives. Soon thereafter Louis signed a lengthy capitulation treaty listing in detail the privileges the city was to enjoy.[3]

Half a century after Lille's conquest, when Louis XV began his personal rule in 1726, the customary exchange of loyalties between the incoming king and his privileged Lillois subjects was transformed. Louis XIV's successors showed little interest in perpetuating a medieval ritual that embedded sovereignty in reciprocal obligations, except to make money. When Louis XV, still burdened by enormous debts accumulated during his grandfather's war, acceded to the throne, he decided that it was time to confirm the privileges of his subjects, for a price. Provincial authorities were informed that it would only cost Walloon Flanders 740,300 *livres* to have provincial prerogatives validated, a sum that also allowed local officials to buy up some very sensitive municipal offices peddled by the royal government to reduce its bloated debt. The estates of Walloon Flanders protested that this practice actually represented a violation of their privileges, but their pleas were to no avail. In the end, they paid.[4] The confirmation of privileges hence stood revealed as naked fiscalism in the hands of a destitute French monarch.

One hundred years after Louis XIV's victory, in August 1767, the town council used the centenary of Lille's annexation to France to express their vision of a legitimate political order. Four statues erected in the town square commemorated the historic event. The first was a figure representing Victory, which recalled Louis XIV's conquest a century ago. The second represented Peace and displayed the peace treaty that had made the annexation final. The third was Justice, which proclaimed the oath taken by Louis XIV to maintain the rights, usages, and privileges of the town. The whole day of 28 August, in fact, was spent in festivities celebrating this crucial vow. After all, observed the town council, it was only "by maintaining the laws proper to the city of Lille that [the city] had reached its current degree of splendor."[5]

Alongside these traditional symbols of distributive justice and princely power, however, was one last statue, that of France. The image, a new one in Lille's festivals, appeared odd among the representations of royally sanctioned urban particularism. Its presence suggested a subtle but significant cultural shift, a redefinition of the basis of political community. The figure of France announced the "protection that she always granted to citizens and in particular to commerce." Somewhere, despite the preoccupation of Lille's ruling elite with the preservation of its own peculiar laws and privileges, a sense of an impersonal state had emerged, a state that transcended the monarchy and knit the localistic Lillois into a larger, national community. France protected citizens and commerce. Protection was traditionally regarded as a kingly duty granted in return for subjects' obedience and loyalty. Now a far more abstract concept of public power, France, was fulfilling the protective role. It is significant that citizens and commerce, and not privileges, were being protected. The pairing implied that utility and productivity, rather than inherited status and localistic customs, were beginning to define membership in the body politic and that individual citizens were replacing corporate groups as fundamental units in the political order. Corporate bodies limited rights and privileges to their own restrictively recruited members. Citizenship implied the extension of civil rights to all Frenchmen. Yet in 1767, the term *citizen* had not yet acquired the explosive anticorporate content that would transform this simple word into a revolutionary slogan.[6] The town council placed the statues of royal Justice and protective France side by side.

When Louis XVI acceded to the throne in 1774, the municipal authorities hoped once more for the traditional confirmation of Lille's privileges. This time the incoming king wisely demanded no payments for validating his subjects' corporate prerogatives. As usual the royal treasury was empty, but Louis XVI and his ministers had become sadly aware of a newly emerging force in public life, that of public opinion. Three years earlier his father had suppressed the highly vocal Parlements and permitted a partial bankruptcy. One significant result had been to demoralize creditors and, in the process, to lay to rest permanently an old, battered mainstay of royal credit, the bonds known as *rentes perpetuelles.*[7] Louis XVI brought back the Parlements, but under the circumstances, it would have been impolitic for royal ministers to demand cash from subjects in order to protect their obviously unstable privileges.

Louis XVI also had no desire to confirm Lille's privileges in the traditional manner, through mutual oaths. Such practices were presumably inappropriate for an "absolute" king answerable to no one but God. They smacked of an unsuitable sharing of power between subjects and king, of quasi-constitutional checks upon royal authority. Several years earlier, in 1766, his father had stated the principles of absolute royal sovereignty in unequivocal terms: "it is in my person alone that sovereign power resides...I alone possess legislative power without sharing it with, or depending for it on, anyone...The whole system of public order emanates from me."[8]

As it became clear that Louis XVI had no interest in Lille's customary confirmation of privileges, Forceville, deputy at the royal court for Lille, offered the following pessimistic appraisal to the municipal authorities: "you should take the precautions necessary to ensure the stability of your constitution, to shelter it from the *révolutions* and consequences that are the fruit of this modern philosophy that tends only to the destruction of old practices."[9]

In 1788 Lille's privileges were under attack again, not by the royal government, but by an unprecedented coalition of guilds, businessmen, lawyers, officeholders, and even nobles and clerics. At issue was the question of representation in the upcoming Estates General and the implicit right of citizens to hold officials accountable for their actions. During this local battle, several guilds demanded that the municipality abolish the old title of urban *bourgeois*, bestowed upon those enjoying full civic rights in the city, and declared henceforth that municipal officials should acknowledge only the name of citizen.[10] By now the meaning of the term citizen had become explicitly egalitarian, part of a battle cry against an old regime resting on the principles of monarchy, estates, orders and corps.

Shortly thereafter, the theoretical and institutional basis of public power was completely transformed. A new legislative body, the National Assembly, claimed that it spoke for the sovereign People and abolished privileges, exemptions, and particularist rights of Frenchmen everywhere. Out of the ruins of the old regime, another society was constructed upon its apparent antithesis. National sovereignty replaced royal absolutism, and equality before the law obliterated the legal basis of social hierarchies and geographical localism. From this nationalizing of civic rights and legislative power emerged a different kind of public authority: one that was democratic and nationalistic. As the National Assembly declared: "Orders, necessarily divisive... were able to stop the development of the national will. The orders exist no longer: they all have disappeared before the honorable quality of citizen... Innumerable privileges, irreconcilable enemies of all good, used to compose our entire public law; they have been destroyed, and at the voice of your Assembly, the provinces most jealous of their privileges applauded their fall."[11] The Revolutionary leaders had begun to rewrite, sometimes with bloody hands, the definition, basis, and content of public law. The public sphere was nationalized and democratized, swept clean of royal and corporate forms of power and status, and opened up to participation and control by citizens. The Revolution of 1789 represented a conscious and determined destruction of virtually all institutions regulating public life in the old regime and the first attempt in history to set up a unified, self-governing nation.

How did a revolution based upon the principles of equality and national sovereignty arise out of a regime resting upon apparently contrary principles of privilege and absolute monarchy? What made it possible for Frenchmen living in a hierarchically ordered and still quite decentralized society to reconstruct their world upon such fundamentally different ideas as those of equality before the law and the sovereignty of a unitary nation? The following study of corporate institutions in Lille is designed to explore this fundamental problem: to examine how privilege operated in the old regime, to ask what trends helped to weaken or perpetuate this kind of organization of power and status, and to trace what ideas were used to attack and defend corporate prerogatives.

The word *privilege* itself stemmed from the Latin for "private laws," that is, laws allowing members of one particular group or territory to enjoy advantages that others did not possess.[12] Some privileges were useful, such as tax exemptions or trial by one's peers, while others were honorific, including the right of nobles to carry swords. Privileges were both disseminated horizontally among territories such as provinces, cities, and seigneuries, and assigned vertically along a hierarchy of social status. In the first case, historians have treated privilege as a dispersion of sovereignty and contrasted it with the attempt of the monarchy to rationalize the state by creating uniform, translocal institutions dependent upon itself. Public power could not be dispensed evenly from the center, because the royal government had to compete and cooperate with pockets of corporately organized authorities such as provincial estates, municipal governments, guilds and all sorts of magistracies. Membership in such privileged bodies, rather than in the state itself, regulated the civil status of individuals. These intermediate groups established civic duties: payment of taxes, obligation for military service, and the right to vote or hold office.

In the second case, historians have stressed the social dimensions of privilege. Privileges established formal status rankings, influenced social mobility, restricted occupational recruitment, and impeded the free disposal of private property. In certain instances, the social realm of the family itself took on a semi-public quality, because special rights were transferred through birth. Overall, privilege made it impossible to distinguish clearly in law between the political and social spheres. Privileges gave a political cast to relationships in civil society and tinged political power with a social hue by basing public authority in property and inheritance.[13]

Privileges in the old regime were generally given institutional expression by groups called orders, corps, and estates (*ordres, corps* and *états*).[14] The tripartite division of society into three orders was justified upon the medieval principle that those who performed specific functions for society – clergymen who prayed, nobles who fought, and commoners who toiled – should form legally distinct spheres enjoying different civil rights, obligations, and rankings. By the eighteenth century, specific functions were no longer correlated clearly with noble rank. Nobles served not only as military officers and proprietors of landed estates, but also as judges, financiers, and even wholesale merchants. The orders were neither social classes, having no necessary relationship to wealth, nor formally constituted political authorities. The seventeenth-century jurist Loyseau defined order as dignity with "*aptitude* for political power."[15] Membership in the order of the nobility, in other words, bestowed upon an individual the requisite dignity for service in a high office of state, but did not confer public power in and of itself. For this reason, it is probably most helpful to say that the term order simply signified juridically recognized social rank or position. Orders were status groups.

French society was further subdivided into a hierarchy of smaller groups usually called corporate institutions or *corps*. Corps were formally constituted groups of individuals who performed the same function in society and received privileges to help them fulfill their tasks. Endowed with legal personality, these public bodies acted as collective units before the law. They could initiate lawsuits, petition authorities, own property, and borrow money. Convents, cathedral chapters, universities, town councils, provincial estates, magistracies, guilds, and chartered companies were all examples of such collective entities that regulated a wide variety of social and political relationships. Many cities also enjoyed corporate status stemming from earlier statutes that empowered them to act as self-governing bodies. Although a variety of superior authorities, including popes and town councils, had a limited right to incorporate groups, this power was usually reserved for the king.[16]

In several ways, corporate organization illustrated the interplay of public and private spheres so common in the old regime. These institutions were a source of social rank, professional advancement, and quasi-autonomous political authority derived from their statutes and regulations. They were given the right to collect dues, fines, and reception fees in order to finance their services on an independent basis, and were able to set restrictive membership requirements. Their social status was correlated both to the dignity of the members' occupation and to their place in the political chain of command. The hierarchy of corps was, of course, far more complicated than that of the three orders and sometimes took precedence over the latter's simple threefold divisions. Magistrates of sovereign courts, for example, enjoyed a rank above all but the most highly esteemed ecclesiastical corps.[17] The reason for the precedence of these laymen over clerics was political: their elevated status expressed their proximity to royal authority, the center of the whole system.

Finally, in the medieval and Renaissance periods, many corporate groups and orders had gained the right to sit in constituted assemblies in order to advise the prince and protect their interests. Corporate bodies with powers of political representation were termed estates (*états*). For the most part, delegates to the estates were chosen from specified corporate bodies and not elected from individuals within an order at large. Representatives of the clergy were chosen from the bishoprics, abbeys, and cathedral chapters. The delegates of the Second Estate were limited to those with specified fiefs or to nobles with several generations of nobility. And the Third Estate was composed largely of representatives from the town councils of major cities, some of whom, like the mayors, were ennobled.[18] The right to sit in a representative body, therefore, was not derived from a delegation of power by individuals to freely elected delegates. Representation was corporate and virtual.[19] Privileged groups claimed the right to speak for others by dint of unaltered patterns of inheritance, property rights, historical precedents, and cooptation.

The monarchy formed the source of unity for this diverse assortment of estates, orders and corps. Two traditions shaped the relationship between the crown and privileged groups: the first evolved out of contractual notions of power that might loosely be called feudal and judicial; the second exemplified a system of domination that Max Weber termed patrimonial and that historians have more frequently called absolutist.[20] The feudal heritage, appropriately symbolized by the statue of Justice erected in Lille in 1767, emphasized authority as a mutual pact between ruler and ruled. The king protected the privileges of his subjects in exchange for their loyalty and obedience. Society was regarded as a hierarchical arrangement of semi-autonomous groups, each of which enjoyed rights and powers that helped to define and limit the prerogatives of other groups beneath and above them. The monarch was a *primus inter pares*: he stood at the top of the social hierarchy and, like those privileged bodies under his rule, had his own proper sphere of activity which he might not transgress. His most important duty was to dispense justice for all members of society, that is, he was to uphold traditional rights and ensure that every group performed its allotted duties. As supreme justiciar of the old regime, he maintained the social equilibrium.[21]

Patrimonialism, by contrast, referred to the management of the royal household and the gradual extension of royal authority beyond the king's domain into other territories. Institutionally, patrimonialism was characterized by the growth of a royal bureaucracy and development of permanent taxation. Unlike modern bureaucratic states with constitutionally delineated public and private spheres, however, the spread of public authority under the king's direction retained a highly personal quality. Paternal and state power flowed virtually as one. The intrusion of royal power into society was characterized less as a contract between the crown and privileged groups, and more as an extension of authority over subordinate subjects. Perhaps most important in this evolution of power was the instability of public norms. On the one hand, just as in the feudal tradition, custom and divine sanction continued to play an essential role in circumscribing royal power. The king, it was believed, ruled on behalf of God and answered ultimately to him. On the other hand, in so far as human agency played a role in constructing social norms, the monarch possessed immense opportunity for arbitrary action, because such norms were seen as a grant from the ruler himself. The claim of Louis XV that "the whole system of public order emanates from me" illustrated perfectly the patrimonial collapsing of the public sphere into the ruler's own person and property.[22]

The Revolution was a fundamental redefinition of the public sphere: it reconstituted the source of public norms, the basis of sovereignty, and the institutionalization of power. "Innumerable privileges," declared the National Assembly, "used to compose our entire public law." The unstable and, as it came to be perceived, inequitable nature of public law formed the basic political problem of the old regime, a society fragmented by privilege and unified politically by the king's personal will. The Revolution was a contested and frequently violent experiment in nationalizing and democratizing public power. It attempted to divest the public realm of personal, transcendent, and customary elements. It tried to make the exercise of political authority predictable and equitable by removing it from the idiosyncrasies associated with royal pleasure, commercial purchase, divine right, tradition, and inheritance. This revolutionary reconstitution of power was made possible, at least in theory, by entrusting sovereignty, the right to make law, to citizens.

Historians have usually traced the origins of the upheaval of 1789 to the long-term effects of three agents of change: the Enlightenment, commercial capitalism, and administrative centralization. Each reputedly undermined corporate structures and fostered a tendency toward individualism, equality, and other liberal practices. Contemporaries of the old regime itself made the case for the corrosive effect of the Enlightenment upon traditional structures. Lille's deputy at court, as we have seen, believed that the diffusion of *lumières* represented a nefarious "modern philosophy" that threatened to annul the validity of centuries of accumulated wisdom. The *philosophes*, it was claimed, were responsible for popularizing a new vocabulary of utility, science, self-interest, liberty, equality, nature, and natural rights that was opposed to the principles of religion, inheritance, tradition, and hierarchy upon which the old regime rested. It seemed logical to conclude that this movement was the source of revolutionary ideology.

The radical nature of enlightened thought, some historians argued, could be traced back in turn to a more fundamental process of socioeconomic change. It was the rise of capitalism and a market economy, they contended, that stimulated an awareness of the autonomy of the individual and loosened corporate bonds based in custom and prescription. Laws of the market were implicit, abstract, and, if allowed to work without legal and institutional interference, uniform in that they fell upon all individuals without respect to personal status. Corporate institutions and related privileges, however, inhibited the working of the market and stymied the development of the commercial bourgeoisie. The anticapitalist corporate "straitjacket" prevented the full emergence of a mobile labor force, cushioned master artisans from the effects of proletarianization, restricted the use of private property, and impeded capital accumulation. Economic impediments to bourgeois dominance were reinforced by political obstacles. A variety of aristocratically controlled corporate bodies including provincial estates, Parlements and officer corps, prevented businessmen from wielding political power commensurate with their growing economic importance. The classic bourgeois revolution, therefore, was anticorporate in both an economic and political sense. The bourgeoisie had to overthrow these intermediate legal bodies to gain political power and to free society from legal barriers to capital accumulation.[23]

The third agent of change, that of centralization, has usually been associated with the name of Alexis de Tocqueville.[24] According to Tocqueville, the monarchy had for centuries been drawing authority away from self-governing corps like town councils, provincial estates, guilds and Parlements, and gradually monopolizing power for itself. Particularly important in this process was the development of a royal bureaucracy of intendants, who were appointed directly by the king to oversee such vital tasks as military recruitment and provincial tax assessment. Through its regulatory apparatus, Tocqueville claimed, the monarchy gradually obliterated the distinctive character of local groups and turned individuals into an ever-more homogenous mass. Royal rule promoted a kind of political and cultural democratization, a harmful transformation whereby healthy corporate initiative was replaced by an unhealthy and conformist individualism. Privileged bodies became hollow shells, mere relics of a bygone glorious past, and played little real role in the old regime. From Tocqueville's view, it was unsurprising that in 1789 a national, egalitarian ethos emerged full-blown from this ostensibly hierarchical society, because for decades individualism and equality had been developing within corps.

Subsequent research has deepened our understanding of each of these three trends, and made their clearcut opposition to corporate institutions more problematic. Privileged groups showed a surprising capacity to absorb and even generate new impulses and to use them to perpetuate their own position. The relationship between corporate groups, enlightened discourse and revolutionary ideology, for example, is still vigorously debated. A new enlightened vocabulary did permeate eighteenth-century France, but royal officials and corporate groups, like the Parlements, were able to employ that vocabulary toward their own ends. Studies of provincial academies revealed, furthermore, that *lumières* emerged from the ranks of the privileged elite: nobles, clerics, and officeholders. Moreover, if enlightened discourse sometimes was used to conservative ends, traditional language associated with the defense of historic corporate liberties could take on radical tones in the context of unsolvable political disputes. Indeed, some historians have suggested that the theoretical underpinnings of the Revolution, in particular the idea of national sovereignty, developed in close connection with actual politics, including the repeated clashes between the king and his Parlements, and owed less to scholarly debate than one might have predicted.[25] Overall, the debate suggests that institutional settings, political battles, and language shaping the choices available to groups were multiple determinants of revolutionary ideology. Nonetheless, there have been few local studies explicitly tracing how political conflict on the local level helped to transform ideas about membership in the body politic. In the search for sources of revolutionary ideology, far greater emphasis has been placed upon studying the norms of formal cultural institutions than upon the constitutional conflicts and routine assumptions of corporate institutions including provincial estates, venal offices, town councils, and guilds.[26]

Decades of study on the composition and income of social groups, secondly, has cast serious doubt on the causal relationship between capitalism, the overthrow of privilege, and revolution. According to revisionist historians, commercial capitalists were more difficult to find in the old regime and less revolutionary than one might have imagined. Nobles and non-nobles alike invested in "proprietary wealth," a combination of land, *rentes*, and offices. Given this shared economic base, it is doubtful that the clash over privilege between Second and Third Estate in 1789 can be located in class conflict arising from their opposing modes of production. Lawyers and venal officeholders, furthermore, and not capitalistic merchants and manufacturers, overwhelmingly represented the Third Estate in 1789. Finally, the Revolution seemed to have done remarkably little to unleash capitalistic impulses in agricultural and industrial production, whose output and organization exhibited a great deal of structural continuity across the revolutionary divide. Perhaps the most that can be said of the Revolution's economic consequences is that the political upheaval changed the laws and institutions governing the economy, and that the destruction of guilds and related regulations purportedly represented bourgeois interest.[27]

Although the evidence of revisionists posed a serious challenge to Marxist interpretations of the Revolution, they were also unable to offer a convincing explanation for the radical institutional cleansing of France in 1789. One reason was that they, like their Marxist opponents, tended to derive political interests from economic ones. For both groups, law and institutions played virtually no role in establishing social identity. The premier critic of Lefebvre's Marxist interpretation, Alfred Cobban, argued that the hierarchical system of orders represented "a formal legal framework which did not correspond to the actual complexity of social life." For others privilege was but a hollow relic "of a vanished social order" and expressed a "traditional vision rather than underlying reality."[28] Rather than posing the question of the independence of the legal sphere, central to understanding the operation of privilege, revisionism gravitated toward a new idea of a class, that of the *notables*. This plutocratic elite, it was argued, transcended corporate boundaries and united all owners of proprietary wealth in the shared defense of their property and privileges.[29] But this line of reasoning left the fundamental questions of the Revolution unanswered: why was there a battle between the Second and Third Estate in the opening of the Estates General? And why did members of the elite itself help to abolish privilege in 1789?

A second question, that of the relationship of economic liberalism to the Revolution, has also been left unanswered by the revisionist challenge. Guilds, regulations, and controlled marketplaces were all abolished in the Revolution, a dramatic institutional overhaul that was logically imputed both by Marxist and liberal analyses to bourgeois motives. Yet if lawyers and officeholders rather than merchants constituted the revolutionary leadership, and if the Revolution was primarily a political transformation, were laissez-faire reforms an integral part of the revolutionary process? Scholars have typically assumed that they were. Yet not all historians agree. The extraordinarily detailed study of French banking by Herbert Luethy, for example, concluded that French *négociants* were ensconced in privileged networks and that liberal impulses came from the royal administration itself.[30] Can it be said, then, that the revolutionary restructuring of economic institutions was implemented on behalf of businessmen? Or did these liberal policies stem from the political and cultural agenda of administrative officials, from their desire to mobilize resources more efficiently and create a unified national spirit? The relationship between economic liberalism, bourgeois agendas, and the nationalization of public power remains open to further investigation.

Finally, work on the finances and bureaucracy of the royal government has enlarged our understanding of the underside of the centralizing monarchy. The insights of Weber and Tocqueville, most often associated with the thesis of centralization, have also helped scholars reassess the ongoing process of decentralization in the ancien régime.[31] As Tocqueville observed, the old order had "two quite contradictory aspects." One tended to create uniformity; the other to expand the role of privilege. The French monarchy had not consistently tried to level all privileges. Under its rule, many privileges had not merely been maintained "but in some respects intensified."[32] The reason may be traced to the fiscal strategies and lack of fixed public norms arising from a patrimonial organization of power.

As recent scholarship has shown, the personalization of royal power in the old regime made a truly public system of credit impossible. Accountable to no one but God, whose day of reckoning somehow seemed easy to ignore, French kings were able to repudiate royal debts, and did so. As a result, even after the "financial revolution" had made public credit available at low interest rates to Dutch and British states under parliamentary supervision, the French crown still struggled to mobilize credit through privileged intermediaries including provincial estates, companies of tax farmers, venal officeholders, and cities. Additional revenues came through the sale of offices, which further blurred public authority with private property. Hence, many so-called "feudal" institutions were actually products of an absolute monarch in search of ready cash. As Tocqueville astutely observed: "when we come across any ancient medieval custom which was maintained, with its worst elements wilfully exploited in defiance of the spirit of the age … we always find, if we go to the root of the matter, some financial expedient that has crystallized into an institution."[33] The ongoing reliance on privileged groups for loans led to institutional rigidity and ultimately to an inability to respond to foreign competitors, especially the English, on their own terms. French defeat in the Seven Years War was followed by a concerted royal effort to rationalize the organization of French society. But some scholars have questioned whether political and financial reform was possible at all in this system, because the chronically impoverished, but absolute, government was unable to find a replacement for its privileged network of creditors.[34]

The monarchy did, in the late 1770s, try to tap international money markets. But it failed to create corresponding mechanisms of public accountability, without which the attempt was doomed. After Terray's partial bankruptcy in 1771, the credit rating of the crown plummeted. Financial ministers like Necker and Calonne were forced to issue annuities whose highly favourable terms were both an indicator of the crown's failure to generate public trust and an inducement to rampant speculation by Genevan bankers.[35] When debt servicing proved to be an impossible task for the highly developed, but convoluted, financial system of the crown, the whole system of public authority, taxation, and credit fell together.

Based on these observations, it might be suggested that the French monarchy was characterized simultaneously both by a desire for rationalization and by an opposing tendency toward corporate "typification."[36] The first trend was visible in the crown's continual attempts to streamline its own financial and administrative operations. This effort reached its apogee in the decades before the Revolution and was evident in the crown's unsuccessful endeavors to suppress the guilds, reorganize municipal administrations and distribute the tax burden more equitably. The second trend arose from the crown's ongoing dependence on privileged corporate groups for credit, a dependency that continually allowed intermediate groups – provincial estates, tax farmers, and all kinds of venal officeholders – to acquire and retain important political and financial power at the monarchy's expense. Such vested interests, fostered by the king's own hand, imparted a cluttered, rigid character to the old regime and precluded a rational reorganization of society.

In this way, the absolute monarchy generated its own internal dynamic opposition. Any attempts to mobilize resources uniformly from all subjects threatened immediately to unleash dangerous resistance from corporate groups to which the crown was also financially beholden. In addition, the very growth of a royal bureaucracy, with its thrust toward regularity and clearly delineated spheres of jurisdiction, tended to foster the idea of an impersonal public sphere, an idea that became ever more pronounced during the Enlightenment. As a result, bureaucratic development, important for solidifying the ruler's authority, had nonetheless the potential to call into question both the secret, personal nature of royal power and the legitimacy of the patrimonial offices that united private property with public service. All in all, the way in which an entrenched process of decentralization clashed with that of centralization appears critical to understanding the preconditions of revolution in France.

Insights from a variety of scholars, then, have demonstrated the complexities of relating the Enlightenment, commercial capitalism, and administrative centralization to the coming of the Revolution. The explosion of 1789 now seems to be the product of longstanding contradictions within corporate and monarchical structures that had reached institutional maturity and become subject to new cultural, financial, and political pressures. The spread of the Enlightened thought within the privileged elite, the prominent role of officeholders in revolutionary agitation, the insecure underpinnings of royal finances that bore the burden of a military revolution without a corresponding financial one – all of these trends point to the importance of a corporate and patrimonial organization of society for understanding the Revolution's origins. Nonetheless, we lack local studies that examine in detail these intermediate bodies and offer systematic evidence for alternative interpretations of the revolutionary outbreak. Exactly what functions did the wide variety of corps perform in the old regime? Who supported their privileges? Who opposed them? And why?

The following study of privileged institutions in Lille is designed to illuminate these issues. The city itself, a prosperous center of trade and textile manufacture, was chosen for two reasons: the possibility of examining the effects of centralization and capitalism on corporate structures. Lille had a long tradition of regional rights and privileges explicitly guaranteed by Louis XIV after the French conquest. Despite its particularism, the city experienced a nationally-oriented municipal revolution similar to those sweeping across all of France in 1789.[37] As a result, it is possible to identify administrative innovations of the French monarchy on a localistic society and to explore how groups eventually mobilized in opposition to monarchical and corporate power. In addition, because Lille was economically highly developed, it had a strong commercial bourgeoisie which, as we will see later, led the municipal revolution in 1789. Unlike most other areas of France, then, Lille appears to fit the classic model of a bourgeois social revolution, in which, businessmen seized power to destroy feudal institutions, like guilds, that were holding back the creation of a capitalist society. The revolutionary activity of Lille's bourgeoisie hence reopens the question of the relationship between economic structures and democratic revolution. Was the political mobilization of these merchants propelled ultimately by their desire to free the economy from its corporate shackles? Can we simply assume, as has often been done, that the political liberalism of businessmen like these was a natural correlate of their capitalist mentality, an understandable offshoot of a mindset concerned above all with winning free markets and deregulating the economy? Or were other issues at stake?

The research was arranged as a series of case studies exploring the relationship of specific corporate institutions to wider social and political trends. These corps included the provincial estates and town council which monopolized local political power; a group of venal officeholders known as the *Bureau des Finances*; the Chamber of Commerce composed of the city's mercantile elite; and several guilds involved in the production and sale of textiles. The first section of the book deals with the relationship of corporate groups to issues of political authority and state finance. The provincial estates held the right to govern the province and consent to all taxes levied within its territory. What was the social composition of the estates, and in whose interest did this privileged body govern? The elite as a whole? Or a smaller group? Next the tension between the bases of royal taxation and credit will be addressed. What taxes were levied and on whom were they placed? Was there an effort to undermine the tax exemptions of the elite and introduce greater equality? Why or why not? The monarchy used a variety of corporate institutions, the city itself as well as venal officeholders and guilds to mobilize credit. How did the reliance upon advances from corporate groups affect the possibility for administrative and fiscal reform in Lille? Finally, political responses to the closed structure of corporate power and rising taxes will be discussed. What groups contested the town council's power in 1789? What issues led to their mobilization?

The second section discusses the problem of a regulated economy from two perspectives: first, that of royal and local officials and second, that of the commercial bourgeoisie. In the hands of government officials, economic policy in the 1760s moved away from mercantilism toward liberalism, a trend that culminated with the abolition of the guilds in 1791. What ethical norms, fiscal interests, and economic motivations underlay the regulatory policies of the municipal magistracy, intendants, and royal ministers? What problems did royal officials encounter in trying to introduce measures based upon the principles of laissez-faire? Why did such reforms fail? Next the stake of merchants and manufacturers in a regulated economy will be explored by looking at their relationship to three textile guilds. Did Lille's commercial bourgeoisie benefit from corporate regulations, or were they uniformly opposed to such economic controls? To what extent was the gradual liberalization of the economy a governmental response to bourgeois interest? What role did battles over economic regulation play in the formation of a revolutionary outlook?

Finally, the last chapter surveys several Napoleonic institutions with an eye to the legacy of the old regime. Did any of the habits, interests, and expectations associated with corporate groups in the old regime survive into the nineteenth century? Were groups able to recreate within an ostensibly egalitarian society an institutional base for their former privileges? If so how? Before turning to these case studies, however, it may be helpful to keep in mind the institutional setting in Lille.

The setting

Lying near the northernmost tip of France, the tiny province of Walloon Flanders occupied only a portion of what is now the department of the Nord. Its territory consisted of three juridically independent cities, Lille,

Douai, and Orchies, and the countryside, or more precisely the feudal territories known as *châtellenies*, surrounding them. Directly to the north lay the Dutch-speaking area of Maritime Flanders, a separate province also under French governance. On the eve of the Revolution, Lille was the seventh largest city in France. From the late seventeenth century to the 1740s, the population grew 15·5 percent, from approximately 55,000 to 63,500. After this decade until the Revolution, Lille's population was virtually stagnant, reaching a height of about 66,000 in 1787.[38] The rather modest rise in urban population was not the consequence of a sluggish regional economy. Rather, it corresponded to dual patterns of rural and urban growth associated with protoindustrialization.[39] The regional population was increasing most rapidly in the small textile villages of the countryside, for which Lille served as a commercial hub. Between 1709 and 1789, the industrious bourg of neighbouring Roubaix grew an astonishing 166 per cent, from approximately 4,500 to 12,000 inhabitants. In 1787 the population density of the *généralité* of Flanders and Artois, based on estimates by Necker, was 89 persons per km², almost double the average density of 46 persons per km² for France overall.[40]

In general, the crowded province was characterized by innovative agricultural techniques, textile manufacturing in both town and country, and commercial connections stretching across Europe and the Atlantic ocean. Lille's manufacturers produced soap and starch, evaporated salt from marshes, refined sugar imported from the French colonies, and pressed coleseed oil in dozens of windmills ringing the city. The city's merchants also sold colonial products like coffee, dyes, sugar and spices imported via Dunkerque.[41] The heart of the city's prosperity, however, had always been in textile production and sales, particularly in the manufacture of linens, woolens, and lace.

Mercantilistic regulations first developed during the fifteenth century still governed economic relations between town and country, especially in matters of cloth production. To the countryside was assigned the task of supplying raw materials and preparing them for manufacturing. To the city was reserved the more complicated and lucrative stages of production and sale, much of which was controlled by Lille's guilds. By the eighteenth century, the enormous growth of rural industry had begun to pose a challenge to the city's domination over its hinterland. Although textile manufacturing in bourgs like Roubaix, Tourcoing, and Lannoy had developed under the sponsorship of Lille's merchants, rural entrepreneurs eventually began to try to cast off their dependence on the urban market.

The privileged economic situation of the city and its elite should not be confused with a higher level of prosperity for urban inhabitants overall. Literacy was highest in the rural areas of the Nord, not in Lille with its crowded, impoverished workforce. The extent of urban poverty and deprivation should not be underestimated. Overall in 1745, 45 per cent of Lille's male taxable population was too poor to pay the *capitation* tax. Most of the poor lived in the disease-ridden textile quarter of St. Sauveur, where two-thirds of the men were incapable of paying this tax. For this two-tiered city with its bustling commerce sector and destitute underclass of casual laborers and indigent workers, it is wise to heed Pierre Deyon's warning, "Let us be suspicious of clichés relative to the 'prosperity' of the eighteenth century; all the cities of the kingdom did not live by the rhythm of Bordeaux, Nantes, Lyon or Paris."[42]

Commerce in Flanders profited from a highly developed network of roads and canals. Lille itself had been founded on the easily defended, but swampy shores of the Deûle river, a geographical location from which it had derived its name, *Lisle*, the island. In 1693 a new canal connected the Deûle and Scarpe rivers, making possible a complete waterway from French Flanders to the rich coal mines in the Austrian Netherlands. In 1750 a second canal and set of locks outside Lille allowed passage through a previously unnavigable section of the Deûle river that had forced merchants to unload and reload all goods transported around the city. Finally, in 1779 a third canal joined the Lys and Aa rivers. With this last canal, the Scheldt, Scarpe, Deûle, and Lys rivers all were interconnected, and, most important, Lille became directly linked by water to the port of Dunkerque.[43] Although there was no *corvée* in Walloon Flanders, taxes set aside for roadwork helped to make the provincial network of paved roads "a model for France." In 1764 communication with Paris was regularized by a stagecoach service that left the capital every other day.[44]

Special tariff arrangements enhanced the opportunity for profitable foreign trade. Under the Spanish Habsburgs, Flanders had traded extensively with Spain and its American colonies, as well as with the Low Countries. After the annexation, both the French and Spanish erected new customs bureaus that cut Flanders off from the Spanish Netherlands. To allay the mounting fears of Lille's merchants, Colbert granted them a *droit de transit*, by which Lille's merchants and manufacturers could both import raw materials from abroad and export finished products to foreign countries without paying duty, or at least only a nominal amount. To enjoy the right of transit, the merchants had to export their products through specified French ports.[45] In spite of the advantages Lille enjoyed in international commerce, trade with the French interior remained quite expensive. Classified as a "province reputedly foreign" (*province réputée étrangère*), Flanders never became integrated into the Five Great Farms, the customs union set up by Colbert that covered approximately two-thirds of France and followed the tariff of 1664. A duty of 12 to 15 percent was levied on most merchandise from French Flanders when it entered the region of the Five Great Farms.[46]

Although Lille has usually been considered a quintessentially bourgeois city, it was also a military one. A border town of critical tactical importance, Lille was forced to support a huge system of fortifications characteristic of the "military revolution."[47] Four months after its conquest by the French, the military genius Vauban began constructing an enormous citadel for the city. In December 1667, four hundred workers broke ground for the ramparts, and the labor of another 1,400 peasants was soon requisitioned. By 1670 the workers had completed the huge pentagonally-shaped fortification capable of holding 12,000 infantry and 1,200 calvary, as well as provisions to withstand a siege for sixty days in the city and another forty days in the citadel itself. Indeed, when the Dutch attacked Lille in 1708, the citadel withstood a siege for 100 days before surrendering, a substantial improvement over the two and a half weeks it had taken Louis XIV to claim victory. During his rebuilding of the city's fortresses, Vauban also increased the size of Lille by one-third, a measure that relieved overcrowding inside the walls and perhaps helped to slow a bit the transmission of diseases that plagued the damp and marshy city.[48]

Political and judicial power in Walloon Flanders was wielded by a small number of closed, privileged corporate groups and royal appointees. The estates of Walloon Flanders, confirmed by Louis XIV's annexation treaty in their "accustomed Rights, Usages, Privileges, Prerogatives, Jurisdiction, Justice, and Administration," formed the most important provincial corps. The estates represented the province to the king, approved and assessed royal taxes, and in general administered most local affairs. Unlike provincial estates elsewhere in France, those in Flanders were not composed of the traditional three orders, but of four "members," which spoke for the interests of three cities and the rural *châtellenie*. Delegates from the town councils of Lille, Douai and Orchies formed the first three members, and four noble *grands baillis* appointed by the four principal *seigneurs hauts justiciers* in the countryside sat collectively as the fourth. Because Douai and Orchies were only small towns, political power in the provincial estates came to rest with the four noble *baillis* and town council of Lille.

The clergy and nobility had no corporate representation in the provincial estates. They did, however, have official assemblies in which they consented to taxes levied on landed property which they farmed themselves. Nonetheless, because they were not included as official "members" in the provincial estates, the nobles and clergy in Walloon Flanders exercised little institutionalized political power.[49]

All provincial business handled by the estates pertaining directly to Lille came under the jurisdiction of Lille's town council, a corps of magistrates bearing the proud title of *Le Magistrat* or *La Loi*. This corps, the most important in the city, managed the city's finances, supervised public works and municipal charity, and issued ordinances governing the moral life of the community. By virtue of their membership in the provincial estates, they had the right to collect all taxes in the city. A subgroup of twelve men on the town council called the *échevins* sat as a court which exercised high, medium, and low justice and enjoyed jurisdiction in the first instance over most of the civil and criminal cases in the city. The capitulation treaty also confirmed the municipal magistrates in their power of "police" over the guilds and the urban economy. By this power, the municipal magistrates were entitled to regulate nearly all aspects of the local economy, including the right to set food prices, to oversee marketplaces, to incorporate guilds by granting them statutes, and to set the cost of the latter's masterships. In short, no part of municipal life was left untouched, in some form or fashion, by the magistrates' all-pervasive authority.[50]

The inhabitants of Lille were divided into two legal categories: the *bourgeois*, who enjoyed a number of civil privileges within the city; and the *manants*, who had no particular rights. The bourgeois of Lille were eligible for a position in the town council, enjoyed modest reductions on certain local sales taxes, had the right to trial before the *échevins*, could not be arrested for debts, and could not have their property seized arbitrarily. Initially, one purchased the status of bourgeois from the town council, who had the right to refuse the request, for the sum of fifteen *livres parisis*. For sons of the bourgeois, the status became hereditary.[51]

At the time of Lille's annexation, there were three secular judicial courts in Lille, in addition to that of *échevins* sitting in the town council. The first court, reputedly created by the Count of Flanders early in the Middle Ages, was a feudal *bailliage* court of minor significance. The second, the *Gouvernance*, was a royal court established by Philippe le Bel in 1314 and had jurisdiction over the villages in the *châtellenie* and royal cases in Lille. The third was the *Chambre des Comptes*, founded by the Duke of Burgundy in 1385 in order to audit the financial records of towns and oversee the ducal domain. This court was relocated in Brussels after Louis XIV's conquest, and in 1692 was replaced in Lille by a *Bureau des Finances*, a similar but less important French court. Cases judged by the *échevins* and *Gouvernance* were appealed to the royal sovereign court (*Conseil Souverain*) of Tournai, established in 1668 and elevated twenty years later to the status of *Parlement*. Later Louis XIV transferred the Parlement to Douai, where it remained until the Revolution. A judicial latecomer to the province, the Parlement of Douai remained one of the more passive high courts in France and played less of a role in the politicization of local populations so common elsewhere in France.[52] The capitulation treaty was designed to guarantee local control over judicial affairs. Judges were required to be "natives of the Low Countries," and

Louis agreed not to sell offices in the judiciary or municipal administration.[53]

Louis XIV established several new institutions in French Flanders. In
1679, he created a mounted police force (*Maréchaussée*) to patrol the
highways and control vagabonds. To mint new coinage, an *Hôtel des
Monnaies* was founded in 1685. (After its annexation, Flanders kept a
separate system of currency based on the *florin*; four *florins* equalled five
livres.) In 1693 two *Maîtrises des Eaux et Forêts* were created with
jurisdiction over the waterways and forests in the countryside.[54] In
addition, two new organizations were founded to promote commercial
interests within the city. In 1714 a Chamber of Commerce was set up so
that merchants and manufacturers in Lille could transmit their opinions
on commerce directly to the intendant or to the controller general, the
king's chief financial minister in Paris. The Chamber of Commerce was
composed of a director and four *syndics*, who were chosen by an electoral
college consisting of twenty of the most prominent merchants in the
city. In 1715 the royal government created a *Juridiction Consulaire*, a
commercial court which arbitrated, at no cost, bankruptcy cases and other
legal disputes between merchants. This court consisted of one judge and
four consuls selected by the same electoral college of merchants.[55]

The provincial particularism of Walloon Flanders was reiterated in
ecclesiastical matters. The province was divided into two dioceses: that of
Arras, whose bishop was appointed by the king of France, and that of
Tournai, controlled by the Austrian Habsburg government. Lille and its
surrounding countryside fell within the diocese of Tournai and hence
remained subject to the spiritual authority of a foreign bishop.
Ecclesiastical revenues collected in Lille supported the seminary of
Tournai in the Austrian Netherlands, where all the clergy of the diocese
was trained. Lille was divided into seven parishes. That of Saint Pierre was
the seat of the important chapter of the college of Saint Pierre, in whose
church the city's official ceremonies were held. In addition, there were
twenty-one convents and nine monasteries within the city walls, a clerical
presence that testified to the intense religiosity and success of the Counter-
Reformation in the region. Article three of the capitulation treaty had
requested Louis to agree that liberty of conscience could never be
permitted in the city, while article four reaffirmed the observance of the
decrees of the Council of Trent.[56]

Two royally appointed officials helped the French monarchy to govern
the province. In 1676 Louis XIV established the post of governor general
over the region of Flanders, Hainaut, and Cambrésis. Although the
governor general was the military head of the province, his functions in
the eighteenth century were largely honorific and the high-ranking dukes

and princes holding the title rarely left the royal court to spend time in Flanders. The governor did serve, however, as an intermediary between the provincial estates and royal officials in Paris or Versailles. The sinecure cost the province of Walloon Flanders 22,175 *livres* a year and represented just one of the new military expenses the region came to support routinely under French rule. In addition to the newly created provincial governor, the citadel of Lille kept its own military governor.[57]

The Intendant of Justice, Police, and Finances was a more important royal appointment. Arriving in 1668, the first intendant was authorized to supervise municipal finances and taxation, to arbitrate disputes between corporate groups, to regulate markets and to oversee other aspects of the urban economy – all functions of the municipal magistrates and provincial estates. It is not surprising that the municipal magistrates greeted the new official coldly, and that the intendant, in turn, found the corps of magistrates "difficult to govern, because it was composed of more than forty heads, among which there were few reasonable ones."[58] Gradually a more harmonious relationship emerged. All important municipal decisions were cleared by the intendants, but the municipal magistrates maintained a high degree of initiative in addressing local concerns.

To aid him in his work, the intendant of Flanders chose two subdelegates, one each from Lille and Douai. Although the intendants were bureaucratic "outsiders" subject to direct recall by the king, the subdelegates were local men enmeshed in the corporate structure of provincial power. It was common for these secondary officials to hold administrative offices in the provincial estates.

As late as 1699 Vauban had noted that Lille's inhabitants felt "little affection" towards France, but the Dutch occupation of Lille from 1708 to 1713 helped to transform their hostility into grudging allegiance. The new conquerors from the Netherlands flooded the city with Dutch merchandise and put heavy tariffs on all products exported from Lille. Calvinist preachers began proselytizing the local populace, and towns-people were horrified when Swiss and Dutch soldiers profaned the sacred host or stoned statues of the Virgin. When the French reconquered Lille, the inhabitants welcomed them back as defenders of the city's commerce and its faith.[59]

Before the Dutch conquest, Vauban had advised Louis XIV that the animosity of the Lillois toward the French might be overcome, if the monarch did not "harm their privileges, place them at the mercy of tax farmers and *traitants*, worse than wolves in their sight, [or] overtax them."[60] The next chapters will discuss whether royal officials followed Vauban's advice, and what the consequences of the fiscal monarchy's policies were.

2   State finance and local privileges

The financial bases of government mirror the priorities and structure of the state itself. Forms of power, systems of social classification, notions of property, and flows of capital are all bound up in a state's fiscal apparatus. In the eighteenth century, the crown's financial problems called into question the political and social foundations of the monarchy. In Flanders, members of the provincial elite, noble and non-noble, challenged a system of royal domination resting upon a bureaucratic network of intendants and a corporately based alliance between the crown and provincial estates. The next four chapters explore contradictions underlying the crown's fiscal and administrative policies and their effects on provincial politics. Reinforcing, and even creating, dispersed corporate privileges at the same time as it fostered egalitarian ideals, the extension of monarchical power ultimately reached an impasse that helped to open the way to a radical reconstruction of the basis of state authority.

Provincial power: crown, municipal magistrates and noble baillis

The estates of Walloon Flanders, as we noted earlier, were controlled by delegates from Lille's municipal magistracy and four noble *baillis* appointed by the principal *seigneurs hauts justiciers* in the countryside. Lille's municipal magistracy was composed of thirty-three temporary officials and ten permanent ones who assisted them. Like other cities in Walloon Flanders, Lille had never had a tradition of municipal elections. Every year, according to the regulations set by the city's medieval charter of 1235, four royal commissioners selected the temporary members of the corps and audited the city's accounts. Under French rule these commissioners were the governor of the province, the intendant, and two noblemen appointed by the king. The thirty-three temporary magistrates included a *rewart*, twelve *échevins*, eight *jurés*, four *voir-jurés*, and eight *prud'hommes*, the latter nominated by the priests of Lille's four oldest parishes. The most important subgroup was the *échevins*, who sat on the regulatory boards of various guilds and formed the court of first instance for most civil and criminal cases in the city. The first *échevin* held the title of mayor, the second that of *cottereau*.

The ten permanent officials included two clerks, three treasurers, a *procureur syndic*, his substitute, and three *conseillers pensionnaires*. These last five officials provided legal counsel for the town council. The *procureur syndic* had to be consulted before any decision of importance was taken, and the first *conseiller pensionnaire* was sent as a deputy to the royal court on matters of extreme urgency. The mayor, *cottereau*, *procureur syndic*, and first *conseiller pensionnaire* sat collectively as the delegates of the town council in the provincial estates.[1]

Originally the permanent officials had been appointed for life by the other members of the town council, but under Louis XIV these posts were transformed into hereditary, venal offices. In 1696 the corps of municipal magistrates was able to purchase the offices of the second and third *conseiller pensionnaire* and later, in 1726, bought up the offices of the treasurers.[2] These posts became commissions granted by the municipal magistrates. The municipal magistrates, however, never succeeded in buying the other offices, which effectively became the property of the families who had purchased them.[3] As a result, the *procureur syndic* and first *conseiller pensionnaire*, who served as permanent delegates to the provincial estates, acquired a substantial degree of political independence.

To become a municipal magistrate, one had to be married, Catholic, and hold the status of *bourgeois* of Lille. In the eighteenth century, the town council was composed almost equally of nobles and non-nobles. Although a few nobles were recruited from old families, most of them were of recent lineage. The non-noble members were chosen from the *rentiers*, officeholders, and wholesale merchants (*négociants*) in the city. According to the city's medieval charter, retail merchants and practicing lawyers could not be appointed to the municipal magistracy.[4] Consequently, although commerce was the lifeblood of the city, commercial groups in Lille wielded far less influence in the town council than their economic importance warranted.

Several regulations were designed to prevent the corps of municipal magistrates from turning into an oligarchic clique. First, family members with close ties were prohibited from serving simultaneously, a regulation that generally was enforced. Distant family ties between those in the magistracy were fairly common, but control never fell into the hands of a few tightly-knit clans. Second, to ensure that one group of officials did not gain too much power, a new corps of magistrates was supposed to be chosen each year. However, to commemorate special events, such as a birth or marriage in the royal family, the king could authorize the "Continuation de la Loi," by which the corps was reappointed for another year without any change. From 1750 to 1789, the king found enough memorable occasions to continue the magistracy twenty-two times. Furthermore, even when a new town council was appointed, the same individual was allowed to rotate from one post to another within the corps. Someone who served as an *échevin* one year, therefore, could become a *juré* the next, a *prud'homme* the following, and then start over again. At the end of the eighteenth century, it was not at all uncommon for an individual to have served fifteen or more consecutive years on the town council.[5] Overall, then, through its combination of royal appointment and sale of offices, the French crown increased both the oligarchic and proprietary character of power in the town council after Lille's annexation.

The four *seigneurs hauts justiciers* who controlled rural seats in the estates were the king, the Prince de Soubise, the Comte d'Egmont, and the Duc d'Orléans, seigneurs of Phalempin, Cysoing, Wavrin, and Comines respectively. The seigneurs leased their offices of *bailli* in the estates for life, with the exception of the *bailli* of Phalempin controlled by the king. After the conquest of Flanders, Louis XIV made this office hereditary and sold it to Diedeman de la Rianderie, whose family remained in office until the Revolution. The nobles controlling the other three seigneuries were not free to lease their offices to whomever they pleased. The provincial governor and the intendant often nominated new *baillis*, and no one was appointed to these powerful offices without the king's approval.[6]

Although their offices were sold for one life only, the *baillis* were often allowed to pass their offices down to their heirs, a practice that allowed a handful of families to remain in power for most of the century. Both the oldest and newest noble families in the province held these offices. Whether the de Muyssarts were already noble in 1096, as members of the family claimed, may be open to question, but they could trace their noble lineage more convincingly back to the fifteenth century. On the other hand, Jean Philippe du Béron was newly ennobled and owed his title to the office of *secrétaire du roi* that he had purchased. A number of *baillis* from older noble families had ancestors who had served on Lille's town council, in some cases as mayor. Some of the *baillis*, notably those appointed by the Prince de Soubise, also exercised important military function. Mengin de Fondragon and Imbert de la Basecque had been *aide major* of Fort St. Sauveur and governor of Lille's citadel, respectively. The father of Bady d'Aymeries had been director of fortifications at Maubeuge for Louis XIV. It is difficult, therefore, to place one clearcut label – old or new, robe or sword – on the noble pedigrees of these men.[7]

The *baillis* controlled a number of important auxiliary offices, those of treasurers, clerks, legal counselors, and the like, that were attached to the provincial estates. In 1694, when Louis XIV turned these posts into hereditary venal offices, the *baillis* purchased them collectively as a corps and then sold them to individuals of their choosing. The officeholders could sell or bequeath their offices, subject to the *baillis'* approval. The vast majority of these officeholders were new nobles: Herts, Imbert de Chereng, Demadre du Grand Hollay, Tesson de la Croix, and Fruict de Riez were all ennobled while they were serving in the estates. The subdelegates of the intendant were also tied into this system of officeholding. For most of the eighteenth century, the subdelegates of Lille came from the d'Haffrenghes family, which also controlled the office of second *conseiller pensionnaire* in the provincial estates. One family, that of Demadre, held an office of *contrôleur* in the estates and *conseiller pensionnaire* in Lille's town council.[8] Just as in the municipal magistracy, officeholding in the estates enhanced familial power at the expense of more impersonal, bureaucratic kinds of authority.

All in all, royal French policy elaborated more fully than ever before a complex, patrimonial organization of power in the estates, which rested upon royal appointment, hereditary fiefdoms, and property in office. This closed and privileged organization of local power lasted for over a century after Lille's incorporation into France. The next sections will suggest some reasons for its continuation and its eventual fall.

The growth of royal impositions

Walloon Flanders enjoyed several important tax privileges. The province was exempt from the salt tax or *gabelle* and from the Farmers General's tobacco monopoly. Flemish inhabitants were permitted to raise their own tobacco, which was taxed by provincial authorities. The province also was allowed to pay a rather nominal subsidy called the *aide ordinaire* in lieu of the royal *taille*. When the king demanded a new tax, the provincial estates had the right to pay the crown an *abonnement*, or fixed payment, and to levy any type of local tax in its stead. Although Lille enjoyed a position more favorable than that of many cities in the French interior, the inhabitants did not escape a rising rate of royal taxation, particularly after the mid-century wars. In the five decades before the Revolution the weight of royal taxes approximately tripled (see Table 1). Privileged groups were obliged to pay a greater share of the taxes created by Louis XIV and his successors. New direct impositions circumvented pre-existing fiscal immunities, while surtaxes on indirect levies tended to hit the population as a whole.

Before Lille was annexed, the city had paid only a very small number of taxes directly to the Spanish Habsburg king. These included the city's

Table 1. *The nominal weight of royal taxation in Lille, 1740–1788*

	1740	1750	1760	1770	1780	1787	1788
1 *octrois* for king	22,594	21,993	22,450	22,704	21,746	23,068	20,763
2 *aide ord.*	45,748	45,509	45,509	45,509	37,509	37,509	37,509
3 *aide extr.*	0	36,790	42,676	0	20,602	0	0
4 *capitation*	57,746	57,600	57,600	57,600	63,360	61,807	61,597
5 *contrôle des actes*	21,094	28,126	28,126	33,976	43,242	53,035	53,035
6 domanial, militia	13,454	11,482	13,508	16,459	19,758	20,558	20,558
7 spl, royal *dixième*	0	9,133	0	0	0	0	0
– royal *vingtièmes*	0	40,587	102,086	106,442	119,747	90,720	99,720
– 3rd *vingtième*	0	0	10,949	0	0	49,756	34,366
8 spl, *octrois*	0	0	8,105	62,934	125,870	157,337	157,337
9 *don gratuit*	0	0	0	12,000	28,880	39,037	39,037
Total (*florins*)	160,636	251,220	331,009	357,624	480,714	532,827	523,922
Total (*livres*)	200,795	314,025	413,761	426,456	601,017	666,034	654,902
Percent change		56%	31%	8%	34%	11%	−1·7%

Source: The table is compiled from the accounts of Lille's three treasurers in the municipal archives of Lille and lists the amounts actually paid to the royal government that year. It does not include the weight of such excise taxes as those levied on soap, playing cards, and leather that were collected by the Farmers General, nor the weight of tariffs on Lille's imports and exports. In the late eighteenth century it was common to apply the local tax assessed for the *aide extraordinaire* (about 30,000 *florins* or 37,500 *livres* per year) toward the debt servicing of the city rather than to turn it over to the royal government. Thus this tax was still collected, even though it was not reported to the center and hence not listed continuously in the table.

quota of the provincial subsidy (*aide ordinaire*) which the estates had paid since 1550, and a small percentage of five *octrois*, the latter totalling about 27,500 *livres*.[9]

The *octrois* formed the basis of the municipal budget and included both tolls placed upon goods entering the city and sales tax collected within the city. These fees were assessed according to the quantity, not value, of goods sold. Local tax farmers submitted bids to the town council for the right to collect a particular *octroi*, or combination of them, for several years. The highest bidder was awarded a lease stipulating the sum he owed to the city and entitling him to keep additional revenues for his expenses and profit.[10]

During the eighteenth century, the ordinary provincial *aide* was usually 250,000 *livres*, of which Lille paid about 57,000 *livres*, slightly less than one-quarter of the total. Lille's municipal magistrates and the *baillis* raised the money for this subsidy by placing local *vingtièmes* or twentieths (not to be confused with the royal *vingtième* discussed below) on the property of inhabitants. Property which nobles worked directly themselves was exempt from the local *vingtièmes*; the rest of their property was taxed. It was customary, however, for the nobility and the clergy to consent to pay local taxes on their personal property at one-half the regular rate. This consent was registered in their annual official assemblies convoked at the same time as the estates. All officeholders were exempt from the ordinary provincial *aide*.[11]

In wartime, the provincial estates had also granted the Habsburgs an additional subsidy called the *aide extraordinaire*. Louis had collected this aide totalling 250,000 *livres* during the War of the Spanish Succession (1701–1713), after which it was discontinued for two decades. The War of the Polish Succession led to its revival in 1735 and subsequent transformation into a permanent annual imposition. In peacetime, however, the king usually allowed the estates to apply the revenue toward servicing the provincial debt or supporting public works projects, such as the construction of barracks.[12] In the eighteenth century, this subsidy was officially 262,000 *livres*, of which Lille paid 60,000 *livres*, not quite one-fourth.

During negotiations between the estates and Louis XIV, the king agreed to let the estates charge all privileged groups for this subsidy. Following provincial custom, it was decided to assess the nobility and the clergy at one-half the regular rate, but to make privileged officeholders pay in full, a ruling that will be examined in more detail later.

Several new taxes, all levied on privileged groups, were created during the wars of Louis XIV and his successors. The *capitation*, a head tax, was established in 1695 and became permanent in 1701. Since professional status or membership in a corps, and not income, was the basis for assessing the tax, it was by no means egalitarian. In Flanders, because nobles were charged for the *capitation* according to the classification of their fiefs, rich nobles did not necessarily pay more than poor ones. The nobility as a whole, furthermore, paid only a very small percentage of the provincial *abonnement*. Members of corps, such as the *Bureau des Finances* or the *Hôtel des Monnaies*, were charged a fixed amount based upon the type of their office.[13] Originally set at 85,183 *livres*, in 1750 Lille's payment for the capitation was reduced to 60,000 *livres*; a surtax of 20 percent (four *sols per livre*) was added for a total of 72,000 *livres*.[14] It remained at that level until the Revolution.

The royal *dixième*, a 10 percent tax on the revenues of all individuals, was created in 1710 during the War of the Spanish Succession. Suppressed in 1717, it was reimposed during the wars of the Polish and Austrian Successions (1733–1737, 1741–1749). The *abonnement* for the *dixième* in the 1740s was approximately 114,000 *livres*.[15] In 1749 the royal *vingtième*, a 5 percent tax on revenues, replaced the *dixième* in Flanders, although the province continued to pay a 10 percent surtax (two *sols per livre*) upon the discontinued abonnement for the *dixième* for about a decade. In 1756, at the beginning of the Seven Years War, the royal *vingtième* was doubled and extended until the Revolution. Twice, from 1760 to 1764 and from 1782 to 1786, the *vingtième* was officially tripled.[16] From 1756 to 1789 the payment to the crown for the two *vingtièmes* remained fairly uniform, between 112,000 and 133,000 *livres*, but it rose to approximately 182,000 *livres* during the creation of the third *vingtièmes*.

The city raised revenue to pay for the royal *vingtièmes* by placing local *vingtièmes* on urban property and also assessing occupational groups, especially guilds.[17] Residents of the city paid taxes on every home that they occupied or rented out. Initially the municipal magistrate used a *cahier* from 1601 to assess taxes on the property of the nobility and clergy, and consequently some lands were under-taxed, or not taxed at all. In 1743, however, the magistrates reformed the *cahier* and included privileged property which had previously been omitted.[18] Overall, this tax appeared to be the most progressive one levied in the city before 1789, and the one felt most acutely by the elite.[19]

The so-called "voluntary contributions," *dons gratuits*, which the royal government exacted in 1758, 1761, and 1768, were designed to squeeze money from cities. Lille was required to pay 200,000 *livres* for the first one, 75,000 for the second, and 140,000 for the third.[20] To reimburse Lille for the first *don gratuit*, the king authorized the municipal magistrates to borrow the necessary funds and to increase the *octrois* levied on meat (known as the *pied fourchu*) by one-third to service the debt. In Lille, as in other French cities, the new *octroi* used to pay the *don gratuit* was to be paid by "all persons of whatever *état*, quality and condition they were."[21]

When new taxes became too difficult to impose, the royal government resorted to surtaxes, the *sols per livre*, on old ones. Beginning in 1705, for example, a 10 percent surtax, two *sols per livre*, was placed on all fees collected by the Farmers General; by 1787 it had risen to 50 percent (ten *sols per livre*). In Lille surtaxes were added to many of the *abonnements* that the city owed the royal government, including the payments for the *capitation, don gratuit*, first royal *vingtième* and the *contrôle des actes*.

The *contrôle*, which officially consisted of registration fees upon deeds and official documents, was imposed in French Flanders in 1696, during the War of the League of Augsburg. In lieu of these fees, the provincial estates paid an *abonnement* generated by placing local *vingtièmes* on the property of everyone in the city. Before the Revolution the *abonnement* itself was 44,196 *livres*, the surcharge on it, 22,097 *livres*.

The surtax on the city's *octrois* constituted the largest royal tax placed

Table 2. *Lease prices of Lille's major tax farms* (*in* florins)

	1740	1750	1760	1770	1780	1788
beer	384,560	377,541	381,020	404,720	447,410	489,420
spirits	169,555	157,148	134,795	132,733	178,169	218,166
wine	24,000	56,000	72,212	69,907	90,800	121,372
meat	34,000	*	35,300	64,000	88,000	127,222
wood & coal	22,750	*	22,400	27,375	29,940	37,187
Total (*florins*)	634,865	*	645,727	698,735	834,319	993,367
Total (*livres*)	793,581	*	807,159	873,419	1,042,899	1,241,709
Percent change:				8·2	19·4	19·1
Percent change, 1740–1788: 56·7						
Percent change, 1770–1788: 42·2						

*Incomplete information
Source: See Table 1.

on Lille; in 1786 it was even greater than the combined weight of the three royal *vingtièmes*. In 1760 the central government placed two *sols per livre*, a 10 percent surtax, on all *octrois* across France; by 1781 the official surtax was ten *sols per livre*, or 50 percent. The provincial estates in French Flanders, however, received a reduction of one-half the official rate.[22] In 1788 Lille's payment for this assessment was about 196,000 *livres*. The town council raised the crown's money by placing their own surtaxes on municipal *octrois*. Like the *octrois*, the surtaxes were flat fees assessed when goods crossed urban boundaries or were sold. Because these fees were placed upon basic necessities like wood, beer, wine, and meat, the surtaxes fell most heavily upon the poor.

As shown in Table 2, the lease prices for the city's major tax farms increased over 40 percent in the two decades immediately preceding the Revolution. It is doubtful that a rising population or increased consumption stemming from economic prosperity mitigated the sizeable increase. Lille, like most French cities, experienced industrial depression in the 1770s and late 1780s, and the city's population was rising only slowly, owing to patterns of rural manufacturing. These additional charges reinforced the regressive nature of urban taxation in the period directly before the Revolution and increased the cost of living for those least able to pay, urban wage workers.

Finally, Lille paid a variety of miscellaneous sums for "domanial" fees, even though these fees represented new kinds of payments rather than old ones traditionally attached to the royal domain. Included in this *abonnement* were funds paid to prevent the creation of offices of wine measurers and inspectors of butchers in the province, as well as money to support the militia and the king's mounted highway police.

Royal financial demands did not end with the *abonnements* paid by the provincial estates to the government. Flemish inhabitants, for example, paid excise taxes on paper and cartons, starch, leather, oil and soap, and playing cards, which were collected directly by the Farmers General. In 1775 the annual product of these indirect taxes in the *généralité* of Flanders and Artois totalled 678,000 *livres*.[23] Although figures are lacking for the period before the Revolution, surtaxes on these indirect taxes would certainly have aggravated their weight, which was felt in urban areas more acutely than the countryside. The amount generated by customs duties on Lille's manufacturing and mercantile activity is also unknown.

Overall, from 1740 to 1788 Lille's total payments to the crown increased about 225 percent, a large portion of which can be attributed to the royal *vingtièmes* and an even greater part to surtaxes on the *octrois* (see Table 1). Without a wage and price series for Lille, it is difficult to compare the nominal rise in the weight of taxation with the real weight measured against cost of living. It has been argued that inflation, measured in terms of grain prices, deflates substantially the nominal tax burden. Based on evidence from over thirty-one *généralités* between a base period of 1726–1741 and that of 1785–1789, Labrousse calculated that average grain prices rose approximately 65 percent across France. Labrousse goes on to show, however, that salaries in this same period were not keeping pace. As a result, even though nominal wages increased slowly, real wages actually declined about 25 percent. With the general shift in France toward indirect taxation after 1760, Labrousse concluded that the central government was trying to tax urban consumption in a period of falling real wages, a strategy unlikely to solve royal financial problems.[24] Based on Labrousse's work, it is likely that the nominal increase in Lille's taxes represented a very important rise in the real weight of taxes on urban wage earners, though less of a real increase for members of the propertied elite.

It has often been argued that French cities were privileged entities that successfully shifted the burden of taxation to peasants.[25] The thesis of the undertaxed city has been challenged on two counts. First, it has been argued that indirect taxation, which fell most heavily on urban consumers, increased more rapidly in the decades before the Revolution than direct taxes borne by peasants. Second, it has been stressed that cities contributed to the crown in more disguised forms, through the sale of offices and other auxiliary measures like loans and subsidies.[26]

The situation at Lille lends weight to both these arguments. Indirect taxes, which were heavily surtaxed, hit consumers in Lille far more than rural producers. In French Flanders, the royal surtax on the *octrois*, a tax rarely discussed in the general literature on finances, helped to shift the weight of royal taxation toward Lille away from the surrounding *châtellenie.* A report by the intendant in 1787 provided a very rough breakdown of royal taxes placed upon Lille and its countryside.[27] Excluding the surtax on *octrois* and the *don gratuit*, the intendant calculated the official *abonnements* for royal impositions for Lille at 443,146 *livres* (31 percent), and the *châtellenie* at 972,046 (69 percent). In 1789 the population of the *châtellenie* was approximately 236,500, and that of the city of Lille about 66,000. Thus although Lille had less than one-quarter of the area's total population, the city paid not quite one-third of the royal *abonnements*. If Lille's contribution to the surtax on the municipal *octrois* and *don gratuit*, both of which were primarily municipal taxes, were added to the above figures, the proportion paid by urban areas would be even higher. The city, moreover, helped out the royal government in other ways, by lending the crown money and by supporting it huge military establishment. The next section looks at these types of financial aid more closely.

Military support and urban debt

Table 3 provides a partial list of the debts on which the municipal government was still paying interest in 1791.[28] Since a number of debts had been contracted and liquidated in the interim, the list does not provide a complete history of urban indebtedness. Nonetheless, several patterns can be detected.

Above all, Lille's debt demonstrated the growing weight of the king's standing army and bureaucracy. Nearly all urban borrowing stemmed from royal requirements. The largest portion of the city's known debt after 1667, just over one-quarter of the total, had been contracted for constructing fortifications and new barracks for royal armies. Another quarter had been raised in order to have municipal privileges confirmed and to purchase venal offices, a practice that one historian called the "war chest" of the French crown.[29] *Dons gratuits* (5·4 percent) were products of the War of the League of Augsburg (1689) and the Seven Years War, while payments for the residences of the provincial governor and the intendant (4·4 percent) attested to ongoing support for the royal bureaucracy. Refinancing charges stemmed from an attempt by the municipal magistrates to meet huge deficits in the municipal treasury in the 1770s, a result of low tax yields and new royal demands, including surtaxes on municipal revenues and the construction of barracks. Sometimes the city benefited from the military needs of the crown. The canal system, responsible for about 10 percent of the city's debt, facilitated Lille's trade. The plans for canals, however, were first launched by Vauban, who saw their utility for military provisioning and strategic

Table 3. *Estimated debt of Lille in 1791*

Total debt: 5,616,399 *florins* (7,020,498 *livres*)
Known debt contracted under the French Bourbons: 3,890,966 *florins* (4,863,707 *livres*)
Source: A.D.N. C 2982

	Year	Sum (in *florins*)
Fortifications	1667	100,000
and barracks	1668	54,000
	1675	60,000
	1685	44,539
	1735	80,000
	1745	50,000
	1755	281,000
	1762	39,850
	1770	160,000
	1771	20,000
	1772	144,000
		Total 1,033,389 *fl.* (1,291,736 *l.*) (26·6%)
Canals	1686	60,000
	1691	40,000
	1750	352,325
		Total 452,325 *fl.* (565,406 *l.*) (11·6%)
Venal offices	1692	160,000
and confirmation	1699	355,920
of municipal	1726	290,402
privileges	1767	28,800
	1758	12,000
	1783	185,600
		Total 1,032,722 *fl.* (1,290,902 *l.*) (26·5%)
Dons gratuits	1689	50,000
	1761	160,000
		Total 210,000 *fl.* (262,500 *l.*) (5·4%)
Grain purchases	1742	320,000
	1770	29,000
	1772	9,000
	1789	40,000
	1790	80,000
		Total 478,000 *fl.* (597,500 *l.*) (12·3%)
Refinancing:	1767–87	170,530 *fl.* (213,162 *l.*) (4·4%)
conversion of		
rentes perpétuelles		
to *viagères*		

Governor's and intendant's *hôtel*	1729	94,000
	1786	160,000
		Total 254,000 *fl.* (317,500 *l.*) (6·5%)
Expansion of urban boundaries	1670	200,000 *fl.* (250,000 *l.*) (5·1%)
Lieu de santé	1672	60,000 *fl.* (75,000 *l.*) (1·5%)

Table 4. *Debt servicing and other payments aiding the state*

	1740	1750	1760	1770	1780	1787	1788
Debt[a]	156,414	221,372	219,111	210,982	255,078	344,695	528,854
Mil./Bur.[b]	160,279	211,843	154,849	245,679	161,134	254,581	213,733
Canals	*	52,711	*	59,794	45,705	44,274	36,112
Total, *florins*	*	485,926	*	516,455	461,917	643,550	778,699
Total, *livres*	*	607,482	*	645,557	577,396	804,437	973,373
livres/head	*	9·3	*	9·9	8·9	12·4	14·9

* Incomplete information
[a] This includes interest payments for all municipal debt, the majority of which was contracted on behalf of the crown, as well as periodic liquidation of specific *rentes*.
[b] This includes all payments for furnishing and maintaining barracks and residences of the governor and intendants, as well as honorariums for military officers, the governor, and the intendant.

maneuvers, such as flooding the path of advancing enemy troops. The expansion of the urban boundaries and the erection of a *lieu de santé* in the newly cleared area, clearly advantageous to the populace's health, was also related to the construction of Lille's citadel under Vauban. On the whole, it seems that only natural disaster, in the form of massive grain shortages, competed with the central government and its wars as a catalyst to urban indebtedness.

Table 4 provides an estimate of the total amount borne by the city for support of the royal army, debt servicing, and maintenance and construction of canals and roads. In the eighteenth century, Lille paid between 200,000 and 300,000 *livres* per year for military and related administrative expenses, a sum that exceeded any one form of royal taxation *per se*. Included in these payments were salaries (*traitements*) and lodging for military officers, honorariums and a lavish residence for the absentee provincial governor, and a fixed annual sum of 66,250 *livres* for the upkeep of fortifications around the city. The city also supplied wood, candles, straw, carts, clean linen, blankets, and food for the garrisons.

When the government demanded that the city undertake construction projects for the crown, the urban expenditures escalated even more. In 1786, for example, the royal government ordered Lille to build a new residence for the intendant. The total cost for military and administrative expenses that year was approximately 547,500 *livres*; of that sum, a total of 213,000 went toward the cost of building and furnishing the intendant's new quarters.

Usually total municipal expenditures for debt servicing, military expenses, and public works ranged annually from 577,000 to 645,000 *livres*. Some of these expenditures were part of the cost of running a city and were not the direct result of royal exactions. Nonetheless, the royal government was clearly able to tap a significant amount of urban revenues for the work of the state. Many of these costs, moreover, remained classified as local expenditures, and did not pass through the hands of tax farmers and *financiers* working for the central government. The purchase of linen, straw, and other supplies for the barracks, for example, was paid directly from municipal *octrois*. For this reason, statements of tax revenues reported to the royal government at the center may well underestimate the financial weight of the French state upon urban society in the old regime.

Although the costs of debt servicing increased between 1740 and 1788, the steep rise in the two years before the Revolution represents a significant departure from the norm. From 1750 to 1780 annual interest payments on all *rentes* usually totalled between 220,000 and 255,000 *florins*. For some unknown reason, in 1787 the municipal magistrates not only made the usual interest payments, but also began to liquidate debts by reimbursing the capital of bondholders (holders of *rentes héritières* described below). Windfall profits do not explain the strange policy; in fact at the end of these years the city was running a slight deficit. More likely, political battles offer the best clue to the new policy. In 1788 the royal government had been forced to call the Estates General because it was unable to service its debt. Consciousness of a national crisis was matched by suspicion of leaders at the local level. For decades in French Flanders the municipal magistrates had been attacked for mismanaging local funds and for failing to pay interest on time. Reimbursing urban creditors may have been a way of reassuring townspeople, who had become highly politicized, that the municipal government was still in good hands. In any case, the abnormal rise in debt liquidation reveals that there was an intense preoccupation in Lille not only with taxes, but also with debt, as the Revolution was about to unfold.

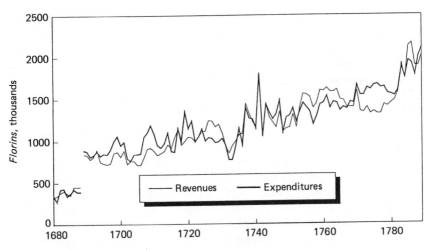

Source: Staquet, *Les finances communales de Lille*, Appendix

Fig. 1. The financial situation of Lille, 1668–1789

The problem of deficits

Municipal credit was based in the sale of bonds (*rentes héritières*) and annuities (*rentes viagères*), whose interest was secured by the *octrois*. In the case of *rentes viagères*, an investor purchased the *rente* issued by the city and was entitled to interest payments, usually 8 percent, for the entire life of the person named in the contract. *Rentes héritières* paid interest in perpetuity to the holder of the *rente*. Throughout the eighteenth century, the annual interest on *rentes héritières* remained at 4 percent.[30]

In the period of Louis XIV when the city contracted a debt, the royal government usually permitted the municipal magistrates to levy a new *octroi* to service that obligation. In the eighteenth century, however, it became common practice for the king simply to let the municipal magistrate pay the interest from existing urban revenues. As a result of enforced urban borrowing on behalf of the crown, urban finances lacked predictability and experienced periodic deficits.

Figure 1, based upon the work of historian René Staquet, shows the periods of deficit in Lille's treasury. Deficits occurred when the city's total receipts, including all revenues from taxes, loans, and urban property, fell short of its obligations. The most important obligations were taxes owed to the royal government, debt servicing, support for the military, salaries of city employees, public works, charities, and subsidies to industries. In periods of shortfall, some people, and from the account books it is not clear who, did not receive what they were owed. The municipal magistrates did not borrow to make ends meet.

Several periods of severe deficit are apparent: during the later wars of Louis XIV and into the regency (1688–1722), during and after the War of the Austrian Succession (1741–1752), and during the whole decade of the 1770s. Perhaps surprisingly, the city did not experience shortages during the Seven Years War or during the period 1782–1787, directly before the Revolution. These last two periods were accompanied by large enough tax increases to cover urban expenditures. In general, municipal deficits arose when the central government placed extraordinary demands upon the city without helping the city find ways to increase its revenues.

During the period of Louis XIV and the regency, the sale of municipal offices played a large role in undermining the stability of urban finances. From 1685 to 1708, the debt of Lille increased approximately 3,750,000 *livres*, and in the 1690s the municipal magistrates suspended some interest payments on municipal bonds. In 1698 the intendant, Dugué de Bagnols, wrote that the continual sale of offices had absorbed urban revenues and would "make it impossible for [the city] to re-establish itself for a long while."[31]

During the regency, the central government used the sale of offices to transfer down to municipalities a portion of its own debt. In 1717 the government suppressed many of the offices created under Louis XIV and reimbursed the municipality with *billets de liquidation*, paper money issued during Law's scheme that was soon worth approximately one-fifth the value of hard currency. After Law's system collapsed, the government in 1722 created new offices in the town halls and guilds, which were, in turn, suppressed two years later and reimbursed with government bonds yielding only 1 percent interest. A year later the municipality was forced to purchase new offices of treasurers.[32] In effect, the continual sale, suppression, and reimbursement of offices with depreciated government securities amounted to a disguised form of royal bankruptcy.

In following wars, the government did not resort to the sale of municipal offices on such a massive scale in Lille, perhaps because local administrators drove harder bargains. During the War of the Polish Succession in 1733, the government wanted the municipal magistrates to pay 996,000 *livres* for offices, but they refused. Thirteen years later during the War of the Austrian Succession, the price was renegotiated and the municipal magistrates contributed only 110,000 *livres*. No municipal offices were created in Lille in 1771 when Terray tried to foist offices on the city as part of his program to salvage a nearly bankrupt monarchy. The last time that the magistrates purchased offices was at the end of the War of the American Revolution in 1783, when they borrowed 232,241 *livres* for those of auctioneers.[33]

In the five decades before the Revolution, the city faced deficits in the 1740s, 1770s, and in 1788–1789, the latter partly resulting from the magistrates' surprising attempt to try to liquidate a portion of the municipal debt. In the mid-1740s, a period punctuated by massive grain purchases, tax increases, and war-related expenses, interest payments on the *rentes héritières* fell four years into arrears. In 1750 the town council decided to divide the *rentes héritières* into two types, new and old, the latter (*rentes héritières dites anciennes*) including all those constituted before 1740. Interest owed on the new *rentes héritières* was paid on time until the Revolution, but that on the old *rentes* remained permanently at least four years in arrears.

Although war ceased in 1748, Lille's obligations to the royal government did not significantly decline, because the city had to bear the cost of preparing for a new war and other public works projects. This expansion was supported by urban loans, not taxes. In 1750 and 1755 the royal government authorized the city to borrow huge sums, 352,325 and 281,000 *florins*, respectively, in order to begin constructing canals and barracks. Thus, even while the weight of royal taxation decreased, the municipal debt rose. There are no records of new *octrois* to secure these loans.

With the Seven Years War came new royal taxes: the second and third *vingtièmes*, the first surtax on the *octrois*, and the *dons gratuits*. The city did not run a deficit, owing to the new influx of revenues from taxes and several loans. The rise in direct taxation placed upon the privileged elite, however, made the political situation more sensitive and later fueled the campaign for political representation. In addition, Lille's debt had risen 31 percent between 1745 and 1772, from 3,980,000 to 5,230,000 *florins*, and no new municipal tolls or taxes had been established to service it.[34]

In the 1770s Lille's finances entered a period of crisis. Expenditures were higher than during the Seven Years War, but receipts fell. Several factors seemed to have been at work. First, even though war had ended and the third *vingtième* was suppressed, the overall burden of royal taxation did not shrink. Lower direct taxation was offset by new taxes on urban consumption, a more regressive, but politically easier, method of tapping private wealth. Within three years, between 1771 and 1774, the *abonnement* for the surtax on the *octrois* doubled, escalating from 62,000 to 126,000 *florins*. The city did not meet the increased demand. By 1776 the magistrates owed M. Thierry, *receveur des domaines du roi*, 197,777 *livres* for the two *abonnements* on the *sol per livre* of the *octrois* and the *don gratuit*.[35]

The chronic deficits of the 1770s may also have reflected a depressed economy.[36] Between 1765 and 1770, municipal funds allotted for the care of abandoned children rose 27,000 *florins*. To alleviate food shortages in

1770 and 1772, the municipal magistrates had been forced to purchase grain. In the same period, unpaid taxes entered in the receiver's account rose from around 8,700 to 45,200 *florins*. Furthermore, the prices for the leases for a number of the city's tax farms, not including the *sol per livre*, were declining or stagnant. Between 1770 and 1775 the lease price for the tax farm on beer (*bière cabaretière*) dropped by 31,000 *florins*.[37] From 1760 to 1770, the only tax farm that was auctioned off for a substantial increase was that on meat (*droit sur le pied fourchu*), but the additional revenue was earmarked for the royal government's *don gratuit*.

Added to the problem of higher surtaxes and economic woes was that of yet another draining military project: the construction of the St. André barracks costing approximately 440,000 *livres* (352,000 *florins*).[38] During this period, interest payments on the old *rentes héritières* fell nine years into arrears and remained between seven and eight years in arrears until the eve of the Revolution. The *rentes viagères* and new *rentes héritières* continued to be paid on time.

In the face of massive deficits, as high as 375,000 *livres* (300,000 *florins*) per year, the municipal magistrates seemed to have no plan. Nor did the intendant provide any guidance, though Caumartin was able to persuade the royal government to reduce its demand for the surtax on the *octrois* by half, from 40 to 20 percent. The municipal magistrates were loath to raise taxes on consumption. In fact, when the crown demanded the first surtax of 10 percent on the city's *octrois*, the municipal magistrates decided to put only a surtax of 5 percent on beer and let the treasury absorb the shortfall.[39] Apparently the intendant never forced them to impose the other 5 percent on this tax farm. New direct taxes were equally repugnant to the magistrates. The city fathers informed the royal government that local *vingtièmes* were already too high to even dream of establishing others, even though the population had supported three *vingtièmes* during the Seven Years War.[40]

Informed of the plight of the city's finances, the controller general in Paris turned a deaf ear and informed the city that cost-cutting measures and new *octrois* were the way to meet the deficit. These measures, he added bluntly, "should not be difficult for a great city like Lille."[41] Eventually the municipal magistrates had no choice but to raise the surtaxes on the city's *octrois*. Even so, they regarded the surtaxes as a blatant violation of article eight of the capitulation treaty, which stated that no imposition would be levied in the province without the consent of the provincial estates. The king, they noted with obvious displeasure, no longer seemed concerned with "observing the legal forms."[42]

The municipal magistrates devised one other financial strategy during these hard times. On 16 May 1767, before the crisis in municipal finances hit with full force, they resolved to begin to transform *rentes héritières* paying 4 percent in perpetuity into *rentes viagères* paying 8 percent for one lifetime. In the transition, any holders of *rentes héritières* would lose 5 percent of their capital, and in 1777, during the height of the municipal crisis, the loss rose to 14 percent. Apparently the magistrates' goal was simply to create a self-extinguishing debt. As Herbert Luethy has observed, owing to the political and institutional makeup of France, most French officials had had no successful experience with amortizing debt except through natural attrition or bankruptcy. Attempts in France to establish viable *caisses d'amortissements* (sinking funds) had failed.[43] No actuarial tables accompanied the magistrates' decision in Lille, so it is not likely that they had calculated the exact cost of this measure for municipal finances overall. Their primary aim was to reduce urban debt and make finances more predictable with the methods at their disposal.

The resolution to increase the proportion of *rentes viagères* did change the composition of Lille's debt. Between 1772 and 1788, the capital invested in *rentes héritières* rose only slightly, from 4,825,000 to about 5,000,000 *florins*. By contrast, in the same period the capital invested in *rentes viagères* rose by a factor of 2·8, from 404,000 to 1,130,000 *florins*.[44] Although a variety of reasons may be offered to explain the shift, which was also occurring on the national level, in Lille it probably stemmed from a lack of confidence in the city's financial future. Why should one hold on to bonds with a dubious rate of return when a more secure alternative was at hand? Even with a reduction of capital, *rentes viagères* probably appeared the wiser investment.[45]

In the 1780s the city technically ceased to run a deficit during most years, but its overall financial situation remained problematic. Expenditures continued to rise as the royal government increased the surtaxes on the *octrois* in 1781 and reimposed a third royal *vingtième* at the end of the American War of Independence (1778–1783). The latter was the only period of warfare during which the municipality was not forced to purchase offices from the royal government. This reflected the new strategy of the finance minister, Necker, who, from 1778 to 1781, tapped international money markets by offering loans at very advantageous, and some would say, ruinous interest rates.[46] Necker's fall and the enormous accumulation of wartime debts by the central government led to a revival of traditional expedients at the local level.[47] In addition to the resurrection of the third *vingtième*, the municipality was obliged to purchase offices of auctioneers. Lille was also compelled to participate in the lavish program of public works that Calonne, controller general from 1783 to 1786, decided to embark upon in order to advertise that the financially strapped royal government was indeed solvent.[48] In 1786 the town council constructed a new residence for the intendant, costing over 200,000 *florins*. Expenditures thus reached their highest point in Lille's history.

Nonetheless, the city did not suffer from the chronic deficits of the 1770s. The reason appears to be that tax revenues, particularly the *octrois*, also reached their highest level to date. It is significant that this crest in taxation occurred when Lille's woolen industry was entering a recession aggravated by the new Anglo-French tariff agreement of 1786.[49] Once again it was urban wage earners who had to bear the brunt of this royal fiscal strategy.

Oddly, despite increased revenues, the municipal magistrates never came to terms with the arrears on the old *rentes héritières*, whose interest payments continued to lag by approximately eight years. We have seen that urban officials began to liquidate debt at a high rate in 1787. Yet the municipal magistrates limited themselves to reimbursing capital on new *rentes héritières*. They made no effort to pay arrears on the old *rentes héritières*, whose delayed payment was either taken for granted or posed such an insurmountable problem that they chose not to address it.

Thus, on the eve of the Revolution the municipal magistrates were in a precarious position. To all appearances, and of course the inhabitants had no way of auditing urban accounts, the municipality was not in a sound financial situation. The city still was in arrears on the old *rentes héritières*, while the rate of taxation had never been greater. Where, Lille's citizens might have rightly wondered, was all their money going? The problems of debt servicing and rising taxes thus set the stage for constitutional battles pitting the privileged elite, who were paying higher taxes than ever and had lost confidence in the old municipal bonds, against the municipal magistracy, whose corps was closed and unaccountable to citizens.

The financial pressure exerted by the royal government on Lille had created a predicament from which the municipal magistrates could not escape. If the magistrates raised taxes, they could meet royal demands and keep the municipal treasury solvent, but they also ran the risk of incurring the wrath of Lille's taxpaying elite, which was battling for political representation. If the magistrates did not increase taxes, their credit rating was bound to suffer, and urban creditors would have all the more reason to demand public supervision of urban financial affairs. Whichever way was chosen to finance the government, loans or taxes, the growth of the state was helping to raise popular consciousness of the need for a public sphere of participation and accountability. Given the growth of public opinion after 1750, officials could not generate a high level of taxation and maintain confidence in their credit without expanding political representation.

It was the paradox of the growth of absolutism in France that it fostered an awareness of an abstract, inclusive state to which all, regardless of estate or personal status, belonged at the same time as its patrimonial underside precluded a truly public realm of authority and membership from emerging. In Lille, new taxes were repeatedly justified by the egalitarian ideal of national unity under the prince. The municipal magistrates, acting as tax collectors for the king, opposed the tax privileges of officeholders and nobles. It would be impossible to pay for the needs of the state unless all privileged groups contributed "in a uniform manner." By contrast, loans supplementing this tax base were often secured by privileged intermediaries, like cities, whose price was royal endorsement of their special prerogatives. The municipality of Lille was only able to extend credit to the crown and perform related services because, as a corporate body, it was authorized to borrow money and collect its own revenues, the *octrois*.

The central government, however, did not rely on the credit of municipalities alone. It also borrowed from other corps in the city – the *Bureau des Finances*, the mint, the *maréchaussée*, and the guilds. It was standard practice, moreover, that after corporate groups had been forced to lend money to the royal government, the king confirmed them in all their rights and privileges. The central government thus found itself in a very contradictory position. It tried to level the tax privileges of corps inside Lille in order to create a wider tax base, but it also promised simultaneously to guarantee the tax exemptions of corps when it wanted to borrow directly from them. The next section explores effects of this double-edged strategy on municipal politics.

Officeholders and tax exemptions

Before the annexation of Flanders to France, venality of offices, that is the sale of administrative or judicial offices, existed neither on the same scale nor in the same form as it did in France. Some offices in Walloon Flanders, notably those of seigneurial *baillis*, had been leased (*engagé*) for life, a practice that stemmed from an earlier feudal tradition. Unlike officeholders in France, those in Flanders did not have the right to sell or bequeath their offices at will. When they died or retired, the office reverted back to the king or seigneur.[50] Offices in the sovereign courts of the Belgian provinces were not sold or even leased for life. The provincial governor chose the officers in the *Gouvernance*, while the Sovereign Court of Malines was a self-recruiting body.

In the first decades after he annexed Flanders, Louis XIV continued to respect the provincial customs for appointing judicial magistrates. Louis XIV, for example, appointed the first magistrates to the *Conseil Souverain* of Tournai for life and they, in turn, coopted new members, subject to the king's approval. These officers do not appear to have paid for their posts.[51] Louis XIV did establish hereditary, venal offices in the new *Hôtel des Monnaies* that was created in 1685. But no widespread sale of offices occurred until a decade later, when provincial custom was sacrificed to the needs of the royal treasury. To raise money for the War of the League of Augsburg, in 1693, Louis XIV made all judicial offices in Flanders venal and hereditary. Previous appointments to the courts were annulled; if an officer wanted to keep his post, he had to purchase it. In order to generate more funds, the king multiplied the number of offices in the courts. In 1686, for example, the Parlement had seven *conseillers*; by 1704 it had thirty-four. And new courts were created. The royal minister Louvois admitted quite frankly that one of the major reasons for establishing the *Bureau des Finances* in Lille in 1691 was financial. The massive conversion, creation, and sale of offices made a sizeable contribution to the French war effort. The official prices for offices established in the *Bureau des Finances* in Lille in 1691 and for those in the *bailliage* and *gouvernance* courts totalled approximately 1,070,000 *livres*. Offices established in the Parlement of Douai in 1693 came to over 885,000 *livres*.[52]

Officers in the Flemish courts were none too pleased at being forced to raise substantial sums to buy their offices, and they wanted concessions in return. Before agreeing to purchase the offices, the provincial estates and the Parlement demanded that Flemish officeholders would be subject neither to the *annuel* nor the *prêt*, fees paid by many officeholders in France to pass down or sell their offices. In order to facilitate the sale of offices, the king agreed to these conditions. Thus, when officers in Flanders wanted to sell or transmit their offices to their heirs, they only had to pay a small *droit de mutation* equal to one year of *gages*, that is, the interest that the government paid on the capital invested in the office.[53] So long as officeholders paid these fees, the offices were treated as part of an individual's property, which he could sell, mortgage, or bequeath at will.

As a second condition for purchasing their offices, the Parlementaires demanded that the king never subject them to *augmentation de gages*, a type of forced loan. When the king raised the *gages*, or interest, paid on the capital invested in an office, he did not pay a higher interest rate on the initial investment. Rather, he required the officeholder to invest more money in his office, on which the royal government then paid interest. Louis XIV quickly consented to a ban on this practice and then, almost as quickly, reneged on his agreement. Soon after the magistrates in the Parlement had purchased their offices, they were required to contribute 100,000 *livres* of *augmentation de gages*.[54] This measure continued to be utilized during royal fiscal crises of the eighteenth century. Following each forced loan, the king solemnly confirmed members of the corps in all their exemptions, rights, and privileges.[55] Confirmation of privileges soon became a routine financial transaction between corporate groups and the

French king, renewed each time that the royal government borrowed money from those groups.

It might be argued, then, that one of the main legacies of Louis XIV for Walloon Flanders was to expand the number of privileged officeholders and to transform their fiscal immunities into virtual property rights.[56] When in 1694, for example, offices in the feudal *bailliage* and *gouvernance* courts were made venal and hereditary, the officers demanded confirmation of their traditional privileges, because they "had paid a considerable sum for their offices."[57] Similarly, when members of the *Bureau des Finances* demanded that the government uphold their stated tax exemptions they stressed that their privileges had been accorded "by paying a considerable finance for our offices, of which the privileges are an integral part."[58] The problem in trying to make royal officeholders pay more taxes, therefore, was not that these individuals were clinging to some archaic feudal tradition in opposition to the rational and progressive policies of the central government. Officeholders were demanding that the government uphold tax privileges that the crown itself had either created, extended, or recently confirmed. The invocation of property rights to justify privilege was not some sort of vague medieval doctrine, but the product of a very concrete commercial transaction between officeholder and king.

It was also the royal government which allowed the municipal magistrates to expand the urban tax base to include privileged groups. In 1699, for example, after the municipal magistrates purchased some offices in the guilds that the king's financiers were peddling, Louis XIV allowed the town council to levy several new *octrois* on merchandise to be paid by all groups.[59] The municipal magistrates ignored the officeholders' exemption from *octrois*, clearly stated in the titles to their offices, and demanded that they pay the new fees. The outcome was a long round of court cases. It was not until 1753, for example, that the municipal magistrates finally agreed not to charge the officers in the *Bureau des Finances* for an *octroi* on wood created when the city had purchased offices of wood measurers.[60]

Similarly, in 1725 the officers in the chancellery of the Parlement of Douai and in the *Bureau des Finances* of Lille obtained a parliamentary *arrêt* stating that they were exempt from fees on liquor. The municipal magistrates insisted that no one, not even the old *Chambre des Comptes* in Lille, had enjoyed this privilege and appealed the case to the Royal Council. In 1754, the royal government tried to put an end to the constant quarrels by issuing Letters Patent that minutely specified the exemptions of each corps. Officers in the chancellery of the Parlement and in the *Bureau des Finances*, most of whom were in the process of ennoblement, were granted full exemption on the wine, beer, and liquor that they consumed themselves. Thus, they were granted greater exemptions than the nobility, which by local custom, had to pay a portion of the fees levied on wine and beer.[61]

Corps of officeholders, however, never succeeded in their demands that the central government uphold their exemptions from *aides* and subsidies. Both the local and royal governments argued that the need to assist the state overrode all other immunities and agreements. The municipal magistrates, as we have noted, honored the traditional exemption of officeholders from the ordinary provincial *aide*, but received permission from the king to assess all privileged groups for the extraordinary *aide*. The officers in the Parlement of Tournai and the *Bureau des Finances* in Lille protested against their obligation to pay, and in 1701 took their case to the Royal Council. Although the privileges of the officeholders explicitly included exemptions from *aides*, the royal government decided in favor of the municipal magistrates. Any difficulties in collecting the subsidy, it declared, "could cause considerable harm to the service of the king." The ruling appeared all the more arbitrary to the officeholders, since the same year the king had exacted 100,000 *livres* from the Parlementaires and 48,000 from the *Bureau des Finances* for *augmentation des gages*, after which he had confirmed them in their privileges. Likewise in 1743, after turning over 50,000 *livres* to the king for *augmentation des gages*, the members of the *Bureau des Finances* demanded that the municipality honor their exemption from the extraordinary *aide*. The municipal officers and the central government refused.[62]

To justify their denial of tax exemptions to officeholders, the royal and municipal governments espoused patriotic principles of civic participation and sacrifice. By the second half of the eighteenth century, enforced payments for privileges were explicitly linked to service to the state. In 1771, for example, the government demanded that all those who had been ennobled since 1715 pay 6,000 *livres*, or lose their noble status. The loss of nobility was a form of blackmail to ensure compliance, but the government also offered a more noble reason for paying the fee: "an indispensable and distinctive obligation of the nobility is to serve the State usefully, and it is only by this title that it enjoys all the great privileges and advantages that raise it so high above all other citizens."[63]

The justification for exercising privileges was gradually being altered. One's status in society was to be defended by service to an abstract state, rather than by inheritance, honor, custom or allegiance to a personal king. Privilege and hierarchy were increasingly viewed as politically contingent. The state was the sole agent with the power to confer special rights, privileges, and advantages. It was "only by this title" that such distinctions might be awarded. And what better way could anyone, officeholder or noble, assist the state than by giving it money?

From the argument that all corporate groups had to come to the aid of the state by making special payments, it was perhaps not such a great step – intellectually, if not financially and politically – to arguing that everyone had to serve the state by paying taxes. Taken to its logical extreme, the idea that privilege was dependent upon sovereign power and proof of utility implied that when privilege ceased to be useful, it should be discarded. In the eighteenth century, Lille's municipal magistrates advanced this kind of egalitarian argument. Every subject, they argued, had a duty to support the state financially. Exemptions that the king granted to the nobility, the clergy, and officeholders were valid only for ordinary impositions, which the common people routinely paid. But, they continued:

> If it happens that the State needs extraordinary assistance, then all privileges disappear: all corps must reunite to come to the aid of the Prince and the State, because they are all in the State, and the Prince looks equally to the protection and the safety of all his subjects. Thus, in France, the nobility pays the *capitation* and the *dixième*, although they are exempt from all the ordinary impositions to which the people are subjected; the same in Flanders, although privileged groups are free from the ordinary provincial *aide*, they are not from the extraordinary *aide*.[64]

A similar sentiment was recorded each year during the financial negotiations between the king and the provincial estates. Sporadically before 1750 and routinely thereafter in the register of the estates, article two concerning the terms of the extraordinary *aide* stated: "as all individuals indistinctly are obliged to aid Your Majesty in the needs of the State, and as it would be impossible to find such large sums if those exempt and privileged were not included, the estates ask that it please Your Majesty to declare that all the privileged will be included in the levies and impositions for extraordinary help."[65] In another conflict with the general staff of the army over the *abonnement* for registry fees (the *contrôle*), the municipal magistrates stated that "no one is exempt from payments of this sort of imposition because all individuals are obliged to come to the aid of the king for the needs of the state."[66]

In these cases, one can catch a glimpse of the intellectual foundations of a society of orders being pulled down and that of one based upon egalitarian citizenship emerging. All citizens, by the very fact of belonging to the state, would be subject to taxation. And, by implication, the reverse was also true: all taxpayers might rightly claim the status of citizen, the right to participate in the state. The financial demands of a more complex state combined with an intellectual climate that venerated utility were becoming potent solvents of the corporate order.

There was, however, a paradox. It was a privileged corps, that of the municipal magistrates, who propounded this egalitarian argument. When the municipal magistrates argued that all privileges should disappear before the needs of the state, they were concerned with privilege only in the fiscal realm. They were in no way arguing that political privileges, that is, their own monopoly of political power, should be challenged. There were, therefore, parallels between the central government and the local government in Lille, both of which wished to maintain a closed political system while simultaneously trying to tax privileged elites more heavily. The question that remained to be answered was, could the government impose equality in taxation from above, without allowing for more participation from below? And how would the royal government answer the charges of venal officeholders that their tax exemptions were part of their property? When "all privileges disappeared" in the quest to rescue the state, who would decide where privileges ended and where the rights of property began? The case of the *Bureaux des Finances* illustrates the attempted solution of one set of officeholders to these questions.

3 Corps, bureaucracy and citizenship: the case of the *Bureaux des Finances*

In the eighteenth century, the *Bureaux des Finances* formed one of the many apparently useless collections of corps that lingered on and on for no good reason and hopelessly cluttered up the old regime with their pretensions and inefficiencies.[1] Before the Revolution, there were twenty-nine of these extraordinary judicial courts, which had originally been granted jurisdiction over matters concerning the royal domain. In the great judicial reforms of May 1788 the Keeper of the Seals, Lamoignon, decided to abolish the *Bureaux* along with a number of other expendable and seemingly moribund courts. The measure, like so many other attempts to rationalize the old regime, not only failed, but helped to galvanize the privileged elite into overt opposition to royal "despotism."

Yet, despite its battles against royal arbitrariness, the privileged elite neither developed a unified opposition, nor advanced a successful program of reform of its own. When the Revolution came, the cause of privilege collapsed without effective resistance, and, according to some scholars, it was members of the privileged elite itself who helped to sound its death knell. How might this combination of failed royal reform, politicization, revolution, and ideological division within the elite be explained? A look at the relationship of Lille's *Bureau des Finances* both to the monarchy and to other *Bureaux* across France helps to illuminate these issues.

Before its annexation to France, Lille's most prestigious court had been the *Chambre des Comptes* established by the dukes of Burgundy in 1385 to audit accounts and hear lawsuits concerning revenues attached to the old ducal domain. After French armies conquered Lille in 1667, the old Burgundian court was moved to Bruges, but Louis XIV did not immediately replace it. Only twenty-four years later, in 1691, did he decide to establish a *Bureau des Finances* in Lille, a court less highly ranked than a *Chambre des Comptes*, but one with similar duties.[2] Because the magistrates regarded the new court as the successor of the venerable Burgundian one, they claimed superiority over the other *Bureaux des Finances* in France. The three most prestigious offices in Lille's *Bureau des Finances* – those of the first and second *présidents* and the *chevalier d'honneur* – were filled by noble families who had served in the administration and judiciary since the period of Habsburg rule.[3]

Lille's *Bureau des Finances* consisted of thirty-four offices, only nineteen of which were ennobling and can be considered the true corps. The court in Lille was relatively tiny; only five of the other twenty-eight *Bureaux des Finances* in France were smaller.[4] The decision to keep Lille's court small was deliberate. "Too great a number of *privilégiés* in the city of Lille," as one royal edict noted, "could harm commerce."[5] Although the *Bureaux des Finances* ranked beneath sovereign courts like the Parlements and the *Chambres des Comptes*, in Lille this was the only court with ennobling offices, placing it at the summit of the hierarchy of judicial offices in the city.

The edict of 1691 gave the *Bureau des Finances* in Lille a variety of judicial and administrative tasks. Its officials had jurisdiction over cases concerning the royal domain in the provinces of Flanders, Hainaut, Artois, and Cambrésis. They registered letters of provision for new officeholders, received surety deposits from officials who handled public funds, supervised the maintenance of royal roads, and received the fealty and homage from all the fiefholders of the king. Among their most important functions was the power to audit the accounts of the *octrois* in the towns under their jurisdiction and to oversee the assessment of some very important indirect taxes in Hainaut and Maritime Flanders.[6]

The edict of 1691 accorded the officeholders of Lille's *Bureau des Finances* the same honors, dignities, and privileges as those in the Parlement of Flanders. These included important fiscal immunities, such as exemptions from the *taille*, the salt tax, *lods et ventes*, municipal tolls, subsidies, gifts, and loans to the king, and, perhaps most important, the privilege of ennoblement.[7] Offices in most *Bureaux des Finances* ennobled in the second degree, that is, both the father and son had to serve twenty years or die in office in order to transmit nobility to their descendants. Because the privileges of Lille's court were stated to be the same as those of the Parlement of Flanders, which ennobled in the first degree, the magistrates in Lille claimed this right. The king, however, never recognized their case.[8]

Few families were ennobled through the *Bureau des Finances* in Lille. Of the sixty-five families who served in the nineteen ennobling offices of the court, eleven were already noble when they entered the offices and nine completed the process of ennoblement. In 1790, five magistrates were noble, five were *roturiers* in the second generation, nearing the goal, and nine were in the first generation.[9] The surprising number of nobles serving in these ennobling offices may be traced to local pride in the court's Burgundian heritage and a long tradition of administrative service. The non-nobles looked to the court to provide them with an honorable profession, a variety of tax exemptions, and an avenue into the ranks of the nobility.

Prior to Lille's annexation, *Bureaux des Finances* elsewhere in France had experienced a steady loss of administrative and judicial functions. In 1557, in order to raise money for the royal treasury, the monarchy made the offices in these courts venal, and, during the next century, multiplied their number to generate more revenue. Because the sale of offices increased the courts' administrative independence, the crown created new agents, like the intendants, whom it could control more directly. The *Bureaux des Finances* had originally been given jurisdiction over various taxes including the *taille*, internal duties (*traites*), fees placed on wine and other goods circulating within France (*aides*), and municipal tolls (*octrois*). In the *pays d'élection*, however, the crown undercut these duties by authorizing the intendants to supervise the assessment of the *taille* and to audit the accounts of the municipal *octrois*. The royal council itself took over awarding leases for the tax farms of the *aides*, and later, with the formation of the Five Great Farms, it also extended its control more firmly over internal tariffs.[10] By the time of Lille's conquest, these venal offices had become administratively insignificant.

Nonetheless, the royal government continued to multiply the number of these offices, because their sale generated sorely needed revenue. When the *Bureau* was created in Lille in 1691, the royal minister Louvois observed that the sale of the offices would raise over 700,000 *livres* for the government, as well as attach new officeholders and their families more firmly to the service of the French crown.[11] In 1691, thirty offices, eighteen of them ennobling, were created and sold for a total of 690,525 *livres*. Four more offices, including the one of *chevalier d'honneur*, were created from 1692 to 1702.[12]

The initial purchase of an office was a kind of loan to the central government. The buyer invested his capital in the office, and, in return, the king granted him the right to exercise the functions, collect the fees, and enjoy the privileges attached to the office. In many offices, the king also paid a specified amount of interest (*gages*) on the capital investment. In Lille's *Bureau des Finances*, the *gages* was set at 3 and one-third percent. *Gages* and fees collected for services (*emoluments*) took the place of a set salary and, in strict economic terms, brought a low rate of return. But officeholders were not seeking mere economic advantage. As one historian has noted, the purchase of an ennobling office was, above all, an "investment in standing."[13]

By paying additional fees, the officeholder was allowed to transmit his office to a designated successor, a practice that effectively made venal offices the private property of the officer. Besides the famous *annuel* or *Paulette*, a yearly fee equal to one-sixtieth of the value of the office, there was a much heavier, supplementary payment called the *prêt* created in 1620. At times the king allowed, or forced, officeholders to buy off the *annuel* and *prêt* in return for a lump sum of money. Another set of offices, the *offices à survivance*, such as those in the Parlements, were exempt from both the *annuel* and the *prêt*. Instead, these officeholders had only to pay a *droit de mutation*, equal in 1709 to one-eighth of the official value of the office, upon its sale or transfer.[14] Owing to negotiations by the estates of Walloon Flanders with Louis XIV, the venal offices in that province fell under none of the above arrangements. In order to sell or bequeath an office, the officeholder had only to pay a *droit de mutation* equal to one year of *gages*.[15]

The king raised additional sums from officeholders by exacting forced loans known as *augmentations de gages*, fresh infusions of capital that the king required officeholders to invest in their offices periodically, and by collecting transfer and registration fees.[16] One such fee was the *marc d'or*. All individuals who bought offices were required to pay the ordinary *marc d'or*, equal to one-sixtieth of the value of the office. In addition, after 1771 non-nobles who brought ennobling offices were required to pay the *marc d'or de la noblesse*: 3,000 *livres* for an office that ennobled in one generation, and 1,500 *livres* for an office requiring two generations.[17]

The *Bureau des Finances* at Lille soon experienced the same pattern of administrative decline and fiscal manipulation as other *Bureaux* had. Only one year after its creation, for example, the intendant received the right to audit the accounts of municipal *octrois* in all important towns of the *généralité*, a task originally assigned to the corps. In subsequent decades the intendant's power continued to expand. By the end of the eighteenth century, this official had acquired jurisdiction over disputes concerning the hearth tax in Hainaut and beer fees in Maritime Flanders.[18] Thus, the intendant came to control all significant cases pertaining to local taxation that had originally been under the *Bureau*'s jurisdiction. The duties of the *Bureau des Finances* were further reduced by the powers of the provincial estates, which oversaw the maintenance of royal highways, and by other local courts. In the late eighteenth century, the officeholders complained that the fees received for judging cases pertaining to the royal domain were almost worthless, because other local judges had usurped this function.[19] In addition to undercutting the administrative vitality of this corps, the monarchy also lessened the worth of their tax privileges. New direct taxes, including the *capitation*, the *dixième*, and the *vingtième*, were levied on privileged and unprivileged groups alike. And even extensions of traditional taxes like the provincial *aide extraordinaire* and various *octrois* fell upon members of this corps.[20]

During the seventeenth and eighteenth centuries, therefore, the central government expanded the number of *Bureaux des Finances* to raise cash, but had also left them idling, more or less forgotten, until another fiscal crisis galvanized the crown into demanding some new payment, fee, or loan from them. How the *trésoriers de France* of the *Bureaux* responded to this treatment is illustrated by their reaction to a new royal fee, the *centième denier*, created in 1771 by the controller general Terray.

The years directly preceding Terray's rise to power were stormy ones, politically and financially. France had been humiliated in the Seven Years War. The Parlements were protesting the king's right to levy new taxes and, even more ominous, had started to claim that they represented "the Nation" and had the right to interpret the "fundamental laws" of the realm. Compounding the political ferment was the problem of economic recession. From 1768 to 1771, famine struck various regions of France, a disaster that cut off the flow of tax revenues and made the short-term credit of *financiers* unavailable to the government.[21] In 1769 to meet these crises, the royal government brought in two strong-willed reformers: Maupeou as chancellor and the Abbé Terray as controller general. Maupeou abolished the defiant Parlements and set up new courts in their place. Terray ceased redeeming certain short-term notes, a policy that effectively transformed them into long-term debt, and simultaneously, extended the two *vingtièmes* and made the terms of their collection more rigorous.[22]

It was as part of these dramatic measures that in February 1771 Terray announced that a new fee, the *centième denier*, would replace the *annuel*, the *prêt*, and the *droit de mutation*. The goal of the new fee, according to the royal edict, was to introduce uniformity into the finances of venal offices. All officeholders were to pay the *centième denier*, no matter what previous arrangements had been made with the king, if they wished to sell or bequeath their offices at will. The fee was set at one-hundredth the value of the office, as calculated by the officeholder himself. Since the officeholders had to sell their offices at the price used to assess the *centième denier*, Terray hoped to insure that they would not underestimate their value. In addition, Terray increased the basis for assessing the *marc d'or* from one-sixtieth of the value of a venal office to one-fortieth and placed the *marc d'or de la noblesse* on ennobling offices.[23]

The magistrates in the *Bureaux des Finances* across France were outraged. The *centième denier*, they claimed, annulled their property rights and humiliated their corps. Since sovereign courts, including the Parlements and *Chambres des Comptes*, had been exempted from the *centième denier*, the new fee clearly demonstrated that the *Bureaux des Finances* ranked beneath these courts. Furthermore, only one year before, the *trésoriers de France* had been obliged to raise substantial sums for an *augmentation de gages*, after which the king had solemnly confirmed them in their rights and privileges.[24]

All over France, the magistrates in the *Bureaux des Finances* began to plan their attack on the edict. A number of them began to realize, however, that the defense of their privileges and property rights would not stand a chance unless every *Bureau* in France united and spoke as one to the king. The royal plan for taxing these courts uniformly called for a uniform response. As the magistrates in Lyon wrote to those in Lille, "The lack of union and harmony between the different *Bureaux des Finances* of the kingdom can be regarded as the source of the events which have brought our companies to the test."[25] A movement began, therefore, to try to develop a national bond between all the courts.

Several *Bureaux des Finances* made efforts in 1771 to form a general association which would empower two deputies in Paris to speak for all the courts. The initial effort failed. It was not easy to unite the various *Bureaux*, which had been created at different times and exercised diverse functions, depending on the taxes and the customs of each region. Dumond, *procureur du roi* from the *Bureau des Finances* at Bourges, discovered the problems when he went to Paris to organize an association. In a candid letter to Malus, *procureur du roi* in Lille, Dumond discussed the obstacles to unity. There was, first of all, the sheer problem of a widely dispersed membership. Since few people in any one city had the funds to buy an office in the *Bureau des Finances*, the members of a court could be scattered through small towns, the countryside, and even other provinces. The isolation of the officeholders from each other, according to Dumond, bred selfishness. Men became interested only in the monetary return from their offices; they were not concerned at all with the glory of the *état* or the honor of their corps. As Dumond wrote: "thus each individual has said: my office makes up an important part of my fortune, I would rather pay the *centième denier* than leave myself open to losing it. The government is not ignorant of this way of thinking; it is the basis for a great part of its operation."[26] By holding the officers' property rights hostage, the monarchy had gradually bred a self-serving and narrow kind of individualism. This tendency had to be countered, Dumond believed, by fostering unity, participation, and a sense of service within corps. Dumond had no illusions that uniting the officeholders would be easy, for, he remarked, in his day events were leading men more and more toward *égoïsme*.

By 1774 twelve *Bureaux des Finances* were in favor of countrywide association: those in Auch, Alençon, Grenoble, Montauban, Poitiers, Moulins, Orléans, Soissons, Bordeaux, Rouen, Montpellier, and Lyon.[27] The members discussed various ways to finance an association in an egalitarian manner. The *Bureau* at Montauban suggested, for example, that contributions should be made by head, rather than by *Bureau*, since the movement was as vital to individual members as it was to each court.[28] In November 1774, the courts that had joined the association elected two deputies to serve them in Paris: Dumond from Bourges and Rolland from Grenoble.[29]

The program of the association of the *Bureaux* was gradually enlarged. Although the *Bureaux* were determined, first of all, to try to buy off the *centième denier*, they also decided to try to regain some of the privileges and functions which they had recently lost. Their demands included the re-establishment of the *franc salé* for widows of magistrates, the removal of the eight *sols per livre* surtax imposed on their salt, and restoration of their exemption from *lods et ventes*, a privilege which had been revoked in 1771. They were also going to try to have some of their old powers, and revenues, restored, such as the clergy's obligation to register fealty and homage with them.[30]

The magistrates in Lille's *Bureau des Finances* did not join the association. Individualism, Dumond had noted, was one obstacle to uniting these courts; provincial loyalties were another. When the *Bureau* in Lille was asked to join the association, it declined, stating that it was "in a separate class because of its establishment in Flanders."[31] When a bulletin from Orléans outlined the grievances which the association would present to the king, the magistrates in Lille responded that they had little in common with the other *trésoriers de France*. They were not concerned about the *franc salé*, because the province of French Flanders was exempt from the salt tax. Since the clergy in Flanders was under the Belgian Bishopric of Tournai, the conflict between the *Bureaux* and the French clergy was irrelevant to them. As for the *centième denier* itself, the magistrates in Lille did not want to buy off the fee with an *abonnement*. They wanted complete exemption from it and the reclassification of their offices as *offices héréditaires*. In conclusion, they declared that "we are attached to a province which enjoys the privilege of hereditary offices, and whose right is assured by the capitulation treaty. It is in no way fitting for us to separate ourselves from it in this important circumstance."[32] The magistrates in Lille knew that individual corporate groups had to unite with other corps in order to oppose the king, but they chose to rest their own defense upon the powers and privileges of the province, and not on the association of *Bureaux*.

In arguing that Walloon Flanders should be exempted from the *centième denier*, Lille's *trésoriers* and other officeholders in the province appealed, first of all, to a long series of royal edicts and treaties that guaranteed the province's privileges. The royal edicts of 1691 and 1693 had created offices in the province "en titre d'offices formés et héréditaires." Until 1771 the king had always honored the right of officeholders to sell or bequeath their office without paying the *annuel* or *prêt* owing to special fiscal arrangements between the provincial estates and the king. In return for paying the *aide extraordinaire* after 1701, the crown exempted the province from all other new extraordinary impositions. When Louis XIV imposed a payment for the confirmation of the *droit d'hérédité* in venal offices anyway, the provincial estates protested and cited the conditions of the new *aide*. The province was exempted. In 1713, when Lille was returned to France after the Dutch occupation, the Treaty of Utrecht confirmed the province in its privileges, customs, exemptions, and "*offices héréditaires.*" A royal declaration of 9 August 1722, reimposing the *annuel* on many officeholders, did not include Walloon Flanders. Finally, in December 1743, when a royal edict made officers in the *Bureaux des Finances* buy off the *annuel*, the controller general Orry exempted Lille's court.[33] It made sense, therefore, for the *Bureau des Finances* in Lille to turn to the province once more for protection.

The initial appeals to have the *centième denier* suppressed in Flanders were to no avail. In 1773 Terray told the *Bureau des Finances* in Lille that the object of the law was uniformity, and that Flanders would be subject to the new payment. All venal offices ultimately derived their authority from one source, the king as sovereign, and all officers were, therefore, uniform. Terray stated it bluntly: "those given offices do not hold their offices from the constitution, or the privileges, or the uses and customs of the province; they hold them from the king based upon a *finance* like all the officeholders of the kingdom, and since nothing differentiates them there is no reason why they are not ruled by the same laws."[34] The battle between the officers in Flanders and the king, therefore, came to rest upon opposing conceptions of how sovereignty should be expressed, one defined by the king and another by his Flemish subjects. Did sovereign power legitimately enable the king to revoke at will contracts, historical precedents, and property rights, or did these stand beyond his legislative power?

The provincial estates and the magistrates in Flanders readily admitted that the king was sovereign, that he was the ultimate authority and source of civil law. But royal sovereignty was embedded in, and limited by, a long tradition of reciprocal duties between the ruler and his subjects. As the Parlement of Douai observed, the predecessors of Louis XV had upheld Flanders' privileges, and the province, in turn, had rendered, "the most respectful fidelity, the most prompt obedience, and the most complete sacrifices."[35] Now these allegiances were being called into question.

"What confidence," they continued, "could they have in the sacred word of the king if the agreements made so solemnly with their sovereign were not respected?" Or as the provincial estates, which had a long experience with the Bourbon tradition of fiscal demands and broken promises, sadly reflected, "the seal of the prince and that of time are equally without credit, everything is becoming arbitrary."[36]

Drawing upon constitutional arguments centuries old, the magistrates in the *Bureau des Finances* in Lille argued that royal sovereignty was limited by two concepts: the sanctity of property and that of contract.[37] The magistrates described the problem in the following manner: "if it is a principle that the title [*titre*] of all his offices belongs to His Majesty, being a portion of his power which cannot be taken away, at least he had agreed that we could freely dispose of our capital investment [*finances*], and it is under the sacred guarantee of his royal word, that we have always envisioned the price of our offices as the most essential part of our patrimony."[38] The magistrates divided a venal office into the *titre* and the *finance*, each of which, they claimed, existed in a separate juridical domain. The *titre*, the title to the functions of the office, was openly conceded to be the king's sole prerogative, because "all types of public power reside in the person of the king."[39] The *finance*, the capital investment, was a form of private property, which officeholders in Flanders could transfer at will.

According to the magistrates, the king had, in effect, given up his right to grant offices to whomever he wished by making offices in Flanders "*héréditaires*." The king could not introduce new conditions, such as the payment of the *centième denier*, on property in offices that he had already sold under other conditions. As the Parlement of Douai declared: "*cette hérédité* [the right to bequeath an office to one's heir] cannot be regarded as a simple privilege, but as a veritable right of property founded on the most sacred titles, on a contract that Louis XIV resolved of his own accord to make with his newly conquered subjects."[40] The members of the provincial estates agreed completely. The finance of the office was entirely in the buyer's hands: "it belongs to him without reserve."[41] Sometimes the right to bequeath property in offices was likened to the hereditary nature of "all property [*fonds*] of whatever nature it is." In this case the estates contended that "the heredity of offices is not any more contrary to the authority of the sovereign than those of the *fonds des terres*." At other times, the right to pass down offices was qualified: "But if the offices of Flanders are not hereditary by their nature, they are by virtue of their original title."[42]

The original title to the office was a contract guaranteed by the sovereign's authority. Terray might dismiss disdainfully the "so-called titles" of these officeholders, but the provincial estates described the creation of *offices héréditaires* in Flanders as a "primordial contract whose reciprocity linked the buyer and seller."[43] The magistrates in the *Bureau des Finances* stated that if the king wanted to impose new conditions upon venal officers, he could, but then "the primitive contract is annulled, and it is a question of forming a new contract."[44] The only just way for the king to impose the *centième denier* was for him to buy back the offices and then sell them again under the new conditions.

In their fight against the *centième denier*, the *Bureaux des Finances* in other parts of France, like the one in Lille, appealed to the contractual and property rights of citizens. Although the offices in the *Bureaux des Finances* in other parts of France had not been created with hereditary offices, most of the officers had, in 1709, 1722, or 1743, paid the king a lump sum of money to buy off the *annuel*. The magistrates argued that from the time of this payment, their offices had become their patrimony, which they could transmit to whomever they wished, and which even the king could not legally touch. The payment represented a contract, which "fixed forever the property of the *finance* of the *Trésoriers de France*." Therefore, "in the eyes of Justice, this patrimony, acquired under public faith, can never be burdened with suppressed fees that one would like to revive."[45] The sovereign had the right to delegate public functions to whomever he wished, but, the *trésoriers* proclaimed: "indeed if the rights of the sovereign are inalienable in the eyes of his subjects, the property of... these same subjects is equally sacred in the eyes of a just king who wants to reign only by the laws. [The law] of property, that fundamental law of the happiness of States, should it be less inviolable for the *Trésoriers de France* than for the rest of the Subjects?... The rights of the sovereign and those of his subjects are equally imprescriptible."[46]

Because most of the *Bureaux des Finances* did not have the financial credit of the province like Walloon Flanders to fall back upon, they had to argue their case from the credit of the courts in association. The association of *Bureaux* attempted to show that the king would lose more money than he would gain by imposing the new tax. The credit of the *Bureaux des Finances*, they pointed out, was necessary to the king. Within twenty-seven years, from 1743 to 1770, the *trésoriers de France* claimed that they had raised eight million *livres* in *augmentations de gages* alone. Furthermore, a continual turn-over in the buying and selling of offices was to the king's financial advantage. Non-noble purchasers of ennobling offices had to pay two variants of the *marc d'or*; by 1771 these two fees could cost as much as 5,521 *livres*. When an office was sold, there was a *droit de mutation* equal to one-sixteenth the value of the office. For an office valued at 40,000 *livres*, this would total 2,500 *livres*. The seller of the office also had to pay 1,360 *livres* for his *lettres d'honneur*, which entitled him to enjoy his titles and tax privileges after he had served twenty years.[47]

Now, however, since the *Bureaux des Finances* were "covered by objects of disgrace and titles of surtaxes and impositions," and since the new *centième denier* had stripped them of their property rights and placed them in a class with "subaltern" courts, no one would be foolish enough to want these offices. Not only would the government lose money from the diminished sale of offices, but, the *Bureaux des Finances* claimed, they had the right to reimbursement for the money that they had paid to buy off the *annuel*.[48]

The argument that the *Bureaux des Finances* would lose their credit seemed at one point to have had some effect. A letter from one representative working for the *Bureaux* in Paris noted that the sale of their offices had become almost impossible, and that the king's ministers were as anxious as the officeholders to have the stalemate broken.[49] The good news for the corps finally came during Turgot's regime. In November 1775 the new controller general decided to revoke the *centième denier* for the *Bureaux des Finances*. Since Turgot wanted to restore the sound administration of these courts, he also planned to suppress a number of the superfluous offices that had been created solely to raise money.[50]

As of 1775, the officeholders in Walloon Flanders had been unsuccessful in their attempt to have the *centième denier* suppressed for themselves. Although the *trésoriers de France* in Lille had not supported the association of the *Bureaux des Finances*, they still reaped the benefits of the association's efforts. For the moment it appeared that the magistrates in Lille owed more to the united interests of a country-wide association of *Bureaux* than to its membership in a privileged province.

Unfortunately for the *Bureaux des Finances*, Turgot's decision was reversed in August 1776, soon after his downfall. Once more these courts fell victim to the government's need for funds. The unnecessary offices in them would not be suppressed, because the king could not reimburse the capital.[51] In yet another series of reversals, in 1777 the province of Walloon Flanders was completely exempted from the *centième denier*. The special status of French Flanders stemmed, once again, from the government's financial dependence on the province. In 1776 the king had demanded a joint loan of 20 million *livres* from the two provincial estates of Maritime and Walloon Flanders. The estates used the occasion to ask the government to revoke the *centième denier* in Walloon Flanders, and to maintain all venal officeholders in their original prerogatives, including the "*droit d'hérédité*." The next year the royal council suppressed the new fee and declared that the "principle of uniformity [was] irreconcilable with the constitution ... of Flanders."[52] The allegiance of the Flemish *trésoriers de France* to their province, rather than to a country-wide association of *Bureaux des Finance*, was vindicated.

The anger and frustration of the *Bureaux des Finances* in the rest of France toward the king revived. As the magistrates in Bordeaux remarked, "Such changeable conduct [can] only tend to alter the respect due to the orders of His Majesty and extinguish the just confidence that his people owe to his sacred word."[53] The same magistrates called for the immediate reimbursement of the funds used to buy off the *annuel* and *droit de survivance*. If this was not met, honor would force them to ask the king "to take back an *état* that far from honoring us, degrades us in the eyes of the public and our own, and to reimburse our offices, that we have only taken in virtue of the privileges, established by the diverse edicts of their creations, the annihilation of which should equally annihilate the primitive contract."[54] The magistrates at Metz wrote that the revocation of their prerogatives made it impossible "to exist honorably." Unless both their original privileges and functions were restored, they "could only prefer an entire suppression."[55] The officers from Rouen noted that in towns where the *Bureau des Finances* was the only ennobling office, men might still be willing to buy this fragile office. In Rouen, however, where a number of ennobling courts existed, the *Bureaux des Finances* could no longer compete and could not support a new fee. Their offices had simply become a "source of hardship and worries," and they too were ready to petition the king for their own suppression: "we would desire it like men weary of a sad life desire the peace of the tomb."[56] In Caen the officers reported that, in 1777, four of their twenty-five offices were vacant, and ten magistrates were trying unsuccessfully to sell their offices.[57]

To fight the *centième denier* some magistrates made efforts to revive the old committee of representatives in Paris. The attempt to unite the *Bureaux*, however, was continually hampered by divisions between the courts. Only in 1786 did these officeholders succeed in buying off the *centième denier*. This time the payment cost them 1 million *livres*. As Dumond observed earlier concerning the royal government, "it only keeps the privileges that are able to furnish money."[58]

After the question of the *centième denier* had been settled, some deputies asked that a committee remain in Paris, because the king's council was going to discuss the functions of the *Bureaux des Finances*. Since the powers of these courts had been steadily weakened, it was absolutely essential, many magistrates believed, to regain their old functions. Divisions among the *Bureaux* generated during the dispute over the *centième denier* still lingered. Some persons wanted one deputy to negotiate for all the courts; others were in favor of a large, representative committee. A group of deputies in Paris proposed a compromise. All of the *Bureaux des Finances* might elect one deputy at large to be their spokesman, and the other deputies who had been sent to Paris from the provinces would form an advisory committee.[59] Above all, it was important to put aside old animosities. Only by developing a uniform *espirt de corps* could the *trésoriers de France* arrest the decline of their administrative activities and their status. It was necessary for each *Bureau* to have "the same principles, the same usages, and the same habits."[60]

The magistrates barely had time to consider these proposals when the next blow fell. On 8 May 1788, Lamoignon suppressed the *Bureaux des Finances* and a number of other courts. The excessive number of offices, the government declared, was an obstacle to justice, and their tax exemptions a burden to the French people. The suppression would eliminate useless officials who clogged the administrative hierarchy, and allow the government to distribute the burden of taxation more fairly. All officeholders in the *Bureau des Finances* would have to pay the basest of taxes, the *taille*, unless they had served in office for twenty years.[61]

Once again a number of *Bureaux*, led by the one at Lyon, demanded the formation of a national lobby: "It is of the greatest importance that our procedures be absolutely uniform."[62] The magistrates from Lyon asked each court to send a deputy immediately to Paris. By late November, however, only twelve other *Bureaux des Finances* had responded to their plea: those in Paris, Soissons, Grenoble, Montauban, Amiens, Rouen, Poitiers, Tours, Moulins, Limoges, Toulouse, and Alençon.[63] The magistrates in Lille once more demonstrated their provincial isolation and haughtiness by identifying themselves with the ancient Burgundian *Chambres des Comptes*. "This *Bureau*," they declared, "has nothing to do with the other *Bureaux des Finances*."[64]

With the suppression of the *Bureaux*, confidence in the equity of the king ebbed. The biggest worry of the officeholders, and of their creditors, was reimbursement for their offices. Where would a nearly bankrupt government find the huge sums necessary to buy back all these offices? Officeholders in Poitiers pointed out that although the king had suppressed over 700 offices, which formed the major part of many families' fortunes, he had presented no certain method for refunding the capital: "a manifest surprise by His Majesty who declared that he wants to reign by law."[65] Those in Bordeaux claimed that the reimbursement would amount to 26,000,000 *livres* in all.[66] In Lyon officials were openly cynical: "the confidence that the promise of His Majesty inspires does not permit us to doubt the certainty of reimbursement."[67] The magistrates in Soissons summed up the government's dilemma: "It is without doubt advantageous to the People to diminish the number of *privilégiés*; but this principle of administration is subordinate to the inviolability of property."[68]

In the edict of 1788, the government claimed that the *gages* and tax exemptions of the *Bureaux* exceeded the revenues which the government could obtain from the capital investment. The magistrates disagreed. Their reception fees, the officers in Lyon emphasized, were ample indemnity for their exemptions, and the corps had been forced to borrow money to meet the king's numerous *augmentations de gages*. Their interest had been reduced to a mere 2 percent, and the royal *vingtièmes* were deducted from that interest.[69]

As for the tax privileges of the corps, the magistrates differed as to their worth and importance. The officers at Soissons, for example, defended their privileges and wanted to see them restored. Marriage alliances, they pointed out, were contracted on the basis of the financial worth of their prerogatives, and lands had been bought on the assurance of the exemptions they would receive. The loss of their privileges would cause confusion in social rankings, and upset the social order.[70] For magistrates in other *Bureaux*, the steady erosion of their privileges before their suppression made those privileges seem of less and less concern. In Lille, the son of the *procureur général* Malus wrote: "as for privileges, they are a consideration of little importance, some distinctions more personal than transmittable, exemptions that are reduced to nothing for someone who is not a peasant [*laboureur*], finally purely honorific qualifications which excite more envy than they warrant: there, *Monseigneur*, is just about what remains for the *Trésoriers de France* of their old splendor."[71] For Malus, it was more important to defend the utility of the *Bureaux des Finances* than their tax privileges. The professional status of the magistrates, their *état*, was what was at stake: "but at least it [the office] was an *état*; the father transmitted it to his son as a way of establishing himself, and, however little the minister wanted to help their work, they still enjoyed the satisfaction of frequently rendering good and faithful service to the king."[72]

By 1788 a number of magistrates in the *Bureaux des Finances* realized that their survival depended on whether they could prove their usefulness to society. As the court in Lyon argued, the true consideration of magistrates "depends less on the prerogatives and honors attached to their offices than upon the importance and the utility of their functions."[73] The problem was how to convince other citizens and the government that this was indeed the case.

On 23 September 1788, five months after their suppression, the *Bureaux des Finances* and other courts were temporarily re-established. The Estates General, which Louis XVI had decided to call, would determine their fate. The magistrates in Lyon accurately described the obstacles which the *Bureaux des Finances* faced if they were to persuade this assembly not to abolish their offices. Public opinion was ever more hostile to privilege. Many people believed that the privileges of the *Bureaux* were a burden to the state and not merited by useful service. Higher courts disdained them, while lower ones were jealous. Some persons claimed that the functions that the courts still exercised could better be performed by new administrative officials, such as the intendants or members of provincial assemblies. It was not difficult to see that the Estates General might permanently suppress them, or allow them to exist only because reimbursing the officeholder was impossible. The *Bureaux des Finances*, must, therefore, demand back all of their former functions and demonstrate their utility.[74]

To ensure that the Estates General understood the traditional functions of the corps, as well as the financial sacrifices which the officers had made for the king, the officers from Lyon wanted the *Bureaux des Finances* to try to obtain the right to have two representatives at the Estates General. Although their corps had not been represented in the Estates General of 1614, there was historical precedent, based upon the composition of the Estates of Blois in 1576, for sending deputies from their corps. The magistrates also hoped to convince the government that, by providing information on finances and the royal domain, the deputies of the *Bureaux des Finances* could contribute to the deliberations of the Estates.[75]

In December 1788, approximately three months before the elections to the Estates General, the *Bureau des Finances* at La Rochelle proposed "the most noble way" to show the Estates General that these courts were useful and thus should not be suppressed. Since their tax privileges were regarded as detrimental to the nation, they would give them up voluntarily. Their case at the Estates General then would rest upon restoring all of the old activities of the *Bureaux* and revealing how useful they would be to the nation. They also planned to show how much money they had contributed to the government through different surtaxes, registration fees, and refinancing requirements. The renunciation of their tax exemptions would surely bring the Estates to recognize their worth and concern for the general welfare. In a call for other *Bureaux des Finances* to follow their example, they declared: "let us sacrifice the exemptions dearly bought; let us offer to share with our fellow citizens the burden of public taxes...let us remember that before being Magistrates, we must be Men, French, Citizens, and that the prerogatives, the exemptions of a corps must be forgotten when it is a question of the great interest of humanity and *la Patrie*."[76]

After the declaration from La Rochelle was circulated among the *trésoriers de France*, other magistrates decided to give up their tax privileges. Those in Dijon offered to contribute equally to all taxes, and the ones in Soissons, who a few months earlier had defended tax exemptions, now renounced them.[77]

Several groups of magistrates, such as those in Soissons, were worried about the elections to the Estates General. The government had ruled that members of the *Bureaux des Finances* who had not completed the process of ennoblement would sit with the Third Estate, rather than with the nobility. This decision humiliated the *anoblis* in the *Bureaux*, many of whom believed, like those at Orléans, that "we can only sit with the nobility" because of the status of the *Bureaux des Finances* as sovereign courts.[78] Rejected by the Second Estate, these privileged officers were also distrusted by the Third. No unprivileged member of the Third Estate, which was fighting for equal taxation, would vote for a *privilégié* to represent him. Unless they renounced their privileges, the magistrates at Soissons argued, they would have no chance to be elected to the Estates General at all.[79]

In Lille, a special committee was appointed to study the proposals from La Rochelle. Emphasizing that "everywhere reason is combatting privileges, everywhere principles of natural equity are being raised," the committee asked the officers in Lille to give up their tax privileges, to make "the offer, still free and voluntary of all the sacrifices that one will be able to require soon from all privileged corps ... the honor of which will remain with you and will be the source of the most gratifying distinctions."[80] In mid-January 1789, the corps voted to adopt the committee's proposal and sent a memorandum to the Keeper of the Seals and the other *Bureaux des Finances* explaining their decision. "In the general crisis that is currently putting the monarchy to the test," they declared, "all wills, all forces, all interests must reunite to work together for the great work of the regeneration of the state." It would be a "dangerous obstinacy" for privileged groups to sacrifice "the public utility to their particular prerogatives." A large portion of the document was devoted to reclaiming the old functions of the *Bureau des Finances* at Lille, and, if possible, having the *Chambre des Comptes* of the "*provinces Belgiques*" recreated. Since it had been argued that it was less expensive for the intendant than for the *Bureau* to audit accounts, the magistrates offered to audit all accounts without charge. They stressed the need to restore their right to jurisdiction over local taxes, such as the *octrois*, and they hoped to advise the newly formed provincial estates of Hainaut on financial matters.[81]

Furthermore, although previously Lille's *trésoriers de France* had haughtily refused to join a nationwide association of *Bureaux*, they now changed their minds and decided to participate in the national committee representing the *Bureaux des Finances* in Paris. A letter of 2 January 1789 stated that the corps in Lille was afraid of "isolated interests" which could disunite the company during a time when they should have but one goal, "to enlighten the nation on the utility of our constitution and to have our old privileges revived."[82] They endorsed the plan of the *Bureau des Finances* at Lyon and stated that one of them would go to Paris to work on a plan to obtain representation in the Estates General.

Equal taxation and service to the state, this was the program for judicial reform which the magistrates in at least four *Bureaux des Finances* – those in Soissons, La Rochelle, Dijon, and Lille – advanced. How did these magistrates define equality and privilege? How did they view the relationship between their corps and the state? The rhetoric in the memorandums from these courts suggests that some magistrates were in the midst of redefining their allegiances and recasting their notions of privilege. The idea of egalitarian citizenship was emerging within their corps.

"Citizens and Magistrates," the officers from Dijon declared, "let us keep on believing that these two titles can never be separated."[83] The magistrates from Soissons called their renunciation of tax privileges "an act of patriotism" which was done "as Magistrates and as Citizens."[84] The officers from La Rochelle advanced the idea of citizenship even more strongly, "let us remember that before being Magistrates, we must be Men, French, Citizens."[85] The magistrates were moving from a view of society based upon orders and corps to one founded upon the equality of all citizens. Or, perhaps more accurately, many of them were trying to hold on to both ideas of society at once: they were privileged magistrates, and they were citizens.

In the correspondence of the *Bureaux*, the term *magistrate* was associated with privilege and hierarchy. Magistrates were called to defend "the honor of their *état*," a word denoting both social and professional rank. In a society stratified by *états*, there was little sense of civil rights common to all men. Membership in orders and corps, conferred through inheritance, purchase, and professional service, determined social status and legal rights. The magistrates wished to retain honorific distinctions implicit in the corporate hierarchy. Those at La Rochelle stated that they wanted to keep "all the privileges which [they] cannot give up without hurting the dignity of their offices and without renouncing the honor of receiving a status equivalent to the sovereign courts." Since ennoblement was one quality attached to offices in sovereign courts, they were implicitly defending the right to be associated with the nobility, and hence also affirming the legitimacy of hierarchical orders in society.

The term *citizen*, by contrast, implied participation in the state upon the basis of equality. Citizenship flowed from the natural status of individuals untainted by all artificial legal distinctions except for one's primal membership in the state. According to the *Bureau* at Rouen, citizens were "subjects taken without distinction from all classes in society...abstracted from all other civil qualities."[86] Citizenship implied membership in a unified state in which all intermediary bodies were of secondary importance, or even suspect. "The first obligation of the citizen," wrote the *Bureau des Finances* in Dijon, "is that which attaches him to the State. This is the law of every social contract, the spirit of all civilized nations [*nations policées*]." Legal hierarchies were not seen as part of the natural order. They were products of society, subject to renegotiation when the public good demanded it. As the magistrates in Dijon wrote: "if it is important to the glory of the nation that honorific distinctions accorded by birth or by service be conserved, if the order established in society does not permit them to be harmed, the same order also requires that all ranks...identify with each other, so to speak, at the moment when the public situation makes this agreement necessary." The anticorporate thrust of the declaration from La Rochelle was even more forceful: "the prerogatives, the exemptions of a corps must be forgotten when it is a question of the great interest of humanity and *la Patrie*." Because a fiscal crisis threatened the very existence of the state, tax exemptions contributing to that crisis had to be sacrificed.

At the same time as it became common to portray corporate hierarchies as disposable products of society, property emerged as the "natural" foundation of the social order. In the Lockean and physiocratic tradition, the ownership of landed property was regarded as the fundamental bond of society, a mark of true citizenship.[87] The magistrates in the *Bureaux des Finances*, however, regarded their property in offices, their capital investment in the state, as an equally legitimate claim to this title. If as magistrates they had the honor of their *état* to defend, "as citizens they [had] their patrimony to claim."[88] Citizens thus were constitutionally egalitarian, public-spirited, and propertied members of *l'Etat*. By contrast, magistrates were hierarchically stratified, privileged, although also civic-minded, members of an intermediate *état*.

Although hierarchical magistracies and egalitarian citizenship appeared to rest upon logically opposed views of the polity, the rhetoric of some *Bureaux des Finances* tried to reconcile the two. Such an agreement was tentatively formed by reducing privilege to an honorific category of social esteem bearing no claim to tax exemptions, and by justifying social rank upon merit. The link between social status and civil merit suggested an organization of society that was hierarchical in a "modern" sense, because social stratification would rest in utility and be contingent upon the needs of the state. As the officers at La Rochelle wrote: "let us reclaim of our privileges only those which give us the right to be even more useful." A *mémoire* from Lille declared that "it is time to prove that, uniquely jealous of the honor of being useful, we are ready to renounce all the pecuniary exemptions, all the privileges that one could regard as burdensome to the state."[89] The declaration from Soissons similarly stated that: "by renouncing pecuniary privileges, the Magistrate discover, so to speak, all the dignity of his *état*. One must recognize him for the utility of his services."

Overall, then, the magistrates argued that fiscal equality and socio-professional inequality should be the basis of the social order. Since tax privileges harmed the viability of the state, and the state was the citizen's first allegiance, these privileges had to be sacrificed. But honorific distinctions, which were not detrimental to the state, and even helped it to work better by fostering respect for patriotic service, should be preserved. Thus, the magistrates' program consisted of constructing a state with professional, bureaucratic hierarchies, on the one hand, and associational bonds of citizenship implied by equal taxation, on the other.

On 20 April 1789, the first assembly of the general committee representing the *Bureaux des Finances* was held. Malus, who had taken over his father's position as *procureur du roi* in Lille, was present. In all, sixteen corps had sent deputies. There was one representative from each court, rather than several deputies at large, so that "the most perfect equality and the most intimate union [would be] the basis of this assembly."[90] Yet ultimately the movement to unite all the *Bureaux* and to revive their functions failed.

One of the committee's first projects was to draft a memorandum on the fiscal privileges of the *Bureaux*. According to a letter by the committee, although a number of courts had decided to give up their tax exemptions, other courts had refused. In deciding what to do, many magistrates still identified their interests with those of the nobility, even though they had been refused seats in the Estates General with them. According to the general committee, most *Bureaux* believed that because the renunciation of their tax privileges was "commanded by the orders of the nobility," it would bring the magistrates honor.[91] In this case, the sacrifice of tax privileges was a form of paternalism, not egalitarianism. There was no admission that, at root, tax exemptions were unjust.

Other magistrates in the *Bureaux des Finances* wanted to hold onto their privileges. These magistrates simultaneously distrusted the nobility, and yet coveted their privileges. They pointed out that the nobility had only partially renounced their tax privileges and might find a way later to remain exempt, while the *Bureaux des Finances*, having sacrificed their exemptions, would be forced to pay. This group, then, wanted to guard their privileges as long as any other order or corps did.[92]

Again, one of the best examples of the difficulty in achieving unity among the *Bureaux des Finances* was the court at Lille. Letters from Malus indicate that by May 1789 the officers in Lille had completely reversed their position, abandoning that expressed in the *mémoires* of January 1789. The reason is not clear. Among the most progressive magistrates were Malus, father and son. Very likely they had played a large role in convincing the officers in Lille to join the general movement. After Malus *fils* left for Paris to consult with the other deputies, the strong provincial tendencies of the court reasserted themselves. In May 1789 the magistrates at Lille asked Malus not to attend the meeting of the general committee for fear that his ideas would be taken to represent those of their corps. They also declared that they wanted nothing to do with plans that would go against "their particular constitution," and expressed disappointment that the general committee in Paris had not pursued the plan, which they favored, to have representatives at the Estates General. Finally, they retracted their decision to give up their tax privileges, and cautiously decided to wait and see how events would turn.[93]

Events turned against them. There were to be no fiscal privileges, no new *Chambre des Comptes*, no venal offices, and no independent provinces. The night of August 4 was not a reversible decision.

The unsuccessful effort to unite the *Bureaux des Finances* captured the ruptures and contradictions of an absolutist-corporate society that could neither be reformed upon its existing premises nor evolve fully toward a new form of nationally based politics. The monarchy was unable to overcome the contradictions underlying its rule. Successful administrative reform did not merely depend upon the crown's ability to silence corporate opposition, but also on its capacity to reimburse officeholders for their offices and to find new ways to mobilize credit for the central government. On the eve of the Revolution, the impending bankruptcy of the monarchy precluded reimbursement of venal offices, while the loss of confidence in the royal government made borrowing at reasonable interest rates difficult. The legacy of royal debt rendered reform impossible.

Reform was truly a question of property rights, as well as one of equity and efficiency, because the government and elite both regarded the capital investment in a venal office as a legitimate form of property. The disentangling of property from public authority and from privilege was in large part a response to the financial and administrative problems that the monarchy had brought upon itself through its reliance upon venal offices for credit. The controversy over property and privilege in the *Bureaux des Finances* was not a problem related to the rise of the capitalist bourgeoisie, but to the bankruptcy of an absolute monarch whose right to tax was undercut by privileges confirmed in return for loans. The inviolability of property was an urgent question for all venal officeholders who feared the loss of their capital invested in and guaranteed by a state on the verge of financial collapse.

In the face of these royal policies, the habits and assumptions of corps lent themselves both to political isolation and innovation. The failure of the *Bureaux* to act in concert precluded nationwide corporate unity, even though progressive members had a vision of nationally based corps. The court at Lille provided an excellent example of how provincial loyalties and snobbery created divisions among the corps. Such conservative ideals, however, did not simply persist in spite of the monarchy's program for rational reform. Rather, by relying on the financial credit of provinces and by creating layer upon layer of privileged officeholders, the crown had reinforced provincial loyalties and particularistic jealousies. These trends help to explain why even though the magistrates in the *Bureaux des Finances* across France enjoyed the same kinds of privileges, investments, and professional duties, they failed to unite and act together as a "class" before the Revolution. Those who supported the cause of privilege in 1789 were too fragmented by degrees of nobility, local allegiances, and professional snobbery to join together in the defense of the corporate regime. The heritage of individualistic corps along with the crown's manipulation of corporate loyalties precluded the emergence of a unified élite that might simultaneously resist the monarchy and preserve privilege.

Of course, not all members of the *Bureaux* were intent upon preserving privilege. The growth of national unity is usually portrayed as a trend that arose outside of and in opposition to self-centered corps. Corporate interests were reputedly narrow and local; the national interest transcended corps and was embodied in the public sphere of the king's person or, later, the association of the nation. Yet it was members of corporate bodies, as well as those outside corps, who invoked the rhetoric of equality and service to the state. The attempt to form a nationwide association of the *Bureaux des Finances* suggests that national bonds, a sense of a common state community, and egalitarian sentiment were forming within corps themselves, and not simply in opposition to them. It may appear strange to find a corporate political sociability conducive to habits of national participation, but the situation of the *Bureaux des Finances*, even in their failures, suggests that such developments did occur. The search to create a national corporate bond formed a counterpart to the centralizing policies of the absolute monarchy. As the crown undermined privilege and attempted to create a more uniform society, the *Bureaux des Finances*, in turn, attempted to create a nationwide *esprit de corps*. Members debated whether to vote by head or order and what method of representation might best accomplish their tasks. A permanent network of communication began to efface provincial distinctions and inculcate a spirit of broader consensus. At times, then, corporate groups acted as seedbeds for the development of habits of national participation and not just as obstacles to patriotic goals.

Progressive elements within the *Bureaux* strove to adapt the ideals of citizenship and bureaucracy to a corporate framework. These egalitarian and professional goals required that principles underlying traditional corporate organization be transformed. Fiscal immunities had to be sacrificed and status defined as the product of merit and achievement. The attempt to create harmony between equality and hierarchy within the state was not a utopian dream. The Napoleonic French state with its emphasis on bureaucracy and citizenship was built upon similar principles.

The case of the *Bureaux des Finances*, finally, reveals how deep the fissures in the corporate system of allegiances were as the result of the king's violations of contracts, pledges, and privileges. Corporate institutions, like the *Bureaux des Finances*, were becoming estranged from the existing order. The *Bureaux des Finances* were not at the top of the judicial hierarchy, but, with their ennobling offices, neither were they at the bottom. On the eve of the Revolution a good number of the magistrates still looked to the nobility and the clergy for guidance. It was a corps that was, in some respects, embedded in the old regime, but in other fundamental ways had become alienated from it.

When the corporate status, privileges, and duties of the *Bureaux des Finances* had been undermined, so had faith in the king's sacred word – and the king, as Louis XIV had declared, was the state. "All types of public power," Lille's magistrates had agreed, "reside in the person of the king." Although the *Bureaux* still appealed to the king's justice, they were well aware of the blatant reversals of it. Just as the survival of the *Bureaux des Finances* depended upon integrating the abstract principles of citizenship and bureaucratic professionalism into their corps, so the survival of the king depended upon making his power truly public. The king's authority, which was at once personal and public, had to be nationalized in order to make political norms fixed and dependable. When the *Bureaux des Finances* were suppressed in 1788, the court at Montauban protested that the right of property was at stake, but even more, it was a question of "the immediate promise of His Majesty who confers the office and puts it under the auspices of royal faith and public faith. To break or loosen this line, formed of all that which natural right and the political order avow, it would be necessary to suppose a power superior to the sovereign will and to the law."[94]

On more than one occasion, the magistrates in the *Bureaux des Finances* had invoked the principle that the people had certain imprescriptible rights. A statement by the committee in Lille which proposed that the magistrates renounce their tax privileges had declared that "although they [tax exemptions] really made up part of the revenues of our offices, it must be admitted that it is a usurpation that royal authority made over the rights of the people and a sort of injustice which perpetuates them..."[95] Although the idea may never have been fully articulated, the way was being paved toward a notion of popular sovereignty. The king, who too often had defaulted on his obligations to corporate groups and violated his subjects' rights, would no longer be the state; the people would. The king had not been accountable to the people, but a government which received its authority from the people would be.

Perhaps this helps to explain why the old regime collapsed so quickly and why the Revolution of 1789 was so radical. Privileged groups, which were – or should have been – defenders of the old regime and its corporate structures, had already begun to accept premises of the revolutionaries themselves. To avoid the bankruptcy of the state, and to save their offices, some members were willing to sacrifice their privileges. To defend their functions and their property, they were ready to call upon the rights of citizens. The hardheaded experience of political life from underneath, of watching the crown revoke contracts made in good faith and trade privileges for money and status, made the magistrates open to ideas that challenged the structure of the old regime in which their power and status had been based. They, too, wanted a nation of fixed public norms. The experience of the *Bureaux des Finances* helps to shed light on the paradox of why some privileged "insiders," those who appeared to enjoy the benefits of the old order, were ready to accept, and even to promote, ideas of national sovereignty and civic equality.

4   The excluded nobility and political representation

While corps of venal officeholders, such as the *Bureaux des Finances*, saw their functions and privileges whittled away at the hands of the monarchy, corporate bodies with representative functions, such as provincial estates, faced different challenges. The estates of Walloon Flanders, as we saw earlier, had been drawn into a tense alliance with the king. The crown guaranteed their right to rule and closed off access into the corps, but placed growing financial demands on the province. The members of the estates needed the monarchy to uphold their authority, but faced the political consequences posed by royal fiscal requirements. Owing to the monopoly of power by the estates and new forms of taxation, irresolvable constitutional battles plagued the province throughout the eighteenth century. The following account illustrates how closed, royally supported representative bodies, rising taxes, and problems in municipal finances helped to estrange the Flemish nobility from the structures of power in the corporate regime.

Most nobles in Walloon Flanders were of relatively recent origin, their ancestors having engaged in trade or manufacture. In the late eighteenth century the nobility formed approximately one-half of one percent of the population in the *châtellenie* and 1·6 percent of the urban population, but they owned 31 percent of the land in French Flanders. Since many of the nobles had urban and mercantile roots, their holdings were particularly extensive in the area directly surrounding Lille. According to capitation records, the number of noble families in the *châtellenie* rose from 145 to 170 between 1730 and 1789; the number in the city of Lille increased from 151 to 195 between 1695 and 1789. One study tracing the origins of 106 noble families in French Flanders revealed that 15 had been ennobled before 1500, 31 during the period of Spanish Habsburg rule (1500–1667), and 60 during the period of French rule (1668–1789). The majority of those ennobled after Flanders' annexation had purchased the ennobling office of *secrétaire du roi* in the chancellery of a sovereign court or of *trésorier de France* in the *Bureau des Finances* of Lille.[1] Thus, under French rule venality of offices, a fiscal device of the crown, kept paths into the nobility open.[2]

Until 1788, the French monarchy upheld, and even expanded, the estates' governing role. Under Louis XIV, the estates profited from the crown's largescale creation and sale of offices. When in 1693 the royal government made all judicial offices venal and hereditary, the four *baillis* purchased the office of *grand bailli* in Lille's feudal *bailliage* court, joined it to their corps, and rotated it among themselves. They also purchased the office of lieutenant in the same court and selected individuals to fill it. Using their position in this court, the *baillis* tried to extend their control over seigneurial justice in the countryside and increase their income by fining the populace for every possible infraction. In 1693 they also persuaded the monarchy to allow them to hear cases involving debts of rural communities (*faux frais* and *mauvais depens*), a right which the *gouvernance* had previously exercised.[3]

The government restored the authority of the *gouvernance* over such cases several years later, but throughout the eighteenth century, the *baillis* continued to try to gain jurisdiction over rural communities. In 1778, for example, the Baron de Noyelles, one of the most prominent seigneurs in Flanders, took a case against the *baillis* to the Parlement, charging that the *baillis* were usurping seigneurial duties. The officers in the *gouvernance*, which heard appeals from seigneurial courts, supported his cause. The Parlement ruled in favor of the baron, but the *baillis* appealed to the Royal Council. The case was still pending in 1788, when a widespread movement to obtain new provincial estates threatened to undermine the *baillis'* political position completely. The *baillis'* attempt to monopolize administrative and judicial power in the countryside, the nobility charged in 1788, was "a new proof that the *baillis* were multiplying their efforts to unite and concentrate all types of power" in their hands. Only a clear separation of powers, they concluded, could check their pernicious maneuvers.[4]

The other serious clashes between the nobility and the estates concerned questions of taxation and political authority. The continual rise in royal taxation, from which the nobility only partly escaped, continually brought the problem of political participation and accountability to the fore. Nearly every time that the provincial estates levied a new royal tax, another battle over the control of local taxation and administration began.

The first conflict after Flanders' annexation broke out in 1694, when the nobility claimed that the *baillis* and Lille's municipal magistrates were attempting to degrade their status and level them to the position of commoners. By custom when the nobility and clergy consented to their quota of the ordinary provincial *aide*, which took the place of the royal *taille*, the contract setting their quota stated that their taxes were given "for the relief of the Third Estate, the non-nobles [roturiers], or the taxable estate [l'état taillable]." This perpetuated the notion that the nobility's contribution was not an obligatory tax, but a gift freely given in order to alleviate the fiscal burden legitimately borne by commoners. The provincial estates wanted to remove this clause from the contract, a proposal that outraged the nobility and clergy. To eliminate this qualification, the nobility protested, implied that all orders were "taxable without distinction" when, in fact, the nobility's contribution was always "purely voluntary... uniquely to alleviate [the Third Estate] which alone was obliged to bear all the costs of subsidies." As the dispute grew more heated, the nobility and clergy started a campaign calling for provincial estates based on three distinct orders. In 1707 the case finally reached the Royal Council, which upheld the *status quo*. The *baillis* and municipal magistrates were to exercise sole control over provincial affairs, as before, but they were ordered to recognize the right of the nobility and clergy to consent to taxes levied on their own property.[5]

The creation of new *octrois* in Lille also sparked demands for political participation. In 1735 a controversy arose over whether a nobleman had to pay the *droit de pied fourchu*, a fee levied on cattle entering the city. The issue soon became a test case to determine whether the nobility should enjoy the right to consent to urban *octrois*, as well as to property taxes. The dispute began when Paul Louis de Tenremonde, comte d'Estrée, brought one of his steers into Lille from the countryside and the tax farmer charged him the toll. D'Estrée protested, but the municipal magistrates upheld the tax farmer's right to collect the fee. In reaction, the clergy and the nobility joined with d'Estrée in appealing the case to the Parlement. The nobles argued that the toll in question had been established in 1699 to reimburse the city for offices in the guilds that the municipal magistrates had bought up, a transaction that did not involve the nobility anyway, and furthermore, that they had not consented to the *octroi*.

Past precedents and royal decrees, however, were on the side of the municipal magistrates. Not only the lease for the *octroi* in 1699, but those for other *octrois* from the fourteenth to the seventeenth centuries had expressly stated that the nobility and the clergy had to pay, even though these groups had never given their consent. The only reason that the nobility and the clergy paid lower fees on wine and beer, the municipal magistrates observed, was that these *octrois* had originally been used to furnish provincial *aides* to the crown, and the nobility and the clergy usually paid a reduced rate on these subsidies. The Parlement upheld the municipal magistrates. The nobles had to pay the toll and did not have the right to consent to new *octrois*.[6]

Not only did the nobles lose this case, but, during the eighteenth century, the royal government increased the authority of the *baillis* and the municipal magistrates over the *octrois*. These two corps had always heard cases concerning *octrois* in the first instance, but in 1757 and 1774, the Royal Council granted the *baillis* and the municipal magistrates, respectively, the right to judge claims of less than 125 *livres* without appeal.[7]

The collection of the royal *dixième* and *vingtièmes* led to further disputes over the nobility's and clergy's right to consent to taxes. In 1746, the municipal magistrates altered the rolls used to assess the royal *dixième*, and forced the clergy to pay taxes on property that had not originally been included. When the clergy protested, the magistrates replied that if the clergy was afraid of being overtaxed, it could come to the municipal magistrates "who alone had the right to judge." The clergy, however, thought that the Parlement would give a more impartial verdict. This time the Parlement decided that the magistrates' claims were not based upon legal precedents, because previous statutes and customs had clearly given the nobility and clergy the right to consent to taxes assessed on their property. Thus, these two groups had the right to inspect the tax rolls used to assess the royal *dixième*.[8] A decade later, the magistrates were embroiled in still another controversy with the nobility and clergy, because the magistrates had set up the rolls for the royal *vingtième* without consulting these groups. During that dispute the magistrates were forced to admit that in 1746 the rolls for the royal *dixième* had contained some errors.[9]

In 1757 the nobility and clergy launched their next campaign for political representation. They denounced abuses in the local administration, delays in the interest payments on municipal *rentes*, and the arbitrary nature of power in the provincial estates. The municipal magistrates, they also asserted, were attempting to use the decision regarding the *octroi* on cattle in order to subject the nobility to all taxes without their consent. Even more severe charges were levelled against the *baillis*. These officials were concerned only "with their particular interest and the desire to augment their own power." They had purchased offices in the province "with public funds" in order to build up their own network of patronage. Although the *baillis* claimed that they united the offices that they had purchased to the state, they really only wanted to unite them "to their own persons, which they perpetually confuse with the state." The more impositions rose, the more the *baillis*, who "contributed nothing to the charges of the state," profited by the public misery. For the welfare of all concerned, the power of the *baillis* had to be controlled.[10]

While the estates and the nobility were in the midst of this conflict, the controller general Laverdy unveiled, in 1764, a new program for municipal reform. Laverdy believed that the solution to municipal woes, including endemic constitutional battles, financial problems, and inertia, lay in increasing political participation by the elite. To eliminate oligarchic rule, he decided to suppress venal offices and re-establish municipal elections. To foster local initiative, he made local administrators financially accountable to assemblies of notables, rather than to the intendant alone. The new program called for the creation of town councils composed of a *maire*, chosen by the king, and four *échevins* and six councillors elected in an assembly of notables that represented the major corps and professional groups in the city. One notable had to be selected from the clergy, one from the nobility, one from the *Bureau des Finances*, three from the wholesale merchants, two from the guilds, and so on. These kinds of political changes, Laverdy believed, were necessary to put municipal finances in France back on a sound basis. Political accountability was the key to financial stability: "The liberty to elect municipal officers, the necessity to change them and to allow notables to deliberate in cases that concern the commune, and the form of counting all receipts and expenditures [before the assemblies of notables] seemed to us the most appropriate way to make revenues grow, to decrease expenses, and to restore the order and thriftiness in all public administration."[11]

In Lille, Laverdy's program would have expanded the social basis of recruitment to Lille's town council, but reduced it in size from thirty-three members to twenty-five including the notables. The venal offices held by the ten permanent officials would have been suppressed completely. Because under the traditional system of recruitment the king's own commissioners chose Lille's town council, royal power would also have been substantially reduced.

The nobility and clergy were not interested in having all of Laverdy's proposals implemented in Lille, but several of his principles corresponded nicely to their own attack on the provincial estates. Lille's administration, they argued, was inefficient and unwieldy, and as the continual arrears on the *rentes* clearly showed, its financial situation was deplorable. The city would be governed more effectively and less expensively if the venal officers, that is the permanent members of the municipality, were suppressed and the number of magistrates decreased. The nobility and clergy also hoped to turn Laverdy's method of electing notables through corps to their own ends. Once the traditional structure of the municipality was altered, and the principle of election by corps acknowledged, it would be much easier for the nobility and clergy to reach their true goal – full representation as separate orders in the provincial estates. "All of France aspires to the happiness of seeing the plan for a reformation in finances realized," they declared. The way to achieve this goal was by reestablishing Flanders' "primitive administration...which essentially belongs to all *pays d'etats* properly called, where nothing is done, especially in matters of general expenditures, except by the deliberation and consent of the Three Orders."[12]

The *baillis* and municipal magistrates, in particular the *conseillers pensionnaires* who held venal offices, moved quickly to stop Laverdy's program from being applied in Lille. In February 1766 one of the *baillis* and the first *conseiller pensionnaire* for Lille's town council went to Paris to present their case. The Prince de Soubise, governor of the province, also pledged them his support. In arguing their case, the municipal magistrates, who had stated earlier that privileges in taxation disappeared when the interest of the state demanded it, now resolutely declared that "the least innovation harms our privileges and is always dangerous." When new ideas were substituted for old forms, "a country no longer rests on solid foundations, but on arbitrary law." One could not re-establish elections in Lille, even those organized within corps, because the city had never had them; it had never departed from its "ancient usages."[13]

In response to the nobility's charges of abuses in Lille's administration, the magistrates retorted that the heavy cost of war and numerous surcharges on the city had made it impossible to pay the interest on all municipal *rentes* on time. Only their own careful administration enabled them to pay the *rentes viagères* exactly and to continue to make progress on paying arrears on the *rentes héritières*. Suppressing the venal offices in the municipal corps, they also pointed out, would not help the city financially, because the city would have to reimburse the permanent officials 464,483 *livres* for their offices.[14]

Meanwhile, the municipal magistrates went over every category of municipal expenditure in order to convince the royal government that no waste or abuses existed in their administration. They suppressed one annual banquet costing about 1,200 *florins* that had been given to low-level officers the day of the city's procession and reduced the honorariums of about twenty members of the town council, which were unsalaried positions, by a total of about 8,500 *florins*. The municipal magistrates also emphasized to the royal government that public works projects were often responsible for throwing municipal finances into disarray, but they stated there was little they could do about them. Canals, barracks, fortifications, and roads all had to be kept in good repair.[15] In the end, the royal government never enacted the new program in Lille.

The fight against Laverdy's proposed reforms revealed the municipal magistrates' particularism and their cultural ties to other cities in the Low Countries. To marshal support against the new program, Lille's magistrates did not appeal to other town councils in France. They wrote letters to over twenty cities from the Low Countries, including Ghent, Antwerp, Brussels, and Luxembourg, and asked what form of local government existed there and what changes, if any, had been made in their constitutions. The magistrates' decision to appeal to town councils in the old Burgundian and Habsburg territories was a logical one, because many of these cities enjoyed the same kind of rights and privileges as did Lille. Few town councils inside France wielded such extensive judicial, administrative, and financial powers. As Lille's magistrates anxiously observed, Laverdy's proposals would place "the municipal officers of this city in the same class as those in the interior of the kingdom even though they do not exercise the same rights. The latter do not have judicial power and in matters of police only exercise a precarious authority that is always subordinated to the community. The magistrates of Lille, on the contrary, are members of the Estates of the province; [they] exercise all rights of justice in the city...[and] administer alone all the affairs of police and finance."[16]

Paradoxically, one of the strongest arguments of Lille's municipal magistrates was that their local privileges enhanced the power of the king. Because in most Flemish towns, the king had the right to appoint the municipal magistrates, Laverdy's program "would deprive His Majesty of one of his most important rights." Even more, because notables were to be elected through corps, his reforms would introduce a new and undesirable principle – that of popular consent – into the recruitment of Flemish town councils. As the town council in neighbouring Maubeuge explained, members of town councils in Flanders were called *magistrates* and not simply "municipal officers," because they are "officers of the Justice of Sovereigns or Seigneurs from whom alone they hold their establishment and their nomination, and not at all from the people."[17]

Thus, the municipal magistrates' attacked Laverdy's principle of administrative uniformity by appealing to the customary role of the monarch as judge and guarantor of corporate rights. The king's supreme power to judge and rule had been delegated directly to them, without any intervention by the people. A "judicial" tradition of royal power, in which the king was called upon to preserve particularistic spheres of action, was used to attack an "administrative" one, in which royal reformers tried to mobilize resources by extending controls nationwide.[18] Laverdy's program would not have destroyed the corporate basis of municipal administration, but it would have standardized it. If he had succeeded, the structure of municipal corporations would have become completely dependent upon state policy and ceased to be embedded in historical traditions and special contracts.

Laverdy's reforms, however, went even beyond administrative centralization to introduce a new principle upon which to construct royal power: that of popular participation. Following France's defeat, a number of royal ministers like Laverdy, Turgot, and Necker began to believe that the key to a strong state was not only fostering efficiency from the top down, but developing public cooperation and trust from the bottom up. Government had to be brought into a closer alliance with the people. Reformers like Laverdy sporadically and unsuccessfully tried to increase the scope of elite participation in public affairs. Unfortunately, there was no ongoing commitment to bringing privileged groups into true decision-making with the royal government. In many large cities, as in Lille, Laverdy's reforms were never implemented at all.[19] Increased participation may have been fine in theory, but working with a hand-picked oligarchy certainly offered advantages to the king. Three years after Laverdy's initial proposal, in 1767, the Royal Council again confirmed the magistrates and the *baillis* in the sole right to administer local affairs.

In Lille, Laverdy's principle of broader participation ended up as a vehicle of politicization. The reform stirred up the political consciousness of the urban elite, without satisfying its desire for a share of political power or restructuring oligarchic institutions. Over twenty years later, in 1787, Lille's merchants cited Laverdy's program when they demanded that Flanders' estates be reformed and opened up through elections. The royal government's own proposals for reform, therefore, helped to legitimize the demands of merchants and guild members for political power.

The monarchy's decision to uphold the authority of the *baillis* and municipal magistrates settled little. In 1780 the nobility took another case against the *baillis* to the Parlement, this time charging that the *baillis* had not honored some of the exemptions from *octrois*. The new lawsuit drew an exasperated rebuke from the Prince de Montbarey, secretary of war, who declared that the king had already ruled twice on the question of the provincial estates and had clearly concluded that administrative power resided in the *baillis* and municipal magistrates alone. The nobility and the clergy, furthermore, could not take a case to Parlement that concerned the estates' power over taxation, because this would be opposed "to the authority of the sovereign and the judgment that emanates from his throne." The nobles, subdued but resolute, replied that the question of political authority was not at stake but only personal exemptions from a number of *octrois*. In 1783, the Royal Council reconfirmed these exemptions.[20]

A few years later the century-old conflict was opened again. This time another royal program for administrative reform, the creation of provincial assemblies in all *pays d'élections*, regions that did not have provincial estates, set off the ferment. In June 1787 the royal minister Loménie de Brienne announced that provincial assemblies would be established in all *pays d'élections* in order to assess and collect royal taxes. The assemblies were to retain the traditional distinction of three orders, but the number of members in the Third Estate was to be equal to that of the two other orders combined. Although these assemblies had some of the duties of provincial estates, they did not have the right to consent to taxes and were subject to the authority of the intendants in most administrative matters. Even though the royal government professed its desire to involve more of the citizenry in governmental affairs, the provincial assemblies were actually far weaker institutions than the provincial estates.[21]

Brienne's program did not apply to Walloon Flanders, or any of the other *pays d'états*, but, as with Laverdy's reforms, the nobility and clergy seized upon the government's proposal as a way to demand corporate representation in the provincial estates. In a general assembly held in Lille on 21 November 1787, the clergy of Walloon Flanders and eighty-two nobles voted to demand the creation of a provincial assembly in the province.[22] They did not want an assembly like the ones that Brienne had originally proposed. They wanted provincial estates based upon three distinct orders in which the nobility and the clergy held the right to consent to taxation.

The demands of the nobility and clergy for corporate political representation on the eve of the Revolution were the same as those nearly a century earlier. This time, although the battle started like so many others, it ended quite differently. Four reasons help to explain the difference. First, the royal government, the center of the corporate system, was going bankrupt and was hence unable to support the power of the provincial estates. Until this point, the royal government had consistently upheld the authority of the estates and had even made the traditional structure of authority more rigid. It had been, after all, much easier for the royal government to secure taxes and loans from a limited number of royally recruited officials than from a larger and more autonomous body of nobles and clergy. Now, however, the financial crisis of the monarchy dramatically weakened the century-old alliance.

Second, as a result of rising taxes, chronic constitutional battles, and the political consciousness stimulated in part by the government's own unsuccessful reforms, a wider segment of the elite was putting pressure on the royal and local governments for change. Not only were more nobles involved in this campaign than in the 1760s, but the nobility broadened its basis of opposition by forging a pragmatic alliance with the Third Estate.

Third, solidarity within corporate structures themselves began to disintegrate. Although the *baillis* still firmly defended the traditional political structures, a number of nobles serving in the municipal magistracy joined the movement demanding new provincial estates. Finally, the king convoked a new institution, the Estates General, which eventually provided national direction and a new basis of legitimacy crucial to the course of the Revolution. Without a nationally based alternative to royal sovereignty, municipal revolutions in France might have remained a series of local upheavals, like those of the Dutch patriot revolt in the 1780s, unable to alter the center of power.[23] Sentiment for civic equality and democratic public power generated at the local level thus was given institutional expression and impetus at the national level.

In 1787 the nobles launched their most scathing attack ever against the provincial estates. On 15 May an extraordinary assembly of the deputies of the orders of the clergy and nobility was convened in order to state their grievances against their rulers.[24] The major issues were those of political and financial accountability. All the officials administering the province, they observed, were named by the king. Flanders, therefore, was not really a *pays d'états* with the right to self-government; it was a mere *généralité*, the term given to the regions of France that the intendant administered. The current administration, they continued, was costly, arbitrary, and oppressive. There was no accountability, because the *baillis* and municipal magistrates had the right to consent to taxes, to assess them, and to judge the claims concerning them. Instead of three, there were really six sets of municipal accounts: the official three audited by royal officials and another three that were "private and domestic." The city continually failed to keep up payments of interest on the *rentes*, and the magistrates were constantly borrowing money. Many taxes levied for the king never even reached the royal treasury. The rate of impositions was "exorbitant" and their assessment contained "the most revolting inequality." It was natural, they concluded, to prefer to the current "despotic and onerous regime" an administration that was reconciled to "the will of the Nation."[25]

The municipal magistrates, or at least a portion of them, defended their record just as vigorously. It was true that the city had borrowed money, the magistrates replied, but the loans had been contracted for the service of the king and duly authorized by Letters Patent. Once more they blamed the arrears on the municipal bonds on mounting royal expenses and the demands of previous wars. In spite of these problems, they emphasized that they had in fact paid the *rentes viagères* on time, and were close to paying off arrears on the *rentes héritières* owed since 1781. All arrangements to refinance the city's debt had been approved by the intendant, and not only did all royal taxes enter the king's coffers, but the city was contributing more than ever toward the lodging of troops in the barracks around Lille. The magistrates even furnished a table of the city's *octrois* to show that the nobles had not calculated the resources from these taxes correctly.[26]

The problems about which the nobles and clergy complained – a large municipal debt, arrears on interest payments, rising taxes – did exist. But did they exist because, as the nobility alleged, there were administrative abuses, or because, as the magistrates retorted, municipal finances were not able to meet the increased weight of royal fiscal demands? As we have seen, evidence supports the magistrates' explanation, but the public had no way to verify their claims. The city's financial difficulties may have resulted largely from loans and taxes that the central government passed on to the city in order to conduct its wars and to support its standing army and bureaucracy. Nevertheless, if local elites were persuaded that the city's plight was a consequence of the magistrates' maladministration, then the magistrates still had to face the accusations and take the blame. The gradual transformation of these urban officials into quasi-agents of the crown helps to explain why the power of the royal government and municipal corporations fell together.

By the time of the call for provincial assemblies in 1787, more nobles had mobilized for political reform than ever before. In 1764 two deputies and eight commissioners of the nobility signed a *mémoire* denouncing the power of the estates. These ten nobles all came from old and well-established families, whose nobility could be traced at least to the period of Spanish rule. By contrast, two decades later in 1787, eighty-two nobles signed the petition calling for the creation of a provincial assembly. These nobles included both old and new families, the first and second presidents of the *Bureau des Finances*, the lieutenant of the *gouvernance*, several military officers, and, most striking of all, eight members of Lille's town council and fifteen former members. The nobles who demanded political reform, therefore, came from the whole spectrum of the Flemish Second Estate, and most surprising of all, some had a role in governing the city.[27]

The eight municipal magistrates in favor of a new provincial assembly represented approximately one-half of the nobles serving on the town council in 1787. Many of them had served long, uninterrupted terms.[28] Because *mémoires* issued in the name of the municipal magistrates during the eighteenth century were not signed, it cannot be determined if a portion of the nobles serving on the town council had always supported the demand to reform the local estates, or if, in 1787, some noble magistrates changed their opinion. One charge that the nobility levelled against the town council was that municipal administration was run by a clique of the permanent venal officeholders who did not communicate with the rest of the corps. A possible explanation for the split within the municipal magistracy, then, is that even nobles sitting on the town council felt as if they did not exercise real power and decided that accountability and participation in local political affairs had to be widened.

In contrast to the municipal magistrates, the four *baillis* in 1787 remained united in their opposition to the nobles and clergy. Although several families controlled these offices, the fight of the nobles against the *baillis* cannot simply be explained as a feud between different clans. The brothers Louis and Ferdinand de Madre, for example, controlled the offices of *contrôleur* for the provincial estates and *conseiller pensionnaire* for the city of Lille, respectively. Their names do not appear on the petition calling for new provincial estates, but that of their first cousin, Benjamin de Madre de Beaulieu, does. Those on opposite sides of political struggles were occasionally allied by marriage. For example, DuChambge de Liessart, first president of the *Bureau des Finances* and opponent of the four *baillis*, had been at one time the brother-in-law of the *bailli* Déliot. When they gained or lost control of an office, families, or individuals within families, switched sides in the continuing battle. At the turn of the eighteenth century, for example, Hangourt d'Avelin was a *bailli*, but his son, the Marquis d'Avelin, did not succeed him in the office. In 1764 this son was one of the nobles' commissioners working to break the *baillis'* power. Similarly, in 1764 Déliot Desrobles was one of the nobles actively fighting the provincial estates, but in 1782 his son, Déliot de la Croix, became a *bailli* and defended the office.[29] These kinds of shifting alliances reveal how membership in corporate institutions generated interests independent of those of family or class. The *baillis* did not speak for interests of the nobility as a whole, and sometimes they did not even serve the long-term interests of their own families. Well might the nobility ask the *baillis*, how could they destroy noble privileges, when they might be destroying the special status of their own descendants?[30]

Ideologically, the nobles attacked the estates by appealing both to corporate rights and to the monarchy's own tradition of liberal reform. The estates, in turn, refuted such claims by appealing to royal sovereignty and to its tradition of administrative efficiency. As these battles escalated, arguments tended to go beyond those common to the corporate-absolutist heritage and to invoke principles with potentially more radical implications, including that of popular sovereignty.

On the eve of the Revolution, when the questions of establishing equality in taxation became a burning national issue, the magistrates and *baillis* depicted themselves as progressive administrators who had tried to distribute the tax burden fairly among all groups. Walloon Flanders enjoyed such "precious equality" in its system of taxation, the municipal magistrates argued, because selfish, privileged groups, like the nobility and the clergy, had never been called to the estates. Efficiency, the *baillis* added, depended upon having a streamlined government where a few administrators ran the show. "Isn't it evident," they demanded, "that the simpler the administration of this region is...the quicker the assistance is?"[31] Corporate groups were always jealous of the exemptions and prerogatives, and stopped the government from getting things done.

Perhaps if they had sat in the provincial estates, the nobility and clergy would have tried to throw more of the tax burden onto other groups. The nobility had, after all, just finished a court case against the *baillis* in 1783 in order to receive confirmation of certain exemptions from the *octrois*. But, the nobility and clergy countered, accountability was really the key to an efficient and egalitarian administration. The *baillis* and magistrates also legally enjoyed a number of tax exemptions. Even more serious, the nobles charged, the *baillis* had given themselves exemptions from *octrois* to which they were not entitled at all, and they set up tax rolls arbitrarily, on their own private authority. Without checks on the government, therefore, the equality of which the estates boasted was despotic and hypocritical. The central government's own program for provincial assemblies, the nobility stressed, showed that the central government wanted local inhabitants to exercise increased control over local governments: "According to the light of reason, according to the public will, the Government is convinced that only the surveillance of personal interest can procure for each administration the degree of perfection which it needs in order to assess impositions with *equality*, and to collect them with economy."[32] In addition, it was more critical than ever for the nobility and clergy to gain representation in the local estates, for "the Clergy and the Nobility in paying more than before [have] as a result more interest than before in the good administration of the affairs and finances of the province."[33] Royal programs of reform and payment of taxes hence justified the nobles' right to political participation.

The nobles denied the accusation that they would use political representation to transfer the burden of new taxes down to commoners. The first two orders, they declared, were "always ready to lend themselves to the needs of the state, so long as one does not tax them by right, but with their consent." Nonetheless, their patriotic sacrifice smacked of paternalism and *noblesse oblige*, because they still regarded tax exemptions as their natural due. "The notables of the first two orders [in Paris]," they stated, "represented the general will when they made...the patriotic sacrifice of the exemptions *inherent* in the condition of ecclesiastics and nobles."[34] Thus the nobles' sense of equal taxation did not obliterate their sense of an inherently stratified society. Both nobles and commoners would pay taxes on a uniform basis, but nobles would contribute taxes freely like gifts, while the Third Estate would pay because it had to.

The coherence of different types of corporate hierarchies was a second line of attack used to challenge the estates' monopoly of political power. Depending upon its context, the term *estate* carried different meanings. One common usage signified the customary social ranking of the three estates or orders as status groups; another referred specifically to formally constituted bodies representing subjects to the king. According to the nobility, the social hierarchy of the three estates had to be matched by an identical system of representation giving each estate a distinct political voice. Thus, it was necessary to remove town councillors and seigneurial *baillis* from membership in the provincial estates and to replace them by the more common three-tiered organization of First, Second, and Third Estates.

The *baillis* and municipal magistrates denied that there was an innate correspondence between social and political hierarchies. These rulers contended that "there was only one estate in the region of Lille," that is, that there was but one representative body for the whole province composed of its traditional members, the rural noble *baillis* and town councillors. This estate had the right to speak for everyone in the province, privileged and unprivileged, without distinction.[35] The nobles, they argued, were like privileged non-nobles in the province, such as venal officeholders, who were exempt from taxes but had no additional claim to representative functions. Membership in the order of nobility conferred no political rights: "Thus just as tax-exempt *roturiers* cannot say that they constitute estates, under the pretext that they are required to give their consent to impositions, the ecclesiastics and nobles have no more reason to pretend to be estates."[36]

A third argument utilized by the nobility was that of the "ancient constitution," historic rights so sacred they reputedly took precedence over all other titles and claims. In using this argument, the nobility eventually called into question the legality of the capitulation treaty itself, which had both confirmed the privileges of the province and upheld the sole right of the provincial estates to administer local affairs. According to the nobility, "a more primitive constitution" than the capitulation treaty existed. In 1414 Jean sans Peur, duke of Burgundy, had issued letters declaring that subsidies required not only the consent of the four *seigneurs hauts justiciers*, but also that of "the nobles of the said towns and *châtellenies* or the greatest portion of them." Thus, the capitulation treaty had not confirmed ancient usages. It secured a situation that had arisen only in the later fifteenth and sixteenth centuries, when the four principal seigneurs had gained greater power. To change the capitulation treaty and to give the nobility a place in the estates would be to restore the old and rightful order of things. The rights contained in the "original constitution" of 1414, furthermore, were inalienable: "force could at times rise up against them, but it could not prescribe them."[37]

By 1787 the nobles' feverish attempts to win political representation led them to reject the capitulation treaty even more explicitly – and upon a new principle. They still firmly stressed the need to return to Flanders' "ancient constitution," but they also emphasized that the capitulation treaty was a contract whose validity depended upon the consent of the people, that is, the three orders. The three orders had had "no part in the stipulation of these articles," and thus "*all the orders* of this province recognize that the so-called *Privilege* is onerous for them, and that in consequence, they unite to solicit [its] abrogation as a favor, as an act of Justice and Beneficence."[38]

The nobles denounced the province's onerous political privileges, invoked the principle of contract, and called upon the right of all orders, privileged and unprivileged, to consent to the form of government that ruled them. In the context of the existing political structures, these were radical demands. Since the nobles were working to establish representative estates composed of three orders, however, popular consent and contractual relations did not entail the destruction of hierarchy. On the contrary, they confirmed it. Thus radical and conservative ideas co-existed in the nobles' program for reform. In order to confirm their own position as a distinct, privileged estate, they were willing to invoke contractual theories that might, ultimately, be used to attack the existence of all privileges and estates.

Finally, the nobility appropriated ideas, like those of natural rights, associated with the Enlightenment and turned them to their own ends. The nobles argued, for example, that the right to representation and consent to taxation was a natural right, inherent in the status of nobility. Nature, in other words, justified hierarchy. In 1764 one of their *mémoires* claimed that deliberating on subsidies was an "imprescriptible right" belonging to the nobility; it was "a prerogative attached to the birth of some and the *état* of others, the exercise of this prerogative that proceeds from nature and the law cannot be taken away." Even if the nobility had ceased to practice their rights for a time, they could never lose them. To bolster this point, the nobles' pamphlet, which was actually written by a lawyer, cited *The Rights of Nature and of Men* by the German political philosopher Pufendorf, which had been translated into French by Barbeyrac. According to this reading of Pufendorf, "if a person has not reclaimed his freedom it is because he was ignorant of his true condition and not because he consented tacitly to his enslavement." Thus the "enslaved" nobles held up the inalienable rights, not of all men, but of all noblemen, to participate in the government.[39]

Just as the arguments of the nobility became more explicitly linked to the rights of the people, so did those of the conservative estates. At first in the 1760s, the attempt of the nobility to widen participation in the local estates led the *baillis* and magistrates to defend monarchical absolutism more staunchly than ever. "The government in France is truly monarchical," they declared. In this country, "one only recognizes a unique power that resides entirely in the person of the sovereign, but where the king governs following the law."[40] The *baillis* went on to declare that the king's right of conquest took precedence over any historical customs and privileges, such as the letters of Jean sans Peur, which the nobility might cite in order to justify their right to political participation: "if the province had been subjected without having obtained the capitulation [treaty], the king could have imposed the conditions on it that he would have wanted, that is the right of victory."[41]

After this ringing declaration of monarchical absolutism in the 1760s, it is striking that in 1788, just before the Revolution, the estates were also appealing to the principle of popular consent to justify their own authority. "Everything depended, in the beginning, on the consent of the People and the will of the kings." That the consent of the people could not be documented precisely did not bother the *baillis*: "It is not a question of knowing how in the beginning this way of existing was established. It is only necessary to make sure that it is such and to maintain it." The *baillis* rejected the nobles' claim that all *pays d'états* had to be uniformly composed of three estates. Uniformity in France was impossible because the usages of each province had been shaped by "the spirit, the custom, and the climate of these Provinces." The original, if mythical, consent of the people, the will of the monarch, and the spirit of each province formed the "unshakeable basis of the constitution. It would be as unjust to destroy it because it does not resemble another *province d'états* as to abrogate the custom of Flanders because it differed from that of Brittany."[42]

The *baillis*' argument that their authority rested on popular consent, as well as on the monarch's will, was not logically developed; it appeared amidst a number of other arguments that were by no means internally consistent. Nonetheless, this rhetoric suggested that the ideological foundations of conservatism were shifting before the Revolution and that ruling groups felt the need to justify their power by reference to secular and national principles. A new kind of conservatism, grounded theoretically in popular ratification rather than in tradition or royal authority, may have been developing on the local level. Overall, then, in Lille's constitutional battles the principle of popular consent was used by two sets of privileged groups to defend utterly different ends: to uphold the power of the *baillis* and to destroy it. In neither case did the people's theoretical consent entail the creation of political equality.

Nobles did invoke the concept of equality upon occasion, but it was to argue that different subgroups within the nobility were equal. In general, as one moved along the corporate hierarchy within the Second Estate, subgroups inside the nobility argued for equality when they wanted to enjoy the same status as those above them, but defended the principle of hierarchy to shut out those beneath them.

In 1788 to combat the control of political power by the *baillis* of the four *seigneurs hauts justiciers*, the nobility appealed to the principle that all seigneurs were equal. All nobles who owned fiefs, they contended, were entitled to the same political rights, for "the letters of the same prince [Charles V] on 15 June 1533 confirmed this perfect equality between all Seigneurs." The *baillis* countered this argument with another based upon their property rights. The right of the *baillis* to have representation in the estates was a "right inherent in the land [*glèbe*] of these four seigneuries." It was just like all the other kinds of property rights attached to fiefs, which could not be destroyed. Thus, it was "in vain that these proprietors would say that they are equal to other seigneurs ... it is a chimera to want to bring us back to primitive equality: it is no longer compatible with the social state [*état social*] which cannot subsist if everyone is not maintained in his property."[43]

The social order, the *baillis* argued, was based upon property relations, and the ownership of property, by its very nature, introduced inequality into society. If the property rights attached to the fiefs of the four *Seigneurs Hauts Justiciers* could be destroyed, then those attached to the fief of any seigneur could likewise be abolished. The seigneurs in the province did not wish to probe too deeply into this equation between political representation and *seigneurial* property, because these seigneurs did not want to extend representation to property owners at large. They did not want to acknowledge that nobles who owned property, but who did not specifically own fiefs, were equal to themselves.

Beginning in 1729, fiefowners had tried to exclude newly ennobled individuals, in particular those who had purchased the ennobling offices of *secrétaire du roi*, from membership in their official assembly. The attempts were, at first, unsuccessful. In a case argued before the intendant in 1735, the nobility had to admit that under the Dukes of Burgundy and the Habsburgs, new nobles had always been admitted to the assembly. In another case in 1735 the nobles attempted, unsuccessfully, to prevent Louis Cardon de Garsignies, who had been ennobled through a charge of *secrétaire du roi* from entering their assembly.

In 1778 the nobility again took their case against new nobles to the Royal Council, arguing that it was harmful to receive those ennobled by letters or offices and those without a fief into their corps. If a noble did not own a fief, they claimed, he could not really be concerned with the affairs of the Second Estate. This time they succeeded in obtaining an *arrêt* that declared that only those with four generation of nobility could be called to their assembly.[44] To challenge this decision, the *secrétaires du roi* took their case to the Parlement of Flanders. They contended that their right to participate in the nobles' assembly was one of their property rights, that is, property in office. The privilege of ennoblement in the first degree was "attached to the offices of the chancellery: it is a prerogative of their *état*... an integral part of the property of these offices, and the most distinguished and most gratifying part." One could not make distinctions between different kinds of nobles, because the nobility formed one indivisible estate. According to the *secrétaires du roi*, "some have acquired [nobility] by the services of their ancestors, others by the dignity of the public functions that they perform: all of them owe their *état* to the authority of the king. There is but one *état civil* of the nobility... those whom the king has ennobled are as truly noble today as those who were ennobled before them."[45] Equality of civil rights and uniform authority under the king were to exist not within the state, but within each estate.

Overall then, noble subgroups invoked the principle of equality going up the social ladder and that of hierarchy looking down. The *baillis* who held the reins of power in the province opposed any innovation that would weaken their position. To challenge their rule, the seigneurs argued for the equality of all fiefholders, but tried to exclude new nobles from sitting with them. It was left for the last-arrived *secrétaires du roi* to affirm the equality of all nobles. These officeholders, in turn, had spent enormous sums of money so that they could pull rank on the wealthy non-nobles beneath them.

The argument for equality within the nobility in no way upset the idea of a society based upon three distinct orders, for every noble defended the superiority of the Second Estate. The logic of the argument, however, was susceptible of more radical interpretation if property were stripped of its feudal association with fiefholding and venality of offices. It might just as easily be argued that the ownership of property conferred common civic rights upon all proprietors in the political community. In that case, there would be no need for orders at all. Property alone would define active membership in the state and privileges would be seen as artificial social inventions or usurpations.

Such intellectual currents were circulating in the old regime, particularly among those with physiocratic leanings. In *L'Ami des hommes*, the marquis de Mirabeau contended that landed property formed "the basis and principal bond of a society."[46] Given this premise, there was no longer any justification for the legal distinctions and rights that had been assigned in the past to particular orders and corps. The ownership of property, rather than privilege, conferred the right to political participation and civic existence in the state. This type of reasoning was gaining a wide currency before the Revolution: it informed Calonne's initial proposal for the creation of provincial assemblies composed uniformly of property owners without distinction by order. Proprietary citizenship was competing with, and in Calonne's proposed assemblies replacing, privilege as the basis for civic identity.

Placed in this context, the arguments within the nobility over equality, property, and representation reveal the shifting, but as yet undecided, theoretical bases of civil rights. Nobles mingled notions associated with the traditional discourse of corporate groups – in which rights were a product of history, possession, royal will, and feudal contract – with 'enlightened' discourse, in which rights were associated with the people, property, and nature. They did so in such a way as to hold onto or acquire power within a hierarchical society under attack from a variety of sources. The outcome of this highly fluid mixture of concepts was not predetermined, but shaped through contention for power itself. Conservative nationalism, corporate representation of estates, and democratic rule were all possible outcomes. The very richness of the elite's political vocabulary, as well as the perceived need to utilize ideas susceptible of a far more radical interpretation, illuminates the shifting cultural landscape of pre-revolutionary France and the development of new choices for the political future.

In conclusion, the political and ideological battles within the nobility revealed important fissures in the Second Estate, the most important of which were institutional. The nobles' overt hostility to the corporate structure of political power was the product of almost total exclusion from the formal institutions of power and decision-making under absolute monarchy. In spite of a variety of prior internal divisions, on the eve of the Revolution a large group of nobles had put aside their animosities and formed a broad coalition to press for representation as orders in the provincial estates. In their fight against the noble *baillis* and the municipal magistrates, some of whom had joined the opposition, the nobles had felt compelled to call upon principles, such as the will of the people, contract and property, that were open to broader and more subversive interpretations. By advancing inflammatory ideas for conservative, but ultimately unattainable ends, the nobility politicized other members of society and helped to undermine confidence in the corporate order as a whole. Indeed, to marshal more support, the nobility extended their network of alliances to include members of the Third Estate. The extent to which the programs of these two groups converged and clashed will be the subject of the next chapter.

5   A nation of equals: the demands of the Third Estate

In May 1787 merchants and manufacturers from Lille and the neighboring textile villages of Roubaix, Lannoy, and Armentières asked Lille's Chamber of Commerce to convoke a general assembly to petition for political reform. In a meeting later that month, several of Lille's *négociants* called Calonne's proposal for provincial assemblies and his convocations of the Notables "the hope of France." Walloon Flanders was called a *pays d'états*, the merchants observed cynically, but it was really a *pays d'abonnements*. The taxpayers were not consulted or represented; they had no knowledge of the fate of public monies or control over the administrations' accounts. Interest payments on the bonds were in arrears, and taxes, which fell on the poorest classes, were higher than ever. Citing the letters of Jean sans Peur of 1414, Laverdy's edict of 1766, and the nobility's call for new provincial estates, one merchant, Placide Pankoucke, asked the merchants and manufacturers to support a campaign for new local estates. Approximately forty of them signed his declaration.[1]

During the next year and a half, the royal government seemed unsure how to respond to the political pressure mounting in the province. The situation at Versailles changed almost monthly as royal ministers resorted to one palliative after another in the hopes of shoring up the monarchy a little bit longer. After the crown's impending bankruptcy led to Calonne's fall in August 1788, the Swiss banker, Necker, was recalled to tide the monarchy over until the Estates General met in May 1789. Provincial politics began to become nationalized, as local groups debated who should have the right to sit in the Estates General and how the votes should be tallied.

Traditionally in Walloon Flanders, members of the provincial estates also represented the province as a corporate entity in the Estates General. Had this practice continued in 1789, the power of the highly unpopular provincial estates would have been replicated at the national level, and the *baillis* and municipal magistrates would have actually experienced a rise in political influence. For Lille's non-nobles, the crucial issue over voting at first was not the problem of the doubling of the Third, that is, whether the number of members in the Third Estate would be equal that of the two privileged orders combined. Rather, Lille's Third Estate was afraid that the municipal magistrates might sit as their representative and that members of the Third might not be allowed to vote directly for any representatives at all. Elections to the Estates General posed the fundamental question of whether corporate and virtual representation like that embodied in the Flemish estates was to survive or was to be replaced by individual, democratic representation. This problem was not simply one of class, for the nobility, as we have seen, also lacked a political voice within the estates' collective authority. Initially at stake was the right of individuals from any estate to delegate authority to their own representatives.

When merchants and lawyers heard that the municipal magistrates might serve as their delegates at the Estates General, they were infuriated. In reaction, they began to mobilize the guilds, or, perhaps more accurately, several important merchants and manufacturers in the Chamber of Commerce who were members of guilds helped to organize the others. On 14 and 16 January 1789 deputies from twenty-five professional groups signed a petition that denounced the rule of the municipal magistrates and demanded that the Third Estate have the right to elect their own representative to provincial and general estates. For the most part these deputies came from various guilds in the city, but wholesale merchants, bankers, sugar refiners, and individuals in liberal professions, such as lawyers and doctors, also participated. One week later, after thirty additional guilds decided to join the movement, every important guild and professional group in Lille had pledged its support.[2]

The guilds and merchants spent approximately 8,000 *livres*, most of it advanced by wealthy cloth wholesalers from the guild of dry-goods merchants, during their intense campaign. Five commissioners, named by the guilds, coordinated the effort: Auguste Brame, *doyen* of the grocers; L. J. Dathis, *doyen* of the thread merchant-manufacturers; J. Charvet, *doyen* of the dry-goods merchants; L. J. Duriez-Lecherf, *doyen* of the goldsmiths; and L. Duriez, a notary who was also the official clerk for the guild of dry-goods merchants.[3] Not simple artisans, the guilds' commissioners were highly respected and influential members of Lille's commercial bourgeoisie. Two of them, Brame and Dathis, had served in the elitist Chamber of Commerce.

One more significant group joined the expanding coalition against the provincial estates. In 1787, at least thirty-six *gens de loi*, officials who administered the rural communities and villages, denounced the *baillis'* rule and called for a new provincial assembly.[4] Since the *gens de loi* were appointed by seigneurs to oversee their affairs, it is quite possible that these nobles helped to draw the rural officials into the general political movement. Indeed, some nobles had tried to mobilize the support of the people by publishing libels against the provincial estates and sending emissaries into the parishes to spread seditious ideas.[5] By January 1789, therefore, opponents of the estates were in a coalition that included nobles and non-nobles, merchants and artisans, and rural and urban citizens. What had, until 1787, been a dispute over political power among privileged groups within the elite now exploded into a provincial battle that mobilized individuals from all kinds of corporate and occupational groups.

Although the burst of political activity within the Third Estate was larger in scope and more intense than ever before, it was not the great awakening of a previously lethargic or politically inert group. Groups within the Third Estate had had political grievances before the revolutionary agitation broke out. But many of the conflicts and complaints revolved around local concerns that left few documents or that were ignored because they were so small in scale. What one sees, in part, from 1787 to 1789 is the elevation of these grievances from the obscure level of local politics to the wider and more visible arena of provincial and national politics.

A dispute in 1781 between Lille's magistrates and the guild of dry-goods merchants provides one example. That year, the king called upon the guilds to furnish either men or money for the militia. Leaders of the guild protested vehemently and demanded that the municipal magistrates devise a tax that would fall on "all classes of citizens." When the magistrates refused to establish a more equitable plan, the *doyens* assembled the masters from their guild and drafted a unanimous resolution against the military requisition.[6] The municipal magistrates, apparently, did not respond. Already in 1781, therefore, the *doyens* had mobilized a whole guild to pressure the magistrates for a more egalitarian system of taxation. Eight years later, the leaders of this guild were helping to direct the movement in the Third Estate for new provincial estates, the right to free elections, and the reform of taxation. Until 1787, the masters stood little chance of successfully opposing the magistrates in matters of taxation. The bankruptcy of the monarchy and the attempt of royal ministers to create greater public participation through provincial assemblies provided the opportunity for merchants and guilds to ally with new groups, and gave them the hope of success. The calling of the Estates General, finally, served to nationalize provincial disputes and unleash a new political dynamic.

The nationalization of politics was characterized in part by movements to form associations of corporate institutions across France, an effort already described for the *Bureaux des Finances*. Traditionally, the translocal mobilization of corps had signalled danger for the monarchy. The politics of absolutism relied upon independent bargaining between the crown and corporate groups from a single area. The king, as political center and embodiment of the public welfare, transcended local interests and alone held the right to reconcile opposing particularistic points of view. Associations or leagues of privileged groups that advanced collective interests, such as those formed during the Wars of Religion or the parliamentary Fronde, were a traditional sign of monarchical weakness, an acknowledgement that the center could no longer hold. Political activity in the pre-revolutionary period harked back to this pattern, but the networks were becoming infused with a new political content. They were less "reactive" and more "proactive;" that is, they were less concerned with ridding themselves of an emerging state and more interested in transforming the state by gaining control of its legislative process.[7] No longer was the state to derive its public identity from above, through the monarchy. Citizens, by allying themselves across France, sometimes through corporate networks, were creating a national space for politics from below.

The trend had already become clear among the Parlements that, under Louis XV, formed a union to protest the government's policies in the name of "the nation."[8] Through the rhetoric of the nation, it became possible for individuals and corps to envision a sovereign center independent of the monarchy, one based in secular association rather than personal inheritance or divine will. Because nationally based parlementary solidarity posed a direct threat to monarchical sovereignty, Louis XV had rigorously proscribed the union. Now in 1788 many of the Chambers of Commerce, *Bureaux des Finances*, and municipal governments were involved in some kind of nationwide campaign for political rights and representation.[9]

The passionate debate over how to restructure the estates of Walloon Flanders illustrates the importance of the translocal mobilization of privileged groups and the principle of national homogeneity. In 1788, the nobility justified their right to direct representation in the provincial estates of Walloon Flanders by appealing to the principle of national uniformity, that is, the identity of all *pays d'états*. Flemish nobles were entitled to direct political representation, because all other provincial estates within France were composed of three orders.[10]

There is no indication that the nobility went beyond the theoretical argument and actually tried to ally with nobles in other *pays d'états*. Nonetheless, because in 1787 the royal government itself proclaimed the principle of uniformity, the arguments of the Flemish nobles carried more weight than before. In July 1788 Brienne acknowledged that he would support a proposal to join the estates of Maritime and Walloon Flanders into one representative body with three orders. In a time when the monarchy was trying to give different provinces of the kingdom a consistent plan of administration, he explained, the central government could no longer allow the peculiar structure of Walloon Flanders' estates to persist. The nobles were elated at the news, but the next month, when the government admitted a kind of bankruptcy, Brienne agreed to call the Estates General and soon afterwards resigned. The fate of the estates in Walloon Flanders remained unclear.[11]

The *baillis*, meanwhile, had begun to look for allies outside the royal government. In October 1788 they wrote letters defending the privileges of Flanders and planned to distribute them to other nobles in France, including the princes of the blood, royal ministers, *maîtres des requêtes*, military seigneurs, and noble deputies from other privileged, peripheral regions, such as Languedoc, Brittany, Burgundy, and Artois.[12] Although the *baillis* had argued that their authority was based upon the will of the monarchy, and even that of the people, their plans belied their theoretical claims. As the power of the monarchy crumbled, they tried to bolster their precarious position by appealing to other nobles in autonomous French provinces. If these nobles had supported the *baillis*, they would have relegated most of the Flemish nobility to political insignificance.

There is no evidence that royal ministers were swayed by the *baillis'* arguments. Initially the central government hoped to reorganize the provincial estates into three orders, each composed internally of privileged corporate groups. In one plan, abbeys and ecclesiastical chapters were to select the members of the First Estate, a project that excluded the lower clergy from participation. The four *seigneurs hauts justiciers*, or their *baillis*, were to sit by right in the Second Estate along with those nobles able to demonstrate four generations of nobility. The Third Estate was to be represented by members of Lille's oligarchic municipal magistracy, the mayors of Douai and Orchies, and an undetermined number of representatives from the countryside elected in general assemblies over which the seigneur or his *bailli* presided.[13] According to another proposal, the Third Estate was to be composed of Lille's magistrates, deputies from eight small towns in the *châtellenie*, and fifteen deputies from the countryside. This plan deprived several rapidly growing textile towns – notably Armentières, Roubaix, and Lannoy – of political representation.[14] In both of the proposals, political representation was corporate, exercised by privileged bodies and seigneurs, rather than by elected individuals.

To Lille's inhabitants, representation through the municipal magistracy was outrageous, especially since a nationwide movement championing the rights of the Third had been making rapid progress. The ground had been broken by the Vizelle Assembly in Dauphiné on 21 July 1788. There, representatives from all three orders had demanded the convocation of the Estates General, the formation of new provincial estates, and most significantly, the doubling of the Third and vote by head. The following September, the Parlement of Paris ignored the demand of the Third for equal representation and ruled that the Estates General should be composed in the same manner as it had been in 1614, including vote by order. In response, the Patriot Party in Paris began distributing pamphlets that angrily demanded the doubling of the Third and the renunciation of all tax privileges. The Committee of Thirty, which included liberal nobles like La Fayette and the Duc de la Rochefoucauld, directed one campaign.[15] Municipal governments and local correspondence committees also formed spontaneously across France in order to press for egalitarian reforms. Lille's municipal magistrates received letters from the cities of Etain, Nîmes, Narbonne, Nantes, Quimper, Arras, and Cambrai representing the provinces of Lorraine, Languedoc, Brittany, Artois, and Cambrésis, respectively.[16] The letter from Quimper urged all members of the Third Estate across France to display "the same spirit," so that the demands of the Third for equal representation could not be ignored.[17]

Lille's municipal magistrates remained aloof from the revolutionary agitation. To all the town councils that were supporting a campaign to double the Third, they sent the same response.[18] They could not support this movement because the corporate body of the municipal magistrates spoke collectively for all members of the city as a whole: "we represent the three orders of the clergy, the nobility and the Third Estate of this city in the estates of this province."[19] Not every municipal magistrate supported the status quo. As we have already noted, almost half of the nobles on the town council were in favor of establishing new provincial estates. It is possible that the conservative argument was advanced by the first *conseiller pensionnaire* and *procureur syndic* who sat as the town council's permanent deputies.

The campaign for equal representation of the Third Estate produced a quick, but partial, victory. On 5 December 1788, the Parlement of Paris, now the object of derision and scorn, agreed to double the Third. But the crucial issue of whether voting would be by order or head remained undecided. In Lille, meanwhile, there was still no word on the composition of the Flemish estates nor on the legality of the municipal magistrates' claim to represent the citizens of Lille corporately in the Estates General. In January 1789, therefore, Lille's merchants, lawyers, and guilds escalated their campaign against the town council's pretensions. "The moment so longed for has come," they proclaimed, "the moment to pull ourselves out of the eternal nothingness where the ambition of our municipal magistrates would like to keep us, to the detriment of our rights, our interests, and the common good."[20]

Lille's Third Estate appealed to a variety of principles to justify their demand for political representation. Royal policy, first of all, attested to the legitimacy of their claims. The calling of the Estates General and the creation of new provincial assemblies showed that the king himself wanted "the entire Nation...his subjects of all orders, of all estates, of all conditions, to work under his protection for their own happiness." Secondly, the Third Estate at Lille claimed that the "original" constitution of the city, the medieval charter of the Comtesse Jean in 1215, had granted the people the right of consent. Actually the medieval charter had not allowed the inhabitants of Lille to elect municipal magistrates, but several *curés* had once appointed eight *prud'hommes* to the town council. These *prud'hommes*, they argued, had been the "true delegates of the people by the interposition of their *curés*." Over the centuries, however, these officials had lost their powers; somehow the constitution had "degenerated" and had to be restored to its original purity. Even so, historical traditions and precedents could never determine the proper course for the present generation, because Lille's citizens, thirdly, appealed to their natural rights. Although the past generations may temporarily have ceased to consent to taxes and to elect their town council, the present generation was not bound by these losses, because the rights of the Third Estate were "absolutely inalienable." Fourthly, Lille's commoners invoked the principle of national uniformity: "the rights of all the other provinces are ours; the prerogatives of all the other parts of the Third Estate of the kingdom are ours." For this reason, the new provincial estates in Flanders had to be restructured to conform to those in Dauphiné, where the Third had been doubled. Finally, the citizens of Lille, and their supporters from the neighboring textile villages, similarly excluded from political representation, emphasized their utility to the state, most notably through the taxes that they paid to the king. As the inhabitants of Roubaix pointed out, it was especially important to allow citizens to choose their own representatives when they "participated in all the public charges" and when their trade, manufacture, and sheer numbers contributed to the wealth of the kingdom. The reason for calling the Estates General was to meet the financial needs of the state, and manufacturing villages could help the monarchy achieve this goal more easily than small towns decorated merely with military, civil, and ecclesiastical establishments.[21]

With these arguments, Lille's Third Estate denounced virtual representation through corps and embraced direct democratic representation. No royally appointed, privileged body, like the municipal magistrates, could ever speak for the interests of the urban community. If representatives were to be "trustees of the general will," they had to be "elected by those whom they are representing." They also had to come "from the same order as those whom they are representing," a requirement that nobles in the municipal magistracy did not fulfil. What was at stake was the right of all citizens to enjoy an unmediated civil existence, to hold direct membership in the state. As Lille's Third Estate declared bitterly, "the municipal magistrates want to be US; they want that we have civil existence only in THEM, they want to be deputies for US, they conspire in silence against the most precious of our rights."

Taxation and civic consciousness were closely linked. Taxpayers were entitled to determine their own political destiny, because they furnished the financial underpinnings of the state.[22] Moreover, by generating a sense of cooperation between citizens and their government, political participation would generate new fiscal resources. Citizens directly involved in government, argued Lille's Third Estate, would be willing to contribute freely to the nation. "There will not be a plebian who will not take a more lively interest in the destiny and the fortune of the state and who is not disposed to pay the necessary taxes, without a murmur, and even with a sort of eagerness, because he has the word of His Majesty as a pledge, and he will have the deliberation of the three orders as a guarantee."

But, Lille's Third Estate added ominously, if the municipal magistrates refused to hear their protests and continued to consent to taxes in the name of Lille's Third Estate, then they would consider actions of the magistrates null. Henceforth they would bind themselves only to deliberations taken "either in the Estates General or the Estates of the Province, by the deputies of their choice, elected in a municipal assembly, convoked in the usual manner of most of the cities of the kingdom."

On 17 January 1789, at the request of the deputies of the guilds and professional groups, the royal notary Lys went to the home of Huvino de Bourghelles, mayor of Lille, and when his servant told him that the mayor was not in, the notary gave the servant the petition demanding elections to Estates General instead.[23] In a meeting four days later, the municipal magistrates resolved to regard the protests as void, since according to the constitution of the province, the municipal magistracy "has from all time represented the generality of inhabitants in matters of subsidies."[24]

On 24 January 1789, the king issued letters regulating elections to the Estates General. The regulations put an end to the hopes of the municipal magistrates and *baillis*, who had wanted to represent the province as a corporate entity. All Frenchmen who were at least twenty-five years old, members of the Third Estate, residents of France, and who had paid 6 *livres* in direct taxes that year, were entitled to vote in the Third Estate.[25]

The royal regulations answered the question, who was a citizen of France? In 1789 the answer was all Frenchmen who paid a minimum level of direct taxes. Although elections were based upon the democratic notion of one taxpayer, one vote, the king had still not resolved a critical problem, whether vote should be by order or head.

Once the royal government's policies became clear, the *baillis* abruptly changed course. In February 1789, they renounced their privileged political position and declared that henceforth they planned to sit with the Second Estate in the provincial estates and defend the privileges of the nobility.[26] On 2 March 1789, the royal council finally granted Flanders new provincial estates composed of three orders. It was left to the Estates General to decide the exact composition and system of voting in this body.[27] A letter to Hespel, a noble who had been active in the campaign against the *baillis*, probably captured the sentiments of many other nobles.

Your corps has finally won its suit; the province can bless the name of its king who is granting it provincial estates that proscribes an administration detested by all the taxpayers [*redevables*]... There, then, is the annihilated hydra. The unfortunate part that I find in all this, is that the province has to reimburse the *baillis* their capital [for their offices], as if they had not done it a hundred times by their own hands.[28]

Once the *baillis* were no longer a privileged corps wielding power over the rest of the nobility, many nobles accepted them within their ranks. For the first time since the annexation of French Flanders, the nobility was united politically.

As is evident from their *cahiers de doléances*, lists of grievances forwarded to the king in the spring of 1789, the nobility and Third Estate in Lille shared many important political and economic concerns.[29] On economic matters, in fact, the nobility was perhaps more liberal than the Third Estate. Both estates called for the suppression of all fees and indirect taxes that hindered commerce, though the Third Estate enumerated these in far more exacting detail. They also agreed that exclusive privileges in commerce and freedom of navigation should be suppressed. The Third Estate, however, added the important qualification, "not including the privileges of the *corps en jurandes*," while the nobility said nothing about preserving the guilds. The nobles wanted freedom of the grain trade. The Third Estate was silent on this issue, although it did want each commune to construct warehouses, so that grain could be bought in large quantities when the price was low and sold to the poor at a reduced rate when the price was high. One important exception to the nobles' economic liberalism was their insistence that seigneurial dues be preserved as a right of property.

Fundamentally, the Second and Third Estates in Lille agreed that the government on all levels, municipal, provincial, and national, had to be made accountable to the citizenry, especially in political and financial affairs. Elections of officials by members of each order, public consent to taxation, and publicity in government through the publication of financial accounts were to be the cornerstones of the new system. The nobles, for example, called for the free election of Lille's municipal officers, the abrogation of any privilege proscribing this change, and the public auditing of the municipal accounts by commissioners of the provincial estates, following the form prescribed in 1414 by Jean sans Peur, duke of Burgundy. Lille's Third Estate similarly claimed the right to examine municipal accounts in order to find a way to liquidate the city's debts. While both groups emphasized the principle of consent to taxes and loans, the Third Estate ennumerated in detail a host of vexatious taxes and payments to which they contributed: support for the military; indirect taxes placed upon goods in circulation; surtaxes on urban *octrois*; local tolls; municipal responsibility for maintaining barracks, walls, bridges, roads, and gates at fortified cities; taxes on coal, leather, starch, oil, and sugar; and tariffs at the entrance of the Five Great Farms. Both groups denounced venality of office in the provincial and municipal administrations and demanded that it be illegal to re-establish such a practice. Finally, nobles and commoners wanted the suppression of the intendancies, because their judgements were "arbitrary and clandestine." Overall, the political demands amounted to a dismantling of secret and unaccountable forms of administration upheld or created by the crown: the closed, corporate rule of the provincial estates; venality of office; and administrative centralization through intendancies. This patrimonial system of authority was to be replaced by a national and thoroughly public one, forged by electing officials, disentangling power from private property, and continually overseeing government activity.

Although governmental accountability formed the basis for a coalition between the Second and Third Estates in Lille, the alliance was strained. The corporate power of the *baillis* and municipal magistrates had indeed been broken, but other corporate divisions, notably those of the three orders, remained and, owing to the organization of the Estates General, had taken on even more political importance than ever before. With the calling of the Estates General, nobles across France, for the first time in history, were to form one nationwide, uniformly elected estate exercising political power. Thus, as other corporate divisions lost their significance, the newly institutionalized and rigid division between the Second and Third Estates in the Estates General came to define the central issue of national political equality.

Except for a liberal minority, nobles in Lille largely regarded "the nation" as a hierarchical body formed of separate constitutional orders.

Their *cahier* did use egalitarian rhetoric. According to this document, the
Second Estate wanted

to re-establish the ancient constitution of monarchy, in which the power of the
prince and the rights of the nation were balanced in the most just equilibrium;
where all the citizens were equally protected by the law; where the law was but the
enunciation of the general will [*volonté générale*] of the citizens, expressed by their
representatives, and sanctioned by the prince, sole trustee of executive power;
where no tax was established, levied, and collected except by the free and
voluntary concession of the assembled nation.

How should one interpret this appeal to the "ancient constitution" based
upon such a modern idea as national sovereignty, where "law was but the
enunciation of the general will of the citizens expressed by their
representatives"? Did the appeal to a "general will" imply a common
national spirit arising from an association of all citizens on an equal civil
basis? Were privileged orders then an unacceptable foundation upon
which to construct society?

A small group of nobles in Walloon Flanders was at least moving
toward the idea of the nation as a juridically egalitarian community. These
nobles were sympathetic to a moderate program for a "union of orders"
advanced by a variety of individuals across France. There were several
variations on the general theme of uniting the orders, but, in general, it
was an attempt to reconcile opposition between the privileged orders and
the Third Estate so that the members of the Estates General might stand
as one against ministerial despotism. The movement was based upon a
compromise: the Third Estate would continue to recognize the honorific
distinctions and social prestige of the Second Estate, in return for the
sacrifice of the latter's tax exemptions. The question of the political, as
opposed to fiscal, equality of the Third Estate was less clear. After the
nobility renounced its tax privileges, some more conservative proponents
hoped that the Third Estate would give up its strident demands for
doubling of the Third and vote by head, a policy that threatened to annul
the political significance of orders as constitutive elements of the body
politic. Others wished to grant the Third the political power that its
numbers warranted and engage in common deliberations for true
constitutional equality.[30]

In Lille, the baron d'Elbecq, a *maréchal* in the royal army, proposed
the voluntary sacrifice of the nobles' tax exemptions. It is not possible to
know whether he did so in the hopes of warding off more radical demands
of the Third Estate or because he believed in broad, patriotic cooperation
between the orders. His language was one of reconciliation and respect for
the Third Estate. On 1 April 1789, the week when the nobles were
gathered to draft their *cahier de doléances*, d'Elbecq asked them to
sacrifice their tax privileges:

Now is the time to cement the union of all the orders of the province by a voluntary renunciation of the privileges which until now have kept them separate. This renunciation, dictated by love of the country and by the principles of justice cannot cost an order accustomed to sacrifice everything to the good of the State and the general welfare. I do not, *messieurs*, take credit for this motion; it is suggested by the example of our Princes [and]... by your own statements to share with the class the most valuable to the state by its population, by its work, by its virtues, the honor of defending it and supplying its needs.[31]

The baron's proposal was not patronizing toward the Third Estate. It did not stress that nobles had an inherent right to pay fewer taxes and that, by renouncing their exemptions, they would be doing the Third Estate a favor. Rather, it asserted that equality in taxation was a question of justice, because the commons was the largest and most valuable order in the kingdom.

Unfortunately, the response to this patriotic appeal is not recorded. Since nobles in Walloon Flanders already paid many taxes and the province was exempted from others, giving up noble privileges was not a particularly great economic loss. But tax exemptions also traditionally denoted an elevated social status and implied a kind of political power, even if this power had been severely truncated in practice. Ultimately it was difficult, perhaps impossible, to separate the issue of fiscal equality from questions of social prestige and claims to political power. To agree with the baron's stance on fiscal equality was to acknowledge that the principle of utility, rather than that of inheritance or custom, determined social worth. And if productive activity and financial support for the state established the social value of groups, then how could the Third Estate be denied political power proportional to its resources and labor? The twin principles of fiscal equality and utilitarianism implicitly tended toward social and political equality, even if individuals did not always want to press these premises to their logical conclusion.

A few nobles were probably willing to accept some form of a union of orders based upon the renunciation of tax exemptions. Because the baron d'Elbecq was elected to serve as a substitute deputy of the nobility to the Estates General, his words must have carried some weight. But it seems unlikely that most nobles agreed with his position. The demands in the nobility's *cahier* concerning equality in taxation were less resounding than the baron's ringing motion. Article 69 asked that all tax exemptions attached to offices be suppressed and reimbursed. Because non-nobles, as well as nobles, held offices, this article cannot be considered a renunciation of the nobility's privileges. Article 68 requested the king "to simplify taxation, to establish equality in its distribution and economy both in its collection and in its transfer to the royal treasury." Creating equality in the distribution of taxes implied the abolition of all exemptions, but this article did not specify whether the nobility would grant, collect, and oversee the taxation of nobles as a separate order, or in common with the Third Estate. The debate over voting suggests that most Flemish nobles still saw themselves as members of an inherently more distinguished and constitutionally separate estate.

Some non-nobles in Lille suspected that the nobility's sacrifice of tax exemptions was a ploy to placate the Third Estate without making real concessions in power. As one pamphlet addressed to the nobility in Lille warned:

Generosity and patriotism resound in your resolution to contribute equally with us to the charges and needs of the state. It is the pledge of a durable union between the different orders of the kingdom ... But we should not hide from you, Messieurs, that the condition to vote by order and not by head ... will encounter some obstacles. Our wish, the same as that of all groups in the Third Estate of the kingdom, is contrary to it. Most of the Third thinks that the constitutional equality of its deputies to those of the clergy and the nobility combined cuts short any difficulty on the manner of voting. And in effect, this equality would be illusory if opinions were not counted by head, whether in the Estates General or in the provincial estates.[32]

Lille's Third Estate held that vote by head was the necessary, if still unspoken, conclusion to the government's own program.

In Lille the nobility did not clearly state whether there should be vote by order or head in the estates. Article 7 of its *cahier* simply requested that the new provincial estates of Flanders be organized on the same principles as those which the Estates General adopted for itself in the future. If the Estates General decided to vote by head, then the Flemish nobility would also agree to this measure. By contrast, the clergy of Walloon Flanders unequivocally called for vote by order.

A letter by the liberal Vicomte de Maulde, who had just been appointed *bailli* of Comines by the Duc d'Orléans, helps to interpret the nobility's ambiguous clause. The Vicomte took a philosophical approach to the drafting of the *cahiers*. Appealing to the principle of national unity, he tried to convince the nobles to vote by head, and then described their reaction as follows:

Point de lumières, a complete ignorance of the first elements of a constitution and the tendency to enclose themselves in the narrow circle of their local concerns. When I took the liberty of telling them that the separation of orders was incompatible with the idea of an empire that was but one, I saw myself being understood by only a dozen persons in a meeting of 250 ... I had as many principles as I could inserted in the *cahiers*, but they seemed to want to hold to deliberating by order, and I am learning that this opinion seems that of almost all the kingdom.[33]

Apparently, only a few nobles in Walloon Flanders even comprehended, must less supported, the idea of a unified nation based upon the political equality of all citizens.

The spring of 1789, therefore, saw the Flemish nobility caught in a web of conflicting aspirations and grievances. Owing to the fiscal crisis of both the local estates and the monarchy, the nobles recognized that the "nation" had to have a voice in the political and financial affairs of the state. They rejected both absolute monarchy and a corporate order that had excluded them from political participation. Because they did not wish to preserve the institutions of the past century, they had to create a new program suited to their interests. This program involved social hierarchy, but it was not a return to either feudalism or patrimonialism. The nobility wanted local, provincial, and national assemblies to be elected by the three orders using the Estates General as a model; publicity in government; and the suppression of intendancies and venal offices. In addition, the nobility asked that provincial debts contracted on behalf of the monarchy be taken over by the state. Far from being a decentralized program, the coherence among the various elective levels of government and the assumption of the provincial debt by the nation might be considered a kind of stratified centralization based in the power of the "nation."

The critical debate had come to be how the nation was to be defined, by orders or by citizens. In March 1789, most Flemish nobles envisaged a hierarchically structured nation consisting of three horizontally uniform orders, purged of internal corporate subdivisions. But the principles of justice and national unity, advocated by the Third Estate and some liberal nobles, made it increasingly difficult to defend this position. The Third Estate, after all, constituted the largest group of taxpayers in a nearly bankrupt state. During the drafting of their *cahier*, the nobles took a few ambiguous steps toward national equality. They called for equality in taxation, though they did not specify how taxes would be assessed, and they left the question of vote by order or head to the Estates General. But, in general, it was difficult for many nobles, brought up in a culture in which they were accustomed "to think themselves of another class and even of another nature than other men," to give up the prerogatives of their order.[34]

The fall of the old regime and creation of the new

The drafting of *cahiers* and elections of deputies to the Estates General gave a political voice to more groups, including artisans, than ever before in Lille's history. Direction of the campaign for reform began to spill outside the elite's control. Meanwhile, the morale of the municipal magistrates continued to disintegrate. On 17 March 1789, two members of the town council, Vandercruisse and Vanzeller, tried to hand in their resignations, but the intendant refused to accept them.[35] Two days later, just before the *cahiers* for the Third Estate of the city of Lille were to be drawn up, a group of about forty-five deputies from the different guilds of the city demanded that several grievances be inserted in the official *cahier*. Noting that "abuses of all kinds" were to be found in the municipal administration, they asked that an assembly of elected deputies be convoked as promptly as possible in order to examine the accounts of the city and explore how to liquidate its debts. They also asked that the *octrois* on beer, the largest tax farm of the city, be reduced.[36] While the demand to investigate the city's accounts did appear in the *cahier*, no mention seemed to have been made specifically of decreasing the *octrois* on beer, a concern affecting the lower classes in particular.

Soon after this incident, certain "extraordinary" events during the elections of deputies for the Third Estate to the Estates General left the intendant, the city's merchants and the town councillors in shock. The election of representatives for the Third Estate to the Estates General was done in two stages. On 24 March 1789, in the first stage, the Third Estate of Lille was to assemble and choose thirty-six deputies to act as an electoral body for the next round. These deputies, along with delegates from other nearby towns and villages, then were to elect the final four deputies of the Third Estate from the electoral district (*gouvernance*) of Lille to the Estates General. During the initial elections, conducted largely through the guilds, several lawyers apparently formed a "cabal" with some guild masters and turned the assembly at the town hall into an uproar. In order to humiliate the town council, a process-server walked to the area where the municipal officers were sitting and placed their names, along with those of men from the lowest level of the social scale, in nomination. After each nomination, he broke into peals of laughter. According to the intendant, the municipal officers bore the insults with all the patience that they could muster. As a result of all this, artisans were elected as nearly all of Lille's thirty-six deputies. Appalled, the intendant noted that there were actually saddlers, cabinetmakers, carpenters, barrelmakers, wool combers, candlemakers, and locksmiths representing the city in the next series of elections. Owing to "other motives" that were not spelled out, a number of important merchants in the city, including two leaders of the Chamber of Commerce, were elected but refused to serve. Perhaps they simply did not wish to be associated with the lawyers and artisans who were running the elections.[37]

What happened in the next round of elections is not clear, but Lille's businessmen did succeed in having their interests represented at the Estates General. The four deputies finally elected to the Estates General from the electoral district (*gouvernance*) of Lille were Chombart, mayor of Herlies; Lepoutre, a *propriétaire* from Linselles; Wartel, a lawyer from Lille; and Scheppers, former director of Lille's Chamber of Commerce and current *grand juge* of the *Juridiction Consulaire*.[38]

Having endured taunts in March, the municipal magistrates soon faced another threat to their authority. The winter of 1789 had been exceptionally long and cold, and grain prices had risen steadily. Many workers were unemployed, and the Anglo-French commercial treaty of 1786 had aggravated a recession in the wool industry. On 30 April 1789, the scarcity of food provoked a riot in Lille. The crowd forced farmers coming from the countryside to sell their grain at reduced prices and seized some of the grain without paying for it. Then they stoned the shops of the bakers in the city and carried off their bread. The municipal magistrates ordered guards to patrol the grain markets and shops of the bakers. Later they granted the bakers 10,000 *florins* to indemnify them for their losses.[39]

On 9 May, the *baillis* and municipal magistrates appointed a joint committee of subsistence to supervise the purchase and distribution of grain in the province. On 10 and 11 May, Maracci, a grain merchant, Dominique Dehau, another merchant serving on the town council, and the Vicomte de Maulde were dispatched to buy grain from Holland, Zeeland, and Brussels. Because they could not wait to borrow money through official channels, the *baillis* personally borrowed 250,000 *livres*, using their own property for collateral. Later the king authorized them to unite this loan to the provincial debt. In order to facilitate the transport of grain, the intendant, Esmangart, established freedom of the grain trade within his *généralité*. He temporarily suspended the privileges of Dunkerque's powerful guild of boaters and allowed all boaters and dockworkers to unload and ship grain. He also lifted all fees levied on grain and ordered military commanders in the region to send troops to escort the grain convoys.[40] Grain purchases used up every resource the newly formed committee of subsistence of the provincial estates could muster. By the end of June the committee had spent 220,000 *florins* to feed the inhabitants of the province. One month later the total had escalated to 500,000 *florins*, and when the committee's register ended in January 1790, the outlay had reached the enormous sum of 1,700,000 *florins*.[41]

The severe famine left the city financially destitute. On 30 July 1789, the beleaguered municipal magistrates decided to stop paying all royal taxes and use that money to buy grain instead. Two days later it resolved to ask that all expenses incurred for feeding the populace be made part of the national debt.[42] Famine thus severed completely the frayed financial ties between subject and absolute king.

On 9 July 1789, the beginning of the harvest in the countryside, the ecclesiastical chapter of Saint Pierre in Lille began calculating how much the peasants owed for the tithe. At first all was proceeding peacefully, but a week later, a group of peasants, led by a doctor, Duhem, threatened the canons and refused to pay unless the chapter would return one-third of the tithe as alms for the poor. The canons retreated. The next day, approximately forty women, armed with huge sticks, made the same demand. They were arrested at Frelinghem. The protests grew larger and more menacing. On 21 July, approximately four hundred women entered Lille and demanded alms from the chapter of Saint Pierre, who refused their threats.[43] Soldiers soon scattered the first crowd, but the peasant unrest helped to spark a riot in the city. A hungry and angry crowd gathered in Lille in order to go to the chapter of Saint Pierre again for alms. There they met the commandant of the city and presented a cockade to him. He refused it, and after the commander had the impudence to strike a sympathetic soldier with his cane, the crowd started to stone him. He fled for his life. The crowd then began to sack the homes of several members of the committee of subsistence: Des Oursins, *counseiller pensionnaire* for the town council; Lagache, the sub-delegate; and de Druez, an *échevin*. The residence of the intendant, who had already left, was spared after someone told the crowd that it belonged to the city.

At first the magistrates appeared to be making progress in restoring order. But at three o'clock in the morning, the tocsin suddenly sounded again, and a crowd began pillaging the home of Martel, a very wealthy grain merchant who had refused to give money to the poor. As the riot grew more violent, a group of citizens met in the town hall and began to arm themselves and other citizens. Soon the men began to form companies, and a bourgeois militia was established. No hostilities occurred between the new national guardsmen and the royal troops, all of whom sported cockades.

At ten o'clock that morning, 22 July, a committee of twelve men was formed in order to supervise the new militia. Most of the members on the committee were lawyers, notaries, and merchants, but several nobles, among them Huvino de Bourghelles, mayor of Lille, were also included. The Comte de Thiennes, one of the drafters of the nobility's *cahier*, the Chevalier de Bryan, *Brigadier des armées du roi*, and the Beghein de Beuslin, captain of the canoneers of Lille, were named commanders of the new national guard. The same morning a group of peasants invaded the college of Saint Pierre and forced the canons to give them 15,000 *livres* in money and alms. By the next day, order had finally been restored. No one had been killed during the upheaval, but the *gouvernance* sentenced Charles Monique to be hanged for stealing during the riot.[44] The fury of the crowd made a deep impression upon at least one observer, who wrote: "this confirmed for me how much force a people has. I will always remember this lesson, and I will have it in mind when I treat that which concerns the public."[45]

Unlike some other French cities in July 1789, Lille did not experience a complete change of political power.[46] The municipal magistrates had not been overthrown, but they now shared political and administrative authority with several committees, the most important of which was the spontaneously formed committee of the national guard. The merchants heading this organization looked for ways to create jobs for the unemployed and to set up a system of voluntary public support for the indigent.

A second group also vied for local power: a committee of the three orders of the city. This body, of which little is known, was composed of electors from the three orders chosen during elections to the Estates General.[47] Its members were concerned above all with forcing the municipal magistrates to release the city's accounts so that they could be audited publicly. After the urban riots in July, they became more insistent in their demands, and on 27 July 1789, the municipal magistrates agreed to allow several inspectors to inspect their books.[48] Several weeks later, after members of the national guard attacked the electors for exceeding their constitutional powers, the group decided to disband and consider their mission accomplished.[49] The municipal magistrates, however, continued to furnish information on municipal finances to Lille's deputies in the Estates General.[50]

The constitutional basis of these new committees was not clear. They had been created in response to a generalized power vacuum, a new kind of electoral politics, and violence. It is significant, however, that by the end of the summer, all ruling groups in Lille recognized the sovereignty of the National Assembly and its right to determine what constituted a legitimate or illegitimate exercise of local power. After the committee of electors charged that the national guard had usurped municipal powers without authorization, for example, the national guard asked the Estates General to decide the legality of their future course. "The Estates General is the foundation of the nation," they observed, "it is in its midst that all the individuals who compose it [the nation] come with confidence to put forth their wishes [*voeux*]." Even in the midst of urban upheaval, the sovereignty of the nation and primacy of the National Assembly were never doubted by local patriots. In 1789 there was no question of the disintegration of the state itself under the onslaught of local rebellion, a problem that France had faced in earlier rebellions such as the Fronde. A legitimate, ongoing center for revolutionary activity remained. This potent combination –

local politicization, the collapse of authority, violence, and the recognition of a new sovereign center – propelled the revolution forward into uncharted political waters. To say that the municipal revolution represented a process of decentralization is not completely accurate, for urban revolutionaries believed that local political structures were sanctioned, and could be transformed, by representatives of the nation.

Faced constantly with problems beyond their control and haunted by the recollection of the crowd's rampage in July, the magistrates did not try to hold on to power. In September 1789, the members of the corps, tired and afraid, collectively resigned. "The anarchy that reigns in this city and the effervescence that follows from it," they complained, "makes us continually afraid that people will make an attempt on our lives and our fortunes... The authority that the king confided to us is not only belittled but annulled. Every legal and patriotic administrative act becomes a motive for resentment and vengeance against us; we have, we dare say... lost the confidence of the public animated with a spirit of innovation."[51]

The intendant refused to accept the resignations and urged them to continue to serve. Once the storm passed, he argued unconvincingly, the officers would be honored again. At the end of October, the king reappointed the magistrates until the National Assembly arranged other measures.[52]

Events on the national level completed Lille's municipal revolution and introduced some changes that the city's inhabitants had probably not envisioned. Faced by a recalcitrant nobility, the Third Estate had taken the question of vote by head or by order into its own hands. On 17 June 1789, it had declared itself the National Assembly and assumed sovereignty in the name of the nation. The following week, the vacillating king recognized this illegal act by ordering the other estates to join the Third. The popular uprising in Paris on 14 July and the municipal revolutions and peasant uprisings that swept the country further sapped the monarchy's power and helped to secure the position of the National Assembly. But urban unrest and peasant rebellion, incited by hunger, rumors, and the hatred of crushing taxes and seigneurial dues, threatened to end the life of the new regime almost as soon as it had begun. Hoping to placate the peasants and halt the violent destruction of property, the Vicomte de Noailles, on the night of 4 August, proposed the abolition of tax privileges, the end of all personal forms of servitude, and the right to redeem seigneurial dues by purchase. After the National Assembly had enthusiastically approved this plan, deputies began to sacrifice other kinds of privileges, sometimes completely and other times with qualifications. By the end of the session, seigneurial justices, venality of offices, plurality of benefices, and provincial and urban privileges had all been renounced. The guilds, for the time being, were to be reformed, rather than suppressed.[53] By act of the National Assembly, therefore, Lille and Walloon Flanders lost their privileges.

Critics of Flanders' deputies to the Estates General denounced them for the destruction of provincial prerogatives. The deputies, including the lawyer Merlin of Douai, defended the abolition of the province's special status.[54] The National Assembly had not deprived Walloon Flanders of its privileges, they countered, but made those privileges the common right of all Frenchmen. And because each citizen now was able to defend these rights, they would be more secure than ever. Further, it was absurd to believe that each province should have the right to accept or reject the National Assembly's work. What if each city, in turn, decided to judge the decisions of the province? The result would be anarchy. The crux of the matter was the principle of majority rule: "Is there a society in the world that can exist if each of the members who compose it wants to dominate it, and if the majority of votes does not make the law?" Just as the nobility and clergy no longer had the right to vote by order, so cities and provinces had no legitimate claim to veto national policies. National unity could only exist when all citizens, of whatever former corporate status, were represented in an equal fashion and agreed to bind themselves to the majority's will.

The widespread municipal revolutions of July 1789 made it imperative for the National Assembly to rationalize local governments. On 14 December 1789 the Assembly mandated new municipal elections. The franchise was given to all men over twenty-five years old who had resided in their town at least one year, were not servants, were enrolled in the National Guard, had sworn the civil oath, and paid a direct tax equal to three days of work. According to the new law, each municipality was to be administered by a General Council composed of a mayor, a *procureur*, a corps of municipal officers, and another group of notables. The number of municipal officers and notables varied according to the size of the city. Lille had seventeen officers and thirty-six notables. The new municipal governments were granted a wide range of powers, including administering communal property, supervising roads, setting the local budget, calling out the National Guard, assessing taxes, and even judging some petty offenses. In February 1790 the National Assembly replaced the ancient French provinces by eighty-three departments, which were subdivided systematically into districts, cantons, and communes. Walloon Flanders, Maritime Flanders, and Cambrésis, all of which previously had separate provincial estates, and Hainaut were joined together to form the department of the Nord.[55]

Between 25 January and 12 February 1790, Lille held the first municipal elections in its history. The city, whose population was around 66,000, had only 5,464 active citizens entitled to vote.[56] The result of the elections was a sweeping victory for Lille's commercial bourgeoisie. Fourteen of the seventeen new municipal officers were merchants or manufacturers. At least nine of them, as well as the new mayor, Louis Bonaventure Vanhoenacker, had served in Lille's Chamber of Commerce and the *Juridiction Consulaire*, the court which arbitrated commercial disputes.[57] The municipal election of 1790, therefore, represented a transfer of local power from the nobles and *rentiers* who controlled the old municipal magistracy to the merchants who dominated Lille's economic life.

In 1790 the National Assembly began to overhaul the tax system by suppressing a multitude of hated royal and local taxes and replacing them with more equitable ones.[58] In this sweeping transformation of the tax system, one reform – the abolition of the *octrois* – particularly concerned municipal governments. Because the *octrois* secured the municipal debt and provided the funds necessary for administering the city, they were indispensable to urban officials. But they were also detested by citizens and formed a significant obstacle to freedom of commerce. In many cities, though not in Lille, the *bureaux d'octroi* had been the first victims of the municipal revolutions.[59]

Recognizing the blatant injustice of the *octrois*, the National Assembly proposed their abolition. Not only did the principles of equality in taxation and personal liberty demand this measure, but, as one deputy argued, suppressing the *octrois* would consolidate the Revolution in the cities, just as abolishing seigneurial dues had secured it in the countryside. On 19 February 1791, the proposal was passed. In spite of his physiocratic convictions, Dupont de Nemours argued against the new law. As an *économiste*, Dupont de Nemours favored liberal measures, such as suppressing urban tolls, that would facilitate freedom of commerce, but he also realized that the loss of municipal revenues would have dire fiscal consequences.[60] Petitions from worried municipal governments soon proved him right. Municipal officers from the largest French cities – Nantes, Bordeaux, Rouen, Grenoble, Toulouse, Lyon, and Lille – sent anxious letters to the Committee of Finances describing their financial woes.[61] Rather than consolidating the urban revolution, the new law threatened to bankrupt cities and unleash new upheavals.

According to François Sta, procureur of Lille, the suppression of the *octrois* would cost Lille approximately one million *livres* per year. Since both of the city's major charitable organizations were largely supported by revenues from the *octrois*, there would be little or no money for poor relief, and in 1791 there were 28,000 individuals listed on the rolls of the poor. The city owed its creditors approximately 350,000 *livres* for interest payments due in 1791, and 800,000 *livres* for interest in arrears. Purchasing grain in 1789, reimbursing two municipal treasurers for their offices, and paying various costs of the National Guard had cost the city 666,000 *livres*.[62]

There was, according to Lille's municipal officers, only one solution to their plight: the national government should assume the city's debts. This measure would be an act of justice. The *octrois*, the town council pointed out, were established to indemnify the city for its financial aid to the monarchy. In the eyes of the municipality, urban *rentes* were "incontestably the charge of the state, because they were created for its service."[63] The nationalization of municipal debt provided the financial underpinnings for a new and far more centralized relationship between cities and the state. The monarchy had burdened towns with debts; now cities called on the nation to liquidate that royal heritage. In the process, cities stood to lose a good deal of their corporate identity, particularly in finances, and become more tightly bound than ever into the new nation-state.

The municipal officers in Lyon, which had the largest debt of any French provincial city, helped to orchestrate the campaign to overhaul urban finances.[64] In an address sent to the National Assembly and to cities across France, including Lille, the town council there justified at length the reasons for merging municipal debt with that of the nation. They cast their plea not as the program of an isolated corporate body looking out for its own particular interest, but as an association of public-spirited individuals working toward the common good:

We do not know these divisions anymore, these privileges that made the diverse parts of the empire strangers one to another, and often enemies. The same laws rule us, the same spirit animates us, the same interests link us. Cities are but gatherings [*rassemblements*] of citizens, brought together for the most perfect development of industry... It is, therefore, not as deputies of a commune that is isolated and only looks out for itself that we are coming to express our needs, but principally as citizens, devoted to the public good and taking it as the rule for [our] wishes.

The privileged and corporate identity of cities in the old regime was being cast aside. Cities were no longer isolated enclaves enjoying their own special laws, traditions, and institutions; they were "gatherings of citizens" who were bound together in a utilitarian pursuit, the development of industry. A true harmony of the interests of all citizens in the state, however, was only possible through complete equality, that is, when corporate divisions intensified by royal policies were abolished.

Because the monarchy had forced cities into debts, the state, and not individual cities, should have to bear this burden.

Establishing a new fiscal relationship between the state and its cities, Lyon's officers contended, should be a twofold process: the state should assume urban debts, but cities should also put their communal property on the market or surrender it to the state to help liquidate their obligations. Giving up communal property, in the officers' eyes, was not purely an altruistic measure. Through this measure, cities would not only help to liquidate debts; they "would prevent their return." Municipalities would no longer have independent financial resources for the state to manipulate to its own advantage and the commune's detriment.

On 5 August 1791, the National Assembly answered partially the petitions of the distressed municipal governments. The central government would assume municipal debts contracted for the service of the state, subject to several conditions. First, cities were authorized to sell their communal property to raise capital.[65] That measure taken, they were to add a surtax of 5 percent to the new direct taxes (the *contribution mobilière* and *contribution foncière*) for liquidating debt. When these requirements had been met, the government would take over the remaining debt, subject to proper verification. Two years later, on 15 August 1793, the national government passed a more sweeping motion and assumed municipal debts completely.[66]

Following the government's instructions in 1791, the municipal officers in Lille put the brand new intendant's *hôtel*, valued at 600,000 *livres*, on the market. From the perspective of the town's finances it was sad, but it was also fitting, that no buyers could be found.[67]

The municipal elections in 1790, the suppression of the *octrois*, and the assumption of the municipal debts by the National Assembly abolished the corporate basis of cities and integrated them into the new nation. The structure of debt, as well as taxation, was a critical factor in the transition from a corporate regime to a national state. Loans from corporate groups helped to form the financial underpinnings of the monarchy, and, in the case of cities, led to an exacerbation of a regressive tax structure. Opposition to mounting taxes combined with closed financial accounts and problems in debt-servicing were major reasons for the mobilization of the elite between 1787 and 1789. The public release of financial statements, elections to municipal office, and the abolition of tax privileges were all important political transformations, but they would have been incomplete had the National Assembly left the fiscal underside of the old regime intact. The continued dependence of the crown upon corporate privileges for credit had helped to thwart the systematic reform of municipal taxation and administration. During the Revolution, by contrast, the creation of the national debt laid the fiscal foundations for a permanently centralized French state.

By 1791, then, the political and financial transformation of France was well underway. To what extent was the destruction of guilds and economic regulations an intrinsic part of the revolutionary redefinition of the polity? The next chapter addresses this problem from the perspective of Lille's town council and commercial bourgeoisie.

6 Uses of a regulated economy: the state against itself

For most inhabitants of Lille in the old regime, the idea of an unregulated economy would have seemed preposterous, the occurrence itself highly improbable. The controls were too many, too complex, and too varied. There were import and export duties levied at provincial borders, tolls collected at city gates, subsidized manufactories, obligatory marketplaces, restricted grain sales, municipally regulated industries, and a host of monopolies and quality controls administered by numerous guilds. Any "freedom" in such a system represented a particular right, a product itself of special government dispensation. By the end of 1791, this vast assortment of controls had been dismantled and the economic slate wiped clean, an astonishing accomplishment that has usually been attributed to the rise of the victorious bourgeoisie. Yet in Lille the revolutionary bourgeoisie seemed in no hurry to tear down the guilds, even though it was all too ready for the suppression of vexsome taxes that burdened commerce and industry. In fact, many merchants and manufacturers expressly wanted the guilds' continuation. How is it possible to explain this apparently anomalous position?

The next three chapters look at the relationship of regulation to members of the elite including the municipal magistrates, officials in the royal government, and merchants and manufacturers in the textile industry. Economic regulation, it will be argued, became an unsolvable, contested political issue primarily because of problems generated by the central government itself. The multiplicity of economic controls and the inability of the government to rationalize the economy may be traced back to the fiscalism of the absolutist state, rather than to its organization as a feudal one. In spite of the excessive, useless regulations generated as a by-product of fiscalism, other regulations served the interests of the local elite and were seen as essential components of the urban economy.

The argument follows three interrelated parts. First the position of the municipal magistrates will be addressed. The protectionistic policy of the magistrates might be best described as "mercantilist," in that it attempted to develop urban resources and facilitate native production in order to generate a local tax base. A flexible policy designed to maximize and coordinate urban resources for the benefit of the city as a whole, municipal mercantilism arguably provided the backdrop for what Michael Piore and Charles Sabel have called nineteenth-century "municipalism," a method of mobilizing industrial resources and reconciling disputes between labor and capital through municipal governments and related agencies.[1]

The second part looks at the relationship of the state to economic regulation. After the medieval period, according to Eli Heckscher's controversial interpretation, mercantilism became a tool of statist unification directed against urban particularism.[2] The territorial state replaced municipalities as the unit of economic control and, on paper at least, began a program of consolidation implying the abolition of all sorts of internal barriers to national economic unity. Yet, as Heckscher himself shows, the multitude of particularistic municipal regulations, tolls, and marketplaces never died out. They appeared to be just as strong on the eve of the Revolution as centuries earlier. In addressing this issue, the second section argues that the fiscal bases of the royal government continually relied upon and reinforced regulatory devices in such a way as to preclude later attempts at economic reorganization. Indeed, the royal government's failure to streamline the economy was an integral part of its general political and financial dilemma opening the way to Revolution.

Third, in the following chapter, the relationship of the bourgeoisie to the guilds, their reputed enemies, will be explored. This section suggests that the bourgeoisie opposed economic regulations and related agencies that the central government set up for its own financial gain, such as, tariffs, *octrois*, inspectorships, and enforced sales of masterships, but it supported locally run guilds and regulatory devices that helped merchants and manufacturers to secure profit. The economic liberalism of Lille's bourgeoisie at the time of the Revolution, therefore, had a political cast in that it was directed against state fiscal interference. In their commercial and industrial activities, the mercantile and manufacturing elite displayed far fewer marks of an individualist liberal strategy and relied more upon a corporate policy of collusion than one might have predicted. Finally, a chapter on the abolition of the guilds presents both fiscal and commercial elements involved in their suppression.

The mercantilist policy of the municipal magistrates

The capitulation treaty of 1667 had confirmed the municipal magistrates in their *pouvoir de police*, that is, their right to regulate nearly all aspects of the urban economy. The authority to supervise fairs and markets, to provision the city with food and raw materials, to verify the accuracy of weights and measures, to control prices of food and drink, and to set fair standards of production whether in guilds or without were all included under their traditional regulatory powers. The right to *la police* was not regarded as a separate set of administrative policies, but an outgrowth of the town council's broad judicial functions. The duty of the magistrates was to keep order and to practice distributive justice, that is, to ensure protection under the law to all groups according to their function and station in life.[3]

Three broad aims informed the economic policy of Lille's municipal magistrates. Provisioning the city with an abundant supply of affordable raw materials and foodstuffs needed for work and subsistence was the first goal. If the prices of necessities were routinely too high, the price of the city's manufactured goods would, in turn, fail to be competitive on wider markets. The possibilities of riots by starving citizens, of course, provided another strong motive for securing inexpensive necessities. Requiring the sale of food and raw materials at regulated marketplaces was the most important tool of this policy. Second was a policy of protectionism that reserved all trade and manufacturing for native inhabitants. This concern led to prohibitions against rural manufacturing, as well as to restrictions upon urban commerce by non-native merchants. Third was the aim of stimulating production to assure every producer a livelihood according to his social rank and calling. To this end, the magistrates worked to tame, though never eliminate, competition and to set high standards of workmanship. The attention to trustworthy workmanship, it was believed, would also stimulate exports by guaranteeing the quality of Lille's manufactures. Guilds, which were established by the municipal magistrates, formed the most important means of achieving this goal, but the independent regulatory powers of the town council were also important.[4] The manufacture of woolen *draps*, for example, was classified as a *métier libre*. Although no mastership was necessary to produce this cloth, the municipal magistrates set standards for its size and durability.

In the eighteenth century, there were fifty-five guilds in Lille which regulated a wide range of economic activities – handicrafts, food processing, transportation, construction, certain types of wholesale and retail commerce, and an important part of the textile industry. The statutes of most guilds dated from the sixteenth century.[5] Although to a certain degree guilds were self-regulating bodies, they were far from autonomous. The municipal magistrates established the length of apprenticeships and size of reception fees. These officials also judged cases in the first instance between the guilds and audited the masters' accounts. No guild was able to borrow money or take a case to court without the magistrates' approval. Members of the municipal magistracy also served on the regulatory boards of the city's most important guilds.

Fiscal concerns, of course, underlay all three goals of provision, protection, and production. The success of municipal taxation depended upon sustaining a high level of urban prosperity overall. It was not only municipal services and power that were at stake: the town council was responsible for meeting the fiscal requirements of the king, their uneasy and demanding ally. As a result, fostering urban industry and trade was never an end in itself. The magistrates had to stimulate economic development within city walls so that it might be taxed, whether for local or royal purposes. Taxation, communal rights, and municipal policy were closely related.

Several examples may help to illustrate the application of municipal mercantilist principles. The purpose behind requiring the sale of food and raw materials on markets was to create low prices for consumers. Grain, the staple of society, was the most highly controlled foodstuff. All farmers and merchants were required to sell their grain at the marketplace. To preclude hoarding and price fixing, urban merchants and bakers were prohibited from purchasing grain in the countryside. When the market opened, inhabitants of the city were always allowed to enter first, and only after they had purchased their provisions were the bakers, brewers, flour merchants, and others permitted to follow. Every day, officials carefully recorded the price of grain, so that the municipal magistrates could determine a fair price for bread sold by the bakers.[6]

The policy of provision, which favored consumers and low prices, had to be balanced against the rights of guilds, which protected producers and encouraged higher prices. In Lille, the guild of bakers held the exclusive right to sell bread inside the city and to bake the bread of urban inhabitants who did not own ovens. Individuals were permitted to buy enough flour to make their own bread, but since many of them did not have ovens, they still had to bring their dough to the bakers. According to a municipal ordinance of 1630, residents of Lille were prohibited from buying bread outside the city walls. In 1760, in response to complaints by the bakers, the ordinance was republished. The town council observed that the bakers had to pay high urban rents, follow prices set by the municipal magistrates, purchase masterships, pay local taxes, and buy grain on the market subject to municipal tolls.[7] Protecting the guilds thus formed part of a larger municipal strategy of generating urban taxes and employment.

Overall in matters of food provisioning, supplying consumers at reasonable prices took precedence over guild monopolies. When the communal welfare was at stake, the town council had the right to revoke corporate privileges that harmed the general good. Several different times during the eighteenth century, for example, the guild of butchers refused to sell meat at the legally established price. The guild, whose statutes dated from the thirteenth century, was one of the very few guilds where membership was hereditary through the male line. In 1740 and again in 1771 to force this clan-like guild to bring down its prices, the magistrates gave the right to buy and sell meat to anyone in the city, provided that he conformed to the market regulations and legal prices. When the case was appealed to the Parlement of Douai, the municipal magistrates argued that their regulatory powers, which included setting just food prices and a concern for distributive justice, took precedence over the rights of the guild of butchers. The town council's position was upheld.[8]

The way in which the municipal magistrates regulated access to the mastership was influenced by the same desire to uphold legitimate claims while encouraging urban employment and fair prices. If the reception fees in a guild became too high, entrance would become difficult, and the masters would have more opportunity to set their own prices. Partly for this reason, the magistrates tried to keep the length of apprenticeship reasonable and the cost of becoming a master low. As Table 5 reveals, it cost a good deal less to enter a guild in Lille than in Paris. The length of apprenticeship, furthermore, in all but five guilds in Lille was two years or less, and no journeyman stage was required.[9] Strictly in terms of the time and the financial resources necessary to achieve the mastership, therefore, the guilds in Lille did not suffer from blockage owing to increasingly high reception fees and overly long apprenticeships.

Fiscal considerations also influenced the magistrates' concern for flexible recruitment into the guilds. A large population ensured a high degree of consumption, nearly all of it taxable, within city walls. If guilds became too closed, workers, craftsmen, and entrepreneurs in search of work would be driven away. In some cases, the magistrates lowered reception fees and introduced briefer periods of apprenticeship to induce merchants or craftsmen to locate in the city. An ordinance from 6 July 1720, for example, reaffirmed the municipal magistrates' right "to dispense with the apprenticeship and to receive to the mastership qualified workers and other individuals according to the requirements and circumstances of the cases, following the examples of what our predecessors and we have always done." The goal behind the edict was "to attract good and qualified workers and capable persons in order to maintain and increase the manufactures in this city."[10]

Evidence can be found throughout the eighteenth century of individuals entering the guilds by the magistrates' special dispensation. In 1789, for example, the town council allowed eight persons to enter the guild of grocers without apprenticeships for entrance fees as low as 8 *florins*. In some cases the municipal magistrates conferred with the masters before waiving apprenticeships or reducing reception fees, so that there was no conflict between the masters and magistrates. In one case in 1789 the grocers calculated that because a candidate for the mastership had a

Table 5. *Reception fees for the mastership in Lille and Paris*

Occupations		Fees (in *livres**)	Old fees	New fees (in *livres*)
apothecaries	(a)	115	not listed	
(*apothicaires*)	(b)	120		
bakers	(a)	9	900	400
(*boulangers*)	(b)	24		
	(c)	49		
butchers	hereditary		1,500	800
(*bouchers*)				
shoemakers	(a)	14	350	200
(*cordonniers*)	(b)	35		
	(c)	70		
leather preparers	(a)	32	1,000	600
(*corroyeurs*)	(b)	32		
masons	(a)	42	1,700	800
(*maçons*)	(b)	77		
goldsmiths	(a)	122	hereditary	
(*orfèvres*)	(b)	175		
hatmakers	(a)	15	1,100	600
(*chapeliers*)	(b)	45		
carters	hereditary		1,000	400
(*charretiers*)				
grocers	(a)	57	1,700	800
(*épiciers*)	(b)	63		
pinmakers	(a)	11	500	100
(*épingliers*)	(b)	21		
fruit sellers	(a)	5	900	400
(*fruitiers*)	(b)	5		
carpenters	(a)	28	1,800	800
(*charpentiers*)	(b)	31		
painters	(a)	42 .	500	500
(*peintres*)	(b)	42		
ribbonmakers,	(a)	13	400	400
trimmers	(b)	61		
(*passementiers*)				
tailors	(a)	14	420	400
(*tailleurs d'habit*)	(b)	25		
	(c)	34		

Reception fees in Lille (1767)
(a) son of a masters
(b) resident of Lille
(c) non-resident of Lille

Reception fees in Paris, before and after Turgot's suppression of the guilds in 1776

Source: For Lille, "Etat de ce qu'il coûte pour être reçu à la maîtrise…" A.M.L. A.G. 36, dos. 12. For Paris, Emile Levasseur, *Histoire des classes ouvrières en France depuis la conquête de Jules César jusqu'à la Révolution*. vol. 2 (Paris, 1859), pp. 547–550.

"respectable fortune," was an outsider of the province, but was taking over an established shop, he should pay 40 *florins* to be released from his apprenticeship, a decision which the magistrates approved.[11]

On other occasions, however, the magistrates' desire to open up the guild led to a direct conflict with the masters, who wanted to close off access and to lessen competition between masters. In 1746 the wool weavers (*sayetteurs*) protested against the entry of an individual who had received a mastership in their guild in return for his service in the militia.[12] In 1749 the linen weavers (*tisserands*) protested when the magistrates admitted a new master into their guild, and in 1790 the tailors asked the Parlement of Douai to overrule a decision by the magistrates allowing a member to join.[13]

Reasonable reception rates and brief periods of apprenticeship helped to facilitate membership of masters in two or more guilds at once. The ability to accumulate masterships depended upon the statutes of each guild, and not all corporations allowed the practice. Nonetheless, dual membership was apparently not uncommon. In 1745, for example, of the 78 masters in the guild of candlemakers, 60 were also grocers or tallow workers. Among the 128 masters in the guild of bakers, 50 also belonged to the guilds of grocers or tallow workers. Approximately one-quarter of the tailors were also second-hand dealers. Another *mémoire*, without citing figures, stated that it was common for tanners to be glovemakers, tailors to be shoemakers, wool carders to be candlemakers, and goldsmiths to be wholesale merchants. This merging of tasks suggests far more flexibility and occupational mobility within the guilds than has sometimes been assumed.[14]

Just as fiscal considerations informed the municipal magistrates' policy of protectionism, so merchants and artisans in the city invoked their payment of urban taxes to justify limitation of competition. The linen cloth merchants, who did not form a guild, used this argument when they asked the magistrates to stop *marchands forains* from selling cloth inside the city. Because Lille's merchants "pay the taxes of this city, such as the *tailles*, *vingtièmes*, *capitation*, and generally all other costs...it is a natural right that the inhabitants and *bourgeois* from this city have an incontestable preference over all outsiders in general."[15] In most cases, the municipal magistrates agreed with this stance. In 1760, for example, the magistrates prohibited the guilds from accepting non-natives into their ranks because, "it happens that these non-resident masters, who do not contribute to the taxes of this city, have, nevertheless, the advantage of working here and of introducing their products here, which is very harmful to our inhabitants."[16]

Because fostering the general vitality of the urban economy was the municipal magistrates' overarching goal, they treated the guilds as flexible instruments within a larger plan. Sometimes this meant defending the guilds' monopolies, at other times circumventing them. When it came to rural industry, the magistrates were adamant. The privileges of Lille's guilds, in particular those of the wool weavers, were virtually sacred. As long as the masters in this guild enjoyed the sole right to manufacture specified woolens, rural manufacturers would be less able to lure workers away from the city. At other times in the eighteenth century, however, the magistrates undermined the privileges of Lille's textile guilds by subsidizing entrepreneurs who wanted to set up textile manufactures outside guild control. The goal, nonetheless, was still to encourage urban employment over rural.

In 1714, for example, the magistrates offered 600 *florins* to Jean Gilles Deslobbes to start a rug manufactory that was eventually to employ 300 to 400 workers. The agreement stipulated that he would hire local residents in preference to outsiders. In several other cases the magistrates made entrepreneurs pay fees to the guild of mixed-fabric weavers (described in chapter 7) before setting up shop. In 1756 the magistrates ordered the manufacturer Boussemart to pay 80 *florins* to this guild for the right to make *velours*. Similarly, in 1780 F. J. Flament was required to pay the same guild 20 *patars* per loom on his first twenty looms when he set up a gauze workshop. The royal silk manufactory set up by Albert Cuvelier-Brame, however, was exempted from all guild regulations and fees. He had been granted a subsidy of 50 *livres* per loom from the king, and an additional 40 *florins* from the city for each loom over eight.[17]

In conclusion, no clear-cut label of traditional or progressive can be assigned to the magistrates' policies toward the guilds and urban economy. On the one hand, the magistrates appeared very conservative in their ardent support of Lille's guilds against rural competitors. On the other hand, they seemed quite progressive in their subsidies to capitalist entrepreneurs and flexible entrance policies for the guilds. But it is impossible to evaluate the magistrates' actions from an economic viewpoint alone. Their policies were directed at preserving the city's power, its tax base, and its credit.

Masters, magistrates and the monarchy

Over the centuries, the rise of the absolute monarchy had stimulated economic development, but it had done so on its own terms and for its own purposes – to create taxable wealth. A self-sufficient economy in which goods failed to circulate widely offered monarchs few opportunities for taxation. Regional and long-distance trade in both luxury goods and commodities was essential to enhancing the economic base of royal power. The French monarchy had fostered economic growth with the techniques at its disposal, nearly all of which extended the role of privilege and corporate organizations. Subsidized royal manufactures, chartered trading companies, protectionistic tariffs, and highly-regulated production in guilds were designed to enhance economic performance and increase the state's financial basis.[18]

The collection of taxes was one important reason for the persistence of vexsome economic regulations. The low level of bureaucratic development right up to the Revolution meant that royal tax collection of all sorts could not escape its dependence upon localistic, corporate structures. Indirect taxes levied when goods were consumed or exchanged remained the preferred form of collection in urban areas. To this end the crown had set up or extended its control over tolls, customs bureaus, and marketplaces.[19] Cities, like Lille, found themselves repeatedly constrained to turn over a portion of their local revenues to the central government, a practice that reinforced municipal protectionism. The royal surtax on municipal *octrois*, the heaviest *abonnement* in Lille, showed that the crown's financial dependence upon the privileged urban sector was as strong as ever before the Revolution. Even in direct taxation, the monarchy had found it convenient to enlist the aid of professional and corporate groups. The communal *contrainte solidaire* utilized in gathering the peasants' *taille*, the *abonnements* of provinces, the occupational and status groupings enumerated in the *capitation*, and the reliance on guilds to collect the *vingtième d'industrie* all revealed how difficult it was for the absolute monarchy to part with collective liability in its financial operations.[20]

The monarchy's means of tapping private wealth thus had traditionally been embedded in networks of corporate privilege. From the viewpoint of the state, the introduction or success of a laissez-faire policy of deregulation was not simply a question of removing commercial or industrial regulations in order to generate competition. New ways of channelling back to the state the wealth unleashed by economic freedom had to be devised. To this end there were bureaucratic, fiscal, and political preconditions for the political success of laissez-faire. First, the central government had to have a salaried bureaucracy whose operation was not funded out of particularistic, regional systems of tax farming and the host of tolls and customs on which these depended. Second, it had to devise a way to collect revenues without recourse to indirect taxes on the exchange of goods via tolls or customs or direct taxes through various collective sorts of *abonnements*. The creation of the *dixièmes* and *vingtièmes*, taxes on revenues, represented the first attempts at such a tax. Third, it had to have the cooperation of the populace, especially the privileged elite, in order to reach so systematically and directly into the pocketbooks of its subjects. But none of these political preconditions necessary to clear away the fiscal clutter that had accumulated over centuries and impeded the free exchange of goods was present in France before the Revolution. Bureaucratic sophistication on the part of the government tended to heighten constitutional concerns on the part of society for systems of participation and accountability, and it was actually indirect taxation, dependent upon privileged groups like the Farmers General and cities, that grew most rapidly before the Revolution.[21] Thus, up until the Revolution, privileged corporate groups, with all their corresponding economic impediments, remained integral elements of the fiscal apparatus of the government.

The argument may be pressed even further beyond the question of tax collection and into that of public credit. Loans from corporate groups, including provinces, cities, and corps of tax farmers completely locked particularistic, regional systems of taxation into place.[22] And during wartime, because the government was unable to mobilize credit through a national bank, it resorted to outright fiscalism. *Fiscalism* with its blatant and unadulterated exploitation of a subject population, as Martin Wolfe has observed, may usefully be distinguished from *mercantilism*, in which encouraging the economic prosperity of subjects was seen as the foundation of a stronger tax base. In fiscalism the needs of the treasury took precedence over "the most basic considerations of efficiency, justice, and the crown's ability to control its own bureaucrats."[23]

Fiscalism, rather than mercantilism *per se*, was responsible for the outrageous multiplication of useless regulatory devices. Privileges in the guilds and marketplaces were extended and sold outright, smothering the economy under the weight of all sorts of regulations created solely for their ability to raise revenue. "All these masterships and all these guilds," wrote an exasperated Voltaire at the time of their suppression by Turgot in 1776, "were only invented to take the money of poor workers, in order to enrich government financiers [*traitants*] and to crush the nation."[24] The French monarchy was well known for turning guilds into sources of revenue. Sometimes the royal government had simply created and sold new monopolies for large sums of money. Other times it forced unincorporated groups of merchants and artisans to join guilds and pay reception fees to the royal treasury. Royal financiers also peddled certificates entitling individuals to become masters without paying the regular reception fees. Of the approximately 400 categories of venal offices created by Louis XIV, the majority were related to guilds.[25] Between 1691 and 1714 the crown gained over 86 million *livres* from the sale of these kinds of offices across France.[26]

The financial relationship of the absolute monarchy to the local economy helps to explain why territorial unification was impossible even under a program of laissez-faire. The fiscal apparatus of the central government remained embedded in the corporate framework of local society, which it extended, routinized, and manipulated as necessary. Just as the practice of venality of judicial and administrative offices turned privilege into a rigid form of property, so the crown's reliance upon trade, guilds, and cities for various forms of revenue multiplied the regulatory apparatus of localities and the state. Many economic controls and prerogatives were not hollow shells of a medieval and vestigial past, but by-products of the monarchy's own expansion. They were integral to the way absolute kings financed their operations, even in the eighteenth century when bureaucratic kinds of authority were supposedly rendering corporate forms of organization obsolete.

The process may be illustrated by looking in more detail at several cases. Louis XIV's dealings with the brewers in Lille reveal how a monopoly created for fiscal reasons impeded efficient urban administration. The municipal magistrates, who regulated the price of beer, and the brewers, who did not form a guild, were constantly at war over the price of beer. The brewers had repeatedly tried to organize themselves into a guild so that they could enjoy a monopoly over manufacturing beer, but the municipal magistrates, fearing the consequences, had consistently refused. In 1691 the brewers went over the heads of the municipal magistrates and offered the king 200,000 *livres* to receive the exclusive right to brew beer. The magistrates and the tavernkeepers (*cabaretiers*), who sometimes brewed beer independently for sale in their taverns, were outraged. The magistrates offered the king 200,000 *livres* simply to leave things the way that they were. When the king accepted, the magistrates borrowed the sum, which was secured by a new tax on beer consumed in taverns. In return for this tidy sum, Louis XIV confirmed the municipal magistrates in their regulatory powers and issued Letters Patent which agreed "never to accord the brewers any franchise that would be contrary to [the magistrates'] privileges."[27]

In 1693, however, Louis XIV's pressing financial needs led him to create fifty offices among the brewers anyway. The new offices were given the exclusive privilege over brewing, and the rights of all other groups, such as the tavernkeepers, to brew their own beer were suppressed. Thirty-one of the newly created offices were bought up individually by the established brewers; six more were purchased by other individuals. When it became difficult to sell the rest of the offices, the king was forced to reduce the number of offices from fifty to forty. Finally, after the government put pressure on the brewers to buy the remaining offices, they purchased the last three offices collectively.[28]

For the moment, confusion reigned. Tavernkeepers were thrown out of business, and the revenues from the local beer taxes declined. Now that they had their monopoly, some brewers stopped brewing beer and illegally ceded their rights to tavernkeepers for kickbacks. After more negotiations, the magistrates succeeded in having the offices suppressed five years later. To reimburse the brewers for their offices, an additional tax was placed on beer. A Parisian *financier*, J. B. Dussaussoy, arranged to buy up the brewers' offices in exchange for the right to collect the new beer tax for nine years. To keep the Parisians out of Lille's affairs, it was arranged that a local merchant would pay Dussaussoy 300,000 *livres* and be given the right to collect the beer tax instead. Thus for their efforts to prevent a brewers' monopoly and to restore the local situation to normal, the Lillois emerged with two new taxes on beer and a heavier town debt.[29]

The same year that the brewers' offices were created, the tavernkeepers, who did not form a guild, were threatened by another royal edict which put the exclusive right to manage inns and taverns up for sale. Once again the king agreed to suppress the new privileges in return for money. In order to raise the money, the magistrates created a new guild, the *cabaretiers à bière*, so that under their new corporate status, the members could borrow money to pay off the king. To secure the loans, the magistrates established reception fees. In addition, anyone wishing to sell beer on the premises was required to pay 40 *florins* to the *cabaretiers à biere*.[30] This guild did not constitute a rigidly closed group. There was no apprenticeship and no limit on the number who could join. It simply made the cost of setting up a local tavern more expensive than before. It also led to vigilance on the part of the new guild members to make sure that everyone selling beer had paid their fees.

Another category of offices which proved lucrative for the royal treasury were the local *offices de police*, which included all those posts involved in municipal economic regulation. Weighmasters, measurers, guards at the city gates, messengers, clerks for the city, and numerous transport workers who held the exclusive rights to carry goods to and from the marketplaces – all of these positions fell under the broad title of *offices de police*. As part of their municipal privileges, the magistrates had been granted the authority to appoint individuals to these functions and to set their salaries. When shortly after Lille's annexation, the intendant tried to nominate men to these positions, the magistrates protested, and the royal government upheld the municipality's right.[31]

The magistrates' carefully guarded powers, however, were swept aside by a royal edict in 1695 which made all the *offices de police* venal.[32] A number of other minor regulatory offices were created soon afterward, such as those of wood weighers, weighmasters, and auctioneers (*jurés-priseurs*).[33] The officeholders were granted the exclusive privilege of transporting goods or enforcing specific market and guild regulations. Often they were also given the right to collect fees for their efforts. Everyone, for example, had to use the official grain measurers when they bought grain at the market and pay 2 *deniers* per bushel for their services. In most cases these offices duplicated pre-existing ones, but in others they imposed new regulations and petty fees upon the economic activity. Overall, the offices created by the monarchy led not to a greater concentration, but to more of a dispersion of authority over the local economy than ever.

In order to regain their regulatory power, the magistrates had to buy up the new offices.[34] Because the city's finances were heavily strained at the time, the magistrates sold the offices again. They reserved the right, however, to buy back the offices later when finances permitted, and they placed price controls on the offices, so that no owner could lease his office for more than one-tenth or sell it for more than one-fifth above the original price. The rationale for these measures was, one petition noted, "to follow the order of distributive justice to divide the profit between the owner and the leasee."[35] By 1729 the magistrates had bought back all the offices which they had sold and thus regained control over recruitment.

Buying up these petty venal offices took its toll on city finances. In several cases, after regulatory offices had been bought by the city, the fees for service attached to the offices were joined to the *octrois* of the town. Just as new fees on beer had been established to pay for the brewers' offices, so new fees were levied on coal and wood to reimburse the city for the corresponding offices of measurers of those commodities.[36]

Once the city magistrates had regained control over the *offices de police*, the offices were turned into a way of funding municipal charity. In 1738 royal Letters Patent were issued to establish an *hôpital général*. The new *hôpital général* bought approximately 180 regulatory offices from the city and leased them as a source of revenue. The municipal magistrates kept the right to nominate individuals to fill the posts. According to one estimate in 1738, the offices generated about 10,000 *florins* a year for the charitable institution. The *hôpital général* also received a percentage of certain *octrois*.[37]

This system of financing local charity was jeopardized by new attempts of the royal government to regain control of these offices and collect their fees for the king's profit. In 1768 the central government decided to suppress many of the regulatory offices, which in some parts of France had been created as early in 1571, and ordered that their corresponding fees be turned over to the crown. To reimburse the current officeholders, a portion of the municipal *octrois* was to be transferred to the central government.[38]

The magistrates protested the injustice of shifting urban *octrois*, the mainstay of the municipal budget, to the royal treasury. The administrators of the *hôpital général* observed that the measure would "deprive the poor of a part of their subsistence."[39] But, as it turned out, the royal measure was just another way of forcing the municipality to come up with a subsidy. To have the new edict suppressed, and to furnish a *don gratuit* to the king, the provincial estates of Walloon and Maritime Flanders together paid the crown an *abonnement* of 196,950 *livres* per year for four years. When, in 1773, the royal government again threatened to suppress the offices, the two provincial estates added 100,000 *livres* to the *don gratuit*.[40]

Under the French monarchy, no guild in Lille escaped the multiplication of useless privileges and offices. In 1697 Louis XIV established offices of *syndics* and auditors of accounts in Flanders. Because the municipal magistrates held the right to audit the accounts of the guilds, and collect a fee for their services, the new offices threatened their authority and income. The estates of Walloon Flanders arranged an *abonnement* of 400,000 *livres*.[41] The same edict established offices of syndics for all merchants who were not members of guilds. Lille's merchants protested that wholesale commerce had always been considered a liberal profession (*profession libre*), and had never been subject to corporate controls, such as those implied by the existence of syndics. The petition was to no avail, and the merchants were required to contribute to the general payment to remain independent.[42]

During the eighteenth century the process continued. Upon Louis XV's accession to the throne, the guilds in Walloon Flanders paid 60,000 *livres* for the confirmation of their privileges. In 1747 the guilds and town council furnished 120,000 *livres* to unite new offices of inspectors to their corps, and in 1759 they paid another 60,000 *livres* for refinancing charges on these offices.[43] In 1767 the king created four more *brevets* for each guild in Lille. As no record for an *abonnement* exists, the fate of the latter is unclear.

To raise the capital for buying up various guild offices, the magistrates devised the following plan. The magistrates furnished one-fourth of the total *abonnement* for the offices. In cases where the edicts had created offices in professions outside the guilds, the Chamber of Commerce assessed individuals in the liberal professions. In 1697 and 1727, for example, merchants were charged an additional two years of the *capitation* for their quota. In addition, the magistrates assessed each guild a certain amount based upon its wealth and size. In most cases the guilds borrowed money by selling *rentes* or letters of exchange. To pay the interest, the magistrates allowed the guilds to raise reception fees for the apprenticeship and mastership.[44]

Thus, one result of the monarchy's fiscal manipulation of the guilds was higher reception fees, a pattern replicated in other areas of France.[45] A number of Lille's guilds doubled their reception fees when they were forced to borrow money to pay for the confirmation of their privileges. Because the fees were already low, the increase was hardly excessive. The ribbonmakers raised the cost of becoming a master from 30 to 50 *florins*, the coppersmiths from 24 to 48 *florins*, and the wool combers from a mere 3 to 6 *florins*. The magistrates viewed these increases strictly as a temporary measure. The higher reception fees would cease, the town council informed the king, the day that the guilds' debts were liquidated.[46]

Although ministers in the central government, like Turgot, were quick to blame mismanagement or endless judicial proceedings for corporate debts, in Lille the monarchy probably played the largest role in destabilizing the guilds' finances. The debts of Lille's guilds were generally low, and the municipal magistrates permitted guilds to borrow money only with great reluctance. A survey of the accounts of ten guilds in Lille over ten years, which the royal government asked the municipal magistrates to compile, showed that the annual expenditures of most guilds exceeded their revenues by approximately 50 to 100 *florins*.[47] To meet these shortfalls, the magistrates levied a fee on each master. Borrowing was allowed only as a last resort. In 1782 the dry-goods merchants, for example, petitioned the magistrates for permission to borrow 4,000 *florins* to pay for judicial expenses and to furnish a soldier for the militia. The magistrates refused unless the guild first presented a plan for assessing all the masters.[48]

The magistrates did, however, allow the guilds to borrow funds for the enforced purchase of venal offices. According to an intendant's survey in 1776, forty-seven of Lille's guilds had debts resulting from buying offices or having privileges confirmed. Only eight guilds listed judicial proceedings or "other needs," in addition to venal offices, as reasons for indebtedness.[49] The wigmakers, wool weavers, and mixed-fabric weavers had the largest debts. The wigmakers had been forced to purchase a large number of royal *brevets*. The debts of the two guilds of weavers also resulted from their century-long fight against rural textile manufacturers. Because the magistrates relied upon the weavers' monopolies to fight the growth of rural manufacturing, they did not hesitate to support these legal battles.

The use of guilds as royal credit devices reinforced the closed and defensive attitude for which these corps were so often castigated. Because the guilds helped out the king financially, he owed them protection from competition. Petitions to the municipal magistrates in 1727, when the guilds were forced to give the king money to confirm their privileges, illustrated the pattern. The tavernkeepers, for example, protested that "[the masters] are without privilege because of the continual attacks on them...That is why, in the event that they are required to pay a very considerable sum for the confirmation of their rights and privileges, they have, to make these rights and privileges more explicit [and] more clear,...drawn up a plan for statutes...to preserve the rights of the tavernkeepers, without which their profession will become common and free to everyone."[50] The magistrates accepted their plan to raise their quota, but refused the request for new statutes. Similar requests accompanied other financial proposals. The coopers demanded that their exclusive right to brew vinegar be enforced, the locksmiths asked that iron merchants not be allowed to make retail sales, and the cabinetmakers protested that the carpenters were usurping their monopoly over certain kinds of woodworking.

The requirement to have privileges confirmed appeared most senseless to those individuals at the very bottom of the corporate hierarchy, whose privileges were so minuscule as to be worthless. The guild of fruit sellers, who had to pay 480 *livres*, complained that:

The supplicants, who only sell pears, apples and other common fruit, carry on such a small trade that they cannot be considered for the tax that is being required of them. They are all poor folk, burdened with families who scarcely can subsist, and the majority of their children are obliged to beg. Their guild is open to everyone, one enters by paying 40 *patars* without being subject to any masterpiece. It is the women who carry on the fruit trade, the men work in other guilds to put bread on the table. There are among them several widows who have nothing to live on...it would reduce them to the lowliest misery if one pursued them rigorously for the payment of the right of confirmation for a trade that is of so little value.[51]

The monarchy's quest for funds by squeezing the guilds contributed to the very problems which liberal reformers were attempting to solve. Ministers like Turgot were trying to make the economy more open and competitive, but royal fiscal policies helped to make the guilds more rigid by indebting them, raising their reception fees, and reinforcing the desire for protection. Given the contradictory policies of the central government, it is not surprising that its economic reforms floundered. One so-called reform was the sale of royal masterships, which the government claimed was necessary because excessively high reception fees precluded normal entrance into the guilds. In Lille the cost of a royal mastership usually ran at least 100 *livres* higher than the regular reception fees. In 1727 the municipal magistrates told the intendant that high costs hindered most individuals from purchasing these privileges. The price for a royal mastership in the guild of gunsmiths, for example, was 220 *livres*, while the fee in Lille was about 30.[52] Because no new masters were allowed to enter the guilds at the regular rates until all the royal masterships had been sold for the king's profit, the crown's policy blocked, rather than facilitated, recruitment into the guilds.

The guilds' indebtedness lessened the opportunity for successful economic reorganization. The monarchy was unable to abolish the guilds unless it could reimburse them for their venal offices and had a plan for liquidating other debts resulting from royal policy. This was certainly an important reason why Turgot's attempt to suppress the guilds failed. A letter from Turgot to Lille's intendant on 30 April 1776 noted that the royal government was not suppressing the guilds in many provincial cities, including Lille, until it gained better knowledge of the guilds' finances and the king was "in a position to see to the reimbursement of their debts."[53]

After Turgot's fall, when the guilds were re-established and restructured in Paris and its surrounding provinces, the royal government did assume responsibility for corporate debts there. To liquidate them, the government appropriated three-fourths of the reception fees and the property of the guilds. The king established lower reception fees, ranging from 100 to 500 *livres* for towns of the first order and half this amount for those of the second.[54] One report estimated that from 1776 to 1785 the royal government received over 11,550,000 *livres* from reception fees in Paris and the other provincial towns subject to the reforms.[55] In Paris the reception fees remained at the lower rate only until 1782, when they were raised from 50 to 100 *livres* in exchange for a gift of 1,500,000 *livres* presented by the guilds to the king.[56]

In similar fashion, the central government seemed to have considered taking over the debts of Lille's guilds. A letter to the intendant on 26 August 1776 observed that the crown intended to liquidate the debts of the guilds in all French cities by collecting their reception fees and selling their property. The intendant pointed out, however, that the debts of Lille's guilds outweighed their assets, and that the reception fees were so low compared to those in Paris that they would be of little value to the government. The monarchy, furthermore, could not increase the reception fees in Lille without going against one of its own goals – to reduce admission fees and facilitate recruitment.[57]

The monarchy, then, had helped to create the predicament that its own reformers deplored. Because a variety of economic controls and regulations were actually by-products of royal fiscality, economic reform called for restructuring the financial apparatus giving rise to them. As long as the monarchy was unable to reimburse cities and guilds for their debts, and even continued to borrow from them, liberal economic programs calling for the abolition of corporate structures stood little chance of success. The state as an economic unit had not yet ceased to draw its sustenance from the borrowed and appropriated resources of a host of intermediate units, without which it could not survive.

7   Corporate privilege and the bourgeoisie

In 1789 Lille's revolutionary bourgeoisie called for the preservation of the guilds. By traditional historiographical accounts, this position seems hard to explain. Guilds were reputedly anticapitalist institutions whose regulations retarded the twin processes of capital accumulation and proletarianization. Oriented toward artisanal production, collective interests, and tradition, these bodies encouraged economic statis and stifled technological development. Businessmen, by contrast, were "sturdy individualists." In perpetual search for inexpensive labor and innovative techniques, these capitalists bitterly opposed corporate regulations that limited productive output, impeded the development of new industries, and hindered competition so necessary to the working of a free market.[1]

Two reasons may be suggested for the rather surprising bourgeois defense of guilds. First, guilds and associated regulations may not have been as artisanal, retrograde, and anticapitalist as commonly thought. Second, the bourgeoisie may have been less enamored of free markets and more ready to enhance their economic power through legal monopolies than typically assumed.[2] This chapter will explore both possibilities by looking at the relationship of merchants and manufacturers to several guilds regulating textile production and trade. Included in the study are the guilds of wool weavers (*sayetteurs*); the mixed-fabric weavers (*bourgeteurs*), who worked with linen and silk, as well as wool; the linen thread merchant-manufacturers (*filetiers*); and the dry-goods merchants (*merciers-grossiers*).

These guilds are illuminating for several reasons. First, they regulated the production and local trade of two of Lille's most important industries. For centuries the wool industry had been central to the city's economy, but during the eighteenth century, the manufacture and sale of linen thread experienced unprecedented growth. The guild of dry-goods merchants, meanwhile, held the privilege of selling woolen textiles inside Lille and helped to control the flow of textiles produced in the countryside back into the city. Second, during the eighteenth century, the wool and linen thread industries in Lille followed different economic paths. As a result of rural competition, woolen manufactures in Lille first declined and then stagnated, but production of linen thread continued to rise. Comparing two industries, one waxing and the other waning, makes it clear that the success or failure of any one guild does not represent the fate of them all. Third, this assortment of guilds illuminates the clash and cooperation of a broad spectrum of economic interests: artisanal and bourgeois, urban and rural, industrial and commercial. Finally, these industries were large enough so that they were vital to the urban tax base and played an important role in both royal and urban mercantilist strategies.

Cloth merchants and the guilds of weavers

In the eighteenth century, Lille was the commercial capital of one of the oldest and most highly developed textile-producing regions in Northern Europe. Three guilds regulated weaving in the city. The guild of linen weavers, the *tisserands*, was the poorest of the three and produced linen cloth in competition with weavers from the surrounding countryside. The guild of mixed-fabric weavers, the *bourgeteurs*, a name derived from Bourges, their supposed city of origin, wove cloth primarily from mixtures of wool, silk, cotton, and linen. Most important was the guild of the wool weavers, the *sayetteurs*, who held a monopoly on the production of woolens known as *sayetterie*. The exclusive manufacture of this type of cloth was a privilege of the city as well as the guild, for in 1480, Maximilian of Austria, count of Flanders, had granted Lille the sole right to make such woolen textiles, and, in 1543 the Habsburg emperor, Charles V, formally denied the inhabitants of the countryside the right to weave, full, press, or dye this cloth. Villages in the surrounding countryside were legally limited to spinning raw wool into yarn and to weaving woolen *draps*.[3]

Sayetterie had originated in the thirteenth century with the invention of a new process for combing the wool from sheep fed in permanent pastures. In this process, combs were heated in a furnace and drawn through raw wool to align the long fibers and to separate them from the short "noils" left between the teeth. This process of combing long wools obtained from pasture sheep differentiated *sayetterie* from *draperie*, the latter working with carded, short wools from sheep folded on fallow fields.[4] The long, combed wool used in *sayetterie* could be woven into many varieties of cloth. French regions near Lille provided raw wool of lesser quality used for *sayetterie*, but the highest quality was imported from the Netherlands.[5]

Owing to a host of regulations, the manufacture of woolen textiles had come to be divided into a series of legally distinct stages. The initial step of cleaning and combing the raw wool was performed by wool combers (*peigneurs*), most of whom lived in the neighboring village of Tourcoing. In 1789 there were about 2,000 combers, of whom four-fifths were located in Tourcoing and the rest in Lille, Roubaix, and a few other villages. Inside Lille the small guild of combers had the right to conduct this trade. Because master weavers were prohibited from combing wool, vertical integration of cloth production was impossible. By the mid-seventeenth century, some *peigneurs* were actually merchants who operated lucrative putting-out businesses in which they bought large quantities of raw wool, had it washed and combed, and then sent it to Artois or other neighboring regions to have it spun.[6]

Spinning was a rural activity. Indeed, Lille's sovereigns had even recommended that laborers in the countryside perform these stages preparatory to weaving in order to supply the city with raw materials. In the late seventeenth and eighteenth centuries, Lille's wool was spun by an estimated 20,000 men, women, and children in the region, including the neighboring province of Artois.[7]

The sale of woolen yarn in Lille was governed by local market regulations, a requirement fought by merchant *peigneurs*. The goal of the regulated market was to allow all weavers equal access to raw materials and to prevent hoarding and the consequent rise in prices. When most of the yarn (*filets de sayette*) had been spun by peasants in the surrounding villages, it had not been difficult to require peasants to bring their yarn to the local market. But because the preparation of raw wool had increasingly become specialized by region and the movement coordinated by merchant *peigneurs*, urban market regulations became more difficult to enforce. Merchant *peigneurs* had yarn that was spun in Artois shipped back to their own warehouses, where they set up shop. In 1744, to prevent these merchants from controlling the sale of yarn and potentially fixing higher prices, the municipal magistrates republished the ordinance requiring yarn to be sold on the local market and, to ensure greater compliance, ordered that all yarn coming from Artois had to be unloaded at two specified *cabarets* where the magistrates could monitor the distribution more closely.[8]

Of the three guilds of textile weavers, that of the wool weavers (*sayetteurs*), who made cloth from pure wool, was the most highly regulated. The principle behind the wool weavers' regulations was to maintain each master as an independent, small-scale producer working for his own personal gain. To become a master, one had to serve an apprenticeship of two years. Each master wool weaver could employ only one apprentice at a time and could not operate more than six looms.[9] Cloth production was subject to strict controls. The city magistrates and the intendants, often in collaboration with the cloth merchants, set rigorous standards for the size and number of threads in each piece of cloth. These officials also decided what kinds of textiles each guild could manufacture in the city, though appeals might be made to the Parlement of Douai or Royal Council. Official inspectors checked the cloth by counting the number of threads, issuing seals, and seizing defective merchandise. The regulatory board of the wool weavers, composed of two *échevins*, two cloth merchants, and two master weavers, judged workers accused of violating the rules.[10]

Among the master wool weavers, the production of cloth was a family affair. Even though the apprenticeship was only two years and reception fees were not high, in the 1700s few individuals became apprentices.[11] While the stagnation of the industry partly explains the low numbers, the familial nature of the master's enterprise was also significant. By paying a nominal fee of 12 *deniers*, a master's wife and his children of both sexes had the right to practice the trade without apprenticeship. To aid with menial tasks that an apprentice might otherwise have performed, children, known as *époulmans*, were sometimes hired for a fixed sum. The master's house served as the family workshop, so that living quarters were crowded by as few as one or as many as six looms, the most permitted by law. The master artisan was required to have his own workshop and was prohibited from working for other masters.

The mixed-fabric weavers were governed by corporate restrictions similar to those of the wool weavers, with two important exceptions: there was no legal limitation on the number of looms that each master might operate and rural bourgs had gained the right to make several types of cloth that the mixed-fabric weavers produced. Because it was not always clear which guild possessed jurisdiction over newly invented kinds of cloth, the wool weavers were institutional arch-rivals of the mixed-fabric weavers. Nonetheless, it was not uncommon for an individual to become a master in both guilds, or for a weaver in one guild to marry the daughter of a master in the other in order to practice both trades at once.[12]

Although the corporate regulations of the wool weavers were designed to promote artisanal autonomy, the sale of woolens on international markets, combined with the restrictions on looms, made self-sufficiency illusory. Master weavers had the right to sell the products of their own workshops, but they lacked the resources and experience to participate in international markets. As a result, most wool weavers had become economically dependent on cloth merchants, or *négociants*, outside the guild. These merchants received large orders from abroad, divided up the work among the master weavers, and exported the finished cloth to Spain, the Americas, Italy, Germany, and the French interior.[13] Over half the master wool weavers, the Chamber of Commerce scoffed in the 1770s, could "only be considered as so many workers."[14]

Like weaving, the very lucrative processes of finishing cloth – fulling, pressing, and dyeing – were legally reserved for the city. Until a special agreement was struck between Roubaix and Lille in 1696, it was also illegal to bring *sayetterie* made in the countryside into the city for finishing, a rule that acted as a second check against illicit textile production in rural areas. Although there were two guilds of dyers in Lille, master weavers had the right to dye the cloth that they produced. In practice, however, cloth merchants dictated which finishing processes would be applied, according to the preferences of their customers.[15]

Thus far the relationship between master wool weavers and cloth merchants appears predictable enough. The weavers' familial mode of production was designed to promote artisanal independence and resist capitalist incursions, but it had been eroded as merchants came to control the flow of goods onto international markets. Nonetheless, merchants still had to contend with the tangled legal restrictions of the guilds that raised production costs and reduced efficiency. Until 1738, when the regulation was abolished, for example, master wool weavers could only employ *ouvriers francs*, that is, workers who had served a two-year apprenticeship, in their workshops. Master weavers had to pay the *ouvriers francs* more than other workers and thus had to charge more for their cloth.[16] The cost of food, lodging, and indirect taxes in the city also made labor in the guilds more expensive than that in the countryside.

To reduce the cost of labor and escape corporate constraints, merchants both relied on weavers outside the city and tried to set up large independent workshops inside it. In 1698 the intendant observed that Lille's *négociants* employed thousands of rural weavers, who allegedly were able to charge two to three *florins* less per piece of cloth than the master wool weavers.[17] Meanwhile *négociants* also tried to hire urban workers directly. During the 1770s, for example, the silk merchant-manufacturer, Cuvelier-Brame, waged and won a protracted battle against the guild of mixed-fabric weavers, so that he could set up a new silk manufactory free from the fees, regulations, and inspections that the guild wished to impose. By 1789, Cuvelier-Brame had sixty looms operating in his workshop.[18] Less successfully in 1751, the powerful *négociant* and member of the Chamber of Commerce, Gilles-François Vanhoenacker, petitioned the intendant for permission to make a new kind of woolen cloth (*camelots superfins*) by directly commissioning workers outside the guild of wool weavers. The city magistrates successfully opposed the measure by arguing that "it has never been permitted in Lille for *négociants* to have workers working directly under and for them...this right has always belonged to the masters...*Sieur* Vanhoenacker is proposing an innovation without precedent."[19] These men fit the common picture of the bourgeoisie – entrepreneurs fighting corporate barriers to production and paving the way for proletarian-ization.

The issue, however, is more complex. Merchants, as the old saying goes, not only wanted to buy cheap, they wanted to sell dear. Guilds were not just vehicles of production; they were also tools of exchange. Thus, the same merchants who opposed corporate restrictions on manufacturing were quite willing to support the privileges of commercial guilds that helped them to protect their markets. Many of the cloth merchants in Lille belonged to a guild of dry-goods merchants (the *merciers-grossiers*, discussed below), which enjoyed the privilege of selling woolen textiles in Lille. The highly successful silk merchant-manufacturer, Cuvelier-Brame, fought the guild of mixed-fabric weavers, but, at the same time, he was a member and a staunch defender of the guild of dry-goods merchants. In 1789, he helped to draft its *cahier de doléances*. Similarly, the industrious *négociant*, Gilles Vanhoenacker, as well as two of his sons, Edouard Marie and Louis Bonaventure, belonged. On the eve of the Revolution, Louis Vanhoenacker served as a deputy of the guild.[20] The *cahiers de doléances* of Lille's guilds no longer exist, but other evidence clearly indicates that, in the late eighteenth century, the leaders of the guild of dry-goods merchants supported very conservative commercial policies.[21]

The intricacies of the cloth merchants' attitudes toward guilds do not stop there. *Négociants* were not consistently opposed to corporate restrictions on manufacturing either. First, many merchants looked to the guilds to enforce regulations controlling the quality of exports. By selling durable, reputable merchandise, the *négociants* believed that they would win the confidence of their customers and thereby generate larger markets. The presence of regulations over quality in the 1700s represented a new response to the growth of international trade and the desire to standardize products and predict outcomes. Far from being anachronistic, the attempt to control the productive environment through regulation might be seen as a "scientific" bent of mind, a form of rationalization.

Second, merchants in Lille sometimes supported monopolies in manufacturing as a secondary route toward their primary goal: the limitation of competition in commerce. By relying on guilds to restrict production in the countryside, Lille's merchants could prevent rural manufacturers from turning into commercial rivals. So long as some urban controls dampened industrial activity in the countryside, rural manufacturers would have far more difficulty acquiring the capital to become merchant-manufacturers able to export their wares independently. In short, one might say that in a privileged city, such as Lille, the desire for cheap labor and low prices drew cloth merchants away from corporate forms of organization, but the wish to regulate quality and to control markets led them back.

These competing factors – the desire for inexpensive labor, control of quality, and commercial supremacy – helped to explain why merchants at times supported very liberal and at other times very conservative policies. The controversy over rural industry is a good example of how cloth merchants tried to balance conflicting interests. *Négociants* from Lille promoted rural industry during the seventeenth and eighteenth centuries, but in 1762, when the government legalized the manufacture of all textiles in the countryside, they vociferously opposed the measure and succeeded in delaying its implementation for a decade and a half.

The problem of rural industry

From 1534, when Lille received its monopoly over *sayetterie*, until the late eighteenth century, the city continually fought the attempts of neighboring bourgs to undermine its privilege. Over the years, certain villages, such as Tourcoing, Lannoy, and Roubaix, obtained the right to produce some types of woolen cloth, but Lille still maintained a legal monopoly over the production of *sayetterie* and in particular a popular type of cloth known as *camelots*. To circumvent the legal restrictions, entrepreneurs in outlying bourgs had invented new types of cloth not covered by the regulations, or simply ignored the law.[22] In 1693, there were approximately 1,000 looms in Roubaix and Tourcoing making at least ten different varieties of woolen or silk cloth.[23]

Although the manufacture of woolen cloth in the village was much less regulated than in Lille, even rural manufacturing did not escape corporate regulation. In 1553, for example, the Privy Council of Brussels awarded Roubaix and a number of other privileged villages the right to make several types of cloth (*bouras* and *futaines*) which previously had been the exclusive property of Lille's guild of mixed-fabric weavers. To ensure that rural manufacturers did not produce defective cloth, the Privy Council also established a guild in Roubaix with official inspectors (*égards jurés*) to oversee manufacturing. The guild there, however, was much less strict than the ones in Lille. No restriction was placed on the number of looms a master could operate, and to obtain a mastership one had only to go through the formality of paying the necessary fees.[24]

In deciding whether to permit villages to produce more types of cloth, the royal government weighed fiscal and military, as well as economic, repercussions. The municipal magistrates, always prepared to defend urban resources, never tired of predicting the dire financial and military consequences that would ensue if rural manufacturing were given a free hand to lure laborers away from the city. Officials in the central government, however, did not always agree on what was the most advantageous combination of economic and fiscal policies for the state.

Until the mid-eighteenth century, the government usually supported Lille's privileges in manufacturing in order to preserve the urban tax base and its military obligations. But in the second half of the eighteenth century, some royal ministers articulated new and different grounds for determining the correct relationship between economic planning and state finance. The physiocrats, most notably, believed that the agrarian tax base was more important than the urban one, and that upholding the privileges of cities was harmful to the long-term strength of the state. Instead of relying on urban manufacturing and indirect taxes, they wanted to foster economic growth in the countryside and to create a new system of direct taxation on land that would release the government from its dependence on the privileged, urban sector.

The conflict surrounding freedom of rural manufacturing, therefore, was waged by a variety of interest groups. The municipal magistrates and the guilds of weavers both wanted to restrict manufacturing to the city, the former to generate tax revenue, the latter to preserve their jobs. Rural manufacturers and administrators in the countryside, on the other hand, wanted greater liberty of manufacturing in order to expand production and to increase the rural tax base. The *négociants* from Lille supported or opposed the guilds depending upon whether inexpensive labor or control of trade was more important. The central government mediated the disputes according to its shifting perception of the correct relationship between economic development and fiscal obligations.

One case illustrating the interplay of these concerns occurred in 1696. The last decade of the seventeenth century was a time of particular hardship for Lille. During the War of the League of Augsburg (1688–1697), Walloon Flanders was prohibited from trading with the Spanish Netherlands and experienced a severe crisis in manufacturing. When the war broke out there were 904 looms operating in the wool guild; by its end there were only 568.[25] The city was forced to borrow money to pay for a host of extraordinary royal demands, and in 1693 the harvest failed. According to the master wool weaver Chavatte, the bread for the poor was so rotten that people cried when they saw it.[26]

This was the setting when the intendant, in 1688 and again in 1693, prohibited bringing any *sayetterie* or *bourgeterie* from the villages into Lille to be finished and sold. Since commerce with the Spanish Netherlands was also banned during the war, rural manufacturers were denied both the Low Countries and Lille as outlets for their wares. By closing those markets to rural cloth, the intendant hoped to protect the urban economy; he would force the merchants in Lille to employ weavers in the city. This measure was absolutely necessary, he declared, because over 20,000 persons lived by manufacturing textiles in Lille, and it was they who "produce the revenues of the city by the large quantity of commodities which they consume." Every effort had to be made to prevent workers in the guilds from leaving the city, because they "have no other way of earning their living, while those in the countryside have not only their looms but also the cultivation of the land... by which means they can live more cheaply than those of the city."[27] The need to preserve urban employment and fiscal resources justified the limitation of rural manufacturing.

Acting upon the intendant's prohibition, the guild of mixed-fabric weavers proceeded to seize pieces of cloth (*grisettes* and *calemandes*) which had entered Lille from Roubaix. The move was opposed by Lille's merchants who employed workers in the village, and of course by the manufacturers in Roubaix. The rural manufacturers, meanwhile, offered the municipal magistrates a compromise: they would pay a fee of 2 *patars* per piece in exchange for the right to send their cloth to Lille. The urban treasury would then benefit from rural manufacturing, and the merchants in Lille would not suffer the losses to which the intendant's order condemned them. Without consulting the guilds, the magistrates agreed in 1696 to allow seven types of cloth manufactured in Roubaix, Lannoy, and other privileged villages to enter Lille. The villages were to pay 3 *patars* per piece of cloth to be affixed with the seal of the city.[28] As an intendant wrote several years later, "without the payment of this fee, the magistrates of Lille would not have accorded [the villages] the permission to manufacture these textiles."[29]

Fiscal maneuvering thus broke the magistrates' old alliance with the guilds and forged a new one with the merchants. In 1721, the guilds of weavers petitioned the magistrates to repeal the ordinance of 1696, but the Chamber of Commerce argued in favor of the existing policy. Dyers and merchants, they observed, depended upon the flow of these unfinished textiles into the city.[30] The magistrates' arrangement with the villages served the merchants quite well. It increased the legal basis of textile production in rural areas, but also reinforced the merchants' control over marketing, because cloth had to pass through Lille before it was exported.

The fiscal benefits derived from allowing cloth from Roubaix to enter Lille did not last. When manufacturers from Roubaix made their pieces of cloth longer to reduce the amount paid per unit, the magistrates raised the fee from 3 to 6 *patars*. Roubaix challenged the increase, and in 1728 the Royal Council ruled that the fee could not be levied on cloth coming into Lille from Roubaix.[31] Soon after this ruling, the magistrates, at the request of the Chamber of Commerce, agreed to suppress the *droits sur les changeants*, municipal fees levied on textiles produced by the guild of wool weavers.[32] The petty impositions levied on cloth produced in the city, the merchants complained, made it more expensive and less competitive.

Although Lille lost revenue from the suppression of these taxes, the central government, in important decisions, continued to protect the city's manufacturers. In 1728, the guild of mixed-fabric weavers confiscated some cloth (*calemandilles*) arriving from Roubaix, claiming that their guild had exclusive rights to weave it. The prince de Rohan, *tuteur* of the seigneur of Roubaix, and the manufacturers of Roubaix petitioned the king not only for permission to make this cloth, but also to have presses, rollers, and dyeing equipment for the finishing processes. In fact, some manufacturers, in flagrant violation of the law, had already installed large presses in Roubaix.[33] In his report, the intendant, Bidé de la Grandville, argued that the Royal Council should uphold the privileges of Lille:

It is in vain M. le prince de Rohan and the manufacturers of Roubaix wish to establish that it does not matter to the state whether manufacturers are established in the city or in the countryside, and that exclusive privileges remove the competition among manufacturers so necessary for the growth and profit of commerce. All these reasons have always been known and weighed, and they have not prevented the government at all from granting privileges to the city of Lille, all the sovereigns of Flanders having recognized the necessity of populating such an important city which could only be done by establishing manufacturers.[34]

The intendant further noted that Roubaix already was permitted to manufacture many types of cloth by virtue of previous concessions, and if more were granted, Lille's textile industry might perish entirely. The royal council agreed with the intendant's assessment. The government prohibited manufacturers in Roubaix from having machines to finish cloth and from manufacturing the cloth in question.[35]

Although in 1696 the merchants in Lille had supported the manufacturers in Roubaix, by 1728 they had begun to oppose them. In a letter to the intendant that year, the Chamber of Commerce stressed that only the guild of mixed-fabric weavers in Lille had the right to manufacture the disputed cloth (*calemandilles*) and that Roubaix's manufacturers had no legal claim to it.[36] Why did the *négociants*, at least those represented by the Chamber of Commerce, not favor the development of this cloth in the countryside? Most likely they feared that the rural manufacturers, who wanted both to make and to finish the cloth themselves, were becoming too independent, and that the sale of these new textiles would slip from their hands. It would be safer to protect the guilds in Lille, the sale of whose merchandise they did dictate, rather than to allow possible competitors to arise.[37] During the next decades, economic conservatism became the dominant idiom of Lille's cloth merchants.

Mid-way through the eighteenth century, ministers in the central government influenced by liberal, physiocratic ideas began to advocate greater freedom of commerce and manufacturing. In 1762, an *arrêt* by the

Controller General Bertin granted textile manufacturers in the countryside the right to produce any kind of cloth, as long as they complied with the regulations controlling its quality. In 1763, the government also gave them the freedom to dye and finish cloth themselves.[38]

From 1762 until 1776, the municipal magistrates, the guilds, and the Chamber of Commerce waged a vigorous, but ultimately unsuccessful battle to prevent freedom of rural manufacturing. On the opposite side, rural manufacturers joined with the four noble *baillis*, who represented the countryside in the provincial estates, to have the law implemented immediately. Under pressure from both groups, the central government wavered between executing and suppressing the law in Flanders. In 1762, the royal council agreed to delay applying the law in Flanders until it reviewed the case. In September 1764, it ordered its publication, but after further solicitations from Lille, the Controller General Laverdy decided in July 1765 to suspend it. In 1766, the intendant Caumartin even permitted inspectors from the guilds in Lille to search the countryside to halt the illegal production of cloth. Roubaix appealed once more to the central government, but under Terray, a Controller General who opposed freedom of manufacture, the case for Roubaix and its neighboring villages languished. Only with the arrival of the liberal reformer Turgot did the countryside finally receive, in 1776, the freedom it had demanded. Lille's protests, this time, were in vain.[39]

Although the magistrates and merchants from Lille advanced a number of economic reasons for retaining the city's privileges, the strength of their case rested primarily on the bad fiscal and political consequences that, they claimed, would come from encouraging rural industry. By contrast, strictly economic arguments worked to the advantage of those supporting rural industry. As the manufacturers and *négociants* from Roubaix and the other villages correctly pointed out, it was cheaper to manufacture textiles in the countryside where wages were lower and corporate restrictions did not fragment producers into so many groups.[40] Yet, as Lille's delegates countered, it was precisely because rural manufacturing was economically so attractive that the city needed protection, for the state stood to lose a great deal from the economic decline of such a sizeable city. A heavily fortified garrison town, Lille played a crucial role in defending France, and the tools and machines necessary for manufacturing were best protected within its walls.[41] No less important, without its manufactures the city's tax base would be seriously jeopardized. It would be impossible "to produce the considerable sums that the city pays annually to Your Majesty to meet local expenses, given that there would be an extreme reduction in the product of the *octrois*, and to pay the arrears on its bonds."[42] Lille thus appealed to the city's military position and its subsidies to the royal government, which were generated by municipal bonds and secured by urban sales taxes and tolls, to make its case for economic protection.

How officials of the central government perceived Lille's arguments is not completely clear, although several observations may be made. The intendant, Caumartin, believed in urban protectionism. In fact, when the government asked him to publish the edict permitting rural industry in January 1764 he refused. Only after two additional orders from the Controller General Laverdy did Caumartin reluctantly promulgate the edict in his *généralité* in September 1764.[43] Caumartin thus continued the tradition of previous intendants, such as Dugué de Bagnols and Bidé de la Grandville, who had defended Lille's privileges in order to populate the city.

In Paris, a number of liberal officials, *économistes*, such as the highly influential Trudaines, father and son, the *Intendant des Finances* Tavernier de Boullogne, and several *Intendants du Commerce*, including Boula de Quincy, Michau de Montaran and Jacques-Philippe Pottier, were strong partisans of unshackling rural industry. Influenced by the ideas of Vincent de Gournay and other liberal reformers, these officials believed that the countryside held the key to rejuvenating France, to developing its economic strength, and to guaranteeing its fiscal stability. In their program for reform, they hoped to raise productivity on the land and to restructure the system of taxation completely by imposing a direct tax on land, which they saw as the true source of national wealth. In their view, the state should abolish all arbitrary taxes and privileges which prevented individuals from enjoying their right of property to the fullest.[44] Not surprisingly, when deputies from Lille argued that the city would be depopulated if all rural manufacturing was legalized, Boula de Quincy responded that this was exactly what the government wanted – to have citizens flow back into the countryside to restore its value. On another occasion, Pottier declared that taxes were too high in Lille to be able to manufacture there cheaply, but that was no reason to protect Lille because the magistrates there could always form a common treasury with the *châtellenie* and service debts in common.[45]

Such a view implied a complete financial restructuring of the institutional bases of town and country and a political redistribution of power. Could one, given the maze of impositions, subsidies, venal offices, *abonnements*, *octrois*, and *rentes* of the old regime, reasonably expect urban and rural treasuries to be united and to share each other's debts? In the 1760s and 1770s, the royal government had just begun to impose heavy surtaxes on urban tolls and sales, not to mention the urban *dons gratuits*. Royal policy, therefore, was making municipal taxation more imperative than ever at the same time as the physiocrats were calling for a single land tax as an integral part of their program of laissez-faire. The fiscal underside of the crown remained patrimonial and mercantilist, even as reformist rhetoric and economic policy grew more liberal and anticorporate. The seemingly irresolvable problems of the French government surfaced again. The crown wished to promote economic development and overhaul taxation, but it was unable to dismantle, and even continued to expand, a fiscal apparatus at odds with these progressive goals.

The municipal magistrates from Lille doubted that the government would restructure taxes in tandem with economic liberalization. In 1776, a time when the city was facing enormous annual deficits and new royal surtaxes, the magistrates complained that "this city is considerably indebted; its expenses exceed its resources, it cannot support the mass of impositions that overwhelm it, and to wish to destroy its manufacturers, is to desire its ruin ... It is in vain that one would object that afterward [the government] will reduce these impositions in order to make the inhabitants of the countryside support them in proportion to the gains that freedom [of manufacture] will bring them."[46] If, the *mémoire* continued, the king did levy new taxes on the land, rural workers would simply move across the border to the Belgian provinces to avoid paying them. And, the Lillois were probably thinking, when would the government ever reduce the taxes of any area, rural or urban?

Throughout this period, it fell to rural nobles and administrators to champion the cause of economic liberty. The attitudes of these nobles were a far cry from the position expressed by the conservative Parlement of Paris when Turgot abolished the guilds. At that time the parliamentary nobles argued that removing even one link of the hierarchical chain uniting all corps from the guilds to the king would threaten the very idea of privilege as a constitutive principle of the old regime and upset the whole social order.[47] But in the battle over rural industry the stakes were different. Seigneurs stood to benefit from the introduction of manufacturing into their territories. Over the centuries, princes, dukes and counts had intervened on behalf of their villages to obtain royal permission to manufacture new types of cloth.[48] The rural representatives in the provincial estates of Walloon Flanders supported this position. In 1704, the four noble *baillis* had declared unequivocally that "the soul of commerce is liberty. It is necessary that artisans be able to establish themselves where they want and that distinctions not be made as to where they reside, whether in the town or in the countryside."[49] At one point during the controversy of 1762, even the socially and politically conservative Estates of Artois defended freedom of manufacture, because peasants in Artois spun large amounts of wool into yarn used in Roubaix.[50]

In contrast to this bold seigneurial liberalism, Lille's merchants constituted the cautious party. In 1762 the majority of Lille's *négociants* defended the privileges of the guilds and, in 1764 and 1771, the Chamber of Commerce sent deputies to Paris to plead Lille's cause. No mention of dissent from the conservative position is recorded in the documents surrounding the controversy.[51] Why had Lille's merchants come to oppose this final extension of freedom to rural manufacturers? Evidence suggests that merchants in Lille feared that complete freedom for rural industry would allow manufacturers in the countryside to throw off their dependence on the urban market. In particular, the city's merchants were anxious over the fate of the production and sale of Lille's speciality known as *camelots* and the rise of independent brokers.

Two kinds of *sayetterie* produced in Walloon Flanders during the eighteenth century, *camelots* and *calemandes*, enjoyed important export markets. After 1691, when specific textiles from Roubaix were permitted to enter Lille to be finished and sold, Roubaix became the center for the manufacture of *calemandes*.[52] The manufacture of *camelots*, however, continued even then to be strictly prohibited in the countryside and remained an exclusive speciality of Lille. In 1764, a period when the controversy over rural industry was peaking, there were 866 looms operating in the guild of wool weavers, largely producing *camelots*. Although this number was less than the approximately 1,100 looms operating in the 1680s, demand for this product remained fairly stable. A rough estimate of the number of pieces of cloth produced by the guild at mid-century is available by calculating the average number of seals (*plombs d'outils*) delivered annually to the guild for the four decades 1740–1780:[53]

	1740s	1750s	1760s	1770s
seals/year	30,444	32,100	30,800	24,810

Even in the 1780s, after freedom of manufacturing had been established, there were only twenty-two looms in Tourcoing making *camelots* and a mere eight in Roubaix.[54]

Why did it matter to Lille's *négociants* if this cloth was made in the city or country? One claim was that regulation of quality was an issue, that if the Roubaisiens made *camelots* "this very prosperous manufacture in the city will be ruined by people from the countryside who will pursue it without experience and without regulations."[55] Perhaps, but the assertion seems dubious. Cloth from Roubaix was inspected, and manufacturers there had demonstrated time and again their facility for learning new techniques and even improving on them. Indeed, when Roubaix finally received freedom of manufacturing in 1776, the village's principal manufacturers and administrators vowed to uphold quality controls because their manufactures had only grown through "an exact execution of the regulations."[56] Far more likely, then, control over marketing was at issue. Because only master wool weavers in Lille were permitted to make *camelots*, Lille's *négociants* enjoyed favored access to the sale of this cloth. If complete freedom of rural industry were granted, non-native merchants might be able to hire rural weavers to manufacture *camelots* and export the cloth directly. Furthermore, rural manufacturers had the right to operate as many looms as they wished. Some of these individuals might eventually acquire the resources to export cloth on their own, without recourse to Lille's cloth merchants.[57] Freedom to dye and finish cloth, finally, also made rural industry less dependent on urban guilds and merchants.

While the case between Lille and the countryside was being debated in Paris, the merchants in Lille, working with the municipal magistrates, tried to obtain legal guarantees to keep the sale of *camelots* and *calemandes* under their control. During local negociations between Lille and Roubaix in 1768, Lille's magistrates wanted to require all manufacturers in the *châtellenie* to bring their cloth to a marketplace in Lille, a proposal that never was adopted.[58] Eventually, in 1776, rural merchants and manufacturers technically won the freedom to manufacture, but their commercial liberty was highly restricted. Controls over brokers (discussed in more detail below) remained in effect. Until the Revolution, manufacturers in Roubaix could only sell the products from their own workshops. When they commissioned other weavers to make cloth, they had to deliver that cloth to eight brokers from Lille.[59]

Overall, then, one likely explanation for the change in attitude of Lille's *négociants* from 1696 to 1762 is that urban merchants initially benefited from cheaper labor in the countryside, but as the scale of manufacturing and trade grew, so did competition from rural entrepreneurs. Lille's merchants, therefore, looked to the guild's privileges in manufacturing to prevent others from infiltrating their control over exports. When these privileges were abolished, they tried to restrain competition by other means. Georges Lefebvre observed that rural industry allowed urban *négociants* to concentrate "*en toute liberté*" both the production and sale of cloth in their hands.[60] To keep the cloth trade under their control, however, they frequently had to rely not upon liberty, but upon privilege.

After Lille lost the fight over freedom of rural manufacturing in 1776, the weavers' guilds were hastily reformed. The corporate barriers which had favored the existence of numerous, small-scale artisans were levelled. In 1777, master wool weavers gained the right to buy, comb, and spin wool themselves. Later the same year, the municipal magistrates abolished the regulation limiting master wool weavers to six looms. Finally, in 1779, the magistrates joined the rival guilds of weavers – the wool weavers, the mixed-fabric weavers, and the linen weavers (*tisserands*) – into one guild.[61]

Two of these reforms – removing the limitation on looms and merging the guilds – had been proposed before, but had always failed. The reason for this failure rests partially with the master weavers, who were extremely jealous of their special prerogatives, but it seems likely that the merchants also played a role.

The limitation imposed on the number of looms was designed to foster the independence of the small producer. But by limiting masters to small-scale production, the regulation actually trapped most of them in a cycle of poverty, which made them more dependent than ever on cloth merchants outside the guild. According to one survey from 1775, of 239 masters in the guild, only 20 had six looms and the rest had five looms or less.[62]

By the second half of the eighteenth century, the limitation of looms had created serious problems in woolen manufactures. According to the Chamber of Commerce, masters could not earn enough money by working six looms to cover their expenses or to buy their raw materials in advance. Because large orders had to be divided among so many masters, a process that was time consuming and expensive, merchants did not always meet their deadlines and sometimes lost commissions.[63]

It was not the cloth merchants, however, but a small group of master wool weavers who asked the magistrates in November 1775 for the right to work an unlimited number of looms and to buy, comb, and spin raw wool themselves. Through vertical integration and expansion, these innovative master weavers hoped to meet rural competitors on their own terms. In December 1775 a general assembly of the guild was convoked to vote on the proposals. Of the 239 masters in the guild, 106 attended the meeting, and the overwhelming majority of them voted against the innovations. The loyalty of the wool weavers to the traditional organization of the guild drew the scorn of the Chamber of Commerce: "the inevitable decline of their manufactures does not touch them, as long as equality subsists or rather that poverty is general."[64]

Yet many members of the Chamber of Commerce themselves were peculiarly cautious when it came to removing the cap of six looms permitted each master. At a meeting attended by twenty-three members of the Chamber of Commerce on 19 November 1775, only nine voted to lift the restriction completely. The other fourteen wanted to limit each master to the use of twelve looms. Those in favor of abolishing all limitations pointed out how advantageous the principle of liberty was to economic prosperity. Liberty, they added, was an "incontestable right" of all men, part of "the cry of nature." Those who voted for the restriction to twelve declared that, although the principle of liberty was a truth "for all times and for all places," it could not be applied immediately to the wool guild.[65] Of these fourteen members, at least seven were prominent cloth merchants in the guild of dry-goods merchants; one belonged to the guild of grocers (épiciers).[66]

Why did the Chamber of Commerce, which clearly recognized the problems created by the regulation of looms, not urge complete deregulation? One clue again seems to be the constant preoccupation of Lille's cloth merchants to limit commercial competition. The deliberation by the Chamber of Commerce in November 1775 occurred before the law granting freedom of rural industry was finally registered on 9 November 1777 in the Parlement of Douai. The négociants from Lille were still hoping to prevent Roubaix and other villages from obtaining the right to manufacture camelots. If the limitation on looms was lifted completely, outside merchants might be able to penetrate Lille's monopoly from inside the city. As Lille's merchants stated:

In effect, does not one have to expect that if general liberty is established, opulent négociants, industrious and ambitious outsiders will come with huge firms to seize the manufactures and take advantage of the powerlessness of our unfortunate weavers in order to strip them of their property... thus it is [the weavers'] future that one has to improve by preserving their property and sheltering them from outside incursions.[67]

Very similar sentiments had been expressed by the wool weavers. Raising the permissible number of looms, the masters contended, would be harmful "to the welfare of the guild [communauté] because afterwards one will see powerful persons establish manufactures, which would cause the ruin of many fabricants."[68] Thus, like the wool weavers whom they had scorned, the merchants advanced conservative, artisanal-sounding arguments – but toward their own ends. The merchants in the city had to protect "the little guy" from powerful outsiders who would bring about the loss of artisanal independence. But the merchants would also be shielding themselves from outside rivals. As long as manufacturing was kept on a small scale inside Lille, it would not be possible for new entrepreneurs to set up large enterprises or for successful master wool weavers to supply foreign merchants with large quantities of their cloth. Control over exports, the key to the power of Lille's bourgeoisie, would remain in the hands of established merchants. There would be no challenge to the semi-proletarianized state of the wool weavers and their inability to accumulate capital. Permitting each master the use of twelve looms was a convenient compromise. It would alleviate some of the more pressing problems facing the wool weavers, but still maintain, as much as possible, the commercial *status quo*.

By the time the magistrates acted upon the proposed reforms, the countryside had won its cause. On 20 December 1777 the magistrates unconditionally repealed the statute limiting the number of looms; henceforth wool weavers could operate as many looms as they wished.[69] No member of the Chamber of Commerce seems to have opposed the decision, for now the issue was to make the wool weavers as competitive as possible against rural areas.

A second problem for Lille's wool manufacturers was the division between the guild of wool weavers and that of the mixed-fabric weavers. Every time a new type of woolen-based cloth was invented, the two guilds went to court to fight for the exclusive right to manufacture it. The rivalry made manufacturing in the city less efficient and more expensive. But, as the following example shows, Lille's merchants had not consistently worked to merge the two guilds.

In 1754 the guild of mixed-fabric weavers petitioned for permission to join their guild with that of the wool weavers. The merger would have given the cloth merchants a larger, less regulated and hence cheaper labor force in the city. Yet the Chamber of Commerce argued strongly against the proposal. Protecting the trade in *camelots* largely explains the conservative stance. By 1754 the manufacturers from the village of Lannoy had gained the right to make the same types of cloth as those of the guild of mixed-fabric weavers. But no one other than members of the guild of wool weavers had the right to manufacture *camelots*. If the two guilds of weavers in Lille were merged, the manufacturers in Lannoy would have a pretext for manufacturing *camelots*.[70] Lille's merchants, therefore, decided to uphold the privileges of the master wool weavers in order to guard their commercial monopoly, rather than to streamline urban manufacturing and open themselves up to competition.

As soon as complete freedom of rural manufacturing was granted in 1776, the *négociants* in Lille no longer had any reason to defend the inefficient monopoly of the master wool weavers. Thus, in 1778, when the guild of linen weavers, led by Phillippe Joseph and Charles Joseph Brame, petitioned the magistrates to unite the guilds of wool weavers, mixed-fabric weavers, and linen weavers, merchants in Lille supported the merger. Since the linen weavers were already able to use an unrestricted number of looms, the Brames had fifty to sixty looms under their control. Merging the three guilds would allow entrepreneurs, like the Brames, to expand their production into new areas.[71]

The petitions of the linen weavers attacked the evils of exclusive privileges and benighted guilds by appealing to science, to the *Encyclopédie*, and to the virtues of the selfless citizen in an enlightened age. As one *mémoire* by the linen weavers eloquently proclaimed: "it is to enlightened centuries that useful changes are reserved... Moreover, it is not as linen weavers that the authors of the union have made the proposal: It is as citizens, to whom alone it belongs to determine what concerns the good of commerce in general."[72] Upon first glance, this document seems to be a good example of how a new language, that of the Enlightenment, was involved to attack the corporate structure of society. Yet a further look reveals how individualistic, liberal rhetoric, like that of Turgot's, might be interspersed among quite traditional and apparently contradictory notions. After citing Turgot's reforms and the article on "*privilège exclusif*" in the *Encyclopédie* as proof that privileges were harmful to the state, the petition continued: "in principle, one does not establish exclusive privileges to oppose them one to another, but so that those who have obtained them can be distinguished from those who have none; one does not want to set the privileged against each other, but only defend all of the privileged against all those who are not."

This statement suggests that individuals or groups could invoke progressive concepts, such as freedom of manufacturing, and still perceive the basic structure of society as hierarchical. They might, in fact, use modern-sounding concepts, like liberty, to climb up the corporate hierarchy, and then use traditional ones, like privilege, to shut the door behind them. A similar situation, as we saw earlier, existed among the socially mobile groups in the nobility.[73] The linen weavers wanted to level corporate barriers in order to advance their own position, and then pull up the ladder behind them. After they received the right to manufacture new kinds of cloth in the name of liberty, they would defend all the *privilégiés* "against all those who were not."

The *négociants* received the proposal of the linen weavers warmly. As the Chamber of Commerce remarked, when all weavers were able to manufacture any type of cloth, merchants would be able to fill their orders more promptly and expensive corporate quarrels would finally be laid to rest. In 1779, the municipal magistrates united the three guilds; four years later royal Letters Patent confirmed their action.[74]

By 1783, therefore, it appeared that the corporate structure of the wool industry lay in ruins. The city had lost its monopoly over *sayetterie*. The stages of combing, spinning, and weaving were no longer legally divided. Master weavers could make any kind of cloth they wanted and work as many looms as they wished. Even so, the merchants did not wish to abolish the truncated guild completely. They still relied upon it to regulate quality. It was not master artisans, but merchants and governmental officials, who were responsible for the minute regulations over cloth production so often denounced for impeding progress.

In an age before production was mechanized and centralized in factories, guilds were essential to quality control. Because manufacturing was scattered among so many small-scale artisans, only frequent inspections by officials from the guild ensured that the weavers did not use defective raw materials or skimp on the number of threads per cloth. Because the cloth merchants built up their exports by selling durable, uniform pieces of cloth, they had a strong interest in maintaining quality, a strategy endorsed by the municipal magistrates and intendants. By contrast, weavers stood to gain by cutting back on raw materials and selling defective cloth as if it were perfect.

The long effort of the municipal magistrates and the central government to standardize the production of woolen textiles culminated in the eighteenth century. In 1718, the magistrates, at the request of the Chamber of Commerce, set strict standards for the size of textiles manufactured by the guilds of wool and mixed-fabric weavers. At the demand, once again, of the merchants, the intendant required that all cloth entering Lille from the countryside conform to these standards. Finally, in 1732, the royal council published a complete set of regulations, eighty-nine articles long, which specified the size and number of threads for almost every type of cloth made in Lille or in the surrounding villages.[75]

To enforce these regulations among the master wool weavers, the *doyens* of the guild visited the masters' workshops and placed seals (*plombs d'outils*) upon the pieces of cloth before they were taken off the loom. This practice ensured that cloth from the countryside could not be smuggled into Lille and sold. Before the cloth could be exported or sold locally, it had to be checked again for size and defects at the *bureau de visite* of the guild. The masters had to leave a small portion unwoven at one end of the cloth so that the number of threads could be counted. The officials then applied another seal (the *plomb de visite*) which carried the coat of arms of the city on one side and the name of the cloth on the other.[76] Officials and merchants believed that the strict controls placed on the production of woolen *camelots* were essential to the success of this industry. According to Dieudonné, Prefect of the Nord under Napoleon, it was because of the "strict observation of these regulations before the Revolution, ripened by experience, that the *camelots* of Lille enjoyed a marked preference over the *camelots* of other manufacturers."[77]

The careful controls placed on local manufacturing, however, were threatened by new policies of the central government. Toward the end of the eighteenth century, liberal voices in Paris increasingly deplored what they believed was a surfeit of regulation that stifled innovation. To foster initiative in manufacturing, the king announced a new program in May 1779. The idea was to establish a *régime intermédiaire* between over-regulation and unrestrained liberty, to let manufacturers adapt their production to changing modes and styles. The Letters Patent of 1779 allowed manufacturers whose cloth conformed to the regulations to be given one kind of seal, and those whose cloth did not to be distinguished by another. The seals would also verify that the cloth had been manufactured in France.[78]

The *négociants* in Lille made sure that this option was never offered in Lille. In a meeting in September 1779 all but one of the members of the Chamber of Commerce declared that freedom to make cloth without regulations would seriously undermine Lille's manufactures.[79] Shortly thereafter, the Chamber of Commerce met with the heads and inspectors from the weavers' guilds and under pressure from the merchants "everyone declared that freedom over the dimensions and combinations in regulated cloth would necessarily entail the deterioration of quality and the discredit of their manufactures."[80]

New Letters Patent in June 1780, requiring towns to establish *bureaux de marque*, increased local discontent. The *bureaux* were supposed to apply the new seals that all cloth sold in France or exported abroad had to carry. Originally in 1780, the price was 1 *sol* per piece, but in 1781, it was raised to 15 *deniers* ($1\frac{1}{4}$ *sol*). The yield from the seals and from one-half of the fines for infractions of the rules went to the government; the inspectors (*gardes jurés*), elected by the local manufacturers, kept the other half.[81]

Lille's merchants resisted the creation of a *bureau de marque*. The new institution was, in their eyes, simply a fiscal ploy.[82] The bureau duplicated, at a higher cost, functions which the guilds already performed efficiently, and redirected revenue from local groups to the central government. Because the officials received half of the fines that they imposed, it encouraged them to be arbitrary. Lille's magistrates, by contrast, paid the inspectors for the guilds a set salary. In short, the government's manipulation of cloth regulation for fiscal ends undermined efficient manufacturing and trade. Because the merchants wanted to sell their cloth as cheaply as possible, they seem to have ignored the law. In 1782, for example, two merchants from Lille had their cloth seized in Grenoble by employees of the Farmers General for having neither the new seals nor temporary *plombs de grace*.[83]

The reforms of 1779 and the *bureaux de marque* are sometimes cited as examples of the government's enlightened attempts to break the hold of regulations that were strangling French manufacture and trade.[84] Whatever the intent of the government – and that is, by no means, always clear – in Lille the program of 1779 was a failure. Merchants in Lille did not want more freedom from regulation; they wanted inexpensive, effective regulation. They fought regulation by the *bureau de marque* because they thought it catered unduly to royal finances. Regulation by the guilds, on the other hand, they consistently upheld.

In conclusion, it is evident that merchants were constantly searching for ways to make guilds serve bourgeois needs. When guilds did not serve this purpose, merchants fought them; when they did, they supported them. In the mid-century, the search for profit became more closely connected to protection. The guild of wool weavers had become an instrument for preserving the current social relations of production at a time when economic growth was creating rival, upstart rural entrepreneurs. This concern, along with the bourgeois belief that high standards of artisanal workmanship were essential to success in the market, made the guild of wool weavers a valuable tool of urban commercial interests.

One might argue that merchants in Lille clung to corporate privilege only because the wool industry in the city was declining. Although they relied on privilege, more dynamic groups would have thrived on competition. To test the idea that privilege was tied to older, less vital industries, it is useful to study another guild, that of the thread merchant-manufacturers (*filetiers*).

The guild of linen thread merchant-manufacturers

In the eighteenth century, the manufacture of linen thread (*fils retords*) was one of Lille's most dynamic industries. In 1720 there were 164 mills for twisting thread; by 1789 there were 521.[85] Originally the thread merchants and manufacturers were members of the guild of dry-goods merchants, but in 1691 they established their own corps. The separation can be traced to the plan of a group of thread manufacturers to set up a bleaching works for thread. In order to finance the new enterprise, they received permission from the municipal magistrates to form a guild and to use its entrance fees and annual dues to subsidize the venture.[86] The thread manufacturers thus were able to support a newly developing industry by obtaining corporate status.

To make linen thread (*fils retords*), two or three single strands of linen were put on a mill, which twisted them tightly together. The finished thread was used for sewing, weaving, and making lace. Five workers were needed to operate each spinning mill; in Lille only men worked the mills. The linen strands used in Lille's manufactures were spun by peasants from flax grown in the countryside and sold on the linen market in Lille. Flax was also imported from the Belgian provinces.[87]

The statutes of the guild gave masters the exclusive right to manufacture and sell linen thread in the city. All members of the guild of dry-goods merchants could join the new guild initially and belong to both guilds in return for a small entrance fee and payment of annual dues. Other individuals had to serve an apprenticeship for two years, complete a masterpiece, and pay entrance fees totalling 66 *florins*. Sons of masters paid only one-half of the regular fees, and widows of deceased masters were allowed to carry on the family business. Masters who paid the maximum annual dues could have one apprentice per year; otherwise, they were permitted one every two years.[88]

Unlike the guild of wool weavers, there were no limitations on the number of spinning mills operated by master thread manufacturers. The relationship of merchant-manufacturers to these two guilds, therefore, was quite different. Because the master wool weavers could not work more than six looms, these artisans came to depend on wealthy merchants outside the guild to export their cloth. The wool weavers, generally small-scale and poor, were in one guild, while many of the *négociants* belonged to a different, commercial guild. In the linen thread industry, by contrast, the master thread spinners could expand production inside the guild. As a result, the guild itself included both artisanal masters engaged in limited production and bourgeois merchant-manufacturers involved in manufacturing and export.

Soon after the guild's creation, a number of poorer masters, drawing upon the model of the guild of wool weavers, petitioned the magistrates to limit each master spinner to two mills. The more enterprising merchant-manufacturers – the Bigos, Vanhoenackers, Bonniers, and Mahieus – fought to maintain freedom of manufacturing within the guild. Nothing contributed more toward making commerce flourish, they declared, "than allowing businessmen *une grande liberté.*"[89] In their rebuttal to the small masters, these businessmen emphasized the importance of expansion for independence. If masters could produce only small amounts of thread, none of them would be able to acquire the stocks necessary to engage in foreign trade or to weather economic crises. When master spinners fell upon hard times, they would become dependent on powerful merchants outside the guild for credit, and soon the export of thread would be dominated by merchants who did not even belong to the guild. Thus, when the principal masters in the guild advocated the necessity of "*une grande liberté*" for manufacturing, they were not recommending the destruction of the guild. They wanted freedom inside the guild so that they could use corporate prerogatives to their own advantage.

Because no limitations were imposed, capital accumulation was not impeded by the guild. Over the course of the eighteenth century, the number of masters working only one mill declined and the number of masters working seven mills or more grew (see Table 6). In 1720, masters who operated one mill represented 54 percent of the guild; by 1777, they had fallen to 14 percent. On the other end of the scale, in 1720 only one individual, the widow Bernard Mousson, operated seven or more mills. Her twenty mills represented 12 percent of the total number of mills in the guild. By 1777, 11 percent of the masters worked seven or more mills, which accounted for 39 percent of all mills in Lille.[90] Because large-scale merchant-manufacturers were able to thrive within the guild, they had good reason to perpetuate its privileges.

During the eighteenth century, two issues dominated the policies of the guild. First, like the cloth merchants, the thread merchant-manufacturers were convinced that regulation of quality was the key to stimulating exports. Thus, over the course of the century, the municipal magistrates, the intendants, and the masters constructed a rigorous system of regulation. Second, the guild consistently tried to thwart rural competition. Regulations controlling quality had not been included in the guild's original statutes, but by the end of the eighteenth century, this task was paramount. Thread was measured by wrapping it on skeins of a standard length before it was sold.[91] Buyers could all too easily be cheated if a skein was slightly short. The sturdiness of thread, furthermore, depended upon how evenly and tightly it had been twisted. It would not be difficult to mix good and bad thread together, and sell the whole lot as perfect. To prevent this kind of deception, the magistrates, intendants, and *doyens* of the guild began to establish strict rules.

In 1725, the magistrates regulated lengths of skeins. The following year, at the request of the *doyens*, the magistrates created two inspectors

Table 6. *Spinning mills in the guild of thread spinners*

1720

mills	0	1	2	3	4	5	6	20
masters	0	45	26	3	4	2	2	1

total number of mills: 164[a]
total number of masters: 83
ratio of mills/masters: 2·0

1751

mills	0	1	2	3	4	5	6	14	23	30
masters	1	17	33	4	4	2	2	1	1	1

total number of mills: 200[a]
total number of masters: 66
ratio of mills/masters: 3·0

1777

mills	0	1	2	3	4	5	6	7	8	9	10	11	12	13	14	18	22	24
masters	3	13	53	15	9	7	3	2	3	1	1	0	1	1	1	1	1	1

total number of mills: 413[a]
total number of masters: 116
ratio of mills/masters: 3·6

[a] The number of mills does not include mills owned by the four masters in charge of the guild (*maitres en exercice*). In the accounts of 1720 and 1751 these masters were exempted from the fee levied on mills. In 1777 they were exempted only up to four mills. Since the accounts do not correspond in this respect, I have omitted the mills of the masters in charge in all three cases.
Source: Comptes de la fileterie, 9,278 (1720), 9,293 (1751), 9,319 (1777). After 1777 the receipts from these fees are listed as an aggregate sum, rather than by individual masters.

(*égards*), paid half by the city and half by the guild, to enforce the regulation. In 1733, the intendant, Bidé de la Grandville, established more detailed specifications for twisting thread. In order to identify more easily those who made defective thread, each master was required to put his own seal on packets of thread that he manufactured. Because, according to the intendant Moreau de Sechelles, violations were still occurring, even stiffer regulations were needed. In 1744 he reviewed, modified, and republished all of his predecessors' regulations. New and extremely heavy fines – 100 *florins* for the first offense, 300 for the second, and 1,000 for the third – were imposed on masters who violated the rules. In order to check for imperfect thread that might have been hidden, the inspectors from the guild were authorized to investigate the bleaching establishments, as well as the homes and workshops, of the thread manufacturers. When the inspectors discovered violations of the rules, they seized the imperfect thread and reported the problem immediately to the *doyens* of the guild. Finally, after new *doyens* were elected each year, they were required to read aloud the regulations of the guild to the assembled masters. Reviewing the regulations thus became a kind of annual ritual.[92]

The magistrates soon decided that safeguarding the reputation of Lille's thread manufacturers called for stringent controls over the sale, as well as manufacture, of thread. According to the thread merchant-manufacturers, certain members of the guild of dry-goods merchants in Lille bought cheap, imperfect thread from other towns and then sold it at a higher price, as if it were from Lille. Eventually, the manufacturers complained, this practice would ruin their reputation and individuals would stop buying their thread.[93] To prevent this practice, the magistrates decreed, in 1744, that the guild of dry-goods merchants in Lille could only sell linen thread manufactured according to the regulations. They authorized the inspectors from the guild of thread spinners to search the shops and homes of these merchants. The dry-goods merchants were given "*un tems moral*" to get rid of their defective thread before the inspectors started making their rounds.[94] By the mid-eighteenth century, the linen thread produced in Lille was acquiring a reputation for quality. The preference for thread from Lille over that from Germany or Silesia, the Chamber of Commerce remarked in 1768, was a result of superior standards.[95]

Rural competition did not pose as great a threat to thread manufacturing as it had to weaving. Although peasants could easily spin flax into linen strands, twisting the strands on mills was a complex process which was not easily dispersed in the villages. Bailleul, a small town in the province of Maritime Flanders, approximately 15 miles from Lille, was the guild's major rival. In Bailleul, thread was twisted on ordinary spinning wheels, rather than on mills, and the spinners were predominantly female.[96] Competition was beginning to develop in the region directly surrounding Lille. In 1738, there were only ten spinning mills in the neighboring villages; fourteen years later there were twenty-six.[97] Although Lille's thread manufacturers could do little to stop the production of thread in Bailleul, in 1750 they urged the intendant to ban thread manufacturing in the *châtellenie* of Lille. They also asked the municipal magistrates to bring their case to the king's council.[98]

Unlike the manufacture of woolen cloth (*sayetterie*), which Charles V had prohibited in the *châtellenie*, no sovereign had ever banned the manufacture of linen thread there. Thus the thread manufacturers and city magistrates had to convince the government that protecting the guild would serve the larger interests of the state. Their case rested on two arguments: first, that of state finances, and second, that of society's general need for regulation. The guild stressed that it had been obliged to give the king money for the militia and to buy up venal offices.[99] The municipal magistrates further emphasized that over three thousand persons worked in some way in Lille's thread manufactures, and that if these workers moved to the countryside, urban *octrois* would sharply decrease. Limiting competition in thread manufacturing, therefore, was "for the good of the service of the king."[100]

The guild further insisted that its compliance with a whole series of urban regulations deserved recognition. The masters had to buy their raw materials in official marketplaces where, due to transportation costs and urban tolls, prices were higher. Unlike rural manufacturers, masters in Lille also had to pay fees for apprenticeships, masterships, and salaries of inspectors. Inspections, apprenticeships, market regulations – all, the guild argued, were necessary for the public good. Regulation was part of a well-ordered, moral economy that checked "the greed" of those who wanted to cheat the public in order "to make the biggest profit."[101] Privilege was the corollary of regulation. Those who enforced high standards and maintained public integrity should enjoy advantages.

The intendants favored urban protection. In 1752 Moreau de Sechelles declared that "the conservation of this branch of commerce was of the highest importance."[102] Two decades later, when freedom over rural manufacturing was hotly contested, Caumartin gave three reasons for restricting rural thread manufactures. The first was simply, "the privileges of the city of Lille." The second was that in border provinces, manufactures should be concentrated in fortified cities so that they would not be exposed to enemy attacks. The third was that smuggling and fraud could be practiced too easily in the countryside, which discredited the reputable manufacturers in Lille and would eventually ruin their industry completely.[103]

In 1738, to restrict the growth of thread manufacturing in the countryside, the intendant, Bidé de la Grandville, had prohibited the construction of spinning mills without his permission. Because the four noble *baillis* in the provincial estates protested, the order was not strictly enforced, and during the next decade, a number of new mills were built. Pressed by the guild to halt rural manufacturing, Moreau de Sechelles decreed in 1751 that every rural thread manufacturer had to reapply for permission to operate his mill. To uncover illicit enterprises, he allowed the inspectors of Lille's guild to canvas the villages in the surrounding area. After the search was completed, the intendant shut down the mills of eighteen unauthorized manufacturers and fined them each 100 *florins*.[104]

Two individuals working illegally in the village of Wazemmes, François Petit and Joseph Delobel, were originally master thread spinners from Lille. They argued that since they belonged to the guild in Lille, they should not have to pay their fines, but the municipal magistrates strongly disagreed. Masters from Lille, the municipal magistrates stated, had to remain within the city to exercise their rights and privileges. If masters could move into the countryside, where rents and taxes were lower and surveillance over manufacturing more difficult, the whole guild might try to relocate outside the city.[105] The intendant upheld the fines. Other thread manufacturers, supported by the mayors of Armentières and Roubaix, also asked the intendant to repeal their sentences. Approximately one-half of them were allowed to continue to operate their mills, but only so long as they made types of thread which were not produced in Lille. The rest were ordered to close down their enterprises, but after appeals from Armentières, the sentences were apparently dropped.[106]

In the late 1760s Caumartin took action once again against individuals in the countryside. According to this intendant, merchants in the interior of France were complaining that skeins of thread from Walloon Flanders were too short. Because he believed the problem stemmed from rural manufacturers, he decreed that all rural thread manufacturers had to reapply for written permission to run their mills. In addition, all manufacturers in villages that had no official inspectors would be visited by inspectors from the guild in Lille. Two additional inspectors were to be created to check rural manufactures; the city and the guild would each pay half of the cost. Inspectors from Bailleul were authorized to regulate thread manufacturers in Maritime Flanders.[107]

The intendant's order displeased Lille's guild on several counts. First, the master thread spinners would have to pay for two new inspectors, but the new officials, they contended, would not be able to solve the problem. Short skeins and defective thread came from Bailleul and Armentières, but these towns had their own inspectors and refused to allow officials from Lille into their territory. The charges apparently had some validity. According to the *directeur des fermes* in Walloon Flanders, the *négociants* from Bailleul, a town situated almost directly on the Franco-Belgian border, habitually imported low-grade thread from the Belgian provinces and passed it off as perfect. The inspectors in Bailleul, who were supposed to prevent this type of deception, were really only "tributaries" of the *négociants*.[108] Since no record of payment for the proposed inspectors appears in the guild's accounts, the plan for new inspectors must have been withdrawn.

Several years later, the guild devised another plan. In 1777, Caumartin authorized the inspectors from the guild to enter the customs bureau and check that all thread being exported from Lille conformed to the official regulations. The inspectors could seize thread if it did not meet the official specifications.[109] In 1786, the intendant Esmangart, at the guild's request, made controls over the manufacture of thread even more rigorous. He ordered the municipal officers of every town and village where thread was produced to name inspectors to enforce the regulations. The inspectors were to visit not only the workshops and homes where thread was made, but also all the bleaching establishments, fairs, markets, and warehouses where any thread might be stored or sold. All packages of thread manufactured in Walloon and Maritime Flanders which were being exported from Lille had to be checked and officially sealed by the inspectors from the guild or by a tax official. The guild hired a new inspector in 1788 to perform this task. According to the *directeur des fermes*, the *négociants* from Bailleul, who passed off foreign thread as their own, were none too pleased at having their thread inspected in Lille.[110]

Throughout the eighteenth century, then, the intendants, magistrates and guilds created an elaborate and rigorous system of regulation in order to control quality and to limit rural competitors. To say that regulation was only a thinly disguised ploy simply to prevent rural competition is to ignore the heavy fines, elaborate surveillance, and minute regulations imposed on masters in the city.[111] Nonetheless, the desire for quality was hard to separate from the quest for protection. The manufacturers in the guild of thread manufacturers relied on both to develop their exports and to protect their markets.

Commercial privilege and the guild of dry-goods merchants

The study of corporate privilege in the wool and thread industries has shown how merchants used privileges in production to help them enhance their commercial advantage. To gain a greater understanding of guilds as purely commercial tools, it is helpful to look at the role of the dry-goods merchants (*merciers-grossiers*). "Sellers of all and makers of none" was the motto of the guild, which had the right to sell a wide variety of merchandise inside Lille. Hats, small household items, utensils, stockings, sewing notions, fashion accessories, and textiles all fell under its commercial monopoly. Merchants who did not belong to the guild were prohibited from selling these wares in the city. Artisans of other guilds were permitted to sell their own products. In 1788 the guild contained approximately 600 merchants, a group that ranged from indigent *petits merciers* who peddled their wares in market stalls to wealthy cloth wholesalers who belonged to the elite Chamber of Commerce.

The guild's cloth wholesalers (*grossiers*) had the sole right in Lille to sell fine textiles such as silk, leather goods, and many varieties of woolens, including *camelots*. Some of these cloth wholesalers were rich *négociants* who employed weavers in both Lille and the countryside. The cloth wholesalers were required to serve an apprenticeship of two years and pay 48 *florins* for the mastership, unless one was the son or daughter of a master. The apprenticeship was designed to prevent non-residents from entering the guild.[112]

In the mid-eighteenth century, one of the most important battles that the guild of dry-goods merchants waged was a war against aggressive cloth brokers who delivered cloth from Roubaix to Lille. Initially women, whom no one seemed to have paid much attention to, had gone to Roubaix and brought cloth back to Lille to sell. Some urban merchants also had their own agents to pick up cloth in the villages. Around 1730, approximately the same time that Roubaix's manufacturers asked for the right to have their own finishing equipment, complaints about a new kind of aggressive broker began to appear. The first group to sound the alarm were the wholesalers who sold textiles at warehouses in Lille. According to these merchants, instead of bringing cloth from the countryside back to Lille, audacious brokers were setting up shop in the countryside and offering cut-rate prices. In addition, the brokers attracted customers by extending credit, whereas Lille's warehouse owners generally demanded cash. In 1750 the guild of dry-goods merchants asked the municipal authorities to set up a system of licensed brokers who would be compelled to bring their wares back to Lille and prohibited from practicing commerce for their own profit. The proposal was brought to the Chamber of Commerce which initially opposed the plan and even argued that it might be illegal.

Apparently at this time the Chamber of Commerce thought a system of licensed brokers would hinder freedom of export for Lille's *commissionaires*, wealthy merchants working on commission for foreign correspondents. In return for a 2 percent fee, these individuals had orders filled to meet specifications of merchants abroad. Some *commissionaires* were members of the guild of dry-goods merchants, but membership was not necessary in order to work on commission. A second group of cloth merchants, the *magasiniers* or *marchands en gros*, had somewhat different interests. These wholesalers bought cloth from manufacturers either in Lille or the countryside and sold it at their warehouses for whatever price they chose to set. Selling cloth wholesale inside Lille on a permanent basis required membership in the guild of dry-goods merchants, because non-resident wholesale merchants could only display wares for three days within the city.[113]

In 1750 the Chamber of Commerce feared that the proposed brokerage system might interfere with the right of merchants to buy cloth on commission. The directors observed that the privileges of the guild of dry-goods merchants did not cover *commerce en gros* and exports. Roubaix's manufacturers should be free to take orders from whichever merchant they wanted in Lille or to change their *commissionnaire*, if they pleased. Throughout their report, the Chamber of Commerce seemed to assume that Lille's merchants would naturally control Roubaix's exports. It was just a question of what kind of urban merchant, those who sold on commission or local warehouse owners, would benefit most.[114]

By 1759 the Chamber of Commerce had reversed its earlier opinion and was advocating the licensing of brokers. One possible explanation is that the brokers had begun to infiltrate the network of *commissionnaires*. According to the guild, brokers charged less than 2 percent when they received orders from abroad. Some brokers had started to buy raw wool and dyes in order to employ their own weavers in the countryside and to finish illegally their own cloth. Others were purchasing *camelots* in Lille for export. Several had even started to advertise their services all over France by sending out business cards imprinted with the broker's name, his address, and the type of merchandise in which he dealt.[115]

Alarmed at the progress of these upstarts, the Chamber of Commerce asked for the creation of official cloth brokers and strict rules preventing them from finishing and selling cloth as *commissionnaires*.[116] On 24 January 1759, a municipal ordinance met their demands. The municipal magistrates established eight salaried, licensed cloth brokers (*courtiers de calemandes*) with the sole right to collect cloth from the countryside. The brokers were prohibited from engaging in commerce on their own account and were required to sell their cloth to Lille's merchants. The guild of dry-goods merchants was authorized to check for infractions of the regulations, while the *Juridiction Consulaire*, the commercial court drawn from the mercantile elite of Lille, was empowered to audit the brokers' books.[117] In addition, two members of the Chamber of Commerce, Gilles Vanhoenacker and Gosselin *l'aîné*, backed by funds from the guild of dry-goods merchants, were authorized to spend up to 100,000 *florins* to reimburse the brokers who had made advances to Roubaix's weavers.[118] Then, over the protests of Roubaix, Lille's officials put the new system into effect.

It is not clear exactly what constituted the legal basis of the commercial controls imposed by Lille's magistrates on Roubaix. Until the mid-eighteenth century, royal laws granting Roubaix greater freedom of manufacture had always assumed that finishing and export would be done through Lille. After establishing stringent regulations over cloth production in both Lille and the countryside, the royal *arrêt* of 1732 had stipulated that cloth produced in Roubaix would be inspected in Roubaix and then would "pass freely...into Lille to be dyed, finished and sold wholesale there, as the manufacturers of Roubaix judge appropriate."[119] This important clause was left open to two interpretations: the first stressed that the cloth was to flow into Lille to be finished and sold; the second that the manufacturers of Roubaix had some role in judging who exported their cloth. The municipal magistrates emphasized the first interpretation to justify the power of Lille's official brokers.[120].

The manufacturers in Roubaix protested the injustice of a system that prevented commercial competition and gave the merchants in Lille too much power to fix the price of cloth. They took their case to the Parlement of Douai, which ruled against Lille's magistrates. Nonetheless, the matter did not stop there, as it became pulled into the whole controversy over freedom of manufacturing. In 1768, when the royal government temporarily suspended the law allowing freedom of rural industry, Lille's municipal magistrates resolved to continue to execute the official brokerage system.[121] The Roubaisiens protested to the royal *Conseil du Commerce*, but apparently no decision was made.[122] Even though the legal details of this whole controversy unfortunately remain in shadow, the outcome did not favor Roubaix. As we noted earlier, freedom of manufacturing was granted irrevocably to Roubaix in 1776, but the brokerage system was not entirely dismantled. Until the Revolution, manufacturers in Roubaix who financed the cloth production of other weavers had to sell that cloth to brokers from Lille.[123] Lille's merchants largely kept control of circulating capital, the key to profit in rural industry.

As these incidents show, the entrepreneurs who were demanding freedom of trade were not the wealthy cloth merchants and members of the Chamber of Commerce; they were the aggressive middlemen trying to make their way to the top. The brokers threatened to upset the pre-existing pattern of control over the textile trade and for that reason the cloth wholesalers denounced their actions: "this is no longer liberty, this is an abuse that must be repressed." The brokers had to be put back into their correct place in the corporate hierarchy and be compelled to live within "the just limits of the *état* that they had chosen." The brokers were "insatiable" intriguers, men of "base character" who displayed "unlimited cupidity" and operated in a way "contrary to the rules of a *saine politique du commerce*."[124] Moral indignation and a brokerage system of dubious legality, such was the response of Lille's mercantile elite to those who wished to instill a bit more competition into a protected system of commercial capitalism.

Finally, as the last case shows, the wholesalers were able to keep retailers in the guild of dry-goods merchants under their thumb. Retailers gained some advantages from membership in the guild of dry-goods merchants. The guild helped to combat the presence of itinerant peddlars, *savoyards*, street vendors and others who were the bane of the small shopkeeper's existence. The guild also successfully pressured the magistrates to regulate public auctions (*ventes publiques*) where goods, perhaps stolen, might be sold off at cut-rate prices. When a public auction was established in 1689, the magistrates banned the sale of cloth there, in order to preserve the privilege of the guild of dry-goods merchants. In 1742, the magistrates decided that no new merchandise at all could be sold at public auctions, unless a merchant had died or gone out of business for good.[125]

But it was the affluent wholesalers who benefited most from membership in the guild. In the early eighteenth century, the guild of dry-goods merchants complained that non-resident merchants were selling wares in homes and *cabarets*. In response, the magistrates prohibited any non-guild member from retailing merchandise falling under the corps's commercial monopoly. This measure meant that non-native merchants could only sell merchandise wholesale in Lille. To prevent non-native wholesalers from setting up permanent wholesale outlets, the magistrates decreed that non-resident merchants could stay no longer than three days in Lille to sell their goods. In 1747, to enforce this regulation more strictly, the guild set up a bureau, where all incoming merchants were required to discharge their cargo before selling it. The *doyen* had the right to inspect the wares and to stop defective goods from being marketed.[126] As a result of this system, the well-to-do wholesalers in the guild became privileged middlemen between non-resident wholesalers and retailers in Lille. Because outside merchants were forced to sell goods wholesale in a short period of time, they had to turn to rich wholesalers in Lille to buy out their stock quickly. Local wholesalers in turn, supplied the shopkeepers with the smaller assortment of goods that they needed.

The privileged position of the great merchants at the expense of the lesser ones was not suffered completely in silence. In 1786, a case broke out which pitted a group of shopkeepers against the *doyens* and wealthy merchants in the guild. The trouble began when a cloth wholesaler, Jacques Martin, from a neighboring town of Orchies, brought his cloth into Lille to sell at the bureau of the dry-goods merchants. In the past, he had often sold cloth there which measured approximately 60 to 80 yards. In 1786, however, he decided to sell smaller pieces of cloth, measuring only 12 to 25 yards. The *doyens* of the guild seized the cut cloth on the pretext that Martin would be making a retail sale, a privilege of the guild.[127]

The shopkeepers who wanted to buy the small pieces of cloth from Martin protested. Merchants with limited savings, they pointed out, could not afford to buy the large amounts which non-native wholesalers were required to sell. They were forced, therefore, to go to the *doyens* of the guild, who charged 5 percent more than the original wholesale price. If the *doyens* won this case, they would probably raise their prices even more. Furthermore, the small merchants contended, a royal law had defined a retail sale of cloth as less than 8 yards. Since the pieces of cloth sold by Martin were at least 12 yards, they constituted wholesale merchandise. Adhering to royal legislation, the municipal magistrates ruled that all pieces of cloth at least 8 yards long with a seal at one of the two edges constituted wholesale merchandise. But the magistrates also republished the old ordinances prohibiting outside merchants from making retail sales in Lille.[128]

The small merchants did not just attack economic inequalities; they also denounced the oligarchic structure of political power in the guild and called for democratic representation. They condemned the *doyens* for "abusing the power that had been entrusted to them and sacrificing the general interest to their particular interest."[129] A royal declaration of 4 July 1775 had stated that no judicial proceeding could be initiated in any guild without convoking a general assembly. General assemblies, the small merchants argued, were unknown in the guild of dry-goods merchants. The *doyens* traditionally called together a handful of masters to approve their policies. These leaders might claim that years of service entitled them to act as representatives of the whole guild. But the shopkeepers wanted a whole new definition of representation. A deputy was legitimately so only when he was chosen by "the generality of masters."[130]

The rebuttal by the *doyens* against opening the city to outside wholesalers reiterated the legitimacy and alleged utility of commercial privilege and oligarchic control. The *doyens* simply did not see "that one must admit an outside merchant into competition with the guild of dry-goods merchants under the pretext that he sells at a better price than they." Furthermore, they added, "by according too much favor to outside merchants, by allowing them too great a liberty, one will...destroy the guild of dry-goods merchants." No one could claim, they continued, that guilds were not necessary, because the government itself, after briefly suppressing the guilds in 1776, had hastened to re-establish them.[131] All in all, the economic arguments of the *doyens* rested on little else than the right of the guild to keep out competitors.

The issue of democratic representation within the guild posed a more complex problem. As the *doyens* pointed out, the majority of masters in the guild had signed petitions defending their actions. In 1786, of 483 masters, 255 had defended the action of the *doyens*, while only 59 supported the cause of the small merchants. The rest were neutral. If majority rule was the principle of decision-making, then the *doyens* would still be in charge. The opposition observed that many of the 255 masters who defended the *doyens* did not engage in the kind of commerce that was being contested. It was sufficient, the *doyens* replied, simply to belong to a guild to uphold its rights and privileges.

Although pragmatically the *doyens* realized the benefit of appealing to all merchants in the guild, philosophically they did not want to use democratic representation as the basis of their authority. The royal declaration of July 1775, they contended, did not specify how guilds should choose their representatives and, therefore, "usage has the force of law." To clarify the point, they emphasized that it was "*un usage constant*" only to call former *doyens* of the guild to general assemblies. In sum, tradition and oligarchic control were the principles that the *doyens* defended, and which a large percentage of the guild, in turn, had supported.

Who signed the petition upholding the conservative, traditional policy of the *doyens*? Several of the most powerful *négociants* in Lille headed the list, and at least five of them were members of the Chamber of Commerce: Louis and Edouard Vanhoenacker, Louis Scheppers, J. B. Barrois, and Laurent-Deledicque. The signatures of the successful silk merchant-manufacturer Albert Cuvelier-Brame and the lace merchant Mottez-Gillon also appeared.[132] These men, some of the city's most influential merchants and manufacturers, defended the guilds, supported commercial privilege, and, in 1789, helped to lead the municipal Revolution in Lille. They were, in short, Lille's revolutionary bourgeoisie. Louis Scheppers was elected as a deputy, and Albert Cuvelier-Brame as a substitute deputy, of the Third Estate in Lille to the Estates General. In 1790, Louis Vanhoenacker became the first democratically elected mayor of Lille. Mottez-Gillon was a municipal officer in 1791, and Laurent-Deledicque was a notable in the municipal government in 1790 and 1792.[133] These men did not see any contradiction between waging a liberal battle against the closed, corporate structure of municipal power and supporting traditional, oligarchic practices in the guilds that they controlled. Thus, in 1789, Lille experienced a bourgeois revolution – a revolution made by merchants and manufacturers who were politically liberal and economically conservative.

In conclusion, the case of Lille raises many questions about the assumptions that have influenced interpretations of "reactionary" guilds, the "liberal" bourgeoisie, and the relationship between economic and political interests in the coming of the French Revolution. On the one hand, guilds did not constitute uniform obstacles to economic growth or capitalistic practices. The structure, regulations, and technology in each guild led to different political relationships and potentials for change and growth. On the other hand, merchants and manufacturers had very flexible and instrumental relationships to the guilds. They were ready to prevent the merger of different guilds of weavers, to restrict the number of looms operated by master wool weavers, to keep manufacturing inside the city, and to shut out brokers and non-native wholesalers to maintain their commercial dominance. Far from being sturdy individualists, merchants and manufacturers took advantage of corporate regulations whenever possible to secure profit. They transformed guilds into bourgeois tools.

Lille's revolutionary bourgeoisie did not hold a Smithian worldview. These men did not place their faith in the power of invisible market forces to transform competitive individualism into public felicity. The Chamber of Commerce saw itself as a corps with a code of honor and a rank in society.[134] When these businessmen appealed to liberty, it was often still within the context of a well-ordered, regulated economy. When fighting the brokers, the cloth merchants in the guild of dry-goods wholesalers, for example, gave the following definition of liberty: "The word liberty is a metaphysical term that can be used very badly. In general, liberty does not consist in the unbridled license to do everything that the vagaries of the imagination or the violence of the passions suggests to us, but only in the moderated power to do all that civil law, national law, and religion permit us." True liberty, the merchants concluded, "consists in a perfect submission to legitimate authority."[135] The idea, then, that all groups and individuals had a place in society, that all had to perform their own functions and respect the duties and prerogatives of others, was not limited to small-scale artisans and shopkeepers. Merchants also partook of this vision, and if they stood at the top of the corporate hierarchy, it might well serve them well.

For a variety of reasons, then, the abolition of Lille's guilds during the Revolution was not a bourgeois revolutionary goal. In 1790 the first act of the new bourgeois town council was to reaffirm all of the police regulations of the old municipal magistracy, a measure that implied the direct continuation of all economic controls. The responsibility for dismantling the guilds thus seems attributable to the independent action of the national government, whose motives and political dynamics remain to be studied in depth. The next chapter looks at the fate of mercantilist municipal policy and bourgeois interests as economic regulation was abolished by the national government in the name of liberty and the national interest.

8   The abolition of the guilds

In the earliest stages of the Revolution, many of Lille's citizens continued to regard political and economic liberalism as unrelated principles. Although democratic representation had become the foundations of the newly constituted nation, the townspeople did not believe that this transformation called into question the existence of the city's guilds. The political changes at the national level did, however, provide a new rationale for challenging the oligarchic structure of these corps. In 1790, three years after a group of retailers were denied the right to elect their own *doyens*, another group of approximately forty merchants requested the same changes. Like the masters in 1787, these merchants appealed to the "particular statutes of the *corps*" but they went on to claim that the right to elect officials was "a general principle" and an "imprescriptible right...in accord with reason." They also drew upon the experience of the Revolution itself. The National Assembly was organizing its administration around the principle of democratic election, and local elections for the town council had demonstrated that the right to vote was essential to good government.[1] Thus, the masters' arguments for direct representation acquired a more universalistic character by appealing to principles that the Revolution had enshrined.

Earlier, Louis Vanhoenacker, Lille's new mayor, had supported the oligarchic organization of the guild. His personal opinion on the new petition is not known, but in 1790 the *procureur syndic* of the commune and the municipal officers agreed that the right to vote should be extended to all masters. The town council ordered that new elections be held within the guild that month.[2] The extension of the corporate franchise, however, did not affect the guild's economic monopolies. Democratic practices were to exist within a protectionistic guild.

In March 1791, the Allarde law abolished the guilds as a pernicious vestige of "exclusive privilege." It is somewhat a mystery why, although the abolition of the guilds had been proposed on the night of 4 August 1789, these corps were not suppressed until 1791. One reason may be that opposition to the guilds had not been very strong. In the *cahiers de doléances* of the Third Estate from the largest cities in France, it is impossible to find a generalized bourgeois outcry against these corps.[3] On the contrary, many demands either implied or directly called for their continued existence. The Third Estate in Caen, Reims, Clermont-Ferrand, Rouen, and Paris *intra-muros* (*ville*), for example, asked that widows be reinstated in the right to take over their husbands' businesses without paying additional reception fees, a prerogative that Turgot's reforms had annulled. Like Lille, both Marseille and Nantes called explicitly for preserving the privileges of guilds. By contrast, most opposition to the guilds came from small towns, journeymen, and the countryside.[4] Hostility was generated not from municipalities and businessmen at the top of the economic scale, but from those on the margins of the corporate system who benefited least from its monopolies.

If merchants and manufacturers were not actively pressing for the abolition of the guilds, then their suppression may well have been a result of a new political culture at the national level. The quest to establish national uniformity, to absorb all corps into the body of the nation, and to institutionalize a coherent view of liberty, in part a legacy of physiocracy, seems more critical to understanding the guilds' final demise than the rise of commercial capitalism. As one historian has argued, the night of 4 August and the Declaration of the Rights of Man and Citizen, "doomed the privileges of corporations no less than those of nobles, clerics or provinces."[5]

The specter of corporate debt continued to cast a shadow over attempts to create national uniformity. Significantly, it was the committee on public contributions in the National Assembly, and not the committee on commerce and agriculture, that proposed the guilds' abolition. Because revenues from land taxes and transaction fees were insufficient to cover the needs of the state, the committee on public contributions, headed by Allarde, had begun to consider alternate ways to tap the wealth of merchants and artisans. Requiring all merchants and artisans to purchase a *patente*, or license, seemed to be the most equitable and efficient method of achieving this goal. The committee's proposal did not stop there. The new tax, the members believed, should be linked to another act of "great benefit" to industry and commerce – the suppression of the guilds. Following the arguments of liberal reformers like Turgot, the committee contended that the opportunity to work was one of the rights of man, a right of property. In addition, abolishing high reception fees would make more capital available for investment, while unleashing competition would reduce the price of consumer goods.[6]

The price of the new *patente* was based upon the rent that artisans, merchants and manufacturers paid for their workplaces. Municipal administrators were charged with enforcing the new law. In order to secure their cooperation, the National Assembly allowed them to put 10 percent of the revenues from this tax in the municipal treasury. Since everyone had to register at the town hall to obtain his license, the municipal officers were still able to police the workforce, a measure that some members of the National Assembly believed was important for preserving urban order. In addition, the new law stipulated that each individual who bought a *patente* had to conform to the regulations that governed his profession.[7] The National Assembly, therefore, opened up industry and trade to new recruitment, but left room for municipal authorities to enforce regulations that protected the public welfare.

Although the official reasons for suppressing the guilds in 1791 closely followed those of Turgot fifteen years earlier, Turgot had been unable to reimburse masters who had purchased masterships or offices in the guilds, an omission which had helped to doom his reform to failure. The National Assembly recognized the problem. One member estimated that reimbursing the offices of wigmakers alone would cost 22 million *livres*, and the rest of the offices 15 or 16 million *livres*. As for royal masterships, La Rouchefoucauld evaluated their worth at 80 million *livres*, a figure that was probably high. The National Assembly promised to reimburse the officeholders, using in part, the resources of the new *patente*. It further declared that it was ready to assume the debts of the guilds, a sizeable proportion of which had been contracted for the service of the king.[8] Creditors of the guilds hence became creditors of the state. The guilds were instructed to submit their accounts to the municipal authorities. After being verified by the district and departmental administrators, the accounts were to be submitted to the commissioner in charge of liquidating the public debt. The property belonging to each guild was to be sold, following the form prescribed for the alienation of the *biens nationaux*. Thus continued the drawn-out process whereby the debts of corps – municipalities, provincial estates, the church, and guilds – were nationalized.[9]

Although Allarde remarked that the state should not wage a "war of parsimony" against its citizens, reimbursing masters posed problems. Only 40 million *livres* were allocated to pay back masterships, which represented, at most, two-thirds of their value. The government paid the masters in paper currency, *assignats*, which were already worth less than the money the masters had used to purchase their offices or masterships. The process of liquidating the debts was still not completed in 1794, and by the end of 1793, 100 *livres* in *assignats* were only worth about 30 *livres* in specie.[10] Some masters, therefore, lost over two-thirds of their investment. In some cases, the guilds were to blame for the long delays. In August 1792, the *procureur syndic* of Lille reproved a dozen guilds for failing to turn in their accounts and preventing their creditors from being reimbursed.[11]

The bourgeois town council in Lille was not enthusiastic about executing the Allarde law. After some citizens in Lille heard of the proposal in the newspapers, the municipal officers issued a statement stressing that the law would not go into effect until 1 April 1791 and that until then all regulations were in force. They also warned citizens that the new law did not open trades to everyone without any restrictions, because each individual had to obtain a *patente*.[12] The attempt to force merchants and artisans to purchase these licenses, however, was unsuccessful. In June 1791, and again in January 1793, the *procureur syndic* of Lille complained that few individuals had complied with the law. In 1793 the Convention abolished this form of taxation.[13]

The Allarde law was not a systematic attack on economic regulation *per se*. It was an attack upon the semi-private forms of regulation and the monopolies wielded by guilds. Had all regulation been at stake, the municipality's regulatory authority, its *pouvoir de police*, would similarly have been diminished, but this was not the case. The law of 21 July 1791 concerning *police municipal* authorized municipal administrations to regulate matters including public health, food supply, weights and measures, and the purity of precious metals. To help them in this work, town councillors were allowed to name *commissaires de police*.[14]

When possible, guilds attempted to use the police powers of the municipal administration to preserve remnants of their old corporate organization. The inspectors from the guilds of butchers, goldsmiths, thread spinners, and wool weavers asked the town council to reinstate them under the new title of *commissaires de police*. In each case, the municipal officers agreed.[15] The inspectors from the butchers' guild, for example, were allowed to enter all the shops and homes where meat was sold in order to check its quality and freshness. Thus, by continuing to vest regulatory powers in town councils, the Revolution perpetuated an important strand of municipal mercantilism even as it dismantled the guilds.

The attempt to force merchants and artisans to follow the old regulations met with the same fate as the effort to have them buy *patentes*. In December 1792 the municipal officers lamented that, in spite of the vigilance of their police commissioners, most individuals blatantly ignored all kinds of regulations. Three months later the town council despairingly observed that ever since the establishment of the *patentes*, merchants who sold food and drink rarely had their scales verified and refused to comply with the old rules, even though these were so necessary for maintaining public trust.[16]

Municipal regulation aside, there are few clues as to whether or how guilds kept their corporate identity alive after 1791. The citizen's right to association provided one possible avenue for maintaining a collective life, but the Le Chapelier law had severely curtailed this option and Lille's municipal government was unsympathetic to such attempts. When the carters petitioned for the right to form an association based upon the statutes of their old guild the town council refused without comment.[17]

There were two cases, however, where sustained protest over the abolition of guilds illuminated the multiple interests at stake. The first case, that of inspectors in the textile guilds, illustrates once more the tenacious bourgeois stake in corporate regulation; the second case, that of the boaters, reveals the complicated fiscal and military issues that could come to bear on a seemingly simple economic reform.

The cloth merchants and thread merchant-manufacturers in Lille, as we observed earlier, were avid supporters of the regulations guaranteeing the quality of their exports. These businessmen favored local regulation but opposed fiscally-motivated interference by the royal government. In 1789, although the Third Estate of the *gouvernance* of Lille called for the preservation of the guilds, it also demanded the suppression of the inspectors of manufacturing in the *bureau de marque*, the quasi-fiscal regulatory agency set up by the central government in 1779.[18] Unsurprisingly, when the National Assembly abolished the guilds in 1791, Lille's business community was not at all pleased. By contrast, in October 1790, a group of master weavers had already requested permission from the municipal officers to deregulate their manufactures. The only way that they could compete with the English, they contended, was if they were able to save on the materials used in making their cloth. The petition, predictably enough, was denied.[19]

At first, the abolition of the guilds in March 1791 did not pose a problem for either the cloth merchants or the thread spinners. Because the Allarde law stated that the old regulations were to remain in effect, the inspectors from the guilds in Lille and Roubaix continued to perform their duties, even though the guilds had ceased legally to exist. Only when a second law was passed seven months later was the system of regulation called into question. On 16 October 1791, the National Assembly suppressed both the Chambers of Commerce in France and the unpopular *bureaux de marque*. The new law set off a heated debate. Lille's merchants argued that the law only entailed the destruction of cloth inspectors attached to the *bureaux de marque*. Others, among them master weavers, claimed that the law suppressed all inspectors, including those working for the guilds.[20]

In arguing their case, the cloth merchants and thread merchant-manufacturers distinguished between two aspects of the guilds: their policy of selective recruitment and their regulatory apparatus. It was true, they admitted, that the guilds were an obstacle to liberty, for one should not deprive a citizen of the right to work in the occupation of his choice. But, as the Allarde law itself stated, regulations controlling quality were another matter. Liberty was not the right to do whatever one wanted, but only to do what did not hurt others. Weavers were still free if their work was inspected; they only lost the opportunity to harm society through deception. If merchants could not guarantee the quality of their wares, their sales would decline and commerce as a whole would suffer. The weavers parried these thrusts by denouncing the merchants as "partisans of the ancien régime," because they refused to buy cloth unless it had been properly certified.

Although the municipal authorities wanted to keep the guilds' inspectors, the *procureur syndic* of the district unequivocally ruled against them. There was no doubt, he declared sternly, that the law included the suppression of all types of inspectors. As he warned the *procureur syndic* of Lille: "It is neither up to you, nor to the municipal corps, nor to the administration to interpret or hinder [the execution of this law.] *It is up to us all to obey.*"[21] And so, reluctantly, they did. Thus, the desire of Lille's merchants to preserve local regulation of textile production ended, to their utter dismay, in complete liberty enforced by the state.

Unlike the cloth and thread merchants, Lille's boaters succeeded in preserving their guilds until 1794. The guilds of boaters were particularly strong in the low-lying region of the Nord, where grain supplies, military convoys, and commercial goods moved up and down the intricate network of rivers and canals. The boaters from seven towns – those of Dunkerque, Bergue, Saint-Omer, Aire, Lille, Condé, and Mons (the last in the Belgian province of Hainaut) – formed a federated authority known as "la navigation de Flandre, Artois, et Cambrésis." Each guild held the right to transport, load and unload cargo along different parts of the canals and rivers.

By virtue of their geographical positions and extensive privileges, two guilds, the *bateliers* of Condé and the *belandriers* of Dunkerque, effectively dominated the waterways. After 1699, the boaters of Condé alone enjoyed the lucrative right to carry coal from Belgian Hainaut, one of the richest coal-producing regions in Europe, into France. The boaters of Dunkerque had been granted the exclusive privilege of unloading all merchandise that came into Dunkerque, the major port of the region, and transporting it into the surrounding towns. For most of the eighteenth century, Dunkerque's boaters had been able to transport goods only as far as the town of Saint-Omer in Artois. In 1771 a canal linking the Lys and Aa rivers was completed, and, for a decade, all boaters were allowed to ship goods from Dunkerque through this canal. But in 1781 Dunkerque's boaters succeeded in persuading the royal government to give them the exclusive right to carry cargo from Dunkerque through the new canal and down the Lys and its tributaries. Lille's boaters, therefore, lost most of their business from Dunkerque.[22]

The vast privileges of Condé's and Dunkerque's boaters drew widespread criticism not only from the other boaters, but from many groups that were forced to pay higher prices for transportation in the region. In 1789 the *cahiers* of the clergy, the nobility, and the Third Estate of Lille all demanded freedom of navigation on Flemish waterways.[23] In 1790 the lesser guilds of boaters, along with merchants and administrators from the region, asked the National Assembly to abolish the privileges of the two dominant guilds. Such a move, the request contended, would logically extend the revolutionary principles that had already abolished the privileges of cities and provinces. But, although they attacked their competitors, the lesser guilds of boaters hoped in the end to achieve a peculiar mixture of liberty and protection: they wanted to abolish the special prerogatives of the boaters of Dunkerque and Condé, but to preserve the guilds of boaters themselves. The boaters' guilds, in fact, were some of the most closed and tightly organized of any in the Nord. In Lille, for example, the boaters of the Deûle river only allowed the sons of masters to enter their ranks.[24]

According to Lille's boaters, liberty did not entail the complete freedom of each person to follow his own particular interest. Such a definition of liberty would dissolve "all political association." Rather, article IV of the Declaration of the Rights of Man and Citizen explicitly stated that liberty only allowed one to do that which did not harm another. The National Assembly did not consider man "in the state of pure nature," but proclaimed rights to "the citizen placed in society...bound by the social pact." Exclusive privileges harmed society, but guilds were social servants. Only experienced boaters from the guilds were able to navigate the waterways without mishap. It was foolish to gamble on newcomers when the question of the province's food supply, for example, was at stake.[25]

The officials in Lille's town council, the district, and the directory of the department all came to the same conclusion. The exclusive privileges of the boaters' guilds were unconstitutional and hence had to go, but the guilds themselves were useful bodies that should be preserved. Experienced pilots were necessary to prevent shipwrecks. The guilds contributed to the upkeep of the canals, and too much liberty might eventually allow several wealthy individuals to seize control of transportation on the river.[26]

The boaters from Dunkerque and Condé dismissed these arguments by pointing out that their exclusive privileges were a reward, even a "salary" (*salaire*), in return for their service to the state. During wartime Dunkerque's boaters helped the royal navy defend the port. They had only received their extensive privileges in 1781 after promising the royal government to double their fleet, from 60 to 120 boats. The guild, caught up in a pattern that by now sounds quite familiar, had been forced to borrow large sums in order to meet the king's demand for ships.[27]

Similarly, the boaters in the guild of Condé played a role in war and high finance. They transported troops during campaigns and repaired broken bridges and locks. In addition, their privileges formed part of an international agreement sanctioned in 1699 by both the French monarch and the Habsburg emperor. By this pact, the boaters in Condé and their Belgian counterparts in Mons had been given the right to ship coal from the Belgian mines in Hainaut, through a small section of France via Condé, and then back into the Austrian Netherlands. The Habsburgs paid the French government approximately 400,000 *livres* a year for this right of transit.[28] Abolishing the privileges of the boaters of Condé, therefore, would involve international negotiations and might disrupt a stable source of income for the French government.

Several *mémoires* recognized the validity of these financial claims. If the privileges of Dunkerque's boaters were suppressed, they were admittedly entitled to some sort of indemnity. Nonetheless, regional administrators argued that financial problems such as these should not hinder the revocation of exclusive prerogatives. Lille and other areas, not just the city of Dunkerque, had contributed large sums to the development of new canals. According to Lille's *procureur syndic*, it was completely unjust that "citizens who [partook] equally in the burden of social obligations and public expenses [did] not participate equally in the advantages of the pact that unites them." The monarchy, he lamented, had let fiscal considerations destroy a just balance among the guilds. "Nature and industry have done everything for this fortunate region; the fiscal spirit has done everything against it." But the National Assembly should not allow the dead hand of royal finances to thwart the progress of liberty and equality. If Dunkerque's boaters were justified in demanding the indemnity, then it was "up to the Nation to take upon itself the faults of the [old] government."[29]

A few voices registered their dissent to the preservation of the boaters' guilds. One anonymous individual argued that it was "intolerable under a free constitution" that only the sons of masters were able to become boaters in the guilds, because the principle of birth was "unconstitutional." Another opinion noted that the issue of safety on the waterways was irrelevant, because it was easy to obtain insurance in Amsterdam at low rates, and the trip from Lille to Dunkerque hardly involved high risks.[30] But these sentiments were those of a minority.

The boaters were not included in the general suppression of the guilds. In the spring of 1791, deputies from the guilds of boaters of Lille and Aire successfully presented their case to the National Assembly in Paris. On 4 June 1791 the National Assembly abolished the exclusive privileges of the boaters in Dunkerque and Condé, but preserved the navigational guilds.[31] Until 1794 the boaters in Lille continued to accept only sons of masters into their guild, to hold masses commemorating the death of deceased masters, and to celebrate the feast day of their patron saint. In 1794 these guilds were finally suppressed. The masters were assessed individually for the debts that the "*ci-devant*" guilds had contracted since 1791.[32] Legally, at least, transport by water in the Nord was finally free.

No longer enjoying privileges in law, the guilds of boaters proved difficult to uproot in fact. As late as July 1798 the department of the Nord issued an *arrêt* suppressing corporations of boaters, and in particular the *Chambre d'Assurance de Nord-Libre*, a new version of the guild of boaters of Condé. A year later there were complaints that the boaters from Nord-Libre and their collaborators in Mons were flagrantly violating freedom of navigation on the Scheldt river and its tributaries. In some places, the old *compagnons bateliers* charged excessive fees to pull boats through the locks and fought off new workers with sticks and guns. The government was forced finally to have troops patrol the waterways.[33]

The boaters illustrate an extreme case, but not the only case, of the tenaciousness with which corps tried to hold onto their legally-suppressed privileges. After the radical revolution had passed and Napoleon institutionalized a new regime, other guilds and professional groups tried to revive prerogatives from the old regime. The epilogue addresses the search to recreate hierarchy and professional perquisites within an egalitarian, nationalized public sphere.

9   The corporate heritage and the well-ordered state

For over five hundred years, the city of Lille had held an annual procession dedicated to its divine protectress, Notre Dame de la Treille. In the procession, the city's corporate groups – the guilds with their emblems and images of patron saints, the religious confraternities with their relics, the clergy, the chapter of Saint-Pierre, the municipal magistrates, and the *bailliage* and *gouvernance* courts – wound their way through the city. Valets dressed as fools and madmen roamed among the guildmasters, snapping harmless horsehair whips to keep them in their assigned ranks. Seated on a float in the middle of the procession was a young girl dressed in white, representing the Virgin. For the townspeople, the procession was a time to eat, drink and make merry, and to drink again, much to the dismay of the clergy and delight of the local tax collectors. For many Lillois, the symbol of the procession could have been the Bacchus, who marched with the guild of tavernkeepers and carried a barrel of wine that was consumed and replenished with abandon. In 1767 the clergy insisted that the most scandalous abuses in the procession be suppressed in order to make the procession a purer, holier, and simpler ceremony, closer to its "primitive institution." The procession's route was shortened, the valets and their foolery suppressed, and the drinking curtailed. These reforms accomplished, the tax collectors began to complain. To keep up receipts from the sale of beer and liquor during the festivities, the municipal magistrates began to sponsor games for the people after the procession. Thus the day of the city's procession came to be differentiated more clearly between the sacred and profane, between a more sober and religious procession in the morning and popular amusements, such as shooting, jousting, or archery matches, with plenty to drink, in the afternoon.[1]

The municipal procession recreated each year a symbolic microcosm of the traditional urban order. Corporate bodies, the constitutive elements of society, were arranged in terms of ascending degrees of power within the city. Power radiated up from the guilds, the lowest ranking members, to the municipal magistrates, the corps that had for centuries represented and ruled the urban inhabitants. The municipal magistrates occupied the place of honor directly behind the Virgin, a sign of the interdependence of municipal and divine authority.[2] The other judicial corps followed this sacred center. The hierarchy of power and status represented in this procession appeared static, because the procession celebrated the ideal principles of Lille's medieval constitution. After the city's annexation to France, it does not appear that the judicial corps created by Louis XIV were integrated into the annual pageant. Custom and "immemorial usage" were powerful factors in assigning rank.[3]

With the coming of the Revolution, Lille's annual procession did not end. The old order of rank continued unchanged, though a number of substitutions soon became necessary. In the town procession on Sunday, 6 June 1790, the newly elected bourgeois town councillors marched in place of the former corps of municipal magistrates. That year, not only were newly constituted authorities integrated into traditional forms, but the procession was followed by a very new kind of celebration, the fête of the confederation of the National Guard from the Departments of the Nord, Pas-de-Calais, and Somme.[4] The procession honoring Lille's hierarchical and localistic heritage, therefore, was juxtaposed with a festival that celebrated equality and national unity. "Let the barriers be lowered before this union so sweet," declared Lille's mayor, Louis Vanhoenacker, during his speech that afternoon. "Bizarre usages, oppressive customs disappear: this is a people composed of brothers." The rhetoric and symbols of the revolutionary festival broke with the "bizarre usages" of the past, but the town's annual procession, symbol of the city's corporate identity, was not yet considered such a practice.

In the early stage of the Revolution, then, Lille's citizens did not see corporate institutions *per se* as contrary to national unity. It was only the abuses of those bodies that had to be reformed. Lille's Catholic heritage, moreover, helped to provide legitimacy to a vision of society based upon national brotherhood. In the mayor's speech at the fête of the federation, civic fraternity was hardly distinguishable from the age-old ideal of Christian brotherhood: "These citizens are all His children. One oath binds them; the same faith unites them; the same prayers will reunite them."

In June 1791 the townspeople again held their traditional procession, albeit in a somewhat truncated form. To lend more pomp and prestige to the event, they decided to invite the administrators of the district and judges in the Tribunal of Commerce and the district court to march in the procession. The guilds and religious communities were no longer able to march *en corps*, but the new constitutional clergy helped to fill the gap by carrying the relic shrines of the saints in the same order as before. There was, apparently, one other innovation. The Blessed Sacrament, usually not included in this procession, was carried immediately after the statue of the Virgin. Its presence may have indicated that the procession was becoming more religious.[5] The Popular Society spoke approvingly of the changes: "Today was the solemn procession in honor of the Patroness. The ceremony, formerly gothic, absurd, and most ridiculous, has been, through the care of our municipal officers, transformed into a religious and patriotic ceremony."[6] In 1791, therefore, it was still possible to infuse old corporate forms with national and patriotic sentiment.

In 1793 the annual town procession was suppressed. Egalitarian rhetoric now came to be interpreted with unprecedented literal-mindedness. Officials used processions to eradicate the memory of old corporate hierarchies and to inculcate a utopian vision of society based upon equality and popular sovereignty. To obliterate traditional notions of rank, the processions were ordered around natural, biological categories, such as age and gender.[7] To reinforce the idea that officials were of the people, and not above them, these men often marched among "the mass of people." In the "fête of the death of the last of the tyrants," for example, "all the constituted corps," which were not listed, marched "pêle-mêle" with persons of both sexes, who were ranked by age. In another case, when the Popular Society planned a fête for a Décadi, they expressly asked that "the constituted authorities who are invited to attend this ceremony not come en corps and that all citizens be mixed together without distinction."[8] Yet, lurking beneath this egalitarian vision at the height of the Revolution, one catches, now and then, faint glimpses of the old regime. To celebrate the acceptance of the *Montagnard* constitution of August 1793 the guild of boaters sponsored a jousting march.[9]

With the return of a more moderate regime under Napoleon, vestiges of the old regime began to reappear. Soon after the concordat with the pope ended the bitter schism between the church and state, the procession of Lille in honor of Notre Dame de la Treille was restored. The town's procession was a mere shadow of its former self. The newspaper announcement on 8 June 1806 simply stated that "the clergy from the different parishes of this city will assemble in the parish church of St. Maurice to take part in the procession that will leave precisely at ten o'clock."[10] Perhaps citizens voluntarily joined the clergy, but there is no indication that any civil or military authorities officially participated. The procession thus appears to have been a purely religious ceremony followed by elaborate popular amusements in the afternoon, completing the trend that was already evident in the late eighteenth century. The procession of Lille, as the newspaper commented, had become "a reason for family and friends to get together."[11]

The revival of the annual procession helps to illustrate the significance of the Revolution for Lille. In the old regime, the procession had represented the city's independent corporate identity, and the powerful corps of municipal magistrates had marched in a place of honor. Under Napoleon, the mayor and constituted authorities did not even appear. Lille's procession had ceased to portray the city's autonomy, its honored position in the political space of the old regime. The procession, composed of local and religious elements, hardly found a place in the newly nationalized and secularized public sphere.[12]

One of the most important consequences of the French Revolution was its redefinition of public and private spheres, of the "state" and "civil society." The authority of the state was made more fully public through the theoretical transfer of sovereignty to the people, the nationalization of law and civic membership, and the conscious creation of an impersonal bureaucracy.[13] The personal power of kings and a host of localistic rights and hierarchical privileges no longer enjoyed legal standing in the public arena. Complementing the state's public authority was a sphere of civil rights and freedoms guaranteeing the autonomy of individuals in civil society. Although these rights were actually a product of public legislation, the conditions surrounding work, religious beliefs, and familial status came to be considered a private affair mediated by natural rights and forces, such as those of the market, conscience, and property.[14]

Because interests and practices associated with intermediate bodies no longer enjoyed legal standing, groups wishing to revive such practices had to find new institutional bases and claims to legitimacy. Their search was necessarily governed by the juridical paths laid down by the Revolution. In a political order composed of individual citizens and national authority, intermediate groups might appeal either to the associational right of citizens or to their utility to the state in order to regain a "corporate" niche within an egalitarian nation.

One example of the process is evident in the question of social rank, which continued to preoccupy officials in Napoleonic France. The prefect of the Nord despaired over how hard it was to place the constituted authorities in parades in such a way as to avoid protests over *préséance*.[15] *Préséance*, according to the eighteenth-century jurist Guyot, was defined as "the right to place oneself in an order or rank more honorable than another."[16] Fights over precedence, a hallmark of the old regime, were hardly uncommon in the Nord during Napoleon's reign. The corps of solicitors in the *Tribunal d'Appel* in Douai protested that they had been poorly placed in a cortege. The justices of the peace in Bergue refused to attend a procession in protest against the order of march. The members of the *Cour Prévôtale des Douanes* in Valenciennes fretted that they could not attend ceremonies "*en corps*" because their rank had not been fixed, while the general staff of the army in Lille complained that during the procession of St. Napoléon, several corps that should have followed them, had slipped ahead.[17]

What justified precedence in the Napoleonic era? In 1800, the Minister of Interior explained to the prefect that the key could be found in a law from January 1790: "the government presides over national ceremonies. It directs and rules them; it is thus its immediate agents that must preside over them everywhere."[18] Over the next years, the government set official rules to govern precedence. The law of 18 Germinal X (29 March 1802), regulating services of worship, stipulated that all parish churches reserve a distinguished place for Catholic individuals holding positions of civil and military authority. The law of 24 Messidor XII (13 July 1804) established fixed ranks for public ceremonies.[19] Further decisions refined these laws. One problem, for example, was whether the mayor, his *adjoints*, and the councillors in the municipal administration should all occupy distinguished places in church. The Minister of Ecclesiastical Affairs ruled that the law of 18 Germinal did not apply to "anyone invested with functions but only to whomever is invested with authority."[20] The right to public precedence had become a bureaucratic attribute, tightly bound to the exercise of public authority.

In some respects, the Napoleonic method of ranking groups in relationship to public authority represented a continuation of a general principle developed under absolutism. The jurist Guyot had argued that the right to precedence emanated above all from the king as sovereign lawgiver and as the embodiment of the public sphere. Even though custom, birth, or regional peculiarities might create competing claims to these honors, in the last resort "only the will of the prince can establish precedence." According to this principle, corporate groups or persons that partook of the king's sovereignty were elevated above others in society. This ideal explained why nobles in the Parlements had precedence over *gentilshommes* with far longer lineages. As Guyot argued, "the reason that one gives for this superiority is that the first [the magistrates], being ennobled by their charges are counted equal to *gentilshommes* and that they have, in addition, the honor of being officers of the king, of being invested with public power and of filling a function that simple *gentilshommes* do not." Yet, as Guyot himself also admitted, the principle of lineage continued to intrude upon the question of precedence. Even though men of illustrious old houses who possessed great names could not by right demand precedence in public ceremonies, "an enlightened reason hastens to grant it to them."[21]

In the Napoleonic period, public power continued to confer status in ceremonies of state, but the principles of birth and purchase, implicit in the practice of hereditary aristocracy and venality of office, no longer provided an easily-accessible supplementary route. In theory, precedence after the Revolution was not to be transferred to an individual in his role as a private citizen. The Napoleonic law of 1804 fixing ranks in public ceremonies stipulated that "the ranks and honors granted to a corps would in no case belong individually to the members that composed it."[22] In bureaucratic fashion, the function or office, not the person, was to be honored. Napoleon's eventual creation of a hereditary nobility obfuscated a tidy correlation between rank and civil merit. Nonetheless, the Napoleonic conception of hierarchy drastically reduced the scope of custom and birth as constitutive elements of the public sphere and its bureaucratic ranks.

The structure of municipal power under Napoleon similarly demonstrated the consolidation of bureaucratic authority. After the Revolution, authority moved down in a direct line from the head of state and his ministers to their appointees: the prefects in the departments, the subprefects in the *arrondissements*, and the mayors in the communes.[23] Disseminated uniformly from the center, the state's authority had to compete far less with alternative sources of public power, like that of the powerful provincial estates in the old regime. Under Napoleon, the prefect alone was entrusted with regional administration. The Napoleonic government also chose members of Lille's town council, a practice that was perhaps less striking than in other areas of France, because Lille had never had a tradition of municipal elections. Several *adjoints* assisted each mayor. These men, however, did not deliberate on important questions with the mayor since, by the principles of Napoleonic rule, "administration is the act of one alone."[24]

Individuals filling the positions of mayor and subdelegate were drawn from a larger social pool than under the old regime, but there were striking continuities. The first subprefect in Lille was Albert Scrive, former subdelegate of the intendant of Lille.[25] The mayoralty became progressively less bourgeois. In 1800 Nicolas Gentil-Muiron, a wealthy *négociant* who had served as a municipal officer from 1791–1792 and 1797–1799, was named mayor of Lille. In 1803 he was replaced by Louis Marie Joseph, Comte de Brigode, the son of a former member of the municipal magistracy who had purchased an ennobling office of *secrétaire du roi*. Under the Restoration, Jean Baptiste Joseph, Comte de Muyssart, one of the grands *baillis* of the detested provincial estates of Walloon Flanders, filled the office.[26]

At the local level, electoral colleges of *notables* nominated members for councils sitting at the level of the municipality, the *arrondissement*, and the department. Napoleon made the final selection. The franchise was restricted to the wealthy and measured through the payment of taxes.[27] The three levels of local councils were supposed to assist the prefect, the subprefect, and the mayor by reviewing local budgets and assessing taxes. In fact, they exercised little real power: each council was authorized to meet for no more than two weeks of the year.[28]

Napoleon's system of councils and electoral colleges of *notables* gave institutional expression to the post-revolutionary elite. This elite, defined by wealth, education and property, grouped together those who before the Revolution had been divided by legal privileges and titles. In Lille, many members of old noble families found the new definition of social status distasteful. According to the subprefect Scrive, a number of former nobles refused to attend public ceremonies or go to the theater because special places designating their rank no longer existed. Former nobles, Scrive reported in 1802, still formed the wealthiest group of citizens in Lille, although many merchants also possessed substantial fortunes.[29] Yet, these wealthy ex-nobles spent little on public display or entertainment. The reason, the subprefect believed, was that before the Revolution the nobles had to spend large amounts in order to maintain the pomp and splendor associated with their noble rank. Because after the Revolution they had no special titles, it was not worthwhile to put on a show. Anyone who was rich could spend money lavishly to make a public impression. The ex-nobles preferred to retire from the public eye, rather than to compete with ambitious *parvenus*. Scrive assured his superiors that the rich ex-nobles were not at all dangerous to the government. The government's "true friends," however, were to be found among the upwardly mobile members of the *classe aisée*.[30]

A comparison of the composition of the corps of municipal magistrates in the old regime with the municipal council under Napoleon shows that the social basis of recruitment into government was widened. The corps of municipal magistrates had been dominated by nobles and non-noble *rentiers*; merchants and manufacturers had formed only one-quarter to one-third of the corps. By contrast during Napoleon's rule merchants and manufacturers formed the largest group of the municipal council. In 1810 the social composition of the municipal council was as follows:[31]

merchants and manufacturers	18	60%
propriétaires and *rentiers*	5	17%
legal professions	4	13%
pharmacist/*officier de santé*	2	7%
military officer	1	3%
	30	100%

In Lille, Napoleon had consolidated a bourgeois municipal administration socially, but a bureaucratic one politically, because the new bourgeois municipal councillors exercised little actual power.

The increased transfer of power into the hands of the central government might have been of less consequence if the government spoke for bourgeois interests, particularly for their economic concerns. Indeed, it has sometimes been argued that after the Revolution officials of the state and property owners became co-defenders of a new economic regime based upon laissez-faire principles. In the face of this harshly individualistic, bourgeois climate, artisans and workers alone clung to traditional notions of regulation and corporate solidarity to protect their livelihood.[32] But did Lille's bourgeoisie believe that they would best be served by competitive economic liberalism? Did their expressed interests coincide with programs by the state and its desire for highly centralized authority? Several examples may illuminate this issue more fully.

Mutual aid societies

In tracing the survival of corporate forms of organization, some historians have looked at the formation of mutual aid societies and the continuation of secret journeymen's associations known as *compagnonnages*.[33] Lille was never included in the network of *compagnonnages* so strong in Paris and southern France, but in the eighteenth century, the city did boast one of the largest numbers of mutual aid societies per capita of any city in France.[34] Although evidence on the foundation of mutual aid societies is sparse, it is possible to suggest some relationships between these associations and the guilds of the eighteenth century.

In the eighteenth century, Lille's guilds did not serve as mutual aid societies; that is, they did not provide benefits to widows or assistance to masters in times of hardship or sickness. Nor were there separate religious confraternities attached to each guild offering these services. The guilds themselves took care of both the religious and professional concerns of their members. Corporate funds were used both to reimburse lawyers for their services and to pay priests for saying masses at a variety of ceremonies. Although some guilds engaged in charitable relief, it was not of a form classified as mutual aid. On days dedicated to the Virgin, for example, the guild of apothecaries-grocers distributed money to the poor and needy in the city, but this act of charity was directed at individuals outside the guild, not masters within it.[35]

In discussing the problems of economic aid and the guilds, Vanhaeck, historian of Lille's guild of wool weavers, stressed that much private charitable relief was administered by foundations, and hence did not show up in the regular accounts of the guilds.[36] A foundation was money invested in a *rente*, usually a municipal bond, whose yearly interest was used to provide a hospital bed for a patient, to distribute food to the indigent, to train an orphan in a skilled trade, or to help the poor in similar ways. Some foundations were expressly created to offer aid to needy masters in a particular guild.[37] The principle underlying assistance through foundations, however, was different from that of mutual assistance. Foundations were based upon paternalistic social relations in which the "haves," for whatever reason, left money to the "have-nots." The idea of mutual aid, by contrast, was democratic. All members in the organization contributed equally to the insurance fund, and all members had access to the funds if they fell ill. A member was dependent on his peers, rather than on public charity. In 1737, one reason the workers in the wool industry wanted to form a confraternity for mutual assistance was that "those who fall into poverty and sickness will no longer have to be dependent upon public assistance so often...we will be in a position to provide for them and do them justice."[38] Similarly, in 1783 the municipal magistrates praised these associations, not only because they reduced the burden on the municipal poor rolls, but also because they put their members "beyond the necessity, always humiliating, of having recourse to public alms."[39]

Two letters, the first by Lille's municipal magistrates in 1783, the second by the mayor of Lille in 1804, indicate that mutual benefit societies were proliferating before the Revolution and tended largely to be creations of the eighteenth century.[40] In 1783 the municipal magistrates assured the central government that *compagnonnages*, which were causing unrest elsewhere in France, were unknown in Lille:

...there are, in truth, as in all the cities of Flanders, drinking clubs [*estaminets*] which are open to no other individuals than those who pay the dues, but where nothing happens that is contrary to good order. We also have *associations* whose object is to provide relief to the individuals who compose it in case of sickness, based on a modest contribution to which each of them submits himself each week...These *associations*, finally, if one can call as such the obligation contracted by a number of citizens to aid each other mutually in case of sickness...have no relation to each other or to neighboring towns and do not present, along with the *estaminets*,...any cause for concern with respect to the public order, for which we always have our eyes open.

According to the second letter, by the Napoleonic mayor of Lille, a large number of workers had belonged to mutual aid societies before the Revolution: "These sorts of societies were found in fairly large numbers at the time of the Revolution; they had even acquired a certain stability [*ancienneté*]. There were few workers who were not in one of these societies and sometimes they were in several." The mayor's emphasis on the durability (*ancienneté*) of the societies by 1789 suggests the relative novelty of the organizations, most of which were probably founded during the eighteenth century. Because workers might belong to more than one society, it is likely that most societies in the eighteenth century spanned a number of trades and occupations, a hypothesis supported by other sources.[41] All in all, it appears that mutual aid societies had sprung up before the Revolution as a new form of associational life independent of the guilds. Both before and after the Revolution, Lille's officials used the words *société, association*, and *citoyen* – and not *corps, jurandes, corporation* or *confrérie* – when they discussed these organizations.

In June 1791, three months after the abolition of the guilds, the Le Chapelier law abolished the right of all persons within the same profession to form associations. The new law was, first of all, a response to the threat of strikes launched by various groups of workers.[42] But the policy also reflected a new view of the relationship of the state to society, a position based upon the twin principles of individualism and the primacy of the state. "There are no longer any corporations in the state," the law declared, "there is only the particular interest of each individual and the general interest." For Le Chapelier, even mutual aid societies that assisted the sick detracted from the all-pervasive role of the state: "These *caisses* for assistance seemed useful, but let's not be mistaken on this assertion; it is up to the nation... to furnish work to those who are in need of it."[43] The law expressed the revolutionaries' strong suspicion of all intermediate groups as selfish and particularistic bodies, and a deep faith in the state as the only depository of the general interest.

In Lille, neither philosophical discussions nor the need to repress workers had much to do with the demise of the mutual aid societies. According to the mayor of Lille, the funds of these organizations were lost in the rampant inflation that followed the issuing of the *assignats*.[44] In 1804, mutual aid societies in Lille began to re-establish themselves when, as the mayor saw it, "a more tranquil order of things allowed people to go back to their old habits." The earliest record of a mutual aid society founded after the Revolution was that of the Société de St. Dominique, established in September 1797. In March 1799, the Cercle des Amis des Lois was created, apparently by middle-class men, in order to help the sick.[45] Officials in both the central and municipal governments under Napoleon believed that mutual aid societies were beneficial and should be encouraged. In 1804 Lille's mayor stated that there were seven or eight such societies. Although he willingly granted permission to found new societies, the mayor tried to prevent the groups from turning into what he called immoral "coteries de cabaret." The maximum number of members in each society was about 110, and workers were admitted until they reached the age of forty-five or fifty. In general, only sick benefits, and not old-age pensions, were given. The society of St. Dominique included members from different crafts, a practice that the government generally favored. The diversity of membership inhibited these organizations from being used as incipient unions.[46]

Although he encouraged the creation of legitimate mutual aid societies, the mayor was careful to enforce the law of 22 Germinal XI that prohibited workers from forming coalitions to raise salaries.[47] Upon hearing that the tailors had simultaneously abandoned their workplaces to put pressure on their masters, for example, the mayor ordered the police commissioner to track down the instigators and "to take the most energetic measures to prevent or break up any plans for coalitions on the part of the workers."[48]

Local officials, however, did not necessarily side with employers in all cases. In 1806, for example, the hat manufacturer Antoine Chatelain complained to the mayor that the workers in the hat industry were meeting each Sunday in a *cabaret* and deliberating about ways to force the masters to pay them higher salaries. The mayor, sympathetic to Chatelain's case, called for an immediate investigation because "it was very important not to tolerate an abuse against ... the law of 22 Germinal." After investigating, however, the police commissioner reported that the law did not apply. Chatelain had cut his workers' wages, which were already lower than those that other employers paid. The workers had simply met and decided not to work for him. As for the funds collected, the workers were only preparing to form a society "like those in many trades" where the workers contributed money each month to help those who fell or sick or were unable to find work.[49]

The re-establishment of mutual aid societies in Napoleonic Lille continued a trend begun in the old regime. The societies were not clandestine re-creations of the guilds, because the two forms of organization had already co-existed before the Revolution. The Revolution did not create the open and voluntaristic nature of mutual benefit societies; in Lille these characteristics had already begun to develop before the political upheaval began. Mutual aid societies thus seem to be part of a wider trend toward associational sociability before the Revolution, a trend that encompassed the masonic lodges and academies of the elite and encouraged democratic habits among upper and lower classes before a formal transfer of sovereignty occurred in 1789.[50]

Textile manufacturing

The Revolution dealt a serious blow to Lille's traditional textile manufactures. The woolen industry was decimated during the bombardment of the city of the Austrian Habsburgs in 1792 and never recovered. Napoleon's annexation of Belgium harmed the linen thread industry because finished Belgian thread was no longer banned from entering France. The technology of linen thread spinning remained virtually unchanged and was mechanized only in the mid-nineteenth century.[51]

With their industry in shambles, the thread spinners believed that regulation was the key to revival. In 1797 they asked the Directory to restore the regulations of their old guild. At this time the Minister of Interior seemed amenable to reviving the regulations of 1733 and 1744.[52] Officials were concerned, however, that surveillance over this industry might be too much work for the present police commissioners in Lille. The thread spinners seized on this statement to try to convince the government to recreate the *égards*, or inspectors, of their old guild.[53]

The thread manufacturers were aware that putting the old system back into operation would require certain modifications. First, they realized that they could not actually form a corporation, because, according to the constitution, corporations had been abolished. But, the thread manufacturers observed, the Allarde law abolishing the guilds had also left the regulations in force. Thus, it was constitutionally possible to revive the old regulations without recreating the guild itself. Second, the earlier practice of house visits by inspectors had become illegal. Since this type of control was absolutely necessary to prevent fraud, the thread manufacturers asked that the government create commissioners like those in the national customs bureau, who had special powers to search houses and workshops. The final problem was the fines. In the old system, the third infraction of the rules had entailed the suspension of all trade and manufacturing. Since liberty of commerce now prohibited this, the manufacturers wanted to make their fines so stiff that a third infraction would not occur. With these modifications, the *égard* of the old guild would re-emerge as a *fonctionnaire public* legally endowed with the powers necessary to regulate the industry. Neither the Directory nor the Napoleonic government, however, approved this proposal.[54]

Because the central government was unwilling to hear their pleas, the thread merchant-manufacturers decided to take matters into their own hands. In 1809 they formed an association, a voluntary re-creation of their old guild, to which at least seven-eighths of the manufacturers belonged. All members paid dues and pledged to observe the eighteenth-century regulations. Five commissioners were elected to audit the accounts and receive suggestions for the development of the industry at annual meetings. Two of the commissioners, Dominique Bigo and Flament-Plancq, had been *doyens* of the guild of thread spinners in 1788 and 1790, respectively. Two "visitors" were appointed with the right to enter all places of manufacture and impose fines of 200 francs for infractions of the rules the first time, 400 the second time, and so on with each additional violation. The association was to exist for five years, after which an assembly would vote whether to extend it for another five.[55] Because de Brigode, mayor of Lille in 1809, was convinced that regulation was necessary for the public welfare, he wholeheartedly approved of the new pact and wanted to see its conditions "executed with an exactitude equal to the wisdom that presided when it was drawn up."[56]

The cloth manufacturers of Lille and Roubaix expressed a similar desire for regulation. During Napoleon's reign, Lille's Chamber of Commerce and Roubaix's *Chambre Consultative des Arts et Métiers* asked the government numerous times to place controls on the size and quality of cloth, especially the new cotton textiles that were being produced.[57] Their demands, like those of the thread spinners, were rebuffed. After an audience with the Minister of the Interior in Paris in 1806, a representative from the *Chambre Consultative* told his colleagues, "these *messieurs* would not hide from me that the system of the government, and theirs, is based on completely liberal ideas and the individual liberty of manufacturers will never be subjected to regulations."[58] Certainly Jean Antoine Chaptal, Minister of the Interior from 1800 to 1804, expressed uncompromisingly liberal sentiments. According to Chaptal, "regulations over manufacturing had held our industry captive for more than a century. It remained stationary, while that of our neighbors, released from all fetters, marched with great strides toward perfection." For Chaptal, market forces were the best arbiters of standards. Regulations only stifled competition, prevented innovation, and sheltered unproductive manufacturers.[59]

Lille's prefects disagreed with this assessment. Like the intendants of the old regime, these agents of the central government believed that regulation guaranteed high standards of quality necessary for attracting and keeping a large clientele. As the Prefect Dieudonné wrote in 1805, "The wisdom of regulations [before the Revolution] had inspired the greatest confidence in French commerce. The cloth from Lille, Tourcoing, and Roubaix was used everywhere."[60] Regulation prevented manufacturers from deceiving the public and encouraged trust upon which commerce was built. "With regulation, a newly invented cloth would acquire a new degree of perfection each day. Confidence would be reborn; the manufacturers and workshops of these cities would regain their old splendor." The French needed regulation to compete on the international market: "We can surpass [the English]...we only lack good regulation."

The cloth manufacturers in Roubaix and Lille remained frustrated in their quest to have the central government restore regulation. Their dissatisfaction with the liberal economic policies of the Napoleonic Empire was forcefully expressed in a petition to the Minister of Interior under the Restoration in 1816:

[we have been trying] for a long time to obtain regulations that would prevent cupidity and bad faith from procuring illicit gains by deceiving the confidence of the public ... all these petitions have remained without effect under the government that has just, so happily, disappeared forever. The banal response to these reclamations was that the liberty given to the French was inviolable, that this liberty was the surest way ... to make our manufacturers flourish ... [Dishonest manufacturers] offer, in appearance, the same merchandise at a lower price than the inventor and also obtain the markets that he closes to the other. Such abuse, *monseigneur*, without a doubt has nothing in common with the liberty that commerce needs to enjoy. This abuse only resembles the liberty of a pirate who takes unfair advantage of his resources to strip a man of his rights.[61]

But the government during the Restoration did not appear any more willing than the Napoleonic one to revive regulations.

The cloth manufacturers of Roubaix and Lille may have expressed the same distrust of liberty as other French manufacturers who wanted their industries regulated. By 1801, fourteen departments had requested the Consulate to create inspectors to patrol their manufactures: among them were the silk merchants in Lyon who wished to have the regulations of the silk guild there restored.[62] Thus, although after the Revolution, the central government usually embraced laissez-faire policies in manufacturing, many merchants and manufacturers preferred the familiar path of regulation and protection.

Commercial protection and public auctions

The re-regulation of public auctions illustrates again the persistent desire of both local officials and merchants to limit commercial competition. In 1689, as we saw earlier, Lille's municipal magistrates set up a public auction. To try to prevent the sale of stolen goods, the municipal magistrates commissioned officials to record the items being sold. One group of judicial officers, the bailiffs (*huissiers*) working for the *prevôté* court, were given the sole right to auction off the goods. The municipal magistrates personally received part of the fees collected from the sale of merchandise; the rest went into the city's coffers. The municipal magistrates had been careful not to let these sales undermine the privileges of the city's guilds. In 1742, at the request of the guild of dry-goods merchants, they proscribed the auctioning off of any new merchandise.[63]

Because public auctions generated substantial revenues, it is not surprising that the monarchy eventually decided to tap them. In 1696, Louis XIV created venal offices of auctioneers, *jurés priseurs des biens meubles*, which held the exclusive right to appraise and auction goods and collect a small fee for their efforts. In 1771, all of the old offices were suppressed, and new ones created. Both times, the magistrates purchased the offices. The cost for the first set of offices, including a number of *offices de police*, was 160,000 *livres*, and for the second, 250,000 *livres*.[64] Before the Revolution, therefore, the auctions had become enmeshed in the web of corporate privileges, fees, and regulations that structured public life in the old regime.

In July 1791 the National Assembly abolished the offices of auctioneers and granted notaries, bailiffs, and clerks (*greffiers*) the right to auction goods. Because the municipality had already bought up these offices, the town council paid no attention to the suppression and continued public auctions unchanged. Gradually, however, the regulations were challenged. When the judicial system was restructured, bailiffs from the former *gouvernance* and *bailliage* received the right to work at the auctions.[65] A number of other bailiffs simply went off on their own and set up auctions free from municipal registration and fees. The municipal officers ordered them to stop their auctions at once. According to the town council, even though the law suppressing the guilds had removed all privileges in the professions, individuals still had to conform to police regulations.[66] Not so easily deterred, the bailiffs appealed the decision to the departmental authorities. They argued that the fees collected at the auctions were really *octrois*, which the National Assembly had abolished, and that the municipal officers were overstepping the constitutional bounds of their authority by trying to regulate the public sales. The department ruled in favor of the bailiffs.[67] In 1793 the town council suppressed the official auction entirely. Bailiffs and notaries were permitted to hold auctions, as long as they provided the municipal officials with a complete catalogue of their sale items.[68]

Lille's merchants were none too pleased at the new arrangements. In 1798 a large group of merchants asked the municipal officers to protect them from competition by prohibiting, once more, the sale of new merchandise at all auctions. The municipal officers refused to consider the request. The constitution of the year III, they informed the merchants, had "consecrated as property" the right of citizens to enjoy the fruit of their labor. According to the constitution, "there is neither privilege, nor mastership, nor guild, nor limitation to the liberty of commerce or to the exercise of industry and occupation of any type. This would be to limit liberty of commerce ... and consequently to violate the constitution."[69] The pure devotion to liberty expressed by the town council of 1798, however, did not prevail for long. During the Napoleonic regime, the prefect and mayor were quite willing to limit commercial competition.

In a letter to the prefect in 1803, the mayor de Brigode expressed alarm that public auctions might soon put local shopkeepers out of business.[70] To check this threat, he proposed reviving regulations from the old regime. The mayor observed that it would undoubtedly be preferable to make a new law rather than to resurrect an old one, but such a procedure might be too time-consuming and beyond the legal powers of the mayor. He sent copies of the eighteenth-century municipal ordinances to the prefect and asked for his advice.

Pressure for restricting sales at public auctions was also mounting from the wholesalers in the city. When Napoleon passed through Lille in July 1803, the Chamber of Commerce told him that "honest merchants were not able to sustain the competition" from these sales. Not only were goods sold in wholesale quantities at auctions; wholesalers sometimes sold merchandise to shopkeepers on credit. If an unscrupulous retailer went bankrupt, he could auction off all his merchandise, take the money, and leave his creditors without a cent.[71]

The prefect was sympathetic to the pleas of the mayor and the merchants. "The prefect thinks like you, citizen mayor," wrote the subprefect, "that the abuses existing in the public auctions call for the attention of the police." But, he continued, it was somewhat "inconvenient" to have the texts of the old municipal ordinances reprinted, and "to recall the denominations, the forms, and the dispositions of authorities that no longer exist." Still, the subprefect did not think that this problem was really serious. The law of 22 July 1791 concerning municipal police allowed municipal governments "to borrow from the old regulations all that was in harmony with the principles and spirit of our new legislation." He suggested that the mayor submit an *arrêté* to the prefect that included pertinent sections of all the old regulations, but followed the format of the current municipal *arrêtés*.[72]

The mayor followed the subprefect's instructions precisely. His *arrêté* of 30 March 1804 first cited the regulations relative to the maintenance of public order.[73] Next followed a rationale for the new *arrêté* which was suffused with the principles of the old regime:

Considering that the constant solicitude of the municipal magistrates [before the Revolution] for preserving retail commerce ... shows how important it is for the maintenance of public order and the exercise of distributive justice to re-establish the wise regulations that assure to each protection that the law accords to all in order to repress an abuse that has brought desolation to numerous families who do not have any other means of existence but commerce ...

Not competitive individualism, but distributive justice, was the basis for the mayor's action. The mayor further regarded the *patente*, an obligatory license that a worker needed to practice a trade after 1796, as a kind of mastership that entitled the owner to protection. "If the municipal magistrates believed that they owed the corporations that existed then a special protection for the cost of the mastership ... the current administration owes protection with all the more reason to isolated citizens who contribute each year to the charges of the state by the price of their *patente*."

As in the old regime, fiscal concerns played a role in protectionism. The mayor believed that if small shopkeepers were ruined, an important branch of the state's revenues would perish with them. For all these reasons, the mayor decided to prohibit the sale of all new merchandise in the public auctions. Only in three cases – when a merchant with a *patente* died, went bankrupt, or changed his occupation completely – was it permitted to auction new merchandise. Such limitations may have formed a code common to merchants in other parts of France, for wholesalers in Paris asked for identical controls on public auctions in the capital.[74]

The bailiffs were vehemently opposed to the mayor's restrictive measure. The law of 1 Brumaire VII regulating the *patentes*, they argued, clearly stated that a *patente* of the highest class allowed a person to engage in all forms of commerce without limitation. Since they paid more than small merchants for these licenses, they deserved to have the freedom to sell whatever they wanted. They also noted that the decision of the departmental authorities in May 1792 had authorized them to hold their own sales, and they claimed that the mayor was acting beyond his constitutional authority.[75]

The mayor dismissed their objections. A *patente*, he informed them, was only issued upon the condition that the individual conform to the regulations controlling his profession. The laws of 14 December 1789 and 22 July 1791 had authorized the mayor to make sure that the citizens of his municipality enjoyed the benefits of good policing. "Did not these laws," he asked, "express well enough the intention to maintain the old regulations whose object was the public order?" The decision of the department in 1792 had been made during a period when "a dizziness [*vertige*] dominated the wisest." As for the fiscal arguments, although the few individuals who ran public auctions paid large sums for *patentes* of the first class, this hardly equalled the amount that several hundred small-scale merchants generated in taxes. It was to the advantage of the state, therefore, to protect retailers.[76]

Not only did the prefect, who had earlier sanctioned the mayor's *arrêté*, agree with the mayor, he helped to impose even stricter controls on the auctions. In December 1804, the prefect closed down all auctions except for an official one at the *bourse*. All sale items had to be registered in order to facilitate the collection of registration and stamp taxes for the state. Special *patentes* were required to run an auction.[77] By 1805, the old system of official auctions had essentially been re-established, justified, as in the past, by the need for public order, taxation, and distributive justice.

The restrictions lasted until the Restoration. In 1818, the Minister of the Interior ruled that the mayor's *arrêté* proscribing the sale of new merchandise in public auctions was illegal, and this particular municipal law was repealed.[78] One doubts, however, that this was the final word in the battle to protect retailers.

The persistence of municipal "mercantilism"

Time and again, then, two patterns emerge in post-revolutionary Lille: a long-standing bourgeois concern for controlling competition and quality, and the persistence of municipal mercantilism with its emphasis on protecting native workers, provisioning local markets, and generating urban taxes. Examples pointing to a mercantilistic mentality could be multiplied. In 1803, in response to a petition from Lille's merchants, the mayor Gentil-Muiron prohibited *marchands forains* (peddlars) from displaying their wares in the city.[79] The measure was justified exclusively on fiscal grounds, because the *patentes* for *marchands forains* cost much less than those Lille's merchants were required to buy.[80]

The mayors restored old market regulations, often with bourgeois support. By the end of Napoleon's reign, virtually every local market – poultry, dairy, coal, grain, linen, and fish – had been reregulated. Frequently excerpts from ordinances of the old regime were republished word for word.[81] The return of the linen market provides one illustration of the process. After deregulation during the Revolution, the price of linen strands sold at different markets varied noticeably. As a result of this fluctuation, middlemen, called *recoupeurs*, flocked to the markets, bought up all the inexpensive strands, and sold them later at higher prices. The mayor denounced this maneuver as a dangerous monopoly that drove up the price of raw materials and made it impossible for Lille's manufacturers to compete with foreign producers. To prevent this kind of manipulation, in 1801 he decreed that linen strands had to be sold on the official market and that during the first hour of business only those owning *patentes* of thread spinner, linen weaver, or manufacturers were permitted to buy raw materials.[82] The association of thread spinners agreed to abide by these regulations.

In similar fashion, the system of urban grain provisioning returned to a corporate mold, this time with cooperation from the central government. In 1813, a period of terrible grain shortages, the Napoleonic government required all bakers to obtain special permission from the mayor to engage in this profession. Only those individuals of "good life and morals" who had served an apprenticeship were eligible. A *syndic* and four *adjoints*, elected by the bakers, were charged with inspecting grain supplies.

Napoleon authorized the prefect and the mayor to regulate the local grain market and to set the price of bread as they saw fit.[83]

De Brigode and de Muyssart, mayors under the Empire and Restoration, respectively, were sympathetic to the bakers' demands for protection. Both tried to reduce the number of bakers by refusing to issue new *patentes*. De Brigode planned to decrease the number of bakers from eighty-seven to eighty.[84] In the period 1780 to 1791, the bakers had numbered approximately 110, of which one-half had been recruited from sons of masters.[85] The mayor, therefore, wanted to make the nineteenth-century system more closed than that of the old regime.

Although the bakers supported the reduction to lessen competition, the mayors' decisions sometimes worked against the interests of the bakers' families. Some sons of bakers, for example, were denied licenses, a practice which would have been unlikely twenty-five years before. One person who had been a baker before 1813, but had left the trade for a short period, was not allowed to re-enter.[86] In another somewhat complicated case involving the rights of widows and divorcees, de Brigode declared that: "the widow does not keep the right to exercise the profession of baker after the death of her husband; she no longer has the right to take over the commission after the divorce. The commission is personal, non-transmissible and cannot be divided."[87] The mayors' ruling reflected the individualistic and bureaucratic, as opposed to familial and corporate, principles at work in the new regime: the licenses were "personal" and their transmission controlled by the government. Wives and widows had fewer claims in the sphere of work, because the Revolution had annulled the principle of inheritance integral to a corporate organization of society.

During the Restoration, de Muyssart continued the conservative policies of de Brigode. In August 1820, de Muyssart prohibited all bakers who lived outside Lille from selling their bread in the city, even though the Napoleonic law of 1813 had authorized them to do so. This law remained on the books until 1838. Similarly, in 1821, a *Sieur* Martin asked for the right both to establish a public oven for individuals who wanted to bake their own bread and to sell bread that he made there. The mayor grudgingly gave him permission to build the new oven, but refused to let Martin make any bread for independent sale.[88]

Finally, in 1813, the mayor and prefect tried to re-establish the grain market to ensure lower prices for consumers. The bakers, however, objected that the local market had never been large enough to meet the city's needs. In the end the Minister of Agriculture and Commerce ruled against requiring the bakers to buy their supplies on the market.[89] Although this particular clause from the old ordinances was struck down, from 1816 to 1817 de Muyssart republished other regulations governing the sale of grain. In 1816, for example, he stationed a police commissioner in the market to enforce the municipal ordinance of 1740 that allowed consumers to buy their grain before bakers or merchants.[90]

Some of these restrictions were dismantled during the Restoration. In the early 1820s, protests were raised against the limitation of the number of bakers. After an inquiry, the Minister of the Interior declared that all individuals who wanted to exercise the profession of baker, and could prove sufficient means to do so, must be allowed to establish a trade. The *adjoints* and *syndic* in Lille protested, but 1824 the government was adamant: the government would not tolerate "any limitation or restriction on the free exercise of any industry whatever."[91]

Finally, the occupational monopolies of the old "*offices de police*," the petty market officials and transport workers, were resuscitated. The *préfecture de police* in Paris had made the first move to regulate transport workers in the capital when, in 1801, it required the workers to obtain commissions and wear badges before they could be hired.[92] In Lille in 1803, the prefect initially set up a bureau of weights and measures and required that all those working there receive a commission. Soon Lille's mayor began to award commissions to all workers who transported goods, unloaded cargo, or worked in the local markets. He set up categories of workers, similar to those of the old regime, which enjoyed the exclusive right to carry, weigh, or measure certain goods. The number of individuals in each category was limited, and the fees charged by the workers were fixed. When non-commissioned persons tried to transport goods, the mayor declared that it was important for the safety of the city's inhabitants and for "the preservation of the rights of the established persons" to stop the interlopers immediately.[93] The workers viewed the commissions as a direct continuation of the old venal offices that workers had purchased in the old regime. In January 1819, the mayor had to prohibit the *porteurs du sac* from selling the commissions that the municipality had given them.[94]

Public spirit and the well-ordered state

Despite the republication of municipal ordinances from the eighteenth century, the justification for the revival of protection and professional monopolies was not a simple reiteration of principles from the old regime. Legally, it was no longer possible to rely on privileges, so most groups appealed to such "modern" concepts as public order, regulation, utility to the state, and taxation to defend exclusive practices.[95] The rhetoric was not completely new: guild masters had advanced utilitarian arguments of a similar nature in the old regime. Before the Revolution, it had become common to defend the interests of corporate groups through the principles of the general welfare, that is, by arguing that regulation and controls on competition were necessary to an efficiently run and equitable state. The Napoleonic prefects and the mayors were among those that partook of this vision of the world; they re-established protectionistic policies and regulations in order to prevent disorder, to sanction acquired rights, to practice distributive justice, and to enhance economic performance. Thus, proprietary individualism was not the ubiquitous idiom of agents of the Napoleonic government, nor was corporate rhetoric uniformly the language of opposition to it. Serving as a counterpoint to the language of individualism was the language of *étatisme*, a discourse through which corporate practices of the old regime were recast as utilitarian public services.

Artisans, officials, legal practitioners, and merchants – a whole range of social groups spoke the protectionistic and bureaucratic language of the state. Despite the commitment of some Napoleonic ministers to economic liberalism, many governmental officials in Paris were sympathetic to the creation of professional hierarchies and monopolies by bureaucratic means. The central government grouped members of the auxiliary judicial professions, including solicitors (*avoués*), notaries, and bailiffs (*huissiers*), into "corporations." In each case, the government appointed individuals to these positions, limited the number of persons who could serve, and required the candidates to give a monetary pledge to the government as a guarantee for their good conduct, a policy that introduced practices notoriously similar to venality in offices. In 1800 and 1813, respectively, the government created *chambres des avoués* and *chambres disciplinaires des huissiers* to oversee the discipline of these judicial officials. Barristers (*avocats*) were not subjected to these requirements, but Napoleon did create an "order of *avocats*" which was composed of all lawyers of "good life and morals" who were officially registered on the *tableau des avocats* and had sworn an oath of loyalty to the state. The lawyers elected councils entrusted with preserving the honor of the order.[96] Although notaries had no official disciplinary chamber, in Lille they established regulations to preserve the dignity of their corporation and to maintain a spirit of collegiality.[97] Meanwhile in banking, the government restricted the number of brokers (*agents de change*) and exacted a monetary pledge from each one. Property, exclusion, and legal limitation of competition remained the principles of many bourgeois professions.[98]

Thus, the central government itself abandoned a full-fledged commitment to economic liberty, which was often seen as anarchic and harmful, in order to create its own version of a well-ordered state. Rather than extending greater central control in linear fashion, the Napoleonic bureaucracy at times became more corporate in its organization.

Regulations emanated from the core, but they protected groups that acquired exclusive rights. The French state of the old regime, at once highly centralized and heavily corporate, had begun to reproduce itself in a more nationally uniform, professionalized form.

The co-existence in Napoleonic France of seemingly antithetical policies – in some cases advocating economic liberalism, in others bureaucratic centralization, and yet in still others the protection of acquired rights – was based in differing perceptions of how to create a strong state. The Minister of the Interior, Chaptal, believed that a restricted role for government laid the foundation for economic progress and the overall strength of the state. Market forces, it was assumed, would naturally transform unfettered individualism into the welfare of all. Yet, for Chaptal, economic liberalism was as much a statist as a bourgeois ideology. Intellectuals and government officials had come to realize that the strongest states did not have to compel obedience forcibly, but elicited the cooperation of their citizenry voluntarily through public spiritedness. It would be impossible to foster a general, national interest unless the government destroyed all particularistic privileges and looked to the interest of all citizens equally. As Chaptal observed,

Could a public spirit be formed in a nation where names, titles, and favors classified men;...could a public spirit be established in a country where the law was not equal for everyone, where taxes only weighed on part of the inhabitants, where the favors of the government were the appanage of a small number? Now that our institutions place all Frenchmen under the same law, there will, without doubt, be a public spirit in France, because there will be a common interest, and the cultivator, the merchant and the manufacturer will bless forever the sovereign who consecrated their rights by a solemn act.[99]

Equality, including equal access onto the market, was the fundamental precondition for social bonding. Economic liberalism served the needs of national unification.

In his *Rapport sur les Jurandes et Maîtrises* in 1805, Vital-Roux, a Lyonnais *négociant* who became a regent of the Bank of France, came to a similar conclusion.[100] Guilds would rekindle the development of an "exclusive spirit" and block the direct and beneficial action of the state upon the individual:

... each artisan pays his part of the public impositions to the state that protects him; he is subject to the general laws and rules of the administration. His natural protectors are the magistrates, and we do not see why it would be necessary to guarantee the right of an artisan [to have] a corps or magistracy other than the one that the government has constituted for the guarantee of everyone...By multiplying the intermediaries between the people and the government, one interrupts the march of public administration; one enlarges uselessly the chain that links subjects to the state.[101]

It was the existence of general laws, uniform taxes, and national protection that rendered guilds and other corporate bodies a civic impossibility.

Despite their suspicion of intermediate bodies, many officials were not convinced of the benefits to be gained by unshackling self-interest and letting market forces rule. It was still the role of the government to regulate society; the state had an obligation to balance conflicting claims and to restrain harmful effects of individual license. Saint Jean d'Angély, a member of Napoleon's *Conseil d'Etat*, argued against restoring the guilds, but felt no assurance that invisible market forces would automatically harness individual self-interest to the general welfare. "Personal interest," he cautioned, "is subject to error and injustice... Personal interest must be closely watched by the interest of everyone. It needs a regulator, whether it is giving or requesting, obtaining or producing work."[102]

The central government, of course, was that regulator. Although Napoleon generally favored liberty for commerce and manufacturing, he saw his role as one of harmonizing individual liberty with the public good. Organizing groups along corporate lines was one way to tame individualism. In discussing the situation of the brokers, for example, he argued that despite new theories against corporations, it was necessary to recall the brokers "to the spirit and discipline of corps."[103] Created by and subordinate to the central government, corps like those of the brokers acted as disciplinary arms of the state. In Napoleon's own imagery, the corporation might be described as a satellite revolving around the central government, the hub of the system:

The great order that regulates the whole world must govern each part of the world; the government is at the center of societies like the sun; the diverse institutions must traverse their orbit around it without ever escaping from it. It is necessary then that the government regulate the combinations of each of them in such a manner that they all cooperate in maintaining the general harmony. In the system of the world nothing is left to chance; in the system of societies nothing must depend on the caprice of individuals.[104]

The Napoleonic view of state and society might be described as the transformation of the semi-autonomous corporate regulation of the old regime to the bureaucratic regulation of modern France. The most fundamental change between the two regimes was the creation of constitutional equality, the building block of the modern state. During the Revolution, the nation became the only legitimate *corporation* and either dissolved or assumed the public functions and loyalties of all other corps. As Vital-Roux declared, "it is necessary to call to this universal harmony without distinction all the members of the great family, the only real corporation; it is necessary to call the entire nation to furnish its quota to the happiness of everyone." The nation, the only true corps, transcended, absorbed, and nationalized all prior corporate rights and loyalties. Yet after assimilating the corps of the old regime to itself and consolidating power at the center, the national government deployed that power to balance the interests of groups, to protect acquired rights, and to create social accord – in other words, to recreate routines and practices associated with the corporate regime. The protection of acquired rights was linked both to an ongoing distrust of unfettered individualism and to a heightened faith in the nation as the supreme and disinterested arbiter of the public good. If, in theory, regulation was imposed in the national interest, in practice, it was difficult to prevent regulation from sanctioning virtual monopolies of socio-professional groups. In conclusion, perhaps in the co-existence of modern bureaucratic regulation and the desire of local groups for protection, it is possible to discern the seeds of what has been called "the stalled society" – a society in which the central government ostensibly holds all the power but is still weighed down by a myriad of local interest groups. Given the history of France, it should not be surprising to discover that the central government itself was instrumental in helping to revive, encourage, and legitimate particularistic interests that it continued to decry.[105]

10 Conclusion

In *The Coming of the French Revolution*, Georges Lefebvre argued that "the Revolution of 1789 restored the harmony between fact and law."[1] For Lefebvre, *fact* was to be found in the economy, in modes of production and the social interests arising from them. *Law* was secondary. It consisted of the whole juridical apparatus and norms that legitimated the control of a dominant social class. Fact fundamentally defined social identity; law merely confirmed it.

This study has argued a different case. Law in the old regime, it claims, was constitutive of social identity. Corporate rights and privileges provided differential access to status, power, and wealth within the elite in such a way as to generate independent interests. Rather than legitimating the rule of a dominant class, the juridical framework of society fragmented the elite in such a way as to make a concerted defense of privilege ultimately impossible. And for this reason, in 1789 it was the legal and institutional basis of society that was overturned, not to allow a new class to establish its hegemony, but to transform the ground rules by which political power, analytically distinct from that generated by class relationships, operated within the state. For the men of the eighteenth century, law was very much fact.

The central issue of the French Revolution was how to create new juridical norms that would make both membership in the state and the exercise of political power accessible, principled, and equitable. The constitutional upheaval of 1789 involved a profound redefinition of public norms, of the legal conditions under which people would submit to political authority and the basic rules by which they would conduct their social activities. Political membership and authority became nationalized and democratized, subject in theory to the will of the people. But if this redefinition of political power was not the product of a changing mode of production, to what can it be linked? What were the origins of the Revolution as a political event? The constitutional transformation of 1789, this study has suggested, was the maturation and final collapse of age-old contradictions in a system of patrimonial power. In this political system, public authority was mingled with private rights and personal possession by both the king and other corporate groups in such a way as to create a sense of arbitrary and unprincipled rule. The fluidity and privatization of public norms became untenable in late eighteenth-century France because a new cultural environment, generated by both the Enlightenment and the rise of the state, challenged the personalization of power and because wars world-wide in scope made the rationalization of French administration and finances imperative.

In a variety of ways, the absolute monarchy had generated its own internal dynamic of opposition. The crown tried to close off competing avenues of power, but in the process opened up others. Finances remained its Achilles heel. Public and royal credit remained completely intermixed in a system that allowed the king to act as if he were above the law. Unable to tap financial markets at low rates generated by confidence, the king continued to rely upon loans from officeholders and networks of privileged financiers whose power was as entrenched as ever in 1789. The monarch, absolute though he might claim to be, actually enhanced the dispersion of local power and extended the claims of privileged groups. As a result, the royal government found itself unable to reorganize the economy and administration without provoking stubborn resistance from all sorts of corporate bodies. In fact, traditional resistance by venal officeholders, as the case of the *Bureaux des Finances* revealed, had become more organized and national in scope by the eve of the Revolution than ever before. This point assumes even more significance when one remembers that a good many of those offices, including those in Lille's *Bureau des Finances* itself, had never even existed before the time of Louis XIV.

A second trend of the monarchy had been to coopt the representative and governing corps of localities, such as the estates of Flanders and town council of Lille. Instead of acting as buffers against the intrusion of royal power, they became, wittingly or not, royal allies and tax collectors instead. One consequence was to enhance the political disunity of the local elite. For a time it may have been easier for the king to divide and rule in this fashion, but this practice also had the undesirable effect of encouraging the disaffection of large sectors of the elite with the absolutist-corporate structure of power. In Flanders, nobles outside the provincial estates remained the bitter opponents of those inside. Rising taxes and the elite's political exclusion eventually alienated those whom one might have expected to support the government most strongly.

For this reason, the thesis of the pre-revolutionary formation of a plutocratic class of "notables," a moneyed elite transcending the boundaries between noble and non-noble, appears untenable. Social mobility was not the issue, because movement into the nobility continued as before. But, in the late 1780s, battles between powerful and powerless nobles reached a climax. The elite was deeply fractured, its coherence in disarray by the closure of corporate avenues to power. The selective alliances of the monarchy with representative corporate bodies, like provincial estates and town councils, also help to explain why in 1789 absolute monarchy and local governments fell together. To attack one was implicitly to attack the other.

A third trend was the routinization and permanency of institutions of the monarchy. By the end of Louis XIV's rule, people had come to accept, voluntarily or by force, large standing armies, bureaucratic networks of intendants, and a variety of taxes as ongoing parts of the state's machinery. Such developments helped to foster a new sense of an abstract impartial sphere of authority, a state that superseded both the personal authority of the monarch and the traditional claims of officeholders. In particular, a steady barrage of new taxes helped to give ongoing, concrete meaning to the idea that "all privileges disappeared" in return for the protection of the state. A sense of fiscal equality and the uniformity of law falling on all citizens thus accompanied the rising presence of the state in Lille. Paradoxically, the very bureaucratic success of the monarchy also contained the seeds of its downfall. The impersonal machinery of state helped to stimulate new notions of an abstract and fixed public authority at odds with the personalized power defining royal absolutism.

New expectations for the government, along with the perpetual shipwrecks of royal reform, furthered the conditions for politicization. The monarchy held out the hope for a better society, but also engendered the conditions for its own failure. It established new taxes in order to distribute the tax burden more fairly, but simultaneously extracted loans from officeholders in return for confirming their privileges. Its reformers, like Turgot, wished to open the economy to more competition, but ran up against the debts which guilds had contracted on behalf of the monarchy. Administrators espoused the principle of national uniformity, but were ready to restore Flanders' exemption from the *centième denier* in return for cold cash. The *octrois* drove up the price of urban commodities and fostered protectionism, but they also helped to pay for the king's roads, canals, army, and bureaucracy. The monarchy had no way out of these structural contradictions, except to renounce the foundations of its personalized rule and open up the state to greater participation. Meanwhile, citizens grew more insistent in their demands for political accountability.

Corporate groups have often been cast in the role of villains of the old regime. They were reputedly privileged, selfish, localistic and obscurantist, ready to oppose any kind of rational reform. Thus, not only has the monarchy's role in enlarging the scope of corporate privileges too often been ignored, the positive role of corporate bodies in helping to create the conditions for revolution has also been downplayed. True, some corporate bodies were extremely conservative. But corporate groups of all kinds had also habituated individuals to think in terms of legal rights and to be aware of their erosion. In this way the routine activities of corporate bodies helped to create the juridical terrain from which the claims of citizenship might eventually emerge. Furthermore, when one looks at the corporate regime in terms of the exercise of power, it became clear that many of those who enjoyed some form of privilege – a noble title, office, or membership in a guild – were excluded from important political decision-making. Their privileges were of less and less worth to them, while, in their battles against arbitrary power, their rhetoric took on more universal appeal and their alliances became more national in scope. Mobilization on the eve of the Revolution was not achieved through class alliances, but through corporate networks of town councils, Chambers of Commerce, *Bureaux des Finances* and the like. In Lille, the campaign against the provincial estates was largely funded by the guilds.

Hence corporate groups generated the resources with which to attack the other "despotic" corps and royal bureaucrats governing them. The heart of the matter was the right of individuals to control their own civil existence. As Lille's Third Estate had declared: "But the municipal magistrates want to be US; they want that we only have civil existence in THEM. They want to be deputies for US, they conspire in silence against the most precious of our rights." As the state grew in power and reached more directly into citizens' private lives, in large part through the payment of taxes, groups responded by drawing upon a language of citizenship and claiming an unmediated existence in the state.

There was a paradox, then, in the origins of the Revolution. Just as the extension of an impersonal royal bureaucracy helped to undermine the legitimacy of personal royal rule, so the translocal mobilization of corporate groups and their invocation of more universalistic concepts like those of popular consent, uniformity, rights of property, and citizenship helped to undercut the foundations of their own particularistic privileges. Could a truly public sphere of bureaucracy and citizenship have emerged without the complete destruction of all corporate groups? Comparing political and corporate organization in other countries, particularly decentralized ones, might provide some insights into alternate routes still open in this period. But in France, the contradictions had grown too stark, the financial situation too grim, the politicization too intense. In the end, the corporate regime fell from all directions. It was not only attacked from without, but it also disintegrated from within through the disenchantment of the elite with arbitrary power and through new kinds of mobilization that called into question its own premises. It is perhaps not surprising that the National Assembly finally abolished the whole structure of the old regime. It was not that most of these men were abstract idealists and radical visionaries, but that avenues to reform had repeatedly been cut off by the monarchy, leaving any sort of piecemeal reform impossible.

The social consequences of the Revolution stemmed from its juridical reorganization. When the Revolution reconstituted the basis of political power, it simultaneously redefined the basis of social groupings. By removing private property, personal status, and inheritance from the exercise of public authority, the French Revolution distinguished more clearly than ever before the realm of the state from civil society. The legal order ushered in by the Revolution changed the rules by which social relationships were conducted. It transformed patterns of occupational mobility, definitions of property, investment opportunities, and principles of status because the intermediate institutions conferring such rights had been abolished or nationalized.

A similar observation might be made concerning the relationship of capitalism to the origins of Lille's municipal revolution. Merchants in Lille used their wealth to purchase ennobling offices. Others that remained in commerce and manufacturing showed great skill in using the legal apparatus of the guilds to reinforce their economic domination. Lille's revolutionary bourgeoisie showed no desire to seize political power in order to destroy a corporate straitjacket stifling the economy, because they did not regard the guilds as obstacles to the consolidation of their economic power. Economic liberalism was not the precursor of political liberalism for Lille's bourgeoisie; rather political liberalism coexisted with economic conservatism. The economic demands that were made by Lille's elite, both noble and non-noble, I would argue, were directed against the arbitrariness and insecurity of the economic climate fostered by the absolute state. Unfair taxes, fiscal manipulation of the guilds, and the precarious nature of investments in venal offices, municipalities, and government securities accounted for many of the economically liberal demands of the French elite.

Finally, it is doubtful that the transition from the old regime to modern France can be described as a transition from a society of orders and corps to one of classes. This characterization, I believe, misrepresents the Revolution's profound legal and political consequences. The corporate arrangement of France in the old regime was a legal and political system of rights, obligations, and immunities. These rights may have intersected with, but they were never a substitute for, class interests created in the course of the production and exchange of goods. The Revolution did not directly usher in a class-based society, because its role was institutional. It swept the economic landscape clear of corporate monopolies and placed the regulatory power over the economy firmly in the hands of the state. From a juridical perspective, the destruction of corps in the Revolution brought bureaucracy, a rationalized system of public authority, and citizenship, the rights accorded to members of a state. This institutional transformation provided new possibilities for class formation. After the Revolution, there were fewer institutional obstacles to the emergence of modern classes, because the whole intermediate level of law and power tending to create particularistic interest groups had been stripped away. This destruction created an environment in which translocal economic interests might more readily emerge. But the formation of a society of classes, essentially an economic issue, may best be seen as a problem analytically distinct from the creation of a society of citizens, a matter of political membership.

It might be argued, of course, that bureaucracy and citizenship had no meaning apart from class relationships and that these institutional changes merely confirmed bourgeois interests. But evidence suggests that this was not the case. In Lille it would have been difficult for the state to find one bourgeois class acting in concert to represent. Established cloth merchants in Lille, rising manufacturers in the countryside, and aggressive brokers all had different perspectives on economic regulation. Furthermore, the revival of market regulations, the avowed concern of Lille's mayor for "distributive justice," the comparison of the *patente* to the former guilds, and the concern of professional groups like notaries to protect their honor and income reveals that the state's bureaucratic powers could be turned towards ends reminiscent of the corporate regime. The appeals of these interest groups and the conservative policies of local officials suggest that historians should approach the class-based and bourgeois nature of France after the Revolution with caution. On the local level among the elite, the corporate consciousness of special interest groups often obscured class consciousness. Under Napoleon as during the old regime, institutional arrangements had the capacity to fragment the shared economic base of social classes, and social groups tried to use the power of the state to reinforce special interests.

The Revolution created new possibilities and patterns for mobilization and social conflict. As a result of the Revolution, membership in the national state, or citizenship, became the source of all civic rights. Although in theory the rights of citizens were inalienable and universal, in fact they were inequitably distributed. Thus, after the Revolution, conflict was to revolve significantly around the acquisition and definition of the full rights of citizenship by disenfranchised groups. Some of the battles to acquire political rights were to be class-oriented, such as those fought by workers to redress economic grievances. But not all exclusion from civil rights was class-based. Ethnic groups, religious groups, and women were among those frequently deprived of a voice in the public sphere. Thus the Revolution laid the foundations for future battles waged by disadvantaged groups, whether defined by class, gender, belief or race. Although movements to acquire civil rights might appeal to universal principles, the movements themselves would find it difficult to transcend national borders, for beyond the boundaries of one's state, the rights of citizenship no longer existed. The state remained the dispenser of civil rights and public power. The French Revolution thus ushered in a new era in which aggrieved individuals had to demand rights of citizenship from a bureaucratized national state, their savior and their master.

Notes

1 MONARCHY, PRIVILEGE AND REVOLUTION: THE PROBLEM AND SETTING

1 The best description of the siege is in Alain Lottin, *Chavatte, ouvrier lillois, un contemporain de Louis XIV* (Paris, 1979), pp. 156–162.

2 "Abbrégé de tout ce qu'il s'est passé de plus remarquable au siège de la ville de Lille, l'an 1667, 10 aoust," Georges Lefebvre, ed., *Annales de l'Est et du Nord* 3 (1907), 391, 409.

3 For a published copy of the treaty, see A.N. K 1,161, no. 12.

4 A.D.N. C 237, C 643. Lille's quota of the provincial *abonnement* was 363,002 *livres*.

5 A.M.L. 15,933, registre aux cérémonies, fols. 151v–152r.

6 For definitions of citizenship see Reinhard Bendix, *Nation-Building and Citizenship: Studies of Our Changing Social Order* (Garden City, 1969); and William Rogers Brubaker, "The French Revolution and the Invention of Citizenship," *French Politics and Society* 7 (Summer, 1989), 30–49.

7 Herbert Luethy, *La Banque protestante en France de la Révocation de l'Edit de Nantes à la Révolution*, 2 vols. (Paris, 1961), 2: 470. On public opinion see, Mona Ozouf, "L'Opinion publique," in Keith Baker, ed., *The French Revolution and the Creation of Modern Political Culture*, vol. 1, *The Political Culture of the Old Regime* (Oxford, 1987), pp. 419–434; Keith Michael Baker, "Politics and Public Opinion under the Old Regime: Some Reflections," in Jack Censer and Jeremy Popkin, eds., *Press and Politics in Pre-revolutionary France* (Berkeley, Calif., 1987); Sarah Maza, "Le Tribunal de la nation: les mémoires judiciaires et l'opinion publique à la fin de l'ancien régime," *Annales, E.S.C.* 42 (1987), 73–90; and Thomas E. Kaiser, "Money, Despotism and Public Opinion in Early Eighteenth-Century France: John Law and the Debate on Royal Credit" (unpublished paper, 1988). James Riley observes the rise of the idea of the sacredness of royal debt in *The Seven Years' War and the Old Regime in France: The Economic and Financial Toll* (Princeton, 1986), p. 232.

8 Cited by C. B. A. Behrens, *Society, Government, and the Enlightenment: The Experience of France and Prussia* (New York, 1985), p. 25. It is interesting to recall Bodin's admonition that sovereign princes should "never take an oath to keep the lawes of their predecessors; for otherwise they are not sovereigns."

The Six Bookes of a Commonweale, ed. Kenneth McRae (Cambridge, Mass., 1972), p. 93.

9 A.M.L. 318, "Mémoire pour la ville de Lille," June 1774.

10 Maurice Braure, *Lille et la Flandre Wallonne au XVIIIe siècle*, 2 vols. (Lille, 1932), 2:707.

11 A.M.L. A.G. 440, dos. 29, "L'assemblée nationale aux Français," 11 February 1790.

12 William Sewell, Jr., *Work and Revolution: The Language of Labor from the Old Regime to 1848* (Cambridge, 1980), p. 27; C. B. A. Behrens, "Nobles, Privileges, and Taxes in France at the End of the Ancien Régime," *Economic History Review*, 2nd ser. 15 (April 1963), 452.

13 On political categories of public and private see Jürgen Habermas, *The Structural Transformation of the Public Sphere*, trans. Thomas Burger, (Cambridge, Mass., 1989).

14 Throughout this discussion I draw on the insights of Emile Lousse, *La Société d'ancien régime. Organisation et représentation corporatives* (Louvain, 1943).

15 Charles Loyseau, *Traité des ordres et simples dignitez* (Paris, 1610), p. 4.

16 According to Antony Black, the Roman legal tradition (utilized by French kings) asserted the authority of the prince to incorporate groups, whereas the Germanic tradition stressed "the self-authorizing rights of the customary group." *Guilds and Civil Society in European Political Thought from the Twelfth Century to the Present* (Ithaca, New York, 1984), p. 18.

17 Joseph Guyot, *Répertoire universel et raisonné de jurisprudence civile, criminelle, canonique, et bénéficiale* (Paris, 1784), 13: 467–485 (entry for "Préséance").

18 For example, E. Appolis, "Les Etats de Languedoc au XVIIIe siècle. Comparaison avec les états de Bretagne," and Louis de Cardenal, "Les dernières réunions des trois ordres de Périgord avant la Révolution," both in *L'organisation corporative du Moyen Age à la fin de l'Ancien Régime. Etudes présentées à la commission internationale pour l'histoire des assemblées d'états* (Louvain, 1937); and Armand Rébillon, *Les Etats de Bretagne de 1661 à 1789* (Paris–Rennes, 1932), p. 83. A table showing the social composition of provincial estates in France is supplied by John Bosher, *The French Revolution* (New York and London, 1988), pp. 89–90.

19 François Furet, "La monarchie et le règlement électoral de 1789," in Baker, *Political Culture*, pp. 375–377. For examples of the corporate organization of estates across Europe, see R. R. Palmer, *The Age of the Democratic Revolution*, vol. 1, *The Challenge* (Princeton, 1959).

20 On feudal and patrimonial structures of domination, see Max Weber, *Economy and Society*, ed. Guenther Roth and Claus Wittich, 2 vols. (Berkeley, Calif., 1978), 2:1,006–1,110. The term *absolutism* unfortunately tends to conjure up the image of a modern dictator. The term *patrimonialism* captures the absolute, but personal, quality of royal legislation in its pre-modern economic and social setting. In addition, it offers the advantage of describing the simultaneous growth of a royal bureaucracy and proliferation of venal or patrimonial offices as a logical, but contradictory, extension of one system, rather than the grafting of a new bureaucratic form onto an older "feudal" one.

21 On the king as judge see J. H. Shennan, *The Parlement of Paris* (London, 1968), pp. 151–156; William Church, *Constitutional Thought in Sixteenth*

Century France (Cambridge, Mass., 1941), pp. 99–120; Roland Mousnier, "Comment les Français voyaient la constitution au XVIIe siècle," *XVIIe Siècle* (1955), 11–28.

22 Weber, *Economy and Society*, 2: 1,012–1,015; Bendix, *Nation-Building*, pp. 39–57. For further discussion of the personalization of public power see Andrew Vincent, *Theories of the State* (Oxford, 1987), pp. 42–64; Herbert H. Rowen, *The King's State: Proprietary Dynasticism in Early Modern France* (New Brunswick, 1980), pp. 75–92; and Nannerl O. Keohane, *Philosophy and the State in France: The Renaissance to the Enlightenment* (Princeton, 1980), p. 17.

23 Standard Marxist accounts include Georges Lefebvre, *The French Revolution*, 2 vols., trans. Elizabeth Moss Evanson, vol. 1, and John Hall Stewart, vol. 2 (New York, 1962, 1964); and Albert Soboul, *The French Revolution, 1787–1799*, trans. Alan Forrest and Colin Jones (New York, 1975). See also Geoffrey Ellis' review article: "The 'Marxist Interpretation' of the French Revolution," *English Historical Review* 93 (1978), 353–376.

24 *L'Ancien Régime et la Révolution* (Paris, 1856); English translation by Stuart Gilbert, *The Old Régime and the French Revolution* (New York, 1955).

25 According to George Taylor the radical Declaration of the Rights of Man and Citizen was "an adaptation of Enlightenment words, phrases, and concepts to a revolutionary situation that the *philosophes* had neither intended nor foreseen." "Revolutionary and Non-revolutionary Content in the *Cahiers* of 1789: an Interim Report," *French Historical Studies* 7 (1972), 489. R. R. Palmer stressed political conflict as a key to ideology in *The Age of the Democratic Revolution*, 2 vols. (Princeton, 1959). Robert Darnton argued against revolutionary implications of the high Enlightenment in "In Search of the Enlightenment: Recent Attempts to Create a Social History of Ideas," *Journal of Modern History* 43 (1971), 113–132. Daniel Roche treated the integration of academies into the hierarchy of the old regime in *Le Siècle des lumières en province: Académies et académiciens provinciaux, 1680–1789*, 2 vols. (Paris and the Hague, 1978). Other important studies emphasizing the relationship between the intellectual origins of the Revolution and political practice are Dale Van Kley, "Church, State, and the Ideological Origins of the French Revolution: The Debate over the General Assembly of the Gallican Clergy in 1765," *Journal of Modern History* 51 (1979), 630–664; Keith Michael Baker, "French Political Thought at the Accession of Louis XVI," *Journal of Modern History* 50 (1978), 279–303; Keith Michael Baker, "Enlightenment and Revolution in France: Old Problems, Renewed Approaches," *Journal of Modern History* 53 (1981), 281–303; William H. Sewell, Jr., "Ideologies and Social Revolutions: Reflections on the French Case," *Journal of Modern History* 57 (1985), 57–85; Theda Skocpol, "Cultural Idioms and Political Ideologies in Revolutionary Reconstruction of State Power: a Rejoinder to Sewell," *Journal of Modern History* 57 (1985), 86–96; and the collection of essays in Baker, *Political Culture*.

26 One study exploring the links between political and legal disputes of guilds in the old regime and republican ideology in the Revolution is Michael Sonenscher, *Work and Wages: Natural Law, Politics and the Eighteenth Century French Trades* (Cambridge and New York, 1989).

27 Alfred Cobban, *The Social Interpretation of the French Revolution* (Cambridge,

1968) George Taylor, "Noncapitalist Wealth and the Origins of the French Revolution," *American Historical Review* 72 (1967), 469–496. A good summary of the debate is in William Doyle, *Origins of the French Revolution* (Oxford, 1980). On economic consequences see Louis Bergeron, *France Under Napoleon*, trans. R. R. Palmer (Princeton, 1981), pp. 159–191.

28 The quotations are taken from the following authors, respectively: Alfred Cobban, *A History of France, 1715–1799* (Baltimore, 1957), p. 37; Doyle, *Origins*, p. 24; and Pierre Goubert, *The Ancien Régime: French Society, 1600–1750*, trans. Steve Cox (New York, 1969), p. 216.

29 For example, Guy Chaussinand-Nogaret, *The Nobility in the Eighteenth Century. From Feudalism to Enlightenment*, trans. William Doyle (Cambridge, 1985), p. 34; and Theda Skocpol, *States and Social Revolutions* (Cambridge and New York, 1979), p. 59.

30 *La Banque protestante*, 2:14. On the conservatism of businessmen see also Jean-Pierre Hirsch, "Honneur et liberté du commerce: sur le 'libéralisme' des milieux de commerce de Lille et de Dunkerque à la veille des Etats Généraux de 1789," *Revue du Nord* 55 (1973), 333–346; and his "Revolutionary France, Cradle of Free Enterprise," *American Historical Review* 94 (1989), 1,281–1,289.

31 For the revival of Tocqueville see François Furet, *Interpreting the French Revolution*, trans. Elborg Forster (Cambridge and New York, 1981). The use of Weberian categories has been limited to those studying bureaucracy, including John Bosher, *French Finances, 1770–1795: From Business to Bureaucracy* (Cambridge, 1970). Clive F. Church argues for the superiority of Weber's definition of bureaucracy over that of Tocqueville in *Revolution and Red Tape: The French Ministerial Bureaucracy, 1770–1850* (Oxford, 1981). Sharon Kettering's critique of Weber tends to confuse his notion of bureaucracy as an ideal type with historical reality in *Patrons, Brokers and Clients in Seventeenth-Century France* (Oxford, 1986).

32 *The Old Regime*, pp. 77–78.

33 ibid., p. 102.

34 David D. Bien, "The *Secrétaires du Roi*: Absolutism, *Corps*, and Privilege under the Ancien Régime," in E. Hinrichs, et al., eds., *Vom Ancien Régime zür Französischen Révolution* (Göttingen, 1978), pp. 153–168; his "Offices, *Corps*, and a System of State Credit: The Uses of Privilege under the Ancien Régime," in Baker, *Political Culture*, pp. 89–114; Daniel Dessert, "Finances et Société au XVIIe siècle: à propos de la Chambre de Justice de 1661," *Annales E.S.C.* 29 (1974), 847–882; and Gail Bossenga, "Impôt," in François Furet and Mona Ozouf, eds. *Dictionnaire Critique de la Révolution Française* (Paris, 1988), pp. 586–595. For a rural perspective see Hilton Root, *Peasants and King in Burgundy: Agrarian Foundations of French Absolutism* (Berkeley, Calif., 1987). On British politics and the financial revolution see John Brewer, *The Sinews of Power: War, Money and the English State, 1688–1783* (New York, 1989).

35 Luethy, *Banque protestante*, 2: 418ff.

36 Weber, *Economy and Society*, 2: 1,038–1,042.

37 For an overview see Lynn Hunt, "Committees and Communes: Local Politics and National Revolution in 1789," *Comparative Studies in Society and History* 18 (July 1976), 321–346.

38 Estimates are given in Pierre Lefevre, *Le Commerce des grains et la question du pain à Lille de 1713 à 1789* (Lille, 1925), pp. 3–4 and Pierre Deyon,

"Dénombrements et structures urbaines," *Revue du Nord* 53 (1971), 495–508. For a comparative perspective, see Marcel Reinhard, "La Population des villes: sa mesure sous la Révolution et l'Empire," *Population* 9 (1954), 279–288; and Jan de Vries, *European Urbanization 1500–1800* (Cambridge, Mass., 1984).

39 According to Jan de Vries, the net European urbanization of the period 1750–1800 "was disproportionately the result of the growth of smaller cities." *European Urbanization*, p. 258.

40 The population per square kilometer was calculated by Lefevre, *Commerce des grains*, pp. 1–2. For the population of Roubaix see Yves-Marie Hilaire, et al., *Histoire de Roubaix* (Dunkerque, 1984), pp. 76, 98, 112.

41 A.D.N. C 111, "Essai sur le commerce de la ville de Lille," November 1778. See Braure, *Lille*, 2: 369–434 for an overview of Lille's industries. Statistics for most industries in the 1780s are found in C. Dieudonné, *Statistique du département du Nord* 3 vols. (Brionne, 1803–4).

42 "Dénombrement et structure urbaines," p. 498. On literacy see François Furet and Jacques Ozouf, "Literacy and Industrialisation: the Case of the Département du Nord in France," *Journal of European Economic History* 5 (1976), 5–44; and Louis Trénard, "Alphabétisation et scolarisation dans la région lilloise," *Revue du Nord* 67 (1985), 633–648.

43 Braure, *Lille*, 2: 494–502; L. Thbaut, "Les Voies navigables et l'industrialisation du Nord de la France avant 1789," *Revue du Nord* 61 (1979), 149–164. B.M.L. 22.493, *Guide des étrangers à Lille ou description de la ville et de ses environs* (Lille, 1772), p. 63.

44 The quotation is from Dieudonné, *Statistique*, 3:2; see also Braure, *Lille*, 2: 487, 492.

45 Lottin, *Chavatte*, pp. 197–198. On Flanders' *droit de transit* see A.M.L. A.G. 148, dos. 3, 5, 14, and 17; *Encyclopédie Méthodique. Finances*, "Flandre," 2: 219.

46 J. F. Bosher, *The Single Duty Project: A study of the Movement for a French Customs Union in the Eighteenth Century* (London, 1964), pp. 1–7; Braure, *Lille*, 2: 436–441; Moreau de Beaumont, *Mémoires concernant les impositions et droits en Europe*, 4 vols. (Paris, 1769), 3: 506–507, 525.

47 Geoffrey Parker places siege warfare and fortifications at the heart of this transformation in *The Military Revolution* (Cambridge, 1988). A somewhat different view is Michael Roberts, "The Military Revolution" in his *Essays in Swedish History* (London, 1967), pp. 195–225.

48 Maurice Sautai, *L'Œuvre de Vauban à Lille* (Paris, 1911), pp. 12, 144–5.

49 Braure, *Lille*, 1: 234–238. Hubert Couvreur and Michael Montagne, "La Noblesse de la châtellenie de Lille à la fin de l'ancien régime," 2 vols., (unpublished mémoire de maîtrise, University of Lille III, 1970).

50 Paul d'Hollander, "La Composition sociale de l'échevinage lillois sous la domination française, 1667–1789" (unpublished mémoire de maîtrise, University of Lille III, 1968) and his article "La Composition sociale de l'échevinage lillois sous la domination française, 1667–1789," *Revue du Nord* 52 (1970), 5–15; Albert Croquez, *Histoire de Lille*, 2 vols. (Lille, 1935, 1939), 1: 93–104; and A. Crapet, "La Vie à Lille de 1667 à 1789 d'après les cours de M. de Saint-Léger," *Revue du Nord* 7 (1921), 290–303.

51 Lottin, *Chavatte*, p. 13.

52 Braure, *Lille*, 297–307; Albert Croquez, *La Flandre Wallonne et les pays de l'intendance de Lille sous Louis XIV* (Paris, 1912), pp. 128–151.
53 A.D.N. K 1,161, no. 12, Articles 23, 39, 40.
54 Braure, *Lille*, 1: 314–320; Croquez, *La Flandre Wallone*, pp. 155–159.
55 Henri Convain, *La Chambre ou Juridiction Consulaire de Lille d'après ses registres conservés au greffe du Tribunal de Commerce, 1715–91* (Lille, 1924); *Historique de la Chambre de Commerce de Lille, 1714–1918* (Lille, 1921).
56 Braure, *Lille*, 2: 614–615. Lottin, *Chavatte*, p. 201.
57 Braure, *Lille*, 1:158–160.
58 Croquez, *La Flandre Wallonne*, pp. 80–81.
59 Braure, *Lille*, 1: 70–71, 96–97.
60 ibid., 1: 70–71.

2 STATE FINANCE AND LOCAL PRIVILEGES

1 Braure, *Lille*, 1: 236. A.M.L, A.G, 106, dos. 10.
2 A.M.L. A.G. 106, dos. 8, Arrêt du Conseil d'Etat, 31 July 1696; A.M.L. A.G. 498, dos. 2, 23 April 1726.
3 A.M.L. 18,079, fol. 11, letter of the town council, 6 March 1790; A.M.L. A.G. 423, 'Observations du Magistrat de Lille sur l'édit d'août, 1764.'
4 D'Hollander, "L'échevinage lillois," *Revue du Nord*, pp. 5–7.
5 For one case prohibiting magistrates who were closely related from serving together, see A.M.L., 318, Résolutions du Magistrat, 14 December 1774, fols. 131–140. For continuity in recruitment see A.M.L., 15,443, "Etat alphabétique formé en 1785 de ceux qui ont été dans le corps du Magistrat de la ville de Lille depuis l'année 1765"; and Croquez, *Histoire de Lille*, 1: 104–105.
6 Couvreur and Montagne, *Noblesse*, 1: 228–229; Braure, *Lille*, 1: 234–236; A.D.N. C 226, "Pièces sur les offices de grands baillis;" Croquez, *La Flandre Wallonne*, pp. 86–87.
7 The Hangouarts, followed by the Muyssarts, controlled the office of *bailli* of Wavrin. The interrelated families of Hangouart, de Fourmestraux (*branche des Wazières*), and Imbert de la Basecque held the office in Comines until 1781, when Déliot de la Croix became a *grand bailli*. The Ingiliard family controlled the office of *bailli* of Cysoing for a large portion of the eighteenth century, but at the time of the Revolution, Mengon de Fondragon held the post. In addition to the references cited in the previous note, see A.D.N. C, *registre* 1,509, "Registre aux commissions de Mrs. les Baillis de l'Etat de Lille"; *Calendrier de Lille* (1790); and the genealogies in Paul Dénis du Péage, *Recueil de généalogies lilloises*, in *Mémoires de la Société d'Etudes de la Province de Cambrai* (Lille, 1906–1908), vols. 12–15. For Hangouart, 14: 1,192–1,204; de Muyssart, 13: 780–799; de Fourmestraux, 12: 287–296, Déliot, 12: 37–41; Ingiliard, 12: 83–87; du Béron, 13: 458–459; and Bady d'Aymeries, 12: 8–9.
8 A.D.N. C, *registre* 1509, "Commissions"; Dénis du Péage, *Généalogies*, Herts, 12: 320; Demadre, 14: 1499–1506; Tesson, 13: 600; Fruict, 14: 1471–1473; Cardon, 14: 666; D'Haffrenghes, 12: 63–68. See also the list of nobles in Couvreur and Hubert, "Noblesse," 1: 47–50b.
9 René Staquet, "Les Finances communales de Lille sous l'occupation française de 1668–1789" (unpublished thèse de Doctorat en Droit, University of Lille,

1961), p. 130. Braure, *Lille*, 1: 238–265 also provides a good summary of the major provincial impositions. I have left the figures in tables in *florins*, but give a total in *livres* and cite the amount in *livres* in the text (1 *florin* = 1.25 *livres*).

10 Staquet, "Finances," pp. 27, 87–114.

11 A.M.L. 11,307, "Relève du vingtième, exempts de l'aide ordinaire par leurs charges."

12 Staquet, "Finances," pp. 130–131.

13 A.D.N. C 3,754, letter of Joly de Fleury to the intendant Calonne, 1782. In 1777 the nobility in the *châtellenie* paid only 2,576 *livres* in capitation; the non-nobles there paid 77,537 *livres*. B.M.L. 31,265, "Etat général des Impositions et Droits qui se lèvent sur les Habitants des Châtellenies de Lille, Douay et Orchies, par MM. les Grands-Baillis...1777." For the *capitation* of urban officeholders see A.M.L., 2,368–2,369.

14 A.M.L. A.G. 503, dos. 1.

15 A.M.L. 16,795, account of the *receveur*, 1745.

16 Delays in the payment of the third *vingtième* account for its entry in the accounts closed in 1788 in Table 1.

17 A.M.L. 1,598, accounts for the *vingtième de l'industrie*, 1756–1789; A.M.L. A.G. 901, dos. 16.

18 A.M.L. A.G. 1288.

19 One tax roll indicated that nobles and *négociants* were assessed sums up to 700 *livres* per home in the parish of Saint-Pierre. A.M.L. 1,580, tax roll for 1776. The local *vingtièmes* for the provincial *aides* were not collected in the same manner as for the royal *vingtième*. In the rolls for the *aides*, the occupants residing in homes paid the taxes. In the rolls for the royal *vingtièmes*, the owners paid taxes on all their homes, whether they resided in them or rented them to others.

20 A.M.L. A.G. 1,067, dos. 2, 3.

21 Lettres-patentes du roi, 28 November 1761. Six and Plouvain, eds., *Recueil des édits, déclarations, lettres-patents, etc., enregistrés au Parlement de Flandre*, 12 vols. (Douai, 1785–1790), 6: 773–774. Marcel Marion, *Dictionnaire des institutions de la France aux XVII*e *et XVIII*e *siècles* (Paris, 1923), pp. 186–187.

22 On the *sol per livre* and *contrôle*, Arrêt du Conseil d'Etat, 17 September 1726, Six and Plouvain, *Edits*, 5: 385–387; B.M.L., 31,265, 'Etat des impositions, 1777'; A.D.N. C 3757, Ordinance of the intendant, 19 July 1731; A.M.L. 324, Résolution du Magistrat, 28 November 1781 fol. 113. On *octrois* see also George T. Matthews. *The Royal General Farms in Eighteenth-Century France* (New York, 1958), p. 166.

23 A.M.L. 319, Résolution du Magistrat, fol. 67, "Etat général du produit annuel des differents droits."

24 *Esquisse du mouvement des prix et des revenus en France au XVIIIe siècle*, 2 vols. (Paris, 1933). For a summary see Georges Lefebvre, "The Movement of Prices and the Origins of the French Revolution," in Jeffery Kaplow, ed., *New Perspectives on the French Revolution* (New York, 1965), pp. 103–135.

25 François Hincker, *Les Français devant l'impôt* (Paris, 1971), p. 39; Georges Lefebvre, *Les Paysans du Nord pendant la Révolution française* (Lille, 1924), pp. 175–176. Lefebvre's comment that cities in Walloon Flanders did not pay for the upkeep of provincial roads ignores the fact that each year Lille paid one-

quarter of the *charges communes* of the provincial estates, that is, revenues earmarked for paying inspectors, maintaining bridges and toll booths, and other similar costs. See A.M.L., accounts of Lille's *receveur*.

26 Michel Morineau, "Budgets de l'Etat et gestion des finances royales en France au dix-huitième siècle," *Revue Historique* 264:2 (1980), 289–336; and Nora Temple, "The Control and Exploitation of French Towns during the Ancien Régime," in Raymond Kierstead, ed., *State and Society in Seventeenth-Century France* (New York, 1975), pp. 67–93.

27 E. Van Hende, "Etat de la ville et de la châtellenie de Lille en 1789," *Bulletin de la Commission Historique du Nord* 19 (1890), 251–366; 278.

28 Inadvertently I copied from an archival document 200,000 *florins* for the total borrowed in 1771 for fortifications, instead of 20,000. The erroneous calculation was used in my article, "City and State," in Baker, *Political Culture*, p. 122.

29 Marcel Marion, *Histoire financière de la France depuis 1715*, 5 vols. (Paris, 1914), 1: 44.

30 Staquet, "Finances," pp. 157–158.

31 "Mémoire de Bagnols," pp. 470–471; Staquet, "Finances," p. 157.

32 Croquez, *Histoire de Lille*, pp. 154-156.

33 Ibid.; A.M.L. A.G. 425, dos. 10, "Titres des offices appartenant à la Commune de Lille."

34 Staquet, "Finances," pp. 157–158.

35 A.M.L., A.G., 1,393; A.M.L., 319, Résolution du Magistrat, 27 July 1777, fol. 132.

36 For a general perspective, see J. F. Bosher, "The French Crisis of 1770," *History* 57 (1972), 17–30.

37 A.M.L., 16,570, accounts of the second treasurer, 1773.

38 Staquet, "Finances," p. 166.

39 A.M.L. A.G. 542, dos. 2, letter of municipal magistrates to Caumartin, 6 March 1773.

40 A.M.L. 15,759, "Pièces de 10 Mai 1775 contenant les projets de libération des dettes de l'administration."

41 A.M.L. 15,758, letter from L'espagnol de Grimby, Lille's deputy in Paris, 24 August 1776.

42 A.M.L. A.G. 542, dos. 2, mémoire by the estates, 27 January 1772.

43 *La Banque protestante*, 2:470.

44 Staquet, *Finances*, pp. 157–158.

45 David Weir summarizes familial investment strategies in "Tontines, Public Finance, and Revolution in France and England, 1688–1789," *Journal of Economic History* 49 (March 1989), 95–124. Luethy argues that the royal government's infidelity, rather than a change in public mentality, accounts for the disfavor into which *rentes perpetuelles* fell (2:470).

46 Luethy, *La Banque protestante*, 2: 503–520 is more critical of Necker than Bosher, *French Finances*, and R. D. Harris, *Necker, Reform Statesman of the Ancien Régime* (Berkeley, Calif., 1979).

47 Luethy, *La Banque protestante*, 2: 591.

48 Doyle, *Origins of the French Revolution*, p. 49.

49 Lille produced approximately 30,800 pieces of woolen textiles per year in the

1760s, 24,800 in the 1770s, and 20,000 in the early 1780s. Maurice Vanhaeck, *Histoire de la sayetterie*, in *Mémoires de la Société d'Etudes de la Province de Cambrai*, vols. 16, 17 (Lille, 1910), 16: 284.

50 Croquez, *La Flandre Wallonne*, pp. 86–87, 130–131.

51 Ibid. p. 141; G. M. L. Pillot, *Histoire du Parlement de Flandres*, 2 vols. (Douai, 1849), 1: 212.

52 "Edit portant érection des charges de judicature du Parlement de Tournai et des sièges de son ressort en titre d'offices formés et héréditaires," March 1693, Six and Plouvain, *Edits*, 2: 169–177. On the changing composition of the Parlement, see Pillot, *Parlement*, 1: 148–149, 154, 167, 234, 449. The value of the offices is calculated from the official prices listed in the "Mémoire de Bagnols," pp. 465–469; from Pillot, *Parlement* 1: 113; and from A.D.N. C.B.F. (I).

53 "Conditions acceptés par le Roi…" 26 January 1694, Six and Plouvain, *Edits*, 2: 272–276; "Arrêt du Conseil d'Etat du Roi qui excepte les provinces de Flandres, Haynaut et Artois de l'execution des loix…relativement à l'évaluation et au droit casuel des offices," 4 January 1777, ibid., 8: 70–71.

54 Pillot, *Parlement*, 1: 234.

55 A.D.N. C.B.F. (I) dos. 6; "Edit qui augmente la finance et les gages des officiers des Bureaux des Finances du royaume et les confirme dans leurs privilèges," December 1743, Six and Plouvain, *Edits*, 6: 92–94.

56 On the capitation roles between 1695 and 1787, the number of taxpayers classified as officeholders (*officiers*) increased from 95 to 204, whereas the number of wholesale merchants declined slightly from 107 to 93. P. Thomas, "Textes historiques sur Lille et la Nord de la France avant 1789," *Revue du Nord*, 20 (August 1934) 233–248; 237.

57 "Arrêt du Conseil d'Etat," 1 February 1696, Six and Plouvain, *Edits*, 9: 404–405.

58 A.D.N. C 1,620, *circulaire*, 1748.

59 A.M.L. 15,090, "Registre aux octrois de la ville de Lille," fols. 107–112. For example, the *octroi* authorized in 1699 to pay for a variety of municipal offices was to be imposed on "toutes personnes privilegiez ou non privilegiez."

60 A.M.L. 311, Résolution du Magistrat, fol. 70.

61 A.D.N. C 641; Letters Patent, 21 December 1754

62 A.D.N. C 634, "Extrait des registres du Conseil d'Etat," 19 July 1701; "Arrêt du Conseil d'Etat," 10 December 1737, Six and Plouvain, *Edits*, 10: 403, A.D.N. C 1620.

63 *Edit du roi*, April 1771, Six and Plouvain, *Edits*, 7: 397–403.

64 A.D.N. C 1,620, *circulaire*, 1748.

65 A.M.L. 15,982, "Registre aux cahiers d'aides des états, 1714–1748," fol. 100.

66 A.D.N. C 3,757, 12 July 1755.

3 CORPS, BUREAUCRACY AND CITIZENSHIP: THE CASE OF THE BUREAUX DES FINANCES

1 A slightly different version of this chapter was published as "From *Corps* to Citizenship: The *Bureaux des Finances* before the French Revolution," *Journal of Modern History* 58 (1986), 610–642.

2 Philippe Rosset, "Les officers du Bureau des Finances de Lille (1691–1790)" (Unpublished thesis, University of Lille III, 1977), pp. 34–36.

3 For the genealogies see Eléonore-Paul Duchambge de Liessart, *Notes historiques relatives aux offices et officiers du Bureau des Finances de la généralité de Lille* (Lille, 1855), pp. 67, 87–90, 137–142; Du Péage, *Généologies*, pp. 1,121–1,134; Croquez, *La Flandre Walloone*, p. 19n.

4 Rosset, "Bureau des Finances," pp. 37–38; Jean-Paul Charmeil, *Les Trésoriers de France à l'époque de la Fronde. Contribution à l'histoire financière sous l'ancien régime* (Paris, 1964), p. 18 lists the size of all Bureaux.

5 Cited by Croquez, *La Flandre Walloone*, p. 152.

6 A.D.N., C.B.F. (I), "Edit du Roi portant création d'un Bureau des Finances & Généralité en la ville de Lille," September 1691; Rosset, "Bureau des Finances" pp. 41–43.

7 The *droit des lods et ventes* was a fee paid to a seigneur received when property was sold within his domain. The officers were exempt from this fee in the king's domain. Marion, *Dictionnaire*, p. 339.

8 Rosset, "Bureau des Finances," p. 178.

9 Ibid., pp. 190–194.

10 Charmeil, *Trésoriers de France*, pp. 150, 155–156, 162–163, 166–167, 172–175, 446–447.

11 Croquez, *La Flandre Wallonne*, p. 151.

12 Rosset, p. 37; A.D.N., C.B.F. (I). The sums are based upon the official price of the offices.

13 Taylor, "Noncapitalist Wealth," p. 478.

14 Marion, *Dictionnaire*, pp. 433–434, 452, 523.

15 *Edit du Roi*, March 1693, Six and Plouvain, *Edits*, 2: 175.

16 A.D.N., C.B.F. (I) dos. 6, "Mémoire sur l'état actuel et les fonctions du Bureau des Finances de la ville de Lille."

17 Marion, *Dictionnaire*, p. 361.

18 *Edit du Roi*, 29 April 1692, Six and Plouvain, *Edits*, 9: 367–368. Rosset, "Bureau des Finances," pp. 43–44.

19 24 June 1738, Six and Plouvain, *Edits*, 10: 407–410. A.D.N., C.B.F. (I), dos. 6, "Mémoire sur l'etat…"

20 See chapter 2, pp. 26–29.

21 Bosher, "Crisis of 1770," pp. 17–30; Palmer, *Democratic Revolution*, 1:86–99; William Doyle, "The Parlements of France and the Breakdown of the Old Regime, 1770–1788," *French Historical Studies* 6 (1970), 415–458.

22 Bosher, "Crisis of 1770," p. 27; Marcel Marion, *Histoire financière de la France depuis 1715*, 5 vols. (Paris, 1919), 1: 255–258.

23 Marion, *Dictionnaire*, pp. 78, 435; Marion, *Histoire financière*, 1: 260.

24 Correspondence of the *Bureaux*, A.D.N., C.B.F. 48 (1). The court at Bordeaux referred to an *augmentation de gages* of 4 million *livres*. Marion states that an edict of February 1770 created an *augmentation de gages* of 400,000 *livres*, of which the Bureaux had to pay 200,000 *livres*. *Histoire Financiére*, 1: 256.

25 A.D.N., C.B.F. 48 (1), *circulaire*, December 1774.

26 A.D.N., C.B.F., 48 (i), 17 March 1773.

27 A.D.N., C.B.F., 48 (h), letter from Lyon to Lille, 2 December 1774.

28 A.D.N., C.B.F., 48 (h), letter, n.d.

29 Ibid., *circulaire* from Montpellier, 11 November 1774.
30 Ibid. *circulaire* from Orléans, 24 November 1774.
31 A.D.N., C.B.F., 48 (g), Quoted in a letter of Devillantroye to Malus, 8 March 1772.
32 A.D.N., C.B.F., 4 (h), Response of Lille's Bureau, 9 December 1772, to the letter from Orléans, 24 November 1774.
33 A.D.N., C.B.F., 43 (b), "Pièces Justificatives."
34 A.D.N., C.B.F., 48 (f), letter, 27 September 1773.
35 A.D.N., C.B.F., 48 (l), "Réclamations du Parlement."
36 A.D.N., C.B.F., 48 (d), "Réfutation de la lettre de M. Terray," 19 July 1774.
37 Bodin, for example, argued that contract and property limited sovereign royal power in *Six Bookes of a Commonweale*, pp. 92–93, 204.
38 A.D.N., C.B.F., 48 (f), "Requête au Roi," 30 December 1772.
39 A.D.N., C.B.F., 48 (c), "Mémoire sur l'édit de Fevrier 1771."
40 A.D.N., C.B.F., 48 (l).
41 A.D.N., C.B.F., 48 (d), "Réfutation." See also 48 (f), letter from the Bureau, 27 September 1773.
42 Ibid., "Réfutation."
43 Ibid.
44 A.D.N., C.B.F., 48 (f), "Réflexions" on Terray's letter of 27 September 1773.
45 A.D.N., C.B., 3, dos. 9, "Mémoire des Bureaux des Finances sur l'affaire du centième denier," pp. 48–49.
46 ibid.
47 A.D.N., C.B.F., 48 (e), "Tableau duquel il résulte que la révocation de la survivance des Bureaux des Finances ne peut operer qu'une diminution considerable dans les revenus du roi." Their calculations listed the *marc d'or ancien* at 1,814 *livres*, and the *marc d'or de noblesse* at 2,800 *livres*. These figures included the surtax of 8 *sols per livre* (40 percent).
48 A.D.N., C.B.F., 48 (e), petition of the Bureaux des Finances to the king.
49 A.D.N., C.B.F., 48 (g), letter of Devillantroye in Paris, 16 January 1773.
50 A.D.N., C.B.F., 48 (h), letter of Dumond, 20 August 1776.
51 ibid.
52 A.M.L. 319, Registre aux Résolutions, "Emprunt de vingt millions au profit du roi," fols. 60–70; "Arrêt du Conseil d'Etat du Roi qui excepte les Provinces de Flandres, Haynaut & Artois de l'exécution des loix…," 4 January 1777, Six and Plouvain, *Edits*, 8: 70–71.
53 A.D.N., C.B.F., 48 (n), *circulaire* from Bordeaux, n.d.
54 ibid., *circulaire*, 17 January 1777.
55 A.D.N., C.B.F., 3, dos. 3.
56 A.D.N., C.B.F., 48 (n) *circulaire*, 29 January 1777.
57 ibid., *circulaire*, 11 January 1777.
58 A.D.N., C.B.F., 48 (i), Dumond to Malus, 30 July 1776. Efforts to revive the committee are discussed in letters from Montauban, 16 August 1780, and from Poitiers, 9 August 1778.
59 A.D.N., C.B.F., 3, dos. 13, letter of the *députés réunis* in Paris, 10 September 1786.
60 ibid., *députés réunis*, 10 September 1786.
61 A.D.N., C.B.F., 68, dos. 2.

62 A.D.N., C.B.F., 68, dos. 1, *circulaire*, Lyon, 27 August 1788.
63 ibid. *circulaire*, Soissons, 21 November 1788.
64 A.D.N., C.B.F., 68, dos. 1.
65 ibid., *Arrêté*, n.d.
66 ibid., *Arrêtés*, Bordeaux, 9 and 16 May 1788.
67 ibid., *circulaire*, 11 June 1788.
68 ibid., *circulaire*, 19 May 1788.
69 ibid., 11 June 1788.
70 ibid., 19 May 1788.
71 A.D.N., C.B.F., 3, dos. 13, May 1788.
72 ibid.
73 A.D.N., C.B.F., 3, dos. 13, 2 August 1786.
74 A.D.N., C.B.F., 68, dos. 1, *circulaire*, 17 October 1788.
75 ibid.
76 A.D.N., C.B.F., 68, dos. 5, "Arrêté du Bureau des Finances de la Rochelle," 24 December 1788; Letter, 1 January 1789.
77 ibid., "Arrêté du Bureau des Finances de Dijon," 5 January 1789; "Arrêté du Bureau des Finances de Soisson," 19 January 1789, and letter 31 January 1789.
78 A.D.N., C.B.F., 70, dos. 8, *circulaire*, 31 October 1788.
79 ibid., letter, Soisson, 31 January 1789.
80 ibid., "Rapport fait au Bureau des Finances par les commissaires nommés pour examiner ce qu'il y auroit à faire sur l'arrêté du Bureau des Finances de la Rochelle."
81 ibid., *circulaire*, 17 January 1789.
82 A.D.N., C 4,990.
83 All quotations from the Bureau in Dijon are from their *Arrêté*, 5 January 1789, A.D.N., C.B.F., 68, dos. 5.
84 All quotations from the Bureau in Soissons are from their *Arrêté*, 19 January 1789, A.D.N., C.B.F., 68, dos. 5.
85 All further quotations from the Bureau in La Rochelle are from their *Arrêté*, 24 January 1788, A.D.N., C.B.F., 68, dos. 5.
86 *Circulaire*, 16 November 1787, A.D.N., C.B.F., 70, dos. 8.
87 Keith Michael Baker, "Representation," in Baker, *Political Culture*, pp. 480–484.
88 "Mémoire des Bureaux des Finances sur l'affaire du centième denier," A.D.N., C.B.F., 3, dos. 9.
89 A.D.N., C.B.F., 68, dos. 5.
90 A.D.N., C 3,670, "Projet...proposé à la première assemblée du comité général."
91 A.D.N., C 3,670, Letter of the *députés réunis* to Lille, 29 May 1789.
92 A.D.N., C 3,670, letter of the *comité général*, 13 May 1789.
93 ibid., letter of the *deputés réunis*, 29 May 1789; Duchambge to Malus, 1 May 1789.
94 A.D.N., C.B.F., 68, dos. 1, *circulaire*, 11 June 1788.
95 A.D.N., C.B.F., 68, dos. 5, "Rapport...par les commissaires."

4 THE EXCLUDED NOBILITY AND POLITICAL REPRESENTATION

1 Couvreur and Montagne, "Noblesse," pp. 8–9; Lefebvre, *Paysans*, pp. 22–31.

2 For a look at the process Frenchwide, see David D. Bien "Manufacturing Nobles: The Chancelleries in France to 1789," *The Journal of Modern History* 61 (1989): 445–486.

3 Pillot, *Parlement*, 1: 408–409. Auditing the accounts of the *faux frais* was also a source of revenue for the officers, Lefebvre, *Paysans*, p. 172.

4 A.D.N. C 294, "Réponse des ordres," pp. 103–105; A.D.N. C 311, procès du bailliage contre Duchambge, Baron de Noyelles. A.D.N. C registre Flandre Wallonne, 1509, "Commissions"; *Arrêt du Conseil d'Etat*, 21 May 1698, Six and Plouvain, *Edits*, 10: 462–464; *Arrêt*, 21 January 1700, ibid., 10: 528.

5 A.D.N. C 277, "Factum pour les ordres du Clergé et de la Noblesse de la Province de Lille contre les baillis des quatre Seigneurs Hauts–Justiciers et les Magistrats de ... Lille" (n.d., 1690s); *arrêt* of August 1707, summarized in an *Arrêt du Conseil d'Etat*, 17 January 1767, Six and Plouvain, *Edits*, 10: 716–742.

6 A.M.L. A.G. 1,065, dos. 1, 2.

7 *Arrêt*, 21 March 1757, Six and Plouvain, *Edits*, 10: 619–620; *Arrêt*, 20 October 1774, ibid., 7: 725–726.

8 A.M.L. A.G. 1,288, 1,289.

9 A.M.L. 312, Résolution du Magistrat, 9 November 1758, fols. 154–156.

10 A.D.N. C 282, "Exposition du procès des ordres du clergé et de la noblesse des états contre les baillis et mayeurs et échevins de Lille ..." (1757); the quotations are from A.D.N. C 285, "Défense des droits attachés aux ordres du Clergé et de la Noblesse des Etats de la province de Lille" (1764), pp. 273–289.

11 Maurice Bordes, *La Réforme municipale du contrôleur général Laverdy et son application (1764–1771)* (Toulouse, 1968), p. 301.

12 A.D.N. C 285, "Défense des droits," p. 310; Croquez, *Histoire de Lille*, 1: 158–160.

13 D'Hollander, "L'échevinage lillois" (thesis), p. 123; A.M.L., A.G., 423, "mémoire au roi."

14 A.M.L. A.G. 423, "Autres observations du Magistrat sur les prétendus abus allegués par les ecclésiastiques et nobles," 14 April 1765.

15 A.M.L. 314, 19 May 1766, fols. 55–57.

16 A.M.L. A.G. 423, "Mémoire au roi."

17 A.M.L. A.G. 423, "Mémoire pour montrer l'incompatibilité de l'édit du mois d'aoust 1764 avec les moeurs des Pays Bas"; "Observation touchant l'élection des Magistrats par des notables"; letter from Maubeuge, 12 September 1764.

18 On royal judicial and administrative traditions in political debate see Baker, "French Political Thought," pp. 279–303.

19 Gail Bossenga, "City and State: An Urban Perspective on the Origins of the French Revolution," in Baker, *Political Culture*, pp. 121–130.

20 A.M.L. A.G. 1289, letter of Montbarey to deputies of nobles and clergy, 16 March 1780; letter of nobles to Montbarey, May 1780, in A.D.N. C 294, "Véritable point de vue sous lequel on doit envisager la demande d'une Administration Provinciale faite par les deputés et commissaires des ordres du

Clergé et de la Noblesse," pp. 75–78; *Arrêt du Conseil d'Etat*, 23 January 1783, Six and Plouvain, *Edits*, 11: 215–217.

21 On the provincial assemblies see Pierre Renouvin, *Les Assemblées provinciales de 1787. Origines, développements, résultats* (Paris, 1921).

22 A.D.N., C 294 "Procès-Verbal de l'Assemblée générale du Clergé & de la Noblesse de la Flandre-Wallonne...21 Novembre 1787," in "Réponse des ordres," pp. iii–viii.

23 The point is made by Wayne Te Brake in "Provincial Histories and National Revolution: The Dutch Republic in the 1780s," paper presented at a conference entitled "Enlightenment, Decline, and Revolution, the Dutch Republic in the Eighteenth Century," Washington, D.C., April 1987.

24 A.D.N. C 294, "Résumé des motifs qui déterminent les députés du clergé et de la noblesse de la Flandre Wallonne à supplier Sa Majesté d'établir dans cette province une administration provinciale" (Lille, 1787).

25 ibid.; A.M.L. A.G. 1,289 "Précis pour la Flandre-Wallonne qui demande une administration provinciale."

26 A.N.L. 15,751, "Mémoire pour le Magistrat de la ville de Lille...contre les deputés des ecclésiastiques et nobles de la même province."

27 A.D.N. C 285, "Défense des droits" (1764) lists the names of the deputies. See the list of dates of ennoblements in Couvreur and Montagne, "Noblesse," pp. 47–50b. For the supporters in 1787, see A.D.N., C 294, "Réponse des ordres," pp. iii–viii.

28 For the length of service of municipal magistrates, see A.M.L., 15,443; B.M.L. 799 and 800 "Création de la Loi".

29 The genealogies of Déliot, Hangouart, and DeMadre can be found in Du Péage, *Généalogies*, pp. 37–41, 1,200–1,201,and 1,496, respectively.

30 A.D.N. C 285, "Défense des droits," p. 308.

31 A.M.L. 15,751, "Mémoire pour le Magistrat"; A.M.L. 15,753, "Réfutation des écrits que les députés des Ecclésiastiques et des Nobles de la Flandre Wallonne ont publiés pour prouver que cette Province n'est pas un Pays d'Etats, que les Assemblées Provinciales doivent y être établies, et que l'Administration actuelle est remplie d'abus" (1787), pp. 27–28.

32 A.D.N. C 294, "Réponse des ordres," p. 51

33 A.D.N. C 294, "Résumé des motifs," p. 3.

34 A.D.N. C 294, "Résumé des motifs," pp. 2–3.

35 A.D.N. C 281 "Moiens et objections," p. 37; A.D.N., C. 285, "Défense des droits," p. 40.

36 A.D.N. C 285, "Défense des droits," pp. 205–206; C. 281, "Moiens et objections," pp. 36–37.

37 A.D.N. C 282, "Exposition du procès des ordres du Clergé et de la Noblesse des états contre les Baillis et mayeur et échevins de Lille," (1757), p. 26; A.D.N. C 285, "Défense des droits," pp. 28, 74, 87–100.

38 A.D.N. C 294, "Résumé des motifs," p. 4.

39 A.D.N. C 285, "Défense des droits." On the integration of both individualism and corporate rights into Pufendorf's theory of absolutism, see Leonard Kriegar, *The German Idea of Freedom: History of a Political Tradition* (Boston, 1957), pp. 50–59.

40 A.D.N. C 275, "Réponse pour les Baillis des Quatre Seigneurs Hauts-Justiciers et pour les magistrats de Lille, Douai, et Orchies," p. 2.

41 A.D.N. C 276, "Mémoire," pp. 18–19.
42 A.M.L. 15,753, "Réfutation des écrits," pp. 4–8.
43 A.D.N. C 294, "Réponse des orders," pp. 34–36; A.M.L. 15,753, "Réfutation des écrits," pp. 29–30.
44 The conflicts are summarized in A.D.N., C.B.F. 70, dos. 3, "Précis pour le sieur Renard d'Houchin, écuyer…joint à lui le collège des conseillers secrétaires du roi de la Chancellerie près le Parlement de Flandre," 27 February 1779. See also, A.D.N. C 686, *mémoire* of the nobles to the king, 11 May 1778; Arrêt du Conseil d'Etat, 11 July 1778, Six and Plouvain, *Edits*, 11: 161–163; Arrêt du Parlement de Flandre, 12 May 1778 in A.D.N. C 294, "Réponse des ordres," p. 1v; Couvreur and Montagne, "Noblesse," p. 134.
45 A.D.N., C.B.F. 70, dos. 3, "Précis."
46 Keith Michael Baker, "Representation," in Baker, *Political Culture*, p. 480.

5 A NATION OF EQUALS: THE DEMANDS OF THE THIRD ESTATE

1 A.D.N., MS. 255, "Registre aux délibérations de la Chambre de Commerce," 3 May 1787, fols. 98–99.
2 "Mémoire présenté à la Délibération des Membres du Tiers-Etat de la ville de Lille touchant la Réprésentation qui leur est due aux Etats Provinciaux de la Flandre-Wallonne & aux Etats Généraux" (14 January 1789); "Arrêté et Protestation des Membres du Tiers-Etat de la Ville de Lille, ensuite du Mémoire présenté à leur Délibération le 14 Janvier 1789" (16 January 1789); "Adhésion de différentes Corporations de la Ville de Lille" (21 January 1789). These pamphlets were printed and widely distributed. Copies appear in A.M.L., Don Gentil 1,955; A.M.L., 17,989, dos. 1; A.M.L. A.G. 441, dos. 8; A.D.N. C 296; and B.M.L. 32,398.
3 Payments to the guilds' commissioners were recorded in various accounts of the guilds for 1789. See A.M.L. 9,332 (*filtiers*); 8,127 (*apothicaires-épiciers*); 9,639, fol. 51, (*grossiers-merciers-drapiers*). On 25 June 1789, sixty-five corps and professional groups were assessed for the campaign. See A.M.L., Don Gentil 1,952, "Assemblée généralement convoquée des députés des différentes corporations de la ville de Lille."
4 A.D.N. C 294, "Résumé des motifs," pp. 32–39 of the *pièces justificatives*; Croquez, *La Flandre Wallonne*, p. 89.
5 Couvreur and Montagne, "Noblesse," p. 243.
6 A.M.L. 324, Résolution du Magistrat, 9 May 1781; A.M.L. 669, "Registre aux résolutions des grossiers-merciers," fols. 25–27.
7 On reactive and proactive collective action see Charles Tilly, *From Mobilization to Revolution* (Reading, Mass., 1978), pp. 143–149.
8 Jean Egret, *The French Pre-revolution*, trans. Wesley D. Camp (Chicago, 1977), pp. 138–143.
9 On the national mobilization of the Chambers of Commerce see J. Letaconnoux, "Les Sources de l'histoire du comité des députés extraordinaires des manufactures et du commerce de France (1789–1791)," *Revue d'Histoire Moderne et Contemporaine* (1912) 369–403; J. Tarrade, "Le Groupe de pression du commerce à la fin de l'ancien régime et sous l'Assemblée Constituante," *Bulletin de la Société d'Histoire Moderne et Contemporaine* (suppl. 2 of the

Revue d'Histoire Moderne et Contemporaine) (1970), 23–27; and Jean-Pierre Hirsch, "Les Milieux du commerce, l'esprit de système et le pouvoir à la veille de la Révolution," *Annales E.S.C.* 30 (1975), 1,337–1,370. Correspondence with Lille's Chamber of Commerce is found in A.D.N. C 1,297; A.N. B-III, 169, fols. 475–511; A.D.N. Archives de la Chambre de Commerce, carton 5. Some information on municipal mobilization is found in Egret, *Pre-revolution*, pp. 205–210.

10 A.D.N. C 285, "Défense des droits," p. 7.

11 A.M.L. A.G. 441, dos. 2, Brienne to the deputies of the nobles, 7 July 1788; deputies' response, 14 August 1788.

12 A.D.N. C 260, "Projet de distribution." It is not clear if the letters actually were sent.

13 A.N. K 1,161, "Projet relatif aux plaintes et demandes enconcées dans les mémoires des députés du Clergé et la Noblesse de la Flandre Wallonne."

14 A.M.L. Don Gentil 1,955, "Mémoire présenté," 14 January 1789, p. 6.

15 The role of liberal nobles in the Committee of Thirty was stressed by Elizabeth Eisenstein in "Who Intervened in 1788? A Commentary on *The Coming of the French Revolution*," *American Historial Review* 71 (October 1965), 77–103. See also Daniel Wick, "The Court Nobility and the French Revolution: The Example of the Society of Thirty," *Eighteenth-Century Studies* 13 (1980), 263–284.

16 ibid., A.M.L. 441, dos. 7; 442, dos. 2; Egret, *Pre-revolution*, pp. 205–210. Nantes was particularly important. See Jean Egret, "The Origins of the Revolution in Brittany (1788–1789)" in Jeffery Kaplow, ed., *New Perspectives on the French Revolution* (New York, 1965), pp. 136–152.

17 A.M.L. 205, 17 November 1788.

18 A.M.L. 326, Résolution du Magistrat, 21 January 1789; A.M.L. 205, Registre aux lettres écrites, 29 November 1788.

19 A.M.L. 205, 29 November 1788.

20 A.M.L. Don Gentil 1,955, "Mémoire présenté," p. 1. All quotations of Lille's Third Estate are from the petitions cited in note 2.

21 A.M.L. Don Gentil 1,955, "Délibération des Habitans du Bourg de Roubaix"; "Délibération des représentans du Tiers-Etat de la ville d'Armentières"; "Délibération des Habitans de la ville de Lannoy."

22 See also Régine Robin, *La Société française en 1789; Sémur-en-Auxois* (Paris, 1970), pp. 306–307, 330–333.

23 A.M.L. Don Gentil 1,955, "Arrêté et protestation," p. 6.

24 A.M.L. 326, 21 January 1789, fol. 121.

25 Georges Lepreux, *Histoire électorale et parlementaire du département du Nord. Nos représentants pendant la Révolution (1789–1799)* (Lille, 1898), pp. 2–3.

26 A.M.L. A.G. 441, dos. 10.

27 A.D.N. C 297, "Extrait des registres du Conseil d'Etat," 2 March 1789; B.M.L., Fonds Lillois, 26,134, "Discours de M. l'Intendant," 11 March 1789.

28 Cited in Couvreur and Montagne, "Noblesse," p. 244.

29 The *Cahier* of the nobility was signed by eight nobles including two counts, two barons, and one marquis, that of the Third Estate of the city of Lille by one doctor, four members of the Chamber of Commerce, and five lawyers or notaries. Mavidal and Laurent, *Archives Parlementaires* 3: 526–535.

30 For an overview see Kenneth Margerison, "The Movement for a Union of Orders in the Estates General of 1789," *French History* 3 (1989) 48–70.

31 A.M.L. Don Gentil 1,955, "Motion faite à l'ordre de la noblesse par le Baron d'Elbecq," 1 April 1789.

32 A.M.L. Don gentil 1,955, "Adresse du Tiers Etat du Souverain Bailliage de Lille à la Noblesse du même bailliage," (n.d.).

33 Cited by Lefebvre, *Paysans*, p. 328n.

34 Comment of Lille's subprefect, Scrive, 24 Messidor X (13 July 1802), A.D.N. M, 130, dos. 18.

35 D'Hollander, "L'échevinage lillois" (thesis), p. 141.

36 A.M.L. Don Gentil 1,952, 19 March 1789.

37 A.N. B-III, 72, letter of the intendant to the Directeur Général des Finances, 25 March 1789, fols. 224–225, and "Extrait des registres du Magistrat," 23 March 1789, fols. 229–231; A.M.L. A.G. 439, dos. 3, "Noms des personnes qui ont refusées de faire partie des 36 députés pour l'assemblée des trois ordres."

38 Lepreux, *Histoire électorale*, p. 13.

39 A.M.L. 205, Registre aux lettres écrites, 2 May 1789; A.M.L. 237, Résolution du Magistrat, 18 July 1789, fol. 12.

40 Lefebvre, *Paysans*, p. 345; P. Lefevre, *Commerce des grains*, pp. 118–202; A.D.N. C 692, "Extrait des Registres du Conseil D'Etat," 13 August 1789.

41 A.M.L. 857, Registre aux déliberations du comité de subsistance.

42 A.M.L. 327, Registre aux résolutions, fol. 18.

43 Lefebvre, *Paysans*, pp. 356–359.

44 A.D.N. L 876, "Emeutes"; A.M.L. 15.513, "Enregistrement des pièces relatives à l'establissement, confirmation et renouvellement des officiers généraux et du comité de la garde nationale," fol. 10; A.M.L. A.G. 442, dos. 12, "Récit de ce qui s'est passé à Lille en Flandres" (Lille, n.d.).

45 The comment of Blanquart, *greffier* of the neighboring village of Frelinghem, was cited by L. Théry, "Une commune rurale de la Flandre Française au début de la Révolution: Frelinghem," *Revue du Nord* 9 (1923), 199.

46 See Hunt, "Committees and Communes", 321–346, and Alfred Cobban, "Local Government During the French Revolution," *English Historical Review* 58 (1943) 13–31.

47 A.M.L. 15.513, fol. 8, motion of the committee of the three orders of the city, 31 July 1789.

48 A.M.L. 327, Registre aux résolutions du magistrat, 27 July 1789, fol. 18.

49 A.M.L. 15.513, fols. 30, 34.

50 A.M.L. A.G. 504, dos. 9.

51 A.M.L. 15.443, 21 September 1789. See also D'Hollander, "L'échevinage lillois" (thesis), pp. 143–145.

52 ibid., p. 145; A.M.L. A.G. 482, dos. 26.

53 *Réimpression de l'ancien Moniteur*, 1: 285–293.

54 Letter, 10 December 1789, signed by deputies of the Third Estate from the *gouvernance* of Lille and Cambrésis published in *Réimpression de l'ancien Moniteur*, 2: 345–347; See also the "Réponse des commetans des provinces de Flandres et de Cambrésis à la lettre à eux écrites par sept de leurs commis à l'Assemblée Nationale." Ambrose Saricks, *A Bibliography of the Frank*

E. Melvin Collection of Pamphlets of the French Revolution in the University of Kansas Libraries, 2 vols. (Lawrence, 1960), 2: 448.

55 Jacques L. Godechot, *Les Institutions de la France sous la Révolution et l'Empire* (Paris, 1968), pp. 75–76, 91–112; Lepreux, *Histoire électorale*, pp. 21–22.

56 Croquez, *Histoire de Lille*, 1: 329; A.M.L. Don Gentil, 2054.

57 Two nobles, including Vandercruisse des Waziers, who tried to resign from the municipal magistracy in March 1789, and one *conseiller* from the *Gouvernance* were also elected. The new *procureur* and his substitute were both lawyers. A.D.N. L 606, municipal elections. Lists of the members of the *Juridiction Consulaire* and Chamber of Commerce can be found in Convain, *Juridiction Consulaire*, and A.D.N. MS. 225, "Registre aux délibérations de la Chambre de Commerce."

58 Godechot, *Institutions*, pp. 163–174.

59 On the riots in Paris see, Matthews, *General Farms*, p. 172. Marion cited attacks on the *bureaux d'octroi* in at least 12 cities. After 1 August 1789, collection posts for the *droits des fermes* and the *régie générale* were also destroyed in several provinces. Marion, *Histoire financière*, 2: 7–9; and Bossenga, "City and State," in Baker, *Political Culture*, pp. 134–136.

60 Marion, *Histoire financière*, 2: 225–227.

61 A.M.L. 17,781, dos. 6, "Adresse du conseil général de la commune de Lille à l'Assemblée Nationale sur la suppression ... d'octrois des villes"; "Adresse préliminaire de la commune de Lyon sur la dette de cette ville, sur les dettes des villes en général et sur la nécessité de les joindre toutes à la dette nationale"; Camille Bloch, *Procès-verbaux du comité des finances de l'Assemblée Constituante* (Rennes, 1922), pp. 510, 523; Godechot, *Institutions*, p. 172.

62 A.M.L. 17,781, dos. 6, "Rapport fait par François Sta," 20 April 1791.

63 ibid.

64 A.M.L. 17,781, dos. 6, "Addresse ... de Lyon."

65 Godechot, *Institutions*, p. 172.

66 *Archives Parlementaires*, 29:194, 72:98, 208.

67 A.M.L. 17,781, dos. 3.

6 USES OF A REGULATED ECONOMY: THE STATE AGAINST ITSELF

1 *The Second Industrial Divide: Possibilities for Prosperity* (New York, 1984), pp. 31–33.

2 *Mercantilism*, trans. Mendel Shapiro (London and New York, 1955). Problems with his interpretation are discussed in the volume of essays edited by D. C. Coleman, *Revisions in Mercantilism* (London, 1969).

3 On this definition of *la police* see Martin Wolfe, "French Views on Wealth and Taxes from the Middle Ages to the Old Regime," in Coleman, *Revisions in Mercantilism*, p. 193.

4 The municipal magistrates' policy of protecting small commodity production for political reasons in the seventeenth century is explored by Robert S. DuPlessis and Martha C. Howell, "Reconsidering the Early Modern Urban Economy: The Cases of Leiden and Lille," *Past and Present* 94 (1982) 49–84.

5 A.M.L. A.G. 36, dos. 1, "Noms des arts et métiers érigés en corps." One guild had statutes from the thirteenth century, seven from the fifteenth, thirty-six from the sixteenth, ten from the seventeenth, and one from the eighteenth.

6 Lefevre, *Le Commerce des grains*, pp. 67–73.

7 A.M.L. 568, "Avis du procureur syndic," no. 23.

8 For the decisions of the municipal magistrates, see A.M.L. A.G. 1,063, dos. 1, 7, and A.M.L. A.G. 1,069, dos. 24. For the case before the Parlement, A.D.N. VIII-B, 2,041.

9 A.M.L. A.G. 34, dos. 3, "Déclaration des corps des arts et métiers," 1723.

10 A.M.L. A.G. 1,192, dos. 16.

11 A.M.L. 597, "Avis du procureur syndic."

12 Three times during the eighteenth century the king required the guilds to furnish men for the militia. The municipal magistrates declared that individuals who served three years in the militia for the guilds would be admitted to the guild without apprenticeship. Vanhaeck, *Sayetterie*, 16: 74–75.

13 A.M.L. A.G. 1,192, dos. 16; A.D.N. L 140, "Registre aux décisions sur requêtes du Directoire du département du Nord," fol. 87, no. 206.

14 A.M.L. A.G. 35, dos. 6; A.M.L. A.G. 901, dos. 16. For a similar situation in Dijon see Edward J. Shephard, Jr., "Social and Geographic Mobility of the Eighteenth-Century Guild Artisan: An Analysis of Guild Receptions in Dijon, 1700–90," in Steven L. Kaplan and Cynthia Koep, eds., *Work in France: Representations, Meaning, Organization, and Practice* (Ithaca, 1986), pp. 114–115.

15 A.M.L. A.G. 1,196, dos. 7.

16 A.M.L. A.G. 36, dos. 3.

17 A.M.L. A.G. 1,182, dos. 16; 1,205, dos. 1, 7; 1,203, dos. 9; A.M.L. 322, Résolution du Magistrat, 29 October 1779, fols. 128–129; A.M.L. A.G. 1,206, dos. 4.

18 The classic works on mercantilism under Colbert are Charles Woolsey Cole, *Colbert and a Century of French Mercantilism*, 2 vols. (New York, 1939) and his *French Mercantilism, 1683–1700* (New York, 1943).

19 See Gabriel Ardant, "Financial Policy and Economic Infrastructure of Modern States and Nations," in Charles Tilly, ed., *The Formation of National States in Western Europe* (Princeton, 1975), p. 196.

20 On the relationship between fiscality and corporate peasant liability see Root, *Peasants and King*. For an example of guilds and taxation see the "Arrêt du Conseil d'Etat du Roi, portant nouveau Règlement sur la répartition…des impositions dans les corps…de Paris," 14 March 1779 in *Arts et métiers, 1776–1791* (n.p., n.d.).

21 See Morineau, "Budgets de l'Etat."

22 On the role of the Farmers General as bankers of the king see George T. Matthews, *The Royal General Farms in Eighteenth-Century France* (New York, 1958). Regional tax networks and credit are described in Bosher, *Single Duty Project* and his *French Finances*.

23 Wolfe, "Wealth and Taxes," p. 198. Fiscalism is emphasized to the exclusion of all other elements in mercantilism in Robert B. Ekelund, Jr., and Robert Tollison, *Mercantilism as a Rent-Seeking Society: Economic Regulation in Historical Perspective* (College Station, Texas, 1981).

24 Emile Coornaert, *Les Corporations en France avant 1789* (Paris, 1968), p. 165.
25 Coornaert, *Les Corporations*, pp. 119–153. Etienne Martin Saint-Léon, *Histoire des corporations de métiers depuis leurs origines jusqu'à leur suppression en 1791, suivie d'une étude sur l'évolution de l'idée corporative au XIXe siècle et sur les syndicats professionels* (Paris, 1897), pp. 410–427.
26 Emile Levasseur, *Histoire des classes ouvrières en France depuis la conquête de Jules César jusqu'à la Révolution*, 2 vols. (Paris, 1859), 2: 185; 513–520.
27 Six and Plouvain, *Edits*, February 1692, 2: 126–130; L. Dubois, *Le Régime de la brasserie à Lille, des origines à la Révolution, 1279–1789* (Lille, 1912), pp. xxvi–xxvii.
28 Dubois, *Brasserie*, p. xl.
29 ibid., pp. xlii–xlvi.
30 Six and Plouvain, *Edits*, 3 March 1693, 2: 200; A.M.L. A.G. 35 dos. 6; Dubois, *Brasserie*, p. ciii.
31 A.M.L. A.G. 417, dos. 3.
32 Six and Plouvain, *Edits*, November, 1695, 2: 427–429.
33 ibid., 2: 484–493, 539–541, 545–554, 593–596; Lefevre, *Commerce des grains*, pp. 74–84.
34 A.M.L. A.G. 417, dos. 9, 22.
35 A.M.L. A.G. 417, dos. 11.
36 A.M.L. A.G. 417, dos. 22; Staquet, annexe I.
37 A.M.L. A.G. 417, dos. 16, 21.
38 A.M.L. A.G. 1,076, dos. 2.
39 A.M.L. A.G. 417, dos. 21, "Mémoire des administrateurs de la charité générale." For protests of the provincial estates and the Parlement, see A.M.L. A.G. 1,067, dos. 2.
40 Lefevre, *Commerce des grains*, p. 183; Six and Plouvain, *Edits*, 7: 372–374.
41 A.M.L. A.G. 33.
42 ibid. The Chamber of Commerce wrote similar petitions defending the liberty of merchants in 1727 and 1747. See A.M.L. A.G. 3, dos. 1, and 35, dos. 6.
43 A.M.L. A.G. 2, dos. 3; A.M.L. A.G. 35, dos. 6.
44 A.M.L. A.G. 33, for rolls assessing the guilds in 1697; A.M.L. A.G. 2, dos. 3, and A.M.L. A.G. 3, dos. 1. for rolls in 1726; A.M.L. A.G. 34, dos. 14, for rolls in 1745; A.M.L. A.G. 36, dos. 2 and A.M.L. 312, Résolution du Magistrat, 2 May 1759, fols. 186–190, for policy in 1759.
45 For Lyon, A.M.L. A.G. 33, dos. 7, letter of Lyon's *échevins*. For Paris, René Nigeon, *Etat financier des corporations parisiens d'arts et métiers au XVIII siècle* (Paris, 1934), pp. 20, 31, 58; and Levasseur, *Histoire des classes ouvrières*, 2: 296–300. For Toulouse, F. Dumas, "Les Corporations de métiers de la ville de Toulouse au XVIIIe siècle," *Annales du Midi* 12 (1900) 475–495.
46 A.M.L. A.G. 2, dos. 1, 3.
47 The revenues came primarily from reception fees, from assessments levied on masters according to the number of looms or apprentices in the workshops, and from interest paid by the king on venal offices. The main expenditures included ceremonies, such as masses and funerals; salaries of officials; judicial proceedings; auditing of accounts; and interest payments on money the masters had borrowed. A.M.L. A.G. 36, dos. 7, "Etat des revenues et charges des communautés d'arts et metiers" (1764).

48 A.M.L. 669, "Registre aux résolutions des merciers-grossiers," fols. 27–36.
49 The survey is reproduced in Gail Bossenga, "Corporate Institutions, Revolution and the State: Lille from Louis XIV to Napoleon" (Ph.D. diss., University of Michigan, 1983), pp. 493–497. Unfortunately, the percentage of funds borrowed to meet royal demands, as opposed to judicial costs, was not specified in the survey.
50 A.M.L. A.G. 3, dos. 2, "Requêtes présentées par les differens corps de métiers afin d'être autorisés de lever de l'argent... pour le droit de confirmation."
51 ibid. For a similar case in Paris see Levasseur, *Histoire des classes ouvrières*, 2: 296–297n.
52 A.M.L. A.G. 2, dos. 3, *Mémoire*, 5 April 1727.
53 A.D.N. C 3,982.
54 Levasseur, *Histoire des classes ouvrières*, 2: 402.
55 Nigeon, *Corporations parisiens*, pp. 67–68.
56 Levasseur, *Histoire des classes ouvrières*, 2: 405, 550.
57 A.D.N. C 3982, letter to the controller general, 9 October 1776.

7 CORPORATE PRIVILEGE AND THE BOURGEOISIE

1 On the anticapitalism of the guilds see, for example, Godechot, *Institutions de la France*, p. 20; J. Lambert-Dansette, *Origines et évolution d'une bourgeoisie: Quelques familles du patronat textile de Lille-Armentières, 1789–1914* (Lille, 1954), p. 457; William Reddy, *The Rise of Market Culture* (Cambridge, 1984), pp. 34–38; Peter Kriedte, *Peasants, Landlords and Merchant Capitalists: Europe and the World Economy, 1500–1800*, trans. V. R. Berghahn, (Cambridge, 1983), pp. 11–12; Albert Soboul, *Précis d'histoire de la Révolution française* (Paris, 1962), p. 520. Pierre Goubert calls businessmen "sturdy individualists" in *The Ancien Régime*, p. 215. Portions of this chapter appeared in "Protecting Merchants: Guilds and Commercial Capitalism in Eighteenth Century France," *French Historical Studies* 15 (Fall, 1988), 693–703; and "La Révolution française et les corporations: trois exemples lillois," *Annales, E.S.C.* 43 (1988), 405–426.
2 For two examples of merchants and guilds see Simona Cerutti, "Du corps au métier: la corporation des tailleurs de Turin," *Annales, E.S.C.*, 43 (1988): 323–352; and Hirsch, "Revolutionary France." Charles Sabel and Jonathan Zeitlin look at non-competitive, corporately-based alternatives to mass production under nineteenth-century industrial capitalism in their important article on "Historical Alternatives to Mass Production: Politics, Markets, and Technology in Nineteenth-Century Industrialization," *Past and Present* 108 (1985), 133–176. Sabel and Zeitlin's emphasis on production and technology, however, does not consider the role of merchants who controlled circulating capital so critical to the pre-industrial period. For them "guild industrialization" was formed out of an earlier communitarian and flexible world of petty producers in which "workers and employers often trade places" (p. 174). But the true employers in the eighteenth-century textile industry were merchants, and they rarely traded places with workers.
3 Vanhaeck, *Sayetterie*, 16: 12–20; 17: 309–317.

4 Eric Kerridge, *Textile Manufactuers in Early Modern England* (Manchester, 1985), pp. 1–3.

5 Dieudonné, *Statistique*, 2: 416–417.

6 A.D.N. M 581, dos. 188, *mémoire* to the prefect; Dieudonné, *Statistique*, 2: 415. Most documents for the old regime in the municipal archives of Tourcoing have been destroyed. Paul Delsalle, "Les Enterprises textiles de Tourcoing (XVIIe–XXe siècle)," *Revue du Nord* 69 (1987), 752.

7 Vanhaeck, *Sayetterie*, 16: 20; Dieudonné, *Statistique*, 2: 420.

8 Vanhaeck, *Sayetterie*, 16: 151–158; 17: 155, 326–327.

9 More specifically, master wool weavers (*sayetteurs*) were limited to six looms when they made cloth classified as *changeants*, which included *camelots*. Vanhaeck, *Sayetterie*, 16: 90–115, and Lottin, *Chavatte*, pp. 44–45, 86–105. The *bourgeteurs* had no such limitation.

10 A.D.N. C 1651, Letter to the Chamber of Commerce, 3 January 1782; Vanhaeck, *Sayetterie*, 16: 65–67, 116–147.

11 In the late 1400s and early 1500s the number of apprentices had been between 50 and 150 per year. Vanhaeck, *Sayetterie*, 16: 34–5. According to a survey in the 1775, there were 239 masters. A.M.L., A.G., 1,203, dos. 3.

12 Vanhaeck, *Sayetterie*, 16: 34, 67–77.

13 Pierre Deyon and Alain Lottin, "Evolution de la production textile à Lille aux XVIe et XVIIe siècles," *Revue du Nord* 49 (1967), 24.

14 Vanhaeck, *Sayetterie*, 16: 321.

15 ibid., 16: 308–319.

16 ibid., 16: 42–64.

17 Bagnols, "Mémoire," p. 493. According to Lottin, the amount was exagerrated. *Chavatte*, p. 95.

18 A.M.L. A.G. 1,205, dos. 12; Dieudonné, *Statistique*, 2: 458.

19 Vanhaeck, *Sayetterie*, 16: 84.

20 A.M.L. 11,308, "Déliberation du corps des grossiers-merciers-drapiers du 13 mars 1789." For the genealogy of the Vanhoenacker family, see *Bulletin de la Société de la Province de Cambrai*, 18 (1913), 102–118.

21 See below, pp. 159–166.

22 A. de Saint-Léger, "La rivalité industrielle entre la ville de Lille et le plat pays," *Annales de l'Est et du Nord*, 2 (1906), 367–382.

23 A survey made of rural industry in the *châtellenie* of Lille is reproduced in Lottin, *Chavette*, p. 54.

24 Saint-Léger, "Rivalité," pp. 377–378. Jean Piat, *Roubaix, capitale du textile* (Roubaix, 1968), p. 47.

25 Deyon and Lottin, "Production textile," p. 28n.

26 Lottin, *Chavatte*, pp. 113–114.

27 Ordinance of M. de Bagnols, 19 May 1693, Vanhaeck, *Sayetterie*, 17: 201.

28 ibid., 16: 278n, 206–207. Two different fees (*droits de changeants*) were levied on all pieces of cloth made by the guilds of weavers in Lille, and a *droit de cinq gros* was levied on each piece of cloth leaving the city. A.D.N. C 128; A.D.N. *Placards* 8,559.

29 *Avis* of the intendant (Bidé de la Grandville), 3 July 1732, Vanhaeck, *Sayetterie*, 17: 275.

30 A.D.N. C 124.

31 Vanhaeck, *Sayetterie*, 16: 280–281, 301. This apparently applied only to Roubaix.

32 A.D.N. C 127; *Ordonnance* of the magistrates, 31 October 1731, Vanhaeck, *Sayetterie*, 17: 262.

33 *Avis* of Bidé de la Grandville, 3 July 1732, Vanhaeck, *Sayetterie*, 17: 277.

34 ibid., 17: 276.

35 ibid., 16: 282–283. During the next two decades the intendants continued to support the privileges of Lille in manufacturing. Saint-Léger, "Rivalité industrielle," pp. 392–395; Braure, *Lille*, 2: 382–383.

36 Saint-Léger, "Rivalité," pp. 390–391.

37 This interpretation is supported by the "Mémoire pour les maîtres du corps des marchands grossiers, merciers de la ville de Lille et branches en dépendantes, joints à eux et intervenans les maîtres du corps des sayetteurs, ceux des bourgeteurs, et ceux du corps des peigneurs." (Lille, n.d.), A.M.L., A.G., 150, dos. 22; also in A.D.N. Placards 8,560.

38 ibid., pp. 396–398. *Arrêt*, 12 July 1763. Six and Plouvain, *Edits*, 10: 685.

39 Saint-Léger, "Rivalité"; Hilaire, *Histoire de Roubaix*, pp. 88–94; *Arrêt*, 30 April 1766, Six and Plouvain, *Edits*, 8: 30–32.

40 A.M.L. A.G. 1,200, dos. 2, "Mémoire des habitans, fabriquans, et négocians de Roubaix," July 1764.

41 A.M.L. A.G. 1,203, dos. 12, "Très-humbles et très-respecteuses repré-sentations des Magistrat, négociants et fabricants de...Lille," 1776.

42 Quoted by d'Hollander in "L'échevinage lillois," p. 12.

43 Saint-Léger, "Rivalité," p. 404.

44 On the physiocrats see, Georges Weuleresse, *Le Mouvement physiocratique en France de 1756 à 1770*, 2 vols. (Paris, 1910) and Elizabeth Fox-Genovese, *The Origins of Physiocracy* (Ithaca, 1976).

45 Saint-Léger, "Rivalité," pp. 400–401.

46 A.M.L. A.G. 1,203, dos. 12, "Très-humbles...représentations," p. 11.

47 For the remonstrance see Jules Flammermont, ed., *Remontrances du Parlement de Paris au XVIIIe siècle*, 3 vols (Paris, 1888–1898), 3: 309–354. Rhetoric of the Parlement is analyzed by Steven Laurence Kaplan, "Social Classification and Representation in the Corporate World of Eighteenth-Century France: Turgot's 'Carnival'," in Kaplan, ed., *Work in France*, pp. 176–228. See also Sewell, *Work and Revolution*, pp. 72–77.

48 In 1732 the prince de Soubise, seigneur of Roubaix, supported his village against Lille. A.D.N. C 130. In 1618 the prince d'Egmont, seigneur of Armentières, helped his village obtain the right to make serges. Vanhaeck, *Sayetterie*, 16: 293. For other examples see Saint-Léger, "Rivalité," pp. 372, 375, 483.

49 A.D.N. C 115.

50 The position of the Estates of Artois was cited in a "Mémoire pour les Magistrat, Négociants et fabriquants...de Lille," A.M.L. A.G. 1,203, dos. 12.

51 Anonymous "Observations sur l'arrêt du Conseil du 7 Septembre, 1762," probably by the intendant, noted that the city's *négociants* agreed on the need to preserve guild privileges. A.D.N. C 130.

52 Dieudonné, *Statistique*, 2: 436–439.

53 The number of *plombs d'outils* is listed in Vanhaeck, *Sayetterie*, 16: 284.

54 Deyon and Lottin, "Production textile," p. 28; Dieudonné, *Statistique*, 2: 436.
55 Vanhaeck, *Sayetterie*, 16: 287.
56 Hilaire, *Histoire de Roubaix*, p. 96.
57 In 1779 the wool weavers made reference to manufacturers in Roubaix "who send the shipments abroad themselves without recourse to the *négociants*." A.M.L. A.G. 1,205, dos. 6.
58 J. Flammermont, *Histoire de l'industrie à Lille* (Lille, 1897), pp. 103–104. A.M.L. 315, Registre aux Résolutions, 1 October 1768, fols. 169–175; A.M.L. 320, 20 December 1777, fols. 116–120.
59 Pierre Deyon, "La Diffusion rurale des industries textiles en Flandre française à la fin de l'ancien régime et au début du XIXème siecle," *Revue du Nord* 61 (1979), 92–93.
60 *Paysans*, p. 298.
61 Vanhaeck, *Sayetterie*, 16: 323–339.
62 A.M.L. A.G. 1,203, dos. 3. A total of 239 masters worked 724 looms. The average number of looms per master was three. In 1650, there were 343 masters in the guild working 926 looms, for an average of 2.7 looms per master. See Lottin, *Chavatte*, p. 88. Thus the average number of looms per master had hardly risen over the course of the century.
63 "Deuxième mémoire ou avis de la chambre de commerce," 25 January 1776, Vanhaeck, *Sayetterie*, 17: 373–377.
64 A.M.L. A.G. 1,203, dos. 25; Vanhaeck, *Sayetterie*, 17: 350–351, 362–265.
65 A.D.N. MS. 255, "Registre aux délibérations de la Chambre de Commerce," 19 November 1775, fol. 70; Vanhaeck, *Sayetterie*, 17: 357.
66 The seven *négociants* in the guild of dry-goods merchants were: Laurent Deldique, Pierre Reynard, Scheppers, E. Vanhoenacker, Louis Vanhoenacker, J. B. Barrois, and Burette. In addition Placide Panckoucke is listed on, and apparently crossed off, the rolls for the annual dues in the guild. A.M.L. 9,637, comptes du corps des merciers-grossiers, 1788; *Almanach du Commerce des Arts et Metiers de la Ville de Lille* (Lille, 1787), pp. 46–47. Auguste Brame was an *épicier*, ibid., p. 39. Others who voted for the limitation were: Panckoucke, A. Baillon (sugar refiner), and J. Gossellin. Those who voted for unlimited liberty were: Samin, Le Brun l'aîné, Bosset, Delecourt, Peterninck-Cardon (thread merchant-manufacturer), and Virnot (salt refiner).
67 "Observations...de la Chambre de commerce," 17–29 November 1775, Vanhaeck, *Sayetterie*, 17: 357.
68 A.M.L. A.G. 1,203, dos. 8.
69 Vanhaeck, *Sayetterie*, 17: 378–379.
70 A.M.L. A.G. 1,192, dos. 1.
71 A.M.L. A.G. 1,203, dos. 8, "Observations sur la requête presentée à messieurs du magistrat..."
72 "Mémoire," 1779, Vanhaeck, *Sayetterie*, 17: 394.
73 See chapter 4, pp. 85–87.
74 Vanhaeck, *Sayetterie*, 16: 336–341.
75 Saint-Léger, "Rivalité industrielle," pp. 390–391; Vanhaeck, *Sayetterie*, 17: 236–240, 263–274.
76 ibid., 1: 120–125, 2: 270; Lottin, *Chavatte*, p. 45. The cost for the *plomb de visite* was three *deniers*, all of which went to the municipality. The magistrates

paid the officials who had applied the *plomb de visite* a fixed salary, rather than a percentage of the fines, in order to prevent these officials from fining weavers arbitrarily. The *plomb d'outil* cost six *deniers*, four of which went to the doyens and two to the city.

77 Dieudonné, *Statistique*, 2: 439.

78 *Lettres-Patentes du Roi*, 5 May 1779, Six and Plouvain, *Edits*, 8: 243–250.

79 A.D.N. MS. 255, fols. 78–79.

80 ibid.

81 Six and Plouvain, *Edits*, 8: 300–304; Levasseur, *Classes ouvrières à la Révolution*, 2: 408–409.

82 In 1792, Lille's *négociants* referred to regulation by the *bureau de marque* as a "*loi bursale.*" A.M.L. 17,997, dos. 1.

83 A.M.L. A.G. 1,206, dos. 2.

84 For example, Levasseur, *Classes ouvrières à la Révolution*, 2: 409–410; Godechot, *Institutions*, p. 20.

85 A.M.L. 9,278, 9,319, comptes de la fileterie. The number are based on the fees that masters paid for each mill in operation.

86 A.M.L. A.G. 1,210, dos. 23, 24. Ordinances of the magistrates, 10 April 1691, and 21 July 1691.

87 Dieudonné, *Statistique*, 2: 231–239.

88 A.M.L. A.G. 1,210, dos. 26, "Statuts, Reglemens et ordonnances du corps de la fileterie." Although widows could take over their husbands' businesses, it was much more difficult for daughters to take over their fathers' businesses. In 1780 the daughters of a very successful master, Marie Claire Joseph Bigo and *soeurs*, were allowed to become masters in the guild only after a heated controversy. A.M.L. A.G. 1,214, dos. 17.

89 This paragraph is based on a "Mémoire des maîtres et suppôts du corps des marchands-manufacturiers de fils" and a "Mémoire pour les principaux suppôts du corps des filetiers," A.M.L. A.G. 1,212, dos. 5.

90 A.M.L. comptes de la fileterie, 9,293, 9,319.

91 *Almanach du Commerce* (1789), p. 99. Each type of thread was assigned a number which corresponded to the number of skeins needed to equal one half pound of thread. The finer the thread the higher its number, because more thread would be needed to equal one half pound. Thus, if a merchant ordered three pounds of number 14, he would receive 84 skeins of thread.

92 A.M.L. A.G. 1,212, dos. 6, 7. For the ordinances of Bidé de la Grandville and Moreau de Sechelle on 16 May 1733, and 21 January 1744, respectively, see the statutes of the guild, A.M.L. A.G. 1,210, dos. 26.

93 A.M.L. A.G. 1,213, dos. 13, petition of the guild, 1769.

94 A.M.L. A.G. 1,212, dos. 20, ordinance of the municipal magistrates, 17 February 1744.

95 A.M.L. A.G. 1,212, dos. 13, *Avis*, 21 January 1768.

96 Dieudonné, *Statistique*, 2: 232.

97 A.M.L. A.G. 1,213, dos. 3.

98 ibid.

99 A.M.L. A.G. 1,213, dos. 3, petition of the masters to the municipal magistrates.

100 A.M.L. A.G. 1,213, dos. 3, "Mémoire du Magistrat de Lille concernant les manufactures de fils de lin qui s'establissent dans...le plat pays."

101 A.M.L. A.G. 1,213, dos. 3, petition of the masters.
102 A.M.L. A.G. 1,213, dos. 1, ordinance of Moreau de Sechelle, 3 June 1752.
103 A.M.L. A.G. 1,213, dos. 11, ordinance of Caumartin, 13 March 1767.
104 A.M.L. A.G. 1,213, dos. 3.
105 A.M.L. A.G. 1,213, dos. 3, "Observations en réponse aux requêtes presentés par differens particuliers..."
106 A.M.L. A.G. 1,213, dos. 3 "Réponse aux requêtes..."; A.M.L. A.G. 1,213, dos. 13.
107 A.M.L. A.G. 1,213, dos. 11, 13. Ordinances of Caumartin, 13 March 1767 and 13 December 1769.
108 A.D.N. C 3,171; A.M.L. A.G. 1,213, dos. 14.
109 A.M.L. A.G. 1,214, dos. 6, ordinance of Caumartin, 11 December 1777.
110 A.M.L. A.G. 1,213, dos. 17, ordinance of Esmangart, 27 April 1786; A.M.L. 1,213, dos. 13; A.D.N. C, 3,171, "Observations du directeur des fermes."
111 I have no evidence that Lille's inspectors seized thread from rural manufacturers without just cause, although this may have occurred. In 1759 the intendant upheld the guild's inspectors when they confiscated the thread of a merchant from Armentières who had not followed the regulations and thus was fined 100 *florins*. A.M.L. A.G. 1,213, dos. 13. That the *directeur des fermes* asked the intendant Esmangart to suppress all mills within two leagues of the Franco-Belgian border shows that smuggling was a problem. A.M.L. A.G. 1,214, dos. 14. Apparently in Bailleul the inspectors did harass their competitors. The village of Hazebrouck complained that although they had their own inspectors, those from Bailleul insisted on checking their thread again, charging a fee, and holding up their exports, even though this was against the law. A.D.N. *Archives de la Chambre de Commerce*, Carton 5 (provisional classification), letter from Hazebrouck, 1789.
112 A.M.L. *comptes* 9,638 lists dues-paying members. For a collection of statutes and regulations concerning the guild, see A.M.L. A.G. 1,240, dos. 2.
113 For example, in the mid-eighteenth century when Le Comte, a manufacturer from Roubaix, announced his intention to open a store in Lille to sell cloth from Roubaix *en gros*, the municipal magistrates ruled that only members of the guild of dry-goods merchants had this right. A.M.L. A.G. 150, dos. 13.
114 A.M.L. A.G. 150, dos. 22, Avis de la chambre de commerce, June 1750 and "Mémoire pour les maîtres du corps des marchands grossiers, merciers de la ville de Lille et branches en dépendantes" (Lille, n.d.), p. 14 for the definitions of types of merchants.
115 ibid. On the growth of new forms of advertising in the eighteenth century see Neil McKendrick, John Brewer, and J. H. Plumb, *The Birth of a Consumer Society: The Commercialization of Eighteenth-Century England* (London, 1982).
116 A.M.L. A.G. 151, dos. 2, 18 January 1759.
117 A.M.L. A.G. 151, dos. 1.
118 A.D.N. MS. 255, fol. 48.
119 "...passer librement...à Lille pour y être teintes, apprêtées, et vendues en gros, ainsi que les fabriquans de Roubaix le jugeron à propos..." Articles 87 and 88 of the *arrêt*, 19 April 1732, A.M.L. A.G. 151, dos. 4. For the *arrêt* see Vanhaeck, *Sayetterie*, 17: 263–74.

120 A.D.N. Placards, 8,560, "Mémoire pour les...Grossiers," pp. 19–21.

121 A.M.L. 315, 1 October 1768, fols. 169–175.

122 A.M.L. A.G. 152, dos. 5, the agenda in 1765 for the *intendant du commerce*, M. de Montaran, *père*, lists the issue as one for his next visit in Lille, but I have found no decision on brokers in Pierre Bonassieux, *Conseil du commerce et Bureau du Commerce (1700–1791). Inventaire analytique des procès-verbaux* (Paris, 1900).

123 Deyon, "Diffusion rurale," p. 93. Here Deyon states that "Les roubaisiens ne pouvaient vendre que les produits de leur propre atelier et devaient livrer à huit courtiers lillois tout ce qu'ils avaient acheté ou faire tisser à façon." This seems to contradict his later statement that "Les 'fabricants' roubaisiens ne pouvaient écouler directement que les étoffes qu'ils avaient commanditées et fait fabriquer à façon." "Un modèle à l'épreuve. Le développement industriel de Roubaix de 1762 à la fin du XIXéme siécle," *Revue du Nord* 63 (1981), 59–60. I am following the first statement. In effect the Roubaisiens never lost the right to choose or change their own *commissionnaires*.

124 A.D.N. Placards 8,560, "Mémoire pour les...Grossiers."

125 A.M.L. A.G. 1,240, dos. 13, 15; A.M.L. 669, *registre des merciers-grossiers*, fols. 1–2; ordinances of the municipal magistrates, 18 July 1753 and 28 June 1742 are found in the collection of statutes, A.M.L. A.G. 1,240, dos. 2.

126 A.M.L. A.G. 32, ordinance, 18 September, 1,711; A.M.L. A.G. 1,240, dos. 13, ordinance, 15 February 1747.

127 A.M.L. A.G. 1,242, dos. 6, "Mémoire pour le Sr. Jacques Martin, négociant, demeurant à Orchies...et pour les suppôts du corps des marchands grossiers de cette ville, intervenans...contre les Srs. Roussel-Burrette et Mahieu, marchands grossiers-merciers et maîtres en exercise dudit corps." (Lille, 1786).

128 ibid., pp. 26–34.

129 ibid., pp. 4–5.

130 ibid., p. 13.

131 A.M.L. A.G. 1,246, dos. 6, All quotes are from the "Second mémoire pour les maîtres en exercice du corps des grossiers-merciers de la ville de Lille contre Jacques Martin..." (Lille, 1786). See also the "Mémoire pour les Srs. Roussell et Mahieu, maîtres en exercice du corps des Grossiers-Merciers contre le Sr. Jacques Martin...et ceux des suppôts dudit corps qui se sont rendus intervenans." (Lille, 1786).

132 ibid. See pp. 51–55 of the "Second mémoire" for a copy of the petition.

133 Lepreux, *Histoire électorale*, p. 13; *Almanach de la Garde Bourgeoise et du comité de la ville de Lille* (Lille, 1790), pp. 11–13 (in the Bibliothèque Royale in Brussels); A.D.N. L 606, "Elections des municipalités révolutionnaires"; A.M.L. 413, 11 December 1792, fols. 76–77.

134 Hirsch, "Honneur et liberté."

135 A.D.N. Placards 8,560, pp. 19–20, 25.

8 THE ABOLITION OF THE GUILDS

1 A.M.L. 669, registre des merciers-grossiers, fols. 70–73.

2 ibid.

3 The *cahiers* are published in Mavidal and Laurent, *Archives Parlementaires*, 2: 615 (Lyon); 6: 655 (Paris); 5: 310; 318 (Paris Intra-Muros); 6: 646 (Nancy); 3: 770 (Metz); 3: 132, 140–141 (Dijon); 4: 243 (Nîmes); 5: 785 (Strasbourg); 2: 494 (Caen); 2: 769 (Clermont-Ferrand); 5: 601 (Rouen); 3: 707 (Marseille); 4: 100 (Nantes); 6: 38 (Toulouse); 2: 401 (Bordeaux); 6: 655 (Orléans); 5: 548 (Rennes). In Paris outright denunciation of the guilds was found in the Parisian district of Saint-Louis de la Culture, but not in several of the other electoral districts. Some cities, like Nîmes and Dijon, basically ignored the question of guilds, as did Strasbourg. Because Strasbourg had framed their *cahier* with the demand that Alsace be confirmed in all its privileges, however, it is unlikely that the Strasbourgeois wished to abolish these corps. Both Toulouse and Bordeaux asked that "all exclusive privileges be suppressed," but usually this clause, which appeared frequently in *cahiers*, was linked to the privileges of trading companies, in particular the universally detested *Compagnie des Indes*.

4 Liana Vardi, "The Abolition of the Guilds during the French Revolution," *French Historical Studies* 15 (1988), 708–713.

5 Sewell, *Work and Revolution*, p. 86.

6 Report of M. d'Allarde, 17 February 1791, *Réimpression de l'ancien Moniteur* 7: 396–397.

7 "Décret portant suppression de tous le droits d'aides, de toutes les maîtrises et jurandes et établissement de patentes," 2–17 March 1791. J. B. Duvergier, ed., *Collection complète des lois, décrets, ordonnances...(1789–1824)*, 24 vols. (Paris, 1789–1824), 2: 281–285.

8 Emile Levasseur, *Histoire des classes ouvrières en France depuis 1789 jusqu'à nos jours*, 2 vols. (Paris, 1867), 1: 116–117. Special provisions were made for the Parisian guilds which in 1782 had given the king 1,500,000 *livres* for a new ship, of which 800,000 *livres* remained to be reimbursed. *Moniteur*, 7: 743.

9 A letter to Lille's *procureur syndic*, 22 April 1792, observed that creditors of "the clergy, old *pays d'états*, *Châtellenies*, corporations d'arts et métiers, etc." had to send their titles to M. Dufresne de Saint-Léon, *commissaire liquidateur* in Paris, by 1 May 1792. Claims not exceeding 300 *livres* could be liquidated directly by the directory of the department. A.D.N. L 1738.

10 A.D.N. Levasseur, *Histoire jusqu'à nos jours*, 1: 116–117.

11 A.M.L. 15,862, letter, 11 August 1792. Some guilds in Lille were still submitting tables of debts for verification in 1794. A.M.L. 17,919, dos. 8.

12 A.M.L. 412, municipal ordinance, 29 February 1791, fols. 187–188.

13 A.M.L. 412, municipal ordinance, 7 June 1791; A.M.L. 413, municipal ordinance, 8 January 1793.

14 "Décret relatif à l'organisation d'une police municipale et correctionnelle," Duvergier, *Lois*, 3: 132–149.

15 A.M.L. 349, Registre sur requêtes, fols. 38, 76–77, 158–159, 176; A.M.L. 412, municipal ordinance, 17 June 1791.

16 B.M.L. MS. 312, municipal ordinance, 20 December 1792; 22 February 1793.

17 A.M.L. 349, 19 November 1791, fol. 36.

18 Franc Bacquié, *Les Inspecteurs des manufactures sous l'ancien régime, 1669–1791* (Toulouse, 1927), pp. 357–358. According to Bacquié, the *cahiers* of the *bailliage* of Bordeaux, Rennes, Troyes, Saint-Quentin, Maine, and Toulon

similarly demanded that the inspectors of manufacturing be suppressed and that the guilds or inspectors paid by local inhabitants enforce the regulations.

19 A.M.L. 723, Registre des Tisserands-Sayetteurs-Bourgeteurs, fols. 131–141.

20 For various petitions see A.M.L. 17,997, dos. 1; A.M.L. 17,741; A.D.N. L 1,505, dos. 19; B.M.L. Fonds Lillois 26,151, petition of the thread spinners and merchant-manufacturers of *camelots* and *draps* to the National Assembly. For the opposing view, see the petition by the master weavers, the *citoyens fabricants* of Lille, A.M.L. 17,997, dos. 1.

21 A.D.N. L 1,505, dos. 17, letter of 3 March 1792.

22 Lefevre, *Commerce des grains*, pp. 19–33; Arrêt du Conseil d'Etat, 12 July 1775, Six and Plouvain, *Edits*, 11: 68–69; "Arrêt qui rétablit les belandriers...dans le droit...de charger seuls...les marchandises expédiées de ladite ville," 23 June 1781, ibid., 11: 210–221.

23 Mavidal and Laurent, *Arch. Parl.* 3: 523, 529, 534. Protests had also been registered immediately after the *belandriers* received their exclusive privileges. A.D.N. L 4,726, dos. 2, "Mémoire sur la nécessité de rendre absolument libre la navigation intérieure des provinces de Flandre, Artois, Haynaut, et Cambrésis" (Lille, September 1781).

24 According to reception fees for masters in the accounts of the guild, A.M.L. 3,207–3,210.

25 A.D.N. Placards 8,560, "Mémoire sur la question de scavoir s'il est de l'intérêt de l'état et du commerce de supprimer les corps de navigation" (n.d.).

26 A.D.N. L 4,726, dos. 2, "Rapport sur l'affaire des privilèges des belandriers de Dunkerque, des bateliers de Condé, et autres corps de navigation dans l'étendu du département du Nord.

27 A.D.N. L 4,726, dos. 2, "A l'Assemblée Nationale" by the *belandriers*. The guild claimed the cost of constructing the new ships had been approximately 260,000 *livres*. A.D.N. L, 4,726, dos. 1.

28 A.D.N. L 4,726, dos. 2, "Réponse pour les maîtres en exercice du corps de la Navigation de Condé...presentée à Monseigneur le Directeur Général des Finances pour l'Assemblée de la Nation"; A.D.N. L 4,726 dos. 3, "Abrégé chronologique des services que la navigation de Condé a rendu à l'Etat."

29 A.D.N. L 4,726, dos. 3, Avis du procureur syndic.

30 A.D.N. L 4,725, dos. 2.

31 A.M.L. 3,208, accounts of the boaters, 1792; A.D.N. L 202, Arrêté du département du Nord, 4 August 1791.

32 In 1794 the boaters were 5,641 *livres* in debt, acquired largely after their deputation to Paris in 1791 and for a joust in August 1793. See their accounts in A.M.L. 3,208–3,210. In 1791 the department had ruled that the boaters, and not the nation, would have to pay for any debts incurred while trying to obtain a favorable decree from the National Assembly. A.D.N. L 4,720.

33 A.D.N. L 4,720, *arrêt*, 7 Thermidor VI (25 July 1798); letter of the commandant in Douai, 21 Vendémiaire VII; letter of the Minister of War to Lille's commandant, 8 Vendémiaire VII.

9 THE CORPORATE HERITAGE AND THE WELL-ORDERED STATE

1 Several descriptions of the procession and documents on the controversy with the clergy are found in A.M.L. A.G. 655, dos. 2.

2 Claude Fouret, "Les Fêtes à Lille au XVIIIème siècle" (Mémoire de maîtrise, University of Lille, III 1978), p. 98. In his study of Frankfurt, Gerald Soliday similarly observed that corporate status was associated with political rule: "governing was probably regarded as the most important social function in the community." *A Community in Conflict: Frankfurt Society in the Seventeenth and Early Eighteenth Centuries* (Hanover, New Hampshire, 1974), p. 64.

3 In 1785 the members of the Chamber of Commerce and the *Hôtel de la Monnaie* wanted to have seats of honor as corps in the church choir during a *Te Deum* for the birth of the Duke of Normandy. They were refused because "*usage immémorial*" had given other corps this right. A.D.N. MS. 255, fols. 94–95.

4 B.M.L. MS. 313, "Ordonnance concernant la procession de Lille," 29 May 1790; AML, 15,513, "Enregistrement...de la garde nationale," fols. 178–186 describes the festival of federation and speeches. For further analysis, see Odile Ramette, "La Fédération de Lille, 6 juin 1790," *Revue du Nord*, 64 (July–December 1982), 789–802; and Louis Trénard, "Lille en fête durant la Révolution, 1789–1799," *Revue du Nord* 69 (July–September 1987), 591–604.

5 B.M.L. MS. 313, "Résolution relative aux processions," 20 May 1791; "Ordonnance concernant la procession solennelle de la ville de Lille," 17 June 1791; Croquez, *Histoire de Lille*, 1: 246; E. Hautcoeur, *Histoire de l'église collégiale et du chapitre de St. Pierre de Lille*, in *Mémoires de la Société d'Etudes de la Province de Cambrai*, vols. 4–6 (Lille, 1896–1899), 6: 396–397, A.M.L. 18,261.

6 A.M.L. 18,332, letter 26 June 1791, fol. 24.

7 For similar examples elsewhere in France, see Mona Ozouf, *La Fête révolutionnaire, 1789–1799* (Paris, 1976), p. 134.

8 A.M.L. 413, 10 Pluviôse II (28 February 1794), fols. 170–171; A.M.L. 18,329, *registre* of the popular society, 16 Ventôse II (6 March 1794), fol. 103.

9 A.M.L. 8,210, accounts of the boaters, 1794.

10 A.D.N. Bibliothèque Administrative (cited hereafter as Bib. Ad.), 698, *Feuille du département du Nord*.

11 ibid., 16 June 1805.

12 By 1825 the annual town procession had become a very elaborate and self-conscious celebration of the city's history incorporating both civil and religious elements. See M. Clément, *Histoire des fêtes civiles et religieuses, des usages anciens et modernes du département du Nord* (Cambrai, 1836), pp. 58–67.

13 On the discontinuity between the royal bureaucracy of the old regime and the one formed during the Revolution see Church, *Revolution and Red Tape*, and Bosher, *French Finances*.

14 Habermas, *The Structural Transformation*, pp. 30, 79–88. For a feminist perspective on public and private spheres see Joan Landes, *Women and the Public Sphere in the Age of the French Revolution* (Ithaca, New York, 1988).

15 A.D.N. M 4, dos. 1; letter 18 Fructidor VIII (8 September 1800).

16 J. N. Guyot, *Répertoire universel et raisonné de jurisprudence civile, criminelle, canonique, et bénéficiale*, 17 vols. (Paris, 1784), 13: 467. The article on *préseance* in Guyot's 1784 edition was signed by M. de la Croix, *avocat au parlement*.

17 A.D.N. *Actes de la Préfecture, arrêté* of the prefect, 28 Nivôse XI (19 January 1803), 4: 152; A.D.N. M 4, dos. 2, prefectural correspondence on precedence.

18 A.D.N. M 130, dos. 14 Minister of Interior to prefect, 16 Fructidor VIII (6 September 1800).

19 A.D.N. M 4, dos. 1; A.D.N. *Annuaire Statistique du Département du Nord*, (1804–1805), 3: 94–99.

20 A.D.N. M 4, dos. 1, cited in letter of the Bishop of Cambrai to the prefect, 3 March 1812.

21 Guyot, *Répertoire universel*, 13: 469, 472–473.

22 A.D.N. *Annuaire Statistique*, 3: 96.

23 Godechot, *Institutions*, pp. 586–599.

24 Godechot, *Institutions*, p. 597.

25 A.D.N. *Annuaire Statistique*, an XI (1802–1803), 1: 49–51.

26 A.D.N. L 606, 608; Dupéage, *Généalogies*; de Brigode, 13: 498–501; de Muyssart, 13: 780–799.

27 Bergeron, *France Under Napoleon*, pp. 70–72.

28 Godechot, *Institutions*, pp. 590–594, 597–598.

29 A table of the twenty wealthiest citizens in post-revolutionary Lille, based upon a list in A.D.N. M 130, dos. 13, is reproduced in Bossenga, "Corporate Institutions," pp. 420–421.

30 A.D.N. M 130, dos. 18.

31 A.D.N. *Annuaire Statistique*, "Conseils Municipaux," (1810) 8: 25; A.D.N. M 65, dos. 18, lists of candidates for the municipal councils; A.M.L. Don Gentil 2,422, "Liste des cent plus imposés de la ville de Lille."

32 A classic statement from a Marxist perspective is that of Albert Soboul in *Précis d'histoire de la Révolution française* (Paris, 1962), p. 520. But the general assumptions may be found in other works. "Under the old regime, corporations were legally sanctioned bodies, and their language and institutions recapitulated the hierarchical premises of the traditional monarchy. But after the Revolution, proprietary individualism became the dominant idiom of the state, and the corporate idiom became a language of opposition." Sewell, *Work and Revolution*, p. 162.

33 Sewell, *Work and Revolution*, pp. 162–171; Jean Bruhat, "Le Mouvement ouvrier française du début du XIXe siècle et les survivances de l'ancien régime," *La Pensée*, 142 (Dec. 1968) 44–56. For descriptions of compagnonnage see Cynthia Truant, "Solidarity and Symbolism among Journeymen Artisans: The Case of Compagnonnage." *Comparative Studies in Society and History* 21 (1979), 214–226; and Michael Sonenscher, *Work and Wages*, especially pp. 295–327.

34 Sewell, *Work and Revolution*, p. 231.

35 In the accounts of guilds that I examined, there was no record of economic assistance to sick or indigent masters. My survey included the accounts of the bakers, A.M.L. 8,262–8,275 (1780–1791); boaters, 8,196–8,210 (1780–1794); dry-goods merchants and drapers, 9,639 (1789); apothecaries-grocers, 8,124–

8,127 (1786–1790); and thread merchant-manufacturers, 9,322–9,332 (1780–1790).

36 Vanhaeck, *Sayetterie*, 16: 192.
37 For examples of foundations in the wool guild see Vanhaeck, *Sayetterie*, 17: 184–186.
38 Vanhaeck, *Sayetterie*, 16: 189; 17: 301.
39 A.M.L. A.G. 38, dos. 11, letter 25 February 1783.
40 ibid., A.M.L. 17,989 dos. 6, mayor to subprefect, 27 Messidor XII (16 July 1804).
41 A table furnished by the prefect in 1843 recorded one society founded in 1580, one in 1695, eight societies founded between 1725 and 1792, all of which included "*ouvriers de diverses professions*." Cited in Pierre Pierrard, *La Vie ouvrière à Lille sous le Second Empire* (Paris, 1965), pp. 291–292. The list compiled by the prefect seems to have included only societies founded in the eighteenth century that were reconstituted after the Revolution and thus did not form a complete list. For example, there was the *Société de la Magdelaine* in 1765 which had a master dyer as its treasurer and paid out 279 *florins* in sick benefits, but whose records disappear the next year. AML, 6,636–6,637. I suspect many records of these societies were lost.
42 Godechot, *Institutions*, pp. 216–217.
43 P. J. B. Buchez and P. C. Roux, *Histoire parlementaire de la Révolution française*, 40 vols. (Paris, 1834–1838), 10: 194–195.
44 A.M.L. 17,989, dos. 6, letter of the mayor, 1804.
45 B.M.L. fonds Reybourbon, 83; B.M.L. MS. 312, "Cercle des Amis des Lois," 14 March 1799, fol. 670.
46 A list of the *sociétés des malades* in Lille and the date of their formation is in Pierrard, *La Vie ouvrière à Lille*, pp. 291–292. For the letter of the mayor, A.M.L. 17,989, dos. 6. For statutes of the Société de Saint-Dominique, created in 1797, B.M.L. fonds Reybourbon, 83. The municipal magistrates of the old regime had also opposed the founding of mutual aid societies along craft lines. See Vanhaeck, *Sayetterie*, 16: 189–191; A.M.L. 311, ordinance, 23 December 1752; A.M.L. A.G. 1238, dos. 12. Examples such as these led Maurice Braure to conclude incorrectly that associations of workers were prohibited in Lille before the Revolution. *Lille*, 2: 374.
47 Godechot, *Institutions*, p. 668.
48 A.M.L. 17,998, dos. 3, mayor to police commissioner, 18 June 1807.
49 ibid., mayor to police commissioner, 24 May 1806; police report, 29 May 1806.
50 It does not seem true, as William Sewell argues, that the usage of the word *society* in the old regime was restricted to the educated classes, and that "when the French nation itself was recast as a 'society', formed by voluntary adherence to a social contract, all kinds of other organizations...came to be termed 'societies' as well. Hence, when workers' corporations called themselves *sociétés*, they were simply conforming to general post-revolutionary usage." p. 188. In Lille workers were already using the term *société* in the 1760s to describe mutual aid organizations. If the use of the word *société* implied a new idea of contractual, associational life, then this cultural shift is evident among workers, and not just the elites, before the Revolution in Western Europe. For parallels with English friendly societies see Stephen Yeazell, *From*

Medieval Group Litigation to the Modern Class Action (New Haven and London, 1987) pp. 166–167.

51 A comparison of textile production in 1788 and 1797 in Lille can be found in "Un essai de statistique industrielle en l'an V: L'industrie de la Corrège, de la Creuse, de la Moselle, du Nord, du Pas de Calais, et de la Sarthe en 1797," *Bulletin de la Commission de recherche et de publication des documents relatifs à la vie économique de la Révolution* (1908): 11–295. In 1812 the Nord produced 5,827,000 kg. of cotton thread; the department of the Seine, the next largest producer, produced only 800,000 kg. Jean Antoine Chaptal, *De l'industrie française*, 2 vols. (Paris, 1819), 2: 12–14. On the linen thread industry see Dieudonné, *Statistique*, 2: 233, 238–9; and Jean Lambert-Dansette and Joseph-Antoine Roy, "Origines et évolution d'une bourgeoisie: le patronat textile du bassin Lillois (1789–1914)," *Revue du Nord* 37 (1955), 214.

52 A.M.L. 17,998, 21 Ventôse V (11 March 1797).

53 ibid.

54 ibid.; A.D.N. M 581, dos. 1, correspondence with prefect, 1800–1801.

55 B.M.L. 26,687, "Concordat entre les Fabricans de fils retords de la ville de Lille," 10 February 1809. See also the "Projet de règlement pour la fabrique de fils retords de la ville de Lille," A.D.N. fonds non-classés, registre...de la Chambre de Commerce, fols. 219–223.

56 B.M.L. 26,687, "Concordat."

57 A.D.N. 79-J-35, "Lettres et minutes de la Chambre Consultative (1805 à 1816)"; A.D.N. J-1, "Registre de la Chambre Consultative." A.D.N. fonds non-classés, "Registre aux mémoires de la Chambre de Commerce établi à Lille (3 Nivôse XI à 1816)." These two chambers had been set up by the central government in 1802 and 1803 in order to allow businessmen to transmit their suggestions for improving commerce and manufacturing directly to the Minister of Interior. Members in both chambers were elected by the wealthiest merchants and manufacturers and the prefect was automatically a member. Many of the same families that ran commerce in Lille in the old regime sat in the new chamber of commerce. The members were listed each year in the departmental *Annuaire Statistique*.

58 A.D.N. 79-J-35, doc. 24, 25 April 1806.

59 *De l'industrie française*, 2: 1–2; 205–207, 217–218.

60 A.D.N. 79-J-35, doc. 1, prefect to mayor of Roubaix, 8 Pluviôse XIII (29 January 1805).

61 A.D.N. 75-J-35, doc. 52.

62 Levasseur, *Histoire jusqu'à nos jours*, 1: 253n; 293. For other examples of the demand of merchants and manufacturers in France for the revival of regulation see S. Charléty, "La vie économique de Lyon sous Napoléon," *Vierteljahrschrift für Social-und Wirtschaft Geschichte*, 5 (1906): 365–379; and Chaptal, *Industrie française*, 2: 362–365.

63 A letter of the mayor to the prefect, 2 Prairial XI (22 May 1803), contains extracts of the pertinent municipal ordinances regulating the auctions during the eighteenth century. In 1790, at the request of the guild of dry-goods merchants, the prohibition on selling new merchandise had been reaffirmed. A.M.L. 312, "Ordonnance concernant les corps des grossiers-merciers et drapiers," 15 May 1790, fols. 136–139.

64 Six and Plouvain, *Edits*, 2: 541–544; 7: 380–384; A.M.L. A.G. 417, dos. 22; A.M.L. 324, résolution, 9 January 1783, fol. 273.
65 A.M.L. 349, registre aux requêtes, 23 March 1792, fols. 110–111.
66 A.M.L. 413, ordinance, 10 February 1792.
67 A.D.N. L 8,895, 21 May 1792.
68 A.M.L. 413, ordinance, 27 Brumaire II (17 November 1793).
69 A.M.L. 15,413, fols. 558–559, 27 Thermidor VI (14 August 1798).
70 A.M.L. 18,005, dos. 3, 2 Prairial XI (22 May 1803).
71 A.D.N. fonds non-classés, registre de la Chambre de Commerce, mémoire, 18 Messidor XI (7 July 1803), fols. 12–14.
72 A.M.L. 18,005, 24 Ventôse XII (15 February 1803).
73 A.M.L. 15,413, *arrêté*, 9 Germinal XII (30 March 1804), fols. 755–758.
74 Like Lille's merchants, those in Paris argued that "on a tellement senti les dangers des ventes publiques pour les intérêts du commerce, qu'autre-fois même, ces ventes n'avaient lieu que dans trois cas seulement, en cessation de commerce, par jugement, et après la mort du négociant." *Gazette Nationale ou le Moniteur Universel*, no. 107, 17 Nivôse XI (8 January 1804), 428–429.
75 A.M.L. 18,005, dos. 3, mayor to subprefect 19 Floréal XII (9 May 1804) and mayor to prefect, 16 Ventôse XIII (17 March 1805). The cost of a *patente* was calculated both by the type of occupation and the population of the city in which a worker resided. The *tarifs* for the *patente* are listed in *Actes de la Préfecture*, 5: 5–38.
76 A.M.L. 18,005, dos. 3.
77 A.M.L. 18,005, dos. 2, 16 Frimaire XII (5 June 1804); 18,005 dos. 3, *arrêtés* of the prefect, 10 Nivôse XIII (31 December 1804); 20 Floréal XIII (10 May 1805); 19 August 1806.
78 B.M.L. MS. 312, 11 December 1818, fols. 1,670–1,671.
79 A.M.L. 15,413, *arrêté*, 10 Thermidor XI (29 July 1803).
80 For an identical argument by the Chamber of Commerce in Lyon see *Gazette Nationale ou le Moniteur Universel*, 17 January 1818, p. 74.
81 B.M.L. 312, fols. 1,069–1,081; 1,333–1,345; 1,367–1,368.
82 A.M.L. 15,413, *arrêté*, 24 Fructidor IX (6 September 1801), fols. 693–696.
83 Four of the newly elected officials had the same last names as sons of masters who had entered the bakers' guild in the 1780s. A.M.L. 18,247, dos. 7 and accounts of the bakers, A.M.L. 8,264–8,274 (1780–1790). A.M.L. 18,247, dos. 2 "Extrait des minutes de la Secretairerie d'Etat," 5 April 1813. The Parisian bakers had already been subjected to these restrictions in 1801. Godechot, *Institutions*, p. 680; Duvergier, *Lois*, "Arrêté des Consuls sur le commerce de la boulangerie à Paris," 19 Vendémiaire X (11 October 1801).
84 A.D.N. M 445, cited in letter of de Muyssart to prefect, 21 August 1821.
85 A.M.L. 8,263–8,275, accounts of the bakers.
86 A.D.N. M 445, dos. 1, petition to the prefect, 1821; A.M.L. 18,247, dos. 7. According to the statutes of the guild of bakers in the old regime, individuals had to serve a two-year apprenticeship to become a master, but sons of masters were exempt from this requirement. Lefevre, *Commerce des grains*, p. 98.
87 A.M.L. 18,247, dos. 4.
88 B.M.L. MS. 312, fols. 1,638–1,639, 1,818–1,822, 1,823–1,825; for the *arrêté* allowing rural bakers to sell bread in the city, A.M.L. 15,416, *arrêté du maire*, 10 August 1838.

89 A.D.N. M 445, dos. 1, letter of prefect to the Minister of Agriculture and Commerce, 23 December 1814.

90 B.M.L. MS. 312, "Arrêté qui rappelle plusieurs articles d'ordonnances relatives à la police du marché aux grains," 13 April 1816, fols. 1,368–1,377. See also the *arrêté* of 9 December 1817, fols. 1,589–1,590.

91 A.D.N. M 445, dos. 1, letter from the Bureau de Police to the mayor of Lille, 4 June 1824.

92 Levasseur, *Histoire jusqu'à nos jours*, 1: 287–288. On the central role of the Parisian Prefect of Police in reinstating quasi-corporate structures known as *syndicats* among master employers see Michael David Sibalis, "Corporatism after the Corporations: The Debate on Restoring the Guilds under Napoleon I and the Restoration," *French Historical Studies* 15 (1988), 718–730.

93 B.M.L. MS. 312, *arrêtés* 2 Nivôse XIV (23 December 1805), fols. 910–922; 30 January 1806, fols. 924–927; 24 July 1805, fols. 889–890.

94 B.M.L., MS. 312, fols. 1,674–1,682.

95 On the changed legal and cultural terrain in which labor disputes were contested after the Revolution see Sonenscher, *Work and Wages*, pp. 363–376, and Alain Cottereau, "Justice et injustice ordinaire sur les lieux de travail d'après les audiences prud'hommales (1806–1866)," *Le Mouvement Social* 141 (1987), 25–59.

96 Levasseur, *Histoire jusqu'à nos jours*, 1: 256–257; Godechot, *Institutions*, pp. 622–264. On the monopolistic situation created by Napoleon for the *avoués*, see Isser Woloch, "The Fall and Resurrection of the Civil Bar, 1789–1820s," *French Historical Studies*, 15 (1987), 241–262. On the barristers see Michael Fitzsimmons, *The Parisian Order of Barristers and the French Revolution* (Cambridge, Mass., 1987).

97 B.M.L. 24,262, Henri Pajot, *Le Notariat dans l'arrondissement de Lille* (Lille, 1862), p. 19.

98 See Jean-Pierre Hirsch, "Un fils rompu? A propos du crédit à Lille sous la Révolution et l'Empire," *Revue du Nord* 61 (January–March 1979), 181–193, and Levasseur, *Histoire jusqu'à nos jours*, 1: 258–264. As Gerald L. Geison observed in the introduction to his edited collection, "in the French context, by striking contrast to Anglo-American assumptions, professional 'autonomy' or success went hand in hand with 'dependence' on the state and its bureaucracy." *Professions and the French State, 1700–1900* (Philadelphia, 1984), pp. 3–4. See also J. Léonard, "L'exemple d'une catégorie socio-professionnelle au XIXe siècle: les médecins français," in Daniel Roche and C. E. Labrousse, eds., *Ordres et classes, Colloque d'histoire sociale, Saint-Cloud, 24–25 mai, 1967* (Paris, 1973), pp. 221–234.

99 *De l'industrie française*, p. 222.

100 *Rapport sur les Jurandes et Maîtrises et sur un projet de statuts et règlemens pour les marchands de vin de Paris* (Paris, 1805).

101 ibid., p. 51.

102 *Le Moniteur Universel*, 12 Germinal XI (3 April 1803), pp. 869–870. Regnault de Saint Jean d'Angély was the *rapporteur* for the *Conseil d'Etat* when the government was examining whether or not to regulate industry and manufacturing. His report in April 1803 formed the basis of several important laws, including a law prohibiting coalitions.

103 Levasseur, *Histoire jusqu'à nos jours*, 1: 274n.

104 ibid., 275n.
105 Michel Crozier, *The Stalled Society*, trans. Rupert Sawyer (New York, 1974).

10 CONCLUSION

1 *The Coming of the French Revolution*, trans. R. R. Palmer (Princeton, 1947), p. 2.

Bibliography

UNPUBLISHED SOURCES

ARCHIVES NATIONALES

B III, 72, 169. Collection générale des procès-verbaux, mémoires, et autres pièces concernant les députations à l'Assemblée Nationale de 1789 (Lille)
K 1,161, no. 12. Capitulation treaty

ARCHIVES DÉPARTMENTALES DU NORD

Série C. Records of the Intendant. Cartons 115, 124, 127, 128, 130, 226, 237, 260, 266, 277, 282, 285, 294, 296, 297, 631, 634, 686, 692, 1,297, 1,620, 1,651, 1,708, 3,171, 3,754, 3,757, 3,982
Série C, *registre*
 1,506, "*Registre aux mémoires des Etats*," 1769–1785
 1,509, "*Registre aux commissions des Baillis des Etats*," 1756–1789
Série C, *Archives du Bureau des Finances*. Cartons, 1, 3, 43, 48, 68, 70. Correspondence and documents concerning the privileges and exemptions of the corps
Série L. Documents from the period of the Revolution. Cartons 140, 606, 876, 1,505, 1,738, 2,982, 4,720, 4,726, 4,725, 8,895
Série M. Records of the Prefect and Subprefects. Cartons 4, 65, 130, 445, 581.
J-1. "Registre aux délibérations de la Chambre Consultative des arts et métiers"
79-J-35. "Lettres et minutes de la Chambre Consultative," 1805–1816
Placards 8,560. "Mémoire pour les maîtres du corps des Marchands grossiers"; "Mémoire sur la question de sçavoir s'il est l'intérêt de l'état et du commerce de supprimer les corps de navigation"
Archives de la Chambre de Commerce
 "Registre aux mémoires de la Chambre de Commerce établi à Lille," 3 Nivôse XI à 1816
 Manuscrit 255. "Registre aux délibérations de la Chambre de Commerce de Lille," 1715–1791

ARCHIVES MUNICIPALES DE LILLE

Affaires Générales

The rich collection of 1,297 cartons of materials classified as *Affaires Générales* includes a wide range of documents – *mémoires*, surveys, letters, petitions, edicts, court decisions – on all aspects of municipal life in the early modern period. Used in this study were cartons 2, 3, 33, 34, 35, 36, 38, 106, 148, 150, 151, 417, 423, 439, 440, 498, 503, 655, 901, 1,063, 1,065, 1,067, 1,069, 1,076, 1,182, 1,192, 1,196, 1,203, 1,205, 1,206, 1,210, 1,240, 1,288, 1,289

General Inventory

205–207. "Lettres écrites par le Magistrat," 1788–1790
226–227. "Lettres reçues par le Magistrat," 1788–1789
312–327. "Registre aux résolutions du Magistrat," 1758–1790
347–350. "Registre aux résolutions du Magistrat sur requêtes," 1787–1795
412–413. "Registre aux Ordonnances du Magistrat," 1790–1792
569, 597. "Avis du Procureur Syndic," 1761, 1789
669. "Registre aux déliberations des grossiers-merciers"
723. "Registre aux déliberations des sayetteurs-bourgeteurs-tisserands"
857. "Registre aux déliberations du comité de subsistance," 1789
1,580. Royal vingtième
2,368–2,369. Capitation of officeholders
3,207–10, 8,127–210, 8,124–27, 8,262–75, 9,319–32, 9,637–9. Accounts of guilds
11,307. Exemptions of officeholders for the *aide ordinaire*
11,308. Deputies of the guilds, 1789
15,413. "Recueil aux ordonnances de police," 1790–1804
15,443. List of the municipal magistrates, 1745–1785
15,513. "Enregistrement de la Garde Nationale"
15,751–3. Pamphlets of the estates and nobility on representation
15,862. Suppression of the guilds
15,909. "Registre aux octrois de la ville de Lille"
15,933. "Registre aux cérémonies"
15,982–15,984. "Registre aux cahier d'aides des états," 1714–1786
16,474–16,521. Accounts of the first *trésorier* of Lille, 1740–1790
16,537–16,586. Accounts of the second *trésorier* of Lille, 1740–1790
16,790–16,839. Accounts of the *receveur* of Lille, 1740–1790

Fonds Révolutionnaires

16,771. "Compte final et purgatif des rentes héritières cy devant à la charge de la commune de Lille"
16,860. "Compte final at purgatif des rentes viagères cy devant à la charge de la commune de Lille"
17,741. dos. 4, 6. Industry
17,781. dos. 1, 8. Debts of Lille, 1789; corporations

17,989. dos. 1. Mémoire of the Third Estate
17,989. dos. 6. Associations
17,997–17,998. Manufacture and commerce, 1790–1819
18,005. Public Auctions, 1776–1813
18,008. dos. 3. "Emeutes"
18,079. Deliberations of the municipal council, 1790–1800
18,247. Bakers, 1801–1818
18,329. "Procès-verbaux de la société populaire"
18,332. Letters of the popular society

Don Gentil

1,955. Protests of the Third Estate, 1788–1789
2,054. Active citizens in the Canton of Lille, 1790

BIBLIOTHEQUE MUNICIPALE DE LILLE

Manuscript 312–313. "Suite du Recueil des principales ordonnances du Magistrat." 1790–1825
Manuscript 799–800. "Livre contenant les créations de la Loy et Magistrat de cette ville de Lille," 1344–1786
26,687. "Concordat entre les Fabricans de fils retords de la ville de Lille," 10 February 1809
31,265. "Etat général des Impositions et Droits qui se lèvent sur les Habitants des châtellenies de Lille, Douai, et Orchies."

Fonds Lillois

26,134. "Discours de M. L'Intendant," 11 March 1789
26,151. Petition of the thread spinners to the National Assembly

Fonds Quarré-Reybourbon

83. "Sociétés, cercles."

NEWSPAPERS

Feuille du département du Nord
Gazette nationale, ou le Moniteur universel (*Réimpression de l'Ancien Moniteur.*)

PUBLISHED SOURCES

Almanach du commerce des arts et métiers de la ville de Lille (Lille, 1790)
Annuaire statistique du Département du Nord, vols. 1–12 (Douai, an XI–1814)

Bloch, Camille, ed., *Procès-verbaux du comité des finances de l'Assemblée Constituante* (Rennes, 1922)

Bodin, Jean, *The Six Bookes of a Commonweale*, ed. Kenneth McRae (Cambridge, Mass., 1972)

Bonnassieux, Pierre, *Conseil de commerce et Bureau du Commerce (1700–1791). Inventaire analytique des procès-verbaux* (Paris, 1900)

Buchez, P. J. B., and Roux, P. C., eds., *Histoire Parlementaire de la Révolution française*, 40 vols. (Paris, 1834–1838)

Chaptal, Jean Antoine, *De l'industrie française*, 2 vols. (Paris, 1819)

Collection générale des arrêtés, adresses, proclamations, et autres actes émanés de la Préfecture (Douai, an IX–1815)

Dieudonné, C., *Statistique du Département du Nord*, 3 vols. (Brionne, an XII), reprint edn

Dugué de Bagnols, "Mémoire de Dugué de Bagnols, 1698," *Bulletin de la Commission Historique du Département du Nord* 10 (1868), 450–545

Duvergier, J. B., *Collection complète des lois, décrets, ordonnances, réglemens et avis du conseil d'état depuis 1788 jusqu'à et y compris 1824*, 24 vols. (Paris, 1789–1824)

Encyclopédie Méthodique: Finances, 3 vols. (Paris, 1784–1787)

"Un essai de statistique industrielle en l'an V: L'industrie de la Corrège, de la Creuse, de la Moselle, du Nord, du Pas de Calais, et de la Sarthe en 1797," *Bulletin de la Commission de recherche et de publication des documents relatifs à la vie économique de la Révolution* (1908), 11–205

Flammermont, Jules, ed., *Remontrances du Parlement de Paris au XVIIIe siècle*, 3 vols. (Paris, 1888–1898)

Gerbaux and Schmidt, eds., *Les Procès-verbaux des Comités d'Agriculture et de Commerce de la Constituante, de la Legislative et de la Convention*, 4 vols. (Paris, 1906)

Guide des étrangers à Lille ou description de la ville et de ses environs, B.M.L. 22,493 (Lille, 1772)

Guyot, Joseph N., *Répertoire universel et raisonné de jurisprudence civile, criminelle, canonique, et bénéficiale*, 17 vols. (Paris, 1784)

Isambert, F.-A., Jourdan, A.-J.-L., and Decrusy, eds., *Recueil général des anciennes lois françaises depuis l'an 420 jusqu'à la Révolution de 1789*, 29 vols. (Paris, 1822–1833)

Lefebvre, Georges, ed., "Abbrégé de tout ce qu'il s'est passé de plus remarquable au siège de la ville de Lille, l'an 1667, 10 aoust," *Annales de l'Est et du Nord* 3 (1907), 391–409

Le Peletier de Souzy, "Instructions que je dois donner à M. de Breteuil en luy remettant l'Intendance de Flandre au mois de décembre 1683," *Bulletin de la Commission Historique du Nord* 10 (1868), 373–449

Loyseau, Charles, *Traité des ordres et simples dignitez* (Paris, 1610)

Mavidal, M. J. and Laurent, M. E., eds. *Archives parlementaires de 1787 à 1860*, 82 vols. (Paris, 1879–1913)

Moreau de Beaumont, *Mémoires concernant les impositions et droits en Europe*, 4 vols. (Paris, 1769)

Roux, Vital, *Rapport sur les Jurandes et Maîtrises et sur un projet de statuts et réglemens pour les marchands de vin de Paris* (Paris, 1805)

Six and Plouvain, ed., *Recueil des édits, déclarations, lettres-patentes, etc. enregistrés au Parlement de Flandre*, 12 vols. (Douai, 1785–1790)

SECONDARY WORKS

Agulhon, Maurice, *Pénitents et Francs-Maçons de l'ancienne Provence* (Paris, 1968)
Anderson, Perry, *Lineages of the Absolutist State* (London, 1974)
Babeau, Albert, *La Ville sous l'ancien régime* (Paris, 1884)
Bacquié, Franc, *Les Inspecteures des manufactures sous l'ancien régime, 1669–1791* (Toulouse, 1927)
Baker, Keith, ed., *The French Revolution and the Creation of Modern Political Culture*, vol. 1, *The Political Culture of the Old Regime* (Oxford, 1987)
  "Enlightenment and Revolution in France: Old Problems, Renewed Approaches," *Journal of Modern History* 53 (1981), 281–303
  "French Political Thought at the Accession of Louis XVI," *Journal of Modern History* 50 (1978), 279–303
Behrens, C. B. A., "Nobles, Privileges, and Taxes in France at the End of the Ancien Régime," *Economic History Review* 2nd ser. 15 (April 1963), 451–475
  Society, Government and the Enlightenment. The Experience of France and Prussia (New York, 1985)
Beik, William, *Absolutism and Society in Seventeenth-Century France: State Power and Provincial Aristocracy in Languedoc* (Cambridge, 1985)
Bendix, Reinhard, *Nation-Building and Citizenship: Studies of Our Changing Social Order* (Garden City, 1969)
Bergeron, Louis, *France Under Napoleon*, trans. R. R. Palmer (Princeton, 1981)
  and Chaussinand-Nogaret, Guy, *Grands notables au Premier Empire* (Paris, 1978)
Bertucat, Charles, *Les Finances municipales de Dijon depuis la liquidation des dettes (1662) jusqu'en 1789* (Dijon, 1910)
Bien, David, "La Réaction aristocratique avant 1789: l'exemple de l'armée," *Annales: E.S.C.* 29 (1974), 23–48, 505–534
  "Manufacturing Nobles: The Chancelleries in France to 1789," *Journal of Modern History* 61 (1989), 445–486
Black, Antony, *Guilds and Civil Society in European Political Thought from the Twelfth Century to the Present* (Ithaca, New York, 1984)
Bordes, Maurice, *L'Administration provinciale et municipale en France au XVIIIe siècle* (Paris, 1972)
  La Réforme municipale du contrôleur général Laverdy et son application (1764–1771) (Toulouse, 1968)
Bosher, John, "The French Crisis of 1770," *History* 57 (1972), 17–30
  French Finances. 1770–1795: From Business to Bureaucracy (Cambridge, 1970) 1970)
  ed. *French Government and Society, 1500–1850* (London, 1973)
  The French Revolution (New York and London, 1988)
  The Single Duty Project: A Study of the Movement for a French Customs Union in the Eighteenth Century (London, 1964)

Bossenga, Gail, "Corporate Institutions, Revolution and the State: Lille from Louis XIV to Napoleon" (Ph.D. diss., University of Michigan, 1983)

"From Corps to Citizenship: The *Bureaux des Finances* before the French Revolution," *Journal of Modern History* 58 (1986), 610–642

"Protecting Merchants: Guilds and Commercial Capitalism in Eighteenth-Century France," *French Historical Studies* 15 (1988), 693–703

"La Révolution française et les corporations: trois exemples lillois," *Annales, E.S.C.* 43 (1988), 405–426

Bouvier, J., and Germain-Martin, M., *Finances et financiers de l'Ancien Régime* (Paris, 1964)

Braudel, Fernand, and Labrousse, Ernest, *Histoire économique et sociale de la France*, 2 vols. (Paris, 1970)

Braure, Maurice, *Lille et la Flandre Wallonne au XVIIIe siècle*, 2 vols. (Lille, 1932)

Brewer, John, *The Sinews of Power: War, Money and the English State, 1688–1783* (New York, 1989)

Briggs, Robin, *Early Modern France, 1560–1715* (Oxford, 1977)

Brubaker, William Rogers, "The French Revolution and the Invention of Citizenship," *French Politics and Society* 7 (Summer, 1989), 30–49

Bruhat, J., "Le mouvement ouvrier français du début du XIXe siècle et les survivances de l'ancien régime," *La Pensée* 142 (December 1968), 44–56

Cameron, Rondo, "Economic Growth and Stagnation in France, 1815–1914," *Journal of Modern History* 30 (1958), 1–13

Cavanagh, Gerald, "The Present State of French Revolution Historiography. Alfred Cobban and Beyond," *French Historical Studies* 7 (1972), 587–606

Censer, Jack and Popkin, Jeremy, eds., *Press and Politics in Pre-revolutionary France* (Berkeley, Calif., 1987)

Cerruti, Simona, "Du corps au métier: la corporation des tailleurs de Turin," *Annales, E.S.C.* 43 (1988), 322–352

Charléty, S., "La Vie économique de Lyon sous Napoléon," *Vierteljahrschrift für Social-und Wirtschaft Geschichte* 5 (1906), 365–379

Charmeil, Jean-Paul, *Les Trésoriers de France à l'époque de la Fronde. Contribution à l'histoire financière sous l'ancien régime* (Paris, 1964)

Chaussinand-Nogaret, Guy, *La Noblesse au XVIIIe siècle. De la féodalité aux lumières* (Paris, 1976); trans. William Doyle as *The Nobility in the Eighteenth Century: From Feudalism to Enlightenment* (Cambridge, 1985)

Church, F. Clive, *Revolution and Red Tape: The French Ministerial Bureaucracy, 1770–1850* (Oxford, 1981)

Church, William, *Constitutional Thought in Sixteenth-Century France* (Cambridge, Mass., 1941)

Cipolla, Carlo, ed., *The Fontana Economic History of Europe: The Emergence of Industrial Societies* (Fontana/Collins, 1973)

Clément, M., *Histoire des fêtes civiles et religieuses, des usages anciens et modernes du département du Nord* (Cambrai, 1836)

Cobban, Alfred, "Local Government During the French Revolution," *English Historical Review* 58 (1943), 13–31

A History of France, 1715–1799 (Baltimore, 1957)

The Social Interpretation of the French Revolution (Cambridge, 1968)

Cole, C. W., *Colbert and a Century of French Mercantilism*, 2 vols. (New York, 1939)

French Mercantilism 1683–1700 (New York, 1943)

Coleman, D. C., ed., *Revisions in Mercantilism* (London, 1969)

Cottereau, Alain, "Justice et injustice ordinaire sur les lieux de travail d'après les audiences prud'hommales (1805–1866)." *Le Mouvement Social* 141 (1987), 25–59

Couvreur, Hubert, and Montagne, Michel, "La Noblesse de la châtellenie de Lille à la fin de l'ancien régime," 2 vols. (Mémoire de maîtrise, University of Lille III, 1970)

Crapet, A., "L'industrie dans la Flandre Wallonne à la fin de l'ancien régime. L'organisation du travail," *Revue d'Histoire Moderne et Contemporaine* (1909), 5–29

"La Vie à Lille de 1667 à 1789 d'après les cours de M. de Saint-Léger," *Revue du Nord* 6 (1920), 126–231, and 7 (1921), 290–303

Croquez, Albert, *La Flandre Wallonne et les pays de l'intendance de Lille sous Louis XIV* (Paris, 1912)

Histoire de Lille, 2 vols. (Lille, 1935, 1939)

Crouzet, François, "Wars, Blockade and Economic Change in Europe, 1792–1815," *Journal of Economic History* (1964), 567–88

Crozier, Michel, *The Stalled Society*, trans. Rupert Sawyer (New York, 1974)

Darnton, Robert, "In Search of the Enlightenment: Recent Attempts to Create a Social History of Ideas," *Journal of Modern History* 43 (1971), 113–132

The Business of Enlightenment. A Publishing History of the Encyclopédie, 1775–1800 (Cambridge, Mass., 1979)

The Literary Underground of the Old Regime (Cambridge, Mass., 1982)

Dawson, Philip, *Provincial Magistrates and Revolutionary Politics in France, 1789–95* (Cambridge, Mass., 1972)

Decroix, F., "Hôtel des Monnaies de Lille," *Bulletin de la Société d'Etudes de la Province de Cambrai* (March, 1958), 13–38

Delsalle, Paul, "Les Entreprises textiles de Tourcoing (XVIIe–XXe siècle)," *Revue du Nord* 69 (1987), 752–765

Dessert, Daniel, "Finances et société au XVIIe siècle: à propos de la Chambre de Justice de 1661," *Annales, E.S.C.* 29 (1974), 847–882

Deyon, Pierre, "Dénombrements et structures urbaines," *Revue du Nord* 53 (1971), 495–508

"La Diffusion rurale des industries textiles en Flandre française à la fin de l'ancien régime et au début du XIX ème siècle," *Revue du Nord* 61 (1979), 83–96

"Un modèle à l'épreuve. Le développement industriel de Roubaix de 1762 à la fin du XIXème siècle," *Revue du Nord* 63 (1981), 59–66

and Lottin, Alain, "Evolution de la production textile à Lille aux XVIe et XVIIe siècles," *Revue du Nord* 49 (1967), 23–35

D'Hollander, Paul, "La Composition sociale de l'échevinage lillois sous la domination française, 1667–1789," *Revue du Nord* 52 (1970), 5–15

"La Composition sociale de l'échevinage lillois sous la domination française, 1667–1789" (Mémoire de maîtrise, University of Lille, 1968)

Doyle, William, *Origins of the French Revolution* (Oxford, 1980)

"The Parlements of France and the Breakdown of the Old Regime, 1770–1788," *French Historical Studies* 6 (1970), 415–458

Dubois, Louis, *Le Régime de la brasserie à Lille des origines à la Révolution, 1279–1789* (Lille, 1912)

Duchambge de Liessart, Eléonore-Paul, *Notes historiques relatives aux offices et officiers du Bureau des Finances de la généralité de Lille* (Lille, 1855)

Dumas, F., "Les Corporations de métiers de la ville de Toulouse au XVIIIe siècle," *Annales du Midi* 12 (1900), 475–493

Du Péage, Paul Dénis, *Recueil de généalogies lilloises*, in *Mémoires de la Société d'Etudes de la Province de Cambrai*, vols. 12–15 (Lille, 1906–1908)

DuPlessis, Robert S., and Howell, Martha C., "Reconsidering the Early Modern European Economy: The Cases of Leiden and Lille," *Past and Present* 94 (1982), 49–84

Earle, Edward, ed., *Modern France, Problems of the Third and Fourth Republics* (New York, 1951)

Egret, Jean, *The French Pre-revolution*, trans. Wesley D. Camp (Chicago, 1977)

Eisenstein, Elizabeth, "Who Intervened in 1788? A Commentary on *The Coming of the French Revolution*," *American Historical Review* 71 (October 1965), 77–103

Elbow, Matthew, *French Corporate Theory, 1789–1948* (New York, 1953)

Ellis, Geoffrey, "The 'Marxist Interpretation' of the French Revolution," *English Historical Review* 93 (1978), 353–376

Ekelund, Robert B., Jr., and Tollison, Robert, *Mercantilism as a Rent-Seeking Society: Economic Regulation in Historical Perspective* (College Station, Texas, 1981)

Fitzsimmons, Michael P., *The Parisian Order of Barristers and the French Revolution* (Cambridge, Mass., 1987)

Flammermont, J., *Histoire de l'industrie à Lille* (Lille, 1897)

Fouret, Claude, "Les Fêtes à Lille au XVIIIe siècle" (Mémoire de maîtrise, University of Lille III, 1978)

Fox-Genovese, Elizabeth, *The Origins of Physiocracy* (Ithaca, New York, 1976)

Furet, François, *Penser la Révolution Française* (Paris, 1978), trans. Elborg Forster as *Interpreting the French Revolution* (Cambridge and New York, 1981)

    and Ozouf, Jacques, "Literacy and Industrialization: the Case of the Département du Nord in France," *Journal of European Economic History* 5 (1976), 5–44.

    and Ozouf, Mona, *Dictionnaire Critique de la Révolution Française* (Paris, 1988)

Garden, Maurice, *Lyon et les Lyonnais au XVIIIème siècle* (Paris, 1970)

Geison, Gerald, L. ed., *Professions and the French State, 1700–1900* (Philadelphia, 1984)

Godechot, Jacques L., *Les Institutions de la France sous la Révolution et l'Empire* (Paris, 1968)

Goubert, Pierre, *The Ancien Régime: French Society, 1600–1750*, trans. Steve Cox (New York, 1969)

Gruder, Vivian, "No Taxation without Representation: The Assembly of Notables and Political Ideology in France," *Legislative Studies Quarterly* 7 (1982), 263–279

    "A Mutation in Elite Political Culture: The French Notables and the Defense of Property and Participation, 1787," *Journal of Modern History* 56 (1984), 598–634

"Paths to Political Consciousness: The Assembly of Notables and the 'Pre-Revolution' in France," *French Historical Studies* 13 (1984), 323–355

Guéry, Alain, "Les Finances de la monarchie française sous l'ancien régime," *Annales, E.S.C.* 33 (1978), 216–239

Habermas, Jürgen, *The Structural Transformation of the Public Sphere*, trans. Thomas Burger (Cambridge, Mass., 1989)

Harris, Robert D., *Necker, Reform Statesman of the Ancien Régime* (Berkeley, Calif., 1979)

Hautcoeur, Edouard, *Histoire de l'église collegiale et du chapitre de Saint-Pierre de Lille*, in *Mémoires de la Société d'Etudes de la Province de Cambrai*, vols. 4–6 (Lille, 1896–1899)

Hilaire, Yves, Marie, et al., *Histoire de Roubaix* (Dunkerque, 1984)

Hincker, François, *Les Français devant l'impôt* (Paris, 1971)

Hinrichs, Ernst, et al., ed. *Vom Ancien Régime zür Französischen Revolution: Forschungen und Perspektiven* (Göttingen, 1978)

Hirsch, Jean-Pierre, "Honneur et liberté du commerce: sur le 'liberalisme' des milieux de commerce de Lille et de Dunkerque à la veille des Etats Généraux de 1789," *Revue du Nord* 55 (October–December 1973), 333–346

"Un fils rompu? A propos du crédit à Lille sous la Révolution et l'Empire," *Revue du Nord* 61 (1979), 181–192

"Les Milieux du commerce, l'esprit de système et le pouvoir à la veille de la Révolution," *Annales, E.S.C.* 30 (1975), 1,337–1,370

"Revolutionary France, Cradle of Free Enterprise," *American Historical Review* 94 (1989), 1,281–1,289

Historique de la Chambre de Commerce de Lille, 1714–1918 (Lille, 1921)

Hoffman, Stanley, ed., *In Search of France: The Economy, Society and Political System in the Twentieth Century* (New York, 1965)

Hunt, Lynn, *Revolution and Urban Politics in Provincial France: Troyes and Reims, 1786–1790* (Stanford, 1978)

"Committees and Communes: Local Politics and National Revolution in 1789," *Comparative Studies in Society and History* 18 (July 1976), 321–346

Politics, Culture and Class in the French Revolution (Berkeley, 1984)

and George Sheridan, "Corporations, Association and the Language of Labor in France, 1750–1850," *Journal of Modern History* 58 (1986), 813–844

Hyslop, Beatrice, "French Gild Opinion," *American Historical Review* 44 (1939), 252–271

Kaiser, Thomas E. "Money, Despotism and Public Opinion in Early Eighteenth-Century France: John Law and the Debate on Royal Credit" (unpublished paper, 1988)

Kaplan, Steven, L., *Bread, Politics and Political Economy in the Reign of Louis XV* (The Hague, 1976)

"Réflexions sur la police du monde du travail, 1700–1815," *Revue Historique* 261 (1979), 17–77

and Cynthia J. Koepp, eds., *Work in France: Representations, Meaning, Organization, and Practice* (Ithaca, New York, 1986)

Kaplow, Jeffery, ed., *New Perspectives on the French Revolution* (New York, 1965)

Keohane, Nannerl O., *Philosophy and the State in France: The Renaissance to the Enlightenment* (Princeton, 1980)

Kerridge, Eric, *Textile Manufactures in Early Modern England* (Manchester, 1985)

Kettering, Sharon, *Patrons, Brokers, and Clients in Seventeenth-Century France* (Oxford, 1986)

Kierstead, Raymond, ed., *State and Society in Seventeenth-Century France* (New York, 1975)

Kriedte, Peter, *Peasants, Landlords and Merchant Capitalists: Europe and the World Economy, 1500–1800*, trans. V. R. Berghahn (Cambridge, 1983)

Kriegar, Leonard, *The German Idea of Freedon: History of a Political Tradition* (Boston, 1957)

Labrousse, Ernest, *Esquisse du mouvement des prix et des revenus en France au XVIIIe siècle*, 2 vols. (Paris, 1933)

Lambert-Dansette, Jean, *Origines et évolution d'une bourgeoisie: Quelques familles du patronat textile de Lille-Armentières (1789–1914)* (Lille, 1954)

Lambert-Dansette, Jean and Roy, Joseph-Antoine, "Origines et évolution d'une bourgeoisie: le patronat textile du basin Lillois (1789–1914)," *Revue du Nord* 37 (1955), 199–216; 39 (1957), 21–42; 40 (1958), 49–69; 41 (1959), 23–38

Landes, Joan, *Women and the Public Sphere in the Age of the French Revolution* (Ithaca, New York, 1988)

Leclaire, Edmond, *Histoire de la pharmacie à Lille de 1301 à l'an XI (1803)* (Lille, 1900)

Histoire de la chirurgie à Lille, in *Mémoires de la Société d'Etudes de la Province de Cambrai*, vol. 17 (Lille, 1911)

Lefebvre, George, *The French Revolution*, 2 vols., trans. Elizabeth Moss Evanson, vol. 1, and John Hall Stewart, vol. 2 (New York, 1962, 1964)

Les Paysans du Nord pendant la Révolution française (Lille, 1924)

Lefevre, Pierre, *Le Commerce des grains et la question du pain à Lille de 1713 à 1789* (Lille, 1925)

Lepreux, Georges, *Histoire électorale et parlementaire du département du Nord. Nos représentants pendant la Révolution, 1789–1799* (Lille, 1898)

Letaconnoux, J., "Les Sources de l'histoire du comité des députés extraordinaires des manufactures et du commerce de France (1789–1791)," *Revue d'Histoire Moderne et Contemporaine* (1912), 369–403

Levasseur, Emile, *Histoire des classes ouvrières en France depuis la conquête de Jules César jusqu'à la Révolution*, 2 vols. (Paris, 1859)

Histoire des classes ouvrières en France depuis 1789 jusqu'à nos jours, 2 vols. (Paris, 1867)

Ligou, Daniel, "A propos de la révolution municipale," *Revue d'histoire économique et sociale* 30 (1960), 146–177

Lottin, Alain, *Chavatte, ouvrier lillois, un contemporain de Louis XIV* (Paris, 1979)

"Les Morts chassés de la cité, 'Lumières et prejugés,' les 'émeutes' à Lille (1779) et à Cambrai (1786) lors du transfert des cimetières," *Revue du Nord* 60 (1978), 73–117

Lousse, Emile, *La Société d'ancien régime. Organisation et représentation corporatives* (Louvain, 1943)

Lucas, Colin, "Nobles, Bourgeois, and the Origins of the French Revolution," *Past and Present* 60 (August 1973), 84–126

Luethy, Herbert, *La Banque protestante en France de la révocation de l'Edit de Nantes à la Révolution*, 2 vols. (Paris, 1959–1961)

McKendrick, Neil, Brewer, John, and Plumb, J. H., *The Birth of a Consumer*

Society: The Commercialization of Eighteenth-Century England (London, 1982)

Margerison, Kenneth, "The Movement for a Union of Orders in the Estates General of 1789," *French History* 3 (1989), 48–70

Marion, Marcel, *Dictionnaire des institutions de la France aux XVIIe et XVIIIe siècles* (Paris, 1923)

Histoire financière de la France depuis 1715, 5 vols. (Paris, 1919)

Les impôts directs sous l'ancien régime principalement au XVIIIe siècle (Paris, 1910)

Mathias, Peter, and O'Brien, Patrick, "Taxation in Britain and France, 1715–1810. A Comparison of Social and Economic Incidence of Taxes Collected for the Central Governments," *Journal of European Economic History* 5 (1976), 601–650

Matthews, George T., *The Royal General Farms in Eighteenth-Century France* (New York, 1958)

Maza, Sarah, "Le Tribunal de la nation: les mémoires judiciaires et l'opinion publique à la fin de l'ancien régime," *Annales, E.S.C.* 42 (1987), 73–90

Mendels, Franklin F., "Proto-industrialization: The First Phase of the Industrialization Process," *Journal of Economic History* (1972), 241–261

Meyer, Jean, *La Noblesse bretonne au XVIIIe siècle* (Paris, 1966)

Morineau, Michel, "Budgets de l'Etat et gestion des finances royales en France au dix-huitième siècle," *Revue Historique* 264:2 (1980), 289–336

Mousnier, Roland, *La venalité des offices sous Henri IV et Louis XIII* (Rouen, 1945)

"Comment les Français voyaient la constitution au XVIIe siècle," *XVIIe Siècle* (1955), 11–28

Nigeon, René, *Etat financier des corporations parisiens d'arts et métiers au XVIII siècle* (Paris, 1934)

Olivier-Martin, François, *L'organisation corporative de la France d'ancien régime* (Paris, 1938)

L'Organisation corporative du Moyen Age à la fin de l'Ancien Régime. Etudes présentées à la commission internationale pour l'histoire des assemblées d'états (Louvain, 1937)

Ozouf, Mona, *La Fête révolutionnaire, 1789–1799* (Paris, 1976)

Pajot, Henri, *Le Notariat dans l'arrondissement de Lille* (Lille, 1862)

Palmer, R. R., *The Age of the Democratic Revolution*, 2 vols. (Princeton, 1959)

Parker, Geoffrey, *The Military Revolution. Military Innovation and the Rise of the West, 1500–1800* (Cambridge and New York, 1988)

Piat, Jean, *Roubaix, capitale du textile* (Roubaix, 1968)

Pierrard, Pierre, *La Vie ouvrière à Lille sous le second empire* (Paris, 1965)

La Vie quotidienne dans le Nord au XIXe siècle (Paris, 1976)

Pillot, G. M. L., *Histoire du Parlement de Flandres*, 2 vols. (Douai, 1849)

Piore, Michael and Sabel, Charles, *The Second Industrial Divide: Possibilities for Prosperity* (New York, 1984)

Prévost, M., "Les Elections judiciaires à Lille en 1790," *Revue du Nord* 40 (1958), 357–61

Ramette, Odile, "La Fédération de Lille, 6 juin 1790," *Revue du Nord* 64 (1982), 789–802

Rébillon, Armand, *Les Etats de Bretagne de 1661 à 1789* (Paris–Rennes, 1932)

Reddy, William, *The Rise of Market Culture* (Cambridge and New York, 1984)

Reinhard, Marcel, "Elite et noblesse dans la seconde moitié du XVIIIe siècle," *Revue d'Histoire Moderne et Contemporaine* 3 (1956), 5–37

"La Population des villes: sa mesure sous la Révolution et l'Empire," *Population* 9 (1954), 179–288

Renouvin, Pierre, *Les Assemblées provinciales de 1787. Origines, développements, résultats* (Paris, 1921)

Rezsohazy, Rudolph, *Histoire du mouvement mutualiste chrétien en Belgique* (Paris and Brussels, 1956)

Richet, Denis, "Autour des origines idéologiques lointaines de la Révolution française: Elites et despotisme," *Annales, E.S.C.* 24 (1969), 1–23

Riley, James C., *The Seven Years War and the Old Regime in France: The Economic and Financial Toll* (Princeton, 1986)

Robert, Paul, *Dictionnaire alphabétique et analogique de la langue française. Les mots et les associations d'idées*, 9 vols. (Paris, 1951–1964)

Roberts, Michael, *Essays in Swedish History* (London, 1967)

Robin, Régine, *La Société française en 1789: Semur-en-Auxois* (Paris, 1970)

Roche, Daniel, *Le Siècle des lumières en province. Académies et académiciens provinciaux, 1680–1789*, 2 vols. (Paris and the Hague, 1978)

and Labrousse, C. E., eds., *Ordres et classes. Colloque d'histoire sociale, Saint-Cloud, 24–25 Mai, 1967* (Paris, 1973)

Root, Hilton, *Peasant and King in Burgundy: Agrarian Foundations of French Absolutism* (Berkeley, Calif., 1987)

Rosset, Philippe, "Les officiers du Bureau des Finances de Lille (1691–1790)." 2 vols. (Thèse du troisième cycle, University of Lille III, 1977)

Rowen, Herbert H., *The King's State. Proprietary Dynasticism in Early Modern France* (New Brunswick, 1980)

Ruchenbusch, Janine, "L'Industrie textile dans la région lilloise sous la Révolution et l'Empire" (Mémoire de maîtrise, University of Lille, 1954)

Sabel, Charles, and Zeitlin, Jonathan, "Historical Alternatives to Mass Production: Politics, Markets, and Technology in Nineteenth-Century Industrialization," *Past and Present* 108 (1985), 133–176

Saint-Léger, A., *Histoire de Lille des origines à 1789* (Lille, 1942)

"La rivalité industrielle entre la ville de Lille et le plat pays et l'arrêt du Conseil de 1762," *Annales de l'Est et du Nord* (1906), 367–402, 481–500

Saint-Léon, Etienne Martin, *Histoire des corporations de métiers depuis leurs origins jusqu'à leur suppression en 1791. Suivie d'une étude sur l'évolution de l'idée corporative au XIXe siècle* (Paris, 1897)

Saricks, Ambrose, *A Bibliography of the Frank E. Melvin Collection of Pamphlets of the French Revolution in the University of Kansas Libraries*, 2 vols. (Lawrence, 1960)

Sautai, Maurice, *L'Œuvre de Vauban à Lille* (Paris, 1911)

Sewell, William J., Jr. *Work and Revolution in France: The Language of Labor from the Old Regime to 1848* (Cambridge and New York, 1980)

"Ideologies and Social Revolutions: Reflections on the French Case," *Journal of Modern History* 57 (1985), 57–85

Shennan, J. H., *The Parlement of Paris* (London, 1968)

Sibalis, Michael, "Corporatism after the Corporations: The Debate on Restoring the Guilds Under Napoleon I and the Restoration," *French Historical Studies* 15 (1988), 718–730

Skocpol, Theda. *States and Social Revolutions* (Cambridge and New York, 1979) "Cultural Idioms and Political Ideologies in Revolutionary Reconstruction of State Power: a Rejoinder to Sewell," *Journal of Modern History* 57 (1985), 86–96

Soboul, Albert, *Précis d'histoire de la Révolution Française* (Paris, 1962), trans. Alan Forest and Colin Jones as *The French Revolution, 1787–1799: From the Storming of the Bastille to Napoleon* (New York, 1975)

Soliday, Gerald, *A Community in Conflict: Frankfurt Society in the Seventeenth and Early Eighteenth Centuries* (Hanover, New Hampshire, 1974)

Sonenscher, Michael, *Work and Wages: Natural Law, Politics and the Eighteenth-Century French Trades* (Cambridge and New York, 1989)

Sorreau, E., "La Loi Le Chapelier," *Annales Historiques de la Révolution Française* 8 (1931), 287–314

Staquet, René, "Les Finances communales de Lille sous l'occupation française de 1668–1789" (Thèse de Doctorat en Droit, University of Lille, 1961)

Tarrade, J., "Le groupe de pression du commerce à la fin de l'ancien régime," *Bulletin de la Société d'Histoire Moderne et Contemporaine* (suppl. 2 of the *Revue d'Histoire Moderne et Contemporaine*) (1970), 23–27

Taylor, George, "Noncapitalist Wealth and the Origins of the French Revolution," *American Historical Review* 72 (1967), 469–496

"The Paris Bourse on the Eve of the Revolution," *American Historical Review* 67 (1962), 951–977

"Revolutionary and Non-revolutionary Content in the *Cahiers* of 1789: an Interim Report," *French Historical Studies* (1972), 479–502

Te Brake, Wayne "Provincial Histories and National Revolution: The Dutch Republic in the 1780s." paper presented at a conference on "Enlightenment, Decline and Revolution, the Dutch Republic in the Eighteenth Century," Washington, D.C., April 1989

Théry, L., "Une commune rurale de la Flandre Française au début de la Révolution: Frelinghem," *Révue du Nord* 29 (1934), 193–205

Thomas, Paul, "Textes historiques sur Lille et le Nord de la France avant 1789," *Revue du Nord* 20 (1934), 233–248

Thbaut, L., "Les Voies navigables et l'industrialisation du Nord de la France avant 1789," *Revue du Nord* 61 (1979), 149–164

Tilly, Charles, ed., *The Formation of National States in Western Europe* (Princeton, 1975)

From Mobilization to Revolution (Reading, Mass., 1978)

Tocqueville, Alexis de, *The Old Regime and the French Revolution*, trans. Stuart Gilbert (New York, 1955)

Trénard, Louis, "Alphabétisation et scolarisation dans la région lilloise," *Revue du Nord* 67 (1985), 633–648

"La Crise révolutionnaire dans les Pays-Bas français (Flandre, Hainaut, Artois, Boulonnais, Cambrésis), Etat des recherches," *Annales Historiques de la Révolution Française* (1974), 293–318

"Lille en fête durant la Révolution, 1789–1799," *Revue du Nord* 69 (1987), 591–604

"Notables de la région lillois au seuil du XIXème siècle," *Revue du Nord* 63 (1981), 169–187

Truant, Cynthia, "Solidarity and Symbolism among Journeymen Artisans: The Case of Compagnonnage," *Comparative Studies in Society and History* 21 (1979), 214–226

Tulard, Jean, *Le Consulat et l'Empire (1800–1815)* (Paris, 1970)

Vanhaeck, Maurice, *Histoire de la sayetterie à Lille,* in *Mémoires de la Société d'Etudes de la Province de Cambrai,* vols. 16, 17 (Lille, 1910)

Van Hende, E., "Etat de la ville et de la châtellenie de Lille en 1789," *Bulletin de la Commission Historique du Nord* 19 (1890), 251–366

Van Kley, Dale, "Church, State, and the Ideological Origins of the French Revolution: The Debate over the General Assembly of the Gallican Clergy in 1765," *Journal of Modern History* 51 (1979), 630–664

Vardi, Liana, "The Abolition of the Guilds during the French Revolution," *French Historical Studies* 15 (Fall 1988), 704–717

Vincent, Andrew, *Theories of the State* (Oxford, 1987)

Vries, Jan de, *European Urbanization 1500–1800* (Cambridge, Mass., 1984)

Weber, Max, *Economy and Society. An Outline of Interpretive Sociology,* Guenther Roth and Claus Wittich, eds. (Berkeley, Calif., 1968)

Weir, David, "Tontines, Public Finance and Revolution in France and England, 1688–1789," *Journal of Economic History* 49 (March, 1989), 95–124

Weuleresse, George, *Le Mouvement Physiocratique en France de 1756 à 1770,* 2 vols. (Paris, 1910)

Wick, Daniel, "The Court Nobility and the French Revolution: The Example of the Society of Thirty," *Eighteenth-Century Studies* 13 (1980), 263–284

Witt, Peter-Christian, ed., *Wealth and Taxation in Central Europe: The History and Sociology of Public Finance* (Leamington Spa, U.K., 1987)

Wolf, Philippe, and Dollinger, Philippe, *Bibliographie d'histoire des villes de France* (Paris, 1967)

Woloch, Isser, "The Fall and Resurrection of the Civil Bar, 1789–1820s," *French Historical Studies* 15 (Fall 1987), 241–262

Yeazell, Stephen, *From Medieval Group Litigation to the Modern Class Action* (New Haven and London, 1987)

Index